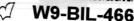

OLD TOWN
Pages 64–83
Street Finder maps 1, 3–4

OLD
TOWN

AROUND
SOLIDARITY
AVENUE

Wista

THE ROYAL
ROUTE

THE ROYAL ROUTE
Pages 112–125
Street Finder maps 1–4, 6

AROUND
MARSHAL
STREET

AROUND
ŁAZIENKI PARK

AROUND ŁAZIENKI PARK
Pages 148–165
Street Finder maps 2, 6

0 kilometers   1

0 miles   1

EYEWITNESS *TRAVEL GUIDES*

WARSAW

EYEWITNESS *TRAVEL GUIDES*

WARSAW

Main contributors:
MAŁGORZATA OMILANOWSKA
JERZY S MAJEWSKI

DK PUBLISHING, INC.

A DK Publishing Book

Produced by Wydawnictwo Wiedza i Życie, Warsaw
SERIES EDITOR Ewa Szwagrzyk
CONSULTANT Dr. Hanna Faryna-Paszkiewicz
JACKET Krzysztof Stefaniuk
DESIGNERS Krzysztof Giedziński, Paweł Pasternak
EDITORS Joanna Egert, Anna Kożurno-Królikowska,
Bożena Leszkowicz, Halina Siwecka

Dorling Kindersley Ltd
CONSULTANT EDITOR Ian Wisniewski
SENIOR DESIGNER Dutjapun Williams
EDITORS Michael Ellis, Peter Preston, Jane Simmonds
US EDITORS Irene Pavitt, Mary Sutherland
RESEARCHER Bogdan Kaczorowski
MANAGING EDITOR Vivien Crump
DEPUTY EDITORIAL DIRECTOR Douglas Amrine
DEPUTY ART DIRECTOR Gillian Allan

PRODUCTION David Proffit
DTP DESIGNER Ingrid Vienings

CONTRIBUTORS
Małgorzata Omilanowska, Jerzy S Majewski, Piotr Bikont

TRANSLATORS
Magda Hannay, PA Szudek

MAPS
Warszawskie Przedsiębiorstwo Geodezyjne

PHOTOGRAPHERS
Hanna Musiał, Maciej Musiał, Agencja "Piękna,"
Mariusz Kowalewski

ILLUSTRATORS
Andrzej Wielgosz, Piotr Zubrzycki
•
Film outputting bureau Graphical Innovations (London)
Printed and bound by G. Canale & C. (Italy)

First American Edition, 1997
2 4 6 8 10 9 7 5 3 1
Published in the United States by DK Publishing, Inc.
95 Madison Avenue, New York, New York 10016
Visit us on the World Wide Web at http://www.dk.com

Copyright 1997 © Dorling Kindersley Limited, London

A CATALOG RECORD IS AVAILABLE FROM THE LIBRARY OF CONGRESS.

Warsaw – 1st American ed.
p. cm. – (Eyewitness travel guides)
Includes index
ISBN 0-7894-1614-X
1. Warsaw (Poland) – Guidebooks. I. Series.
DK4616.W37 1997
914.38'4 – DC21   97–15211
•

Every effort has been made to ensure that the information in this
book is as up-to-date as possible at the time of going to press.
However, details such as telephone numbers, opening hours, prices,
gallery hanging arrangements, and travel information are liable to
change. The publishers cannot accept responsibility for any
consequences arising from the use of this book.

We would be delighted to receive any corrections and
suggestions for incorporation in the next edition. Please write to:
Deputy Editorial Director, Eyewitness Travel Guides,
Dorling Kindersley, 9 Henrietta Street, London WC2E 8PS.

THROUGHOUT THIS BOOK, FLOORS ARE REFERRED TO IN ACCORDANCE WITH
BRITISH USAGE, I.E. "FIRST FLOOR" IS ONE FLOOR UP.

◁ **View of the Old Town Market Square**

CONTENTS

King Zygmunt III Waza

INTRODUCING WARSAW

Flowers in the Botanical Gardens

Madonna and Child by Botticelli,
in the National Museum

Decoration from Wilanów Palace

Palace on the Water in Łazienki Park

Painted Easter eggs

Mead

**Houses in the
Old Town**

HOW TO USE THIS GUIDE

THIS EYEWITNESS Travel Guide enables you to make the most of your time in Warsaw, with the minimum difficulty. It offers knowledgeable recommendations for sights and areas to visit, places to stay, and restaurants, as well as the most useful practical information. *Introducing Warsaw* locates the city geographically, sets modern Warsaw in its historical context, and describes the changing lives of its inhabitants through the seasons of the year. *Warsaw Area by Area* is the main

**Visitors planning
a tour of Warsaw**

sightseeing part of the guide, covering all of the capital's major sights with maps, photographs, and illustrations. It also includes the routes of three guided walks around the city and offers suggestions for day trips outside Warsaw. Specially selected information about hotels, restaurants, shops, cafés, bars, entertainment, and sports events can be found in the *Travelers' Needs* section.

The *Survival Guide* gives practical information on everyday needs, from making telephone calls to using the city's public transportation system.

WARSAW AREA BY AREA

The center of Warsaw has been divided into seven sightseeing areas. Each area has its own chapter and is color-coded for easy reference. Every chapter opens with a list

of the sights described, which are numbered and plotted on an *Area Map*. Detailed information for each sight is presented in numerical order, making it easy to find within the chapter.

Each area has color-coded thumb tabs.

A suggested route takes in the most interesting and attractive streets in the area.

A locator map shows where you are in relation to other areas in the city center.

Locator map

1 Area Map
For easy reference, the sights are numbered and located on an area map. This map also shows the location of places to park, as well as indicating the area covered by the Street-by-Street Map. The sights are also shown on the Warsaw Street Finder on pages 256–65.

Travel tips help you reach the area quickly by public transportation.

2 Street-by-Street Map
This gives a bird's-eye view of the most important part of each sightseeing area. The numbering of the sights ties in with the area map and the fuller descriptions on the pages that follow.

The list of star sights recommends the places that no visitor should miss.

WARSAW AREA MAP

THE COLOR-CODED AREAS shown on this map (*see inside front cover*) are the seven main sightseeing areas – each covered by a full chapter in *Warsaw Area by Area (pp62–165)*. The seven areas are highlighted on other maps throughout the book. In *Warsaw at a Glance (pp32–51)*, for example, they help locate the top sights, including galleries and museums, palaces and parks, religious buildings and cemeteries. They are also used to show the location of the top restaurants, cafés, and bars *(pp206–7)*, and Warsaw's best hotels *(pp198–9)*.

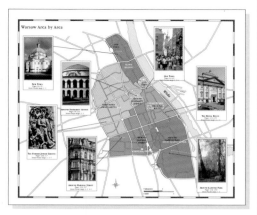

Façades of important buildings are often shown to illustrate their architectural style, and help you to recognize them quickly.

Practical information lists all the information you need to visit every sight, including a map reference to the *Street Finder (pp256–65)*.

Numbers refer to each sight's position on the area map and its place in the chapter.

The visitors' checklist provides all the practical information needed to plan your visit.

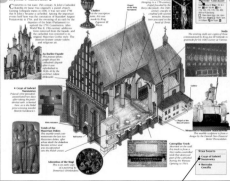

3 Detailed information on each sight
All the important sights in Warsaw are described individually. They are listed in order, following the numbering on the Area Map. Addresses and practical information are provided. The key to the symbols used in the information block is on the back flap.

4 Warsaw's top sights
Historic buildings are dissected to reveal their interiors, while museums and galleries have color-coded floor plans to help you locate the most interesting exhibits.

Stars indicate the features no visitor should miss.

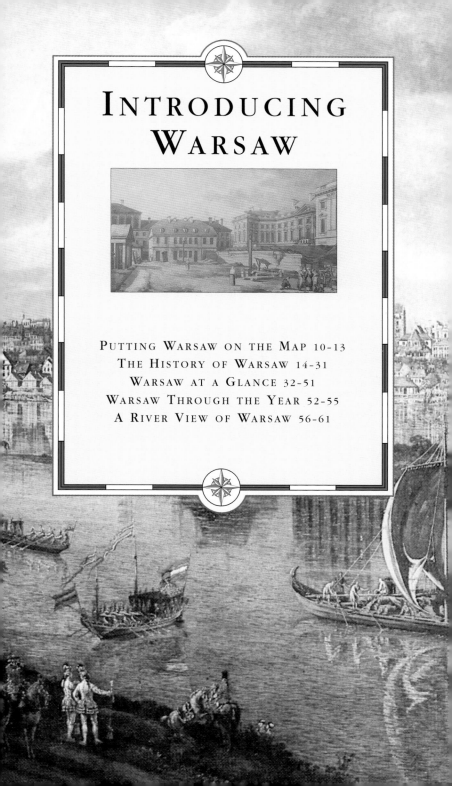

INTRODUCING
WARSAW

Putting Warsaw on the Map

Warsaw, the capital city of Poland, has a population of around 1.5 million and covers an area of 485 sq km (180 sq miles). The city, which is also the capital of the historic district of Mazovia, is located in central Poland on the banks of the River Vistula (Wisła). Warsaw's location makes it an ideal base for visiting other important Polish cities, such as Kraków, Gdańsk, Wrocław, and Poznań.

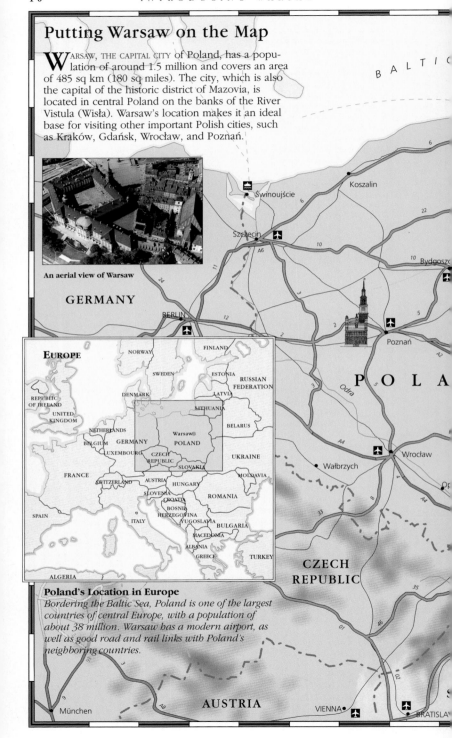

An aerial view of Warsaw

Poland's Location in Europe
Bordering the Baltic Sea, Poland is one of the largest countries of central Europe, with a population of about 38 million. Warsaw has a modern airport, as well as good road and rail links with Poland's neighboring countries.

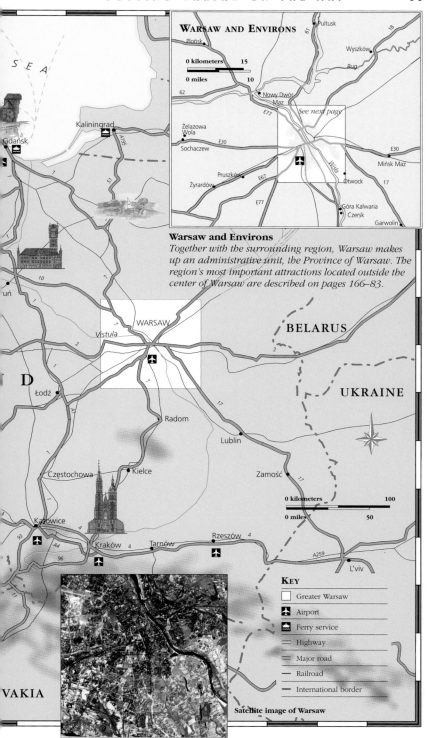

WARSAW AND ENVIRONS

0 kilometers 15

0 miles 10

Pultusk

Płońsk

Wyszków

Bug

Nowy Dwór Maz

See next page

Żelazowa Wola

Sochaczew

E30

Pruszków

Żyrardów

E67

E77

Wisła

Otwock

Mińsk Maz

E30

17

Góra Kalwaria

Czersk

Garwolin

Warsaw and Environs

Together with the surrounding region, Warsaw makes up an administrative unit, the Province of Warsaw. The region's most important attractions located outside the center of Warsaw are described on pages 166–83.

S E A

Kaliningrad

A195

Gdańsk

51

10

uń

WARSAW

Vistula

BELARUS

UKRAINE

D

Łódź

Radom

17

Lublin

Częstochowa

Kielce

Zamość

17

0 kilometers 100

0 miles 50

Katowice

93

A4

96

Kraków 4

Tarnów

Rzeszów 4

A259

L'viv

VAKIA

KEY

☐	Greater Warsaw
✈	Airport
⛴	Ferry service
=	Highway
=	Major road
—	Railroad
—	International border

Satellite image of Warsaw

Greater Warsaw

THE MAJORITY OF ATTRACTIONS listed in this guide are located in central Warsaw and are easily reached either on foot or by public transportation. Moreover, many of Warsaw's most attractive and historic sights are located along what is called the Royal Route, which consists of the main thoroughfares leading from the Royal Castle in the Old Town to Łazienki Park and Wilanów Palace. This book divides the city into seven districts, each of which is detailed within the *Warsaw Area by Area* section.

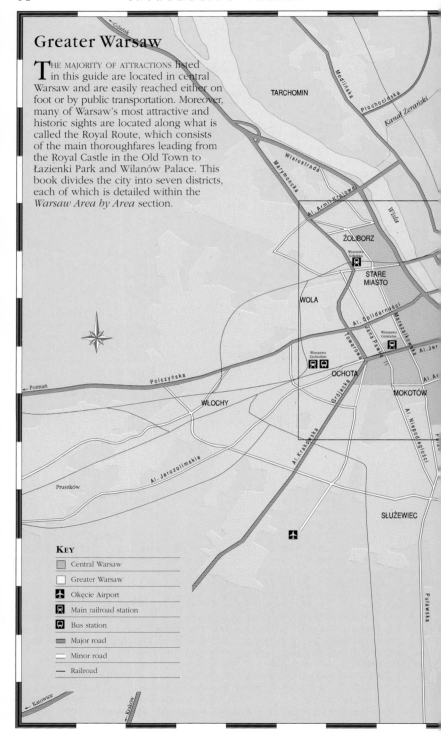

TARCHOMIN

ŻOLIBORZ

STARE MIASTO

WOLA

OCHOTA

MOKOTÓW

WŁOCHY

SŁUŻEWIEC

Pruszków

Poznań

Katowice

Kraków

KEY

	Central Warsaw
	Greater Warsaw
✈	Okęcie Airport
🚉	Main railroad station
🚌	Bus station
▬	Major road
—	Minor road
—	Railroad

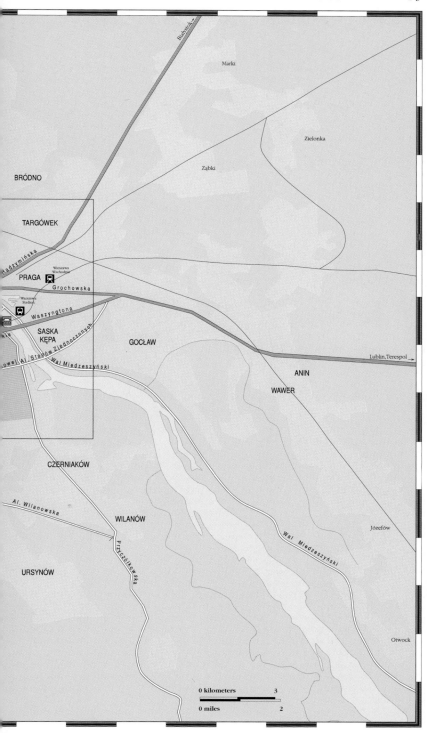

BRÓDNO

Białystok

Marki

Zielonka

Ząbki

TARGÓWEK

Radzymińska

PRAGA

Warszawa
Wschodnia

Grochowska

Warszawa
Stadion

Waszyngtona

SASKA
KĘPA

GOCŁAW

Al. Stanów Zjednoczonych

owej

Wał Miedzeszyński

ANIN

WAWER

Lublin, Terespol

CZERNIAKÓW

Al. Wilanowska

WILANÓW

Przyczółkowska

Wał Miedzeszyński

Józefów

URSYNÓW

Otwock

0 kilometers   3

0 miles   2

THE HISTORY OF WARSAW

WARSAW IS ONE of Europe's youngest capital cities; it became Poland's capital only in the 16th century. But early settlements existed from the 10th century. At the end of the 13th century, Bolesław II, Duke of Mazovia, established a residence and founded what is now known as the Old Town.

The crest of the City of Warsaw

In the early 15th century, Duke Janusz I Starszy established his court in Warsaw, and the town developed rapidly in the late Middle Ages. Although Kraków was the capital, Warsaw remained the seat of the Mazovian dukes. When the dynasty died out in 1526, the king took control of the duchy.

Warsaw's growing status and central position in Poland resulted in Parliament being moved from Kraków to Warsaw in 1569. Warsaw became the capital in 1596, when King Zygmunt III Waza transferred his permanent residence there. In the 17th century, Warsaw continued to develop rapidly, with various churches and palaces being built. But the city's evolution was halted by the Swedish invasion of 1655, known as "the Deluge."

Warsaw continued to grow in the late 18th century during the reign of Poland's last king, Stanisław August Poniatowski. However, the city was occupied by Prussia in 1795. In 1815 Warsaw came under Russian rule. Russian suppression of the 1830 and 1863 insurrections left Warsaw politically weak, but the city still saw rapid industrial growth in that century. Before World War I, Warsaw was Europe's eighth largest city.

When Poland regained independence after World War I, Warsaw was reestablished as the capital. During World War II, Warsaw experienced three dramatic events: the siege of September 1939, the 1943 uprising in the Jewish Ghetto, and the 1944 Warsaw Uprising. Following this last uprising, the Nazis systematically destroyed almost the entire city. Overall, 700,000 of Warsaw's inhabitants (almost half the total) were killed or displaced during the war.

The city came under Communist control in 1945, and a massive rebuilding program restored many of Warsaw's historic monuments. In 1989 the city celebrated the first postwar democratic elections, which ended the Communist era. The pages that follow outline the most important periods of Warsaw's history.

A late-16th-century panorama of Warsaw

◁ **Portrait of King Stanisław August Poniatowski by Marcello Bacciarelli**

Kings and Rulers

WARSAW was originally a seat of the dukes of Mazovia, who were descended from the Polish Piast dynasty. At the beginning of the 15th century, Duke Janusz I Starszy gave Warsaw the status of Mazovia's capital. In 1526, after the death of the last two dukes, Mazovia came under the direct rule of the king, and Warsaw was a royal residence of the Jagiellon dynasty. Warsaw became the capital of the Polish Commonwealth in 1596, under King Zygmunt III Waza, the third king to be elected after the hereditary system was abolished. He and his successors enriched Warsaw with various architectural works. The monarchy ended when Poland lost its independence at the end of the 18th century, and, apart from the Napoleonic era, Warsaw was ruled by occupying powers. From 1918 to 1939, and since 1989, Poland's presidents have governed from Warsaw.

1587–1632
Zygmunt III
Waza
(resident in
Warsaw from
1596)

1518–26
Janusz III

1576–86
Stefan Batory*

1429–54
Bolesław IV

1313–41
Trojden I

1294–1313
Bolesław II

1341–55
Kazimierz I

1573–5
Henryk
Walezy*

1488–92
Janusz II

1200		1300		1400		1500	
DUKES OF MAZOVIA							**JAGIELLONIANS**
1200		1300		1400		1500	

1355–74
Siemowit III

1374–1429
Janusz I Starszy

1471–88
Bolesław V

1492–1503
Konrad III Rudy

1548–72
Zygmunt
August*

1518–24
Stanisław I

Mazovian dukes

1506–48
Zygmunt Stary*
(ruled Mazovia from
1526)

1503–18
Anna Radziwiłł
(Konrad's widow)

*Resident in Kraków

1632–48
Władysław IV
Waza

1764–95
Stanisław
August
Poniatowski

1697–1706
and
1709–33
August II
Mocny

1669–73
Michał Korybut
Wiśniowiecki

1926–39
Ignacy Mościcki

1922–6
Stanisław
Wojciechowski

1947–56
Bolesław Bierut

1918–22
Józef Piłsudski,
Head of State

1989–90
Wojciech
Jaruzelski

1704–9 and
1733–6
Stanisław
Leszczyński

1815–25
Tsar
Alexander I,
King of
Poland**

1881–1894
Alexander III**

00	1700	1800	1900
ECTED KINGS		**ROMANOVS**	**PRESIDENTS**
00	1700	1800	1900

1796–1807
Prussian rule

1674–96
Jan III Sobieski

1855–81
Alexander II**

December 9–16,
1922
Gabriel Narutowicz

1807–15
Fryderyk
August Saski

1825–55
Tsar Nicholas I,
King of Poland
to 1831

1915–18
German
Occupation

1648–68
Jan II Kazimierz Waza

1894–1915
Nicholas II**

1990–95
Lech Wałęsa

1995–
Aleksander
Kwaśniewski

****Resident in St. Petersburg**

1733–63
August III

Warsaw's Origins

A LTHOUGH EARLIER SETTLEMENTS had existed on this site, Warsaw is believed to have been founded at the end of the 13th century, when Duke Bolesław II built a castle. The town expanded under Duke Janusz I Starszy (1374–1429), becoming the Mazovian region's cultural and political center, and the parish church (now St. John's Cathedral, *see pp 76–7*) gained collegiate status. Houses were initially built of wood, which was later replaced by stone. In the late 14th century, the New Town started to develop north of the Old Town, and was granted separate status in 1408.

Warsaw's mermaid

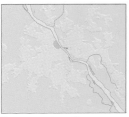

EXTENT OF THE CITY
☐ *ca.1500*   ☐ *Today*

Presbytery of St. John's Cathedral
This is the city's oldest example of Gothic architecture, dating from the first half of the 14th century.

Warsaw Seen from the Vistula *(1581)*
The earliest surviving depiction of Warsaw, a woodcut, documents its Gothic skyline.

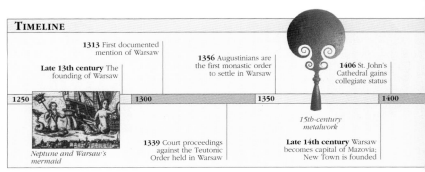

TIMELINE

1313 First documented mention of Warsaw

Late 13th century The founding of Warsaw

1356 Augustinians are the first monastic order to settle in Warsaw

1406 St. John's Cathedral gains collegiate status

| 1250 | 1300 | 1350 | 1400 |

Neptune and Warsaw's mermaid

1339 Court proceedings against the Teutonic Order held in Warsaw

15th-century metalwork

Late 14th century Warsaw becomes capital of Mazovia; New Town is founded

Gothic Portal
This is at No. 21 in the Old Town Market Square.

Duchess Anna Odrowąż
A Mazovian Duchess (1498– ca. 1557).

WARSAW'S LEGENDS

Numerous Varsovian legends were chronicled by the poet Artur Oppman (known as Or-Ot), who lived in the Old Town in the 19th century.

One tale attributes the town's name to the original landowners, Wars and Sawa. Another tells of a mermaid who lived in the Vistula and protected the town, while serenading its inhabitants. Meanwhile, a ferocious monster guarded treasure in the vaults of Zapiecek Square. One look from this monster was lethal, but it was eventually subdued by a cobbler's apprentice. A golden duck was also said to guard treasure in an underground lake beneath the Ostrogski Palace.

Canon Stanisław of Strzelec
As tutor to the last Mazovian dukes, he was buried in the cathedral in 1532.

DUKES OF MAZOVIA
This fragment of a miniature painted in 1449 shows 14th–15th-century Mazovian dukes.

Ducal Seal
Used by the Mazovian Duke Konrad II (1252–94), this seal is in the Raczyński Palace archives (see p92).

Silver Cockerel
This was a symbol of the Brotherhood of Marksmen. It was commissioned in the mid-16th century by a Varsovian aristocrat, Jan Baryczka.

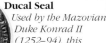

1429 Death of Duke Janusz I Starszy

1454 Construction of St. Anna's Church and Bernardine monastery begins

Gothic door lock and key

1569 Parliament moves to Warsaw from Kraków

1573 First royal election held in Warsaw

1450	1500	1550	1600

1469 Autonomy granted to Jewish Council, which had been founded 100 years earlier

1526 Death of Janusz III, the last Duke of Mazovia

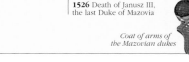

Coat of arms of the Mazovian dukes

Warsaw During the Waza Period

Portrait of King Władysław IV

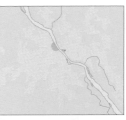

EXTENT OF THE CITY

☐ *1650*   ☐ *Today*

A NEW ERA BEGAN IN 1596 when King Zygmunt III Waza transferred the royal residence from Kraków and made Warsaw the capital. Renowned Italian architects rebuilt the Royal Castle on a grand scale and added several early Baroque buildings. The court also became the intellectual heart of Central Europe, and brought numerous aristocratic families and several monastic orders to Warsaw. The Swedish invasion of 1655 took a heavy toll on the city, however, and was followed by considerable rebuilding work.

Ossoliński Palace
Built in 1641 for the Ossoliński family, this palace was the city's most extravagant and luxurious residence. It was destroyed in 1655.

Queen Cecylia Renata
Queen Cecylia (1611–44) was the first wife of King Władysław IV.

Jesuit Church of Our Lady Mary the Merciful
Built between 1609–26, it has a remarkable dome.

TIMELINE

Artillery of the Waza period in the Polish Military Museum (see p152)

Detail of No. 28 Old Town Market Square

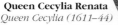

1598 Rebuilding of the Royal Castle begins

	1600		1615

1596 Royal residence moves from Kraków to Warsaw

1597 Jesuits settle in Warsaw

1611 Zygmunt III Waza's triumphal arrival in Warsaw

1607 Devastating fire in the Old Town

Stockholm Scroll
Several meters long, this 17th-century scroll shows the wedding procession of King Zygmunt III Waza.

WHERE TO SEE THE WAZAS' WARSAW

The best example of this period's architecture is the Royal Castle *(see pp70–73)*. Rebuilt after being destroyed during World War II, the Royal Castle contains several royal portraits of the period *(see below)*. Ujazdowski Palace *(p159)* and several burghers' houses in the Old Town, such as the "Little Black Boy House" *(p78)*, also date from this time. Early Baroque churches include the Jesuit Church of Our Lady Mary the Merciful *(p74)* and St. Jacek's Church *(p88)*.

Portraits *of Zygmunt III Waza, Władysław IV, and Jan Kazimierz from the Royal Castle*

A PANORAMA OF WARSAW

This mezzotint, first published in 1696 by Samuel Pufendorf, was based on drawings by Erik Jönsen Dahlbergh, court draftsman of King Charles Gustav of Sweden. It shows Warsaw's Baroque buildings prior to the 1655 Swedish invasion.

King Zygmunt III Waza
Zygmunt's Column, from 1644, is the oldest secular monument in Poland.

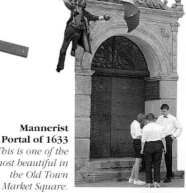

Mannerist Portal of 1633
This is one of the most beautiful in the Old Town Market Square.

The Waza family's coat of arms

1625–6 The worst period of the plague

1632 King Zygmunt III Waza dies

1648 Władysław IV dies

| 1630 | 1645 | 1660 |

1637 Opening of the first permanent theater in the Royal Castle

1644 Zygmunt III Waza's Column is erected

1655 Swedish invasion

Typical Warsaw burghers

Warsaw After the Swedish Invasion

Jan III Sobieski Monument

WARSAW WAS GRADUALLY REBUILT after the devastating Swedish invasion of 1655. The short reign of King Michał Korybut Wiśniowiecki, elected in 1669 after Jan II Kazimierz Waza abdicated, was followed by that of Jan III Sobieski. He was a great patron of the arts, whose election in 1674 inaugurated a new era. Poland's political standing rose, helped by the king's great victory over the Turks at Vienna in 1683.

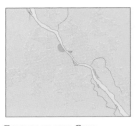

EXTENT OF THE CITY

☐ 1655–1700   ☐ Today

The Daybreak
This work was painted by Jan Reisner, on the ceiling of the queen's chamber at Wilanów.

Krasiński Palace *(1677–82)*
It was designed by the royal architect, the Dutchman Tylman of Gameren, one of many renowned designers brought to Warsaw by Jan III Sobieski.

Field Hetman (Deputy Commander-in-Chief) Stefan Czarniecki
He helped lead Poland to victory over Sweden in 1655–7.

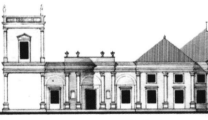

A Noble's Funeral Portrait
In 17th-century Poland, such portraits were specially painted and attached to the coffin while it was displayed before a funeral.

TIMELINE

1661 Founding of *Merkuriusz Polski*, the first Polish periodical printed in Warsaw

1668 Jan II Kazimierz Waza, last in the Waza dynasty, abdicates

1674 Jan III Sobieski elected

1677 Wilanów Palace built

1665	1670	1675

Urn from Ostrogski Palace

Detail from the façade of Wilanów Palace

Queen Marysieńka
Pictured here, together with her children, Marysieńka was the beloved wife of Jan III Sobieski.

Capuchin Church of the Transfiguration
It was founded by Jan III Sobieski in gratitude for his victory over the Turks at Vienna in 1683.

Dome of St. Anthony of Padua Church
Situated on Czerniakowska Street, this church was built in 1687–93 following a design by Tylman of Gameren.

WHERE TO SEE JAN III SOBIESKI'S WARSAW

In addition to Wilanów Palace *(see pp168–71)*, Warsaw has several other buildings from this period. They include the Krasiński Palace *(p102)*, Ostrogski Palace *(p123)*, and St. Casimir's Church *(p90)*, all of which were designed by the court architect Tylman of Gameren.

***Ostrogski Palace** now houses the Frederic Chopin Museum (p123).*

WILANÓW PALACE (1677)
Serving as King Jan III Sobieski's summer residence, surrounded by picturesque gardens, this palace was not used for official functions.

Hussar's Armor
The Polish "winged hussars" won their greatest victories in the 17th century.

17th-century suit of armor

Main altar in St. Anthony of Padua Church

1680	1685	1690

1683 Victory over the Turks in the Battle of Vienna

1692 Construction begins of the Marywil, a covered market area founded by Queen Marysieńka

Saxon Warsaw

IN THE FIRST HALF of the 18th century, two of Poland's elected kings, August II Mocny and August III, were Saxons from the Wettin dynasty. From their court in Dresden, these kings brought the finest Saxon architects and craftsmen to Warsaw, where they created Baroque and Saxon Rococo-style buildings. Despite this, both monarchs spent most of their time in Dresden and dragged Poland into a series of futile wars.

EXTENT OF THE CITY

◼ *1750*　　　　◻ *Today*

Rococo Bureau-Secretary
This fine 18th-century example from the National Museum (see pp154–7) is painted with mythological scenes and features a clock built into its crest.

Meissen Porcelain
Saxon kings were the first to intro-duce Meissen porcelain to Poland; this figurine is in the Royal Castle (see pp70–73).

King Augustus II Mocny

Royal janissaries

Pavilion for the public

Army camp

Dress Sash
Sashes were an essential element of the traditional dress code of Polish aristocrats. This sash can be seen in the National Museum.

Saxon Axis
August II Mocny was inspired by the Versailles of Louis XIV to build an extrav-agant residence surrounded by gardens. This was part of a town-planning scheme.

TIMELINE

Cartridge box of a cavalry officer

1697 August II Mocny elected king of Poland

1704 Stanisław Leszczyński elected king of Poland

1727 Saxon Gardens becomes Warsaw's first public park

1690	1700	1710	1720

1702 Northern War begins

Panorama of Warsaw

1713 Construction of the Saxon Axis begins

1709 August II Mocny becomes king again

Anna Orzelska

August II Mocny gave his daughter Anna a palace, known as the Błękitny (Blue) Palace, as blue was her favorite color (see p106).

Kulawka

A Kulawka wine-glass had no base, so that guests had to drink down each toast in one gulp.

Many of the Saxon buildings in Warsaw, including several palaces and churches on Krakowskie Przedmieście *(see pp112–25)* and Senatorska Street, have been rebuilt since World War II.

Przebendow-ski-Radziwiłł Palace was designed in 1728 by Jan Zygmunt Deybel for King August II's treasurer (see p103).

Standard-bearer opening the royal procession

Polish soldiers

Infantry and cavalry flags

Pulpit in St. Joseph the Guardian's Church

Designed in 1760 by Jan Jerzy Plersch, its boat-like shape symbolized the teaching role of the church.

POLISH AND SAXON REGIMENTS

The summer camp and military displays held on Czerniaków fields in 1732 were in honor of Anna Orzelska's return to Poland from her Grand Tour of Europe.

Personification of Poetry

This is one of many sculptures in the Saxon Gardens from the workshop of Jan Jerzy Plersch. Lactating breasts symbolized the fertility of poetic imagination.

1736 Abdication of Stanisław Leszczyński, followed by the election of August III

Rococo-style crest

1756 Beginning of Seven Years' War, involving large parts of Europe

1740 Collegium Nobilium established

| 30 | 1740 | 1750 | 1760 |

1733 Death of August II Mocny. Stanisław Leszczyński elected king of Poland

1748 Work begins on the city's first opera house

1763 Death of August III

A Rococo commode

Warsaw Under the Last Polish King

POLAND'S LAST KING, Stanisław August Poniatowski, was a great aesthete and patron of the arts who made Warsaw a European cultural center. However, he faced opposition from the aristocracy, making Poland vulnerable, while a lack of military strength meant that the rulers of Prussia, Russia, and Austria were able to divide Poland among them.

The royal coat of arms

EXTENT OF THE CITY

▨ *1770*   ☐ *Today*

Hugo Kołłątaj
A prominent intellectual and figure of the Enlightenment, he was also involved in drafting the Polish Constitution of 1791.

The election field
contained the throne for the future king.

1791 Constitution
This bill of human rights, ratified on May 3, was the first in Europe.

The Voivode (Lord Lieutenant) of the Płock region hands over his region's vote to the marshal of the Sejm (Parliament).

Knights' Hall in the Royal Castle
The king redecorated this hall, and the entire first floor of the Royal Castle, in an early Neo-Classical style.

TIMELINE

Detail from Theater on the Island in Łazienki Park

1764 Stanisław August Poniatowski elected to the Polish throne

1770 Permanent street names are confirmed

1772 Restyling of the Palace on the Water begins in Łazienki Park

1760		1770		178

1765 Military Academy founded

1772 First Partition of Poland

1773 National Ministry of Education established

Bacchus Room in the Palace on the Water in Łazienki Park

1779 National Theater opens

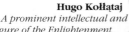

King Stanisław August Poniatowski
In this portrait, the king is depicted deep in thought, contemplating Poland's fate a few months before the Second Partition, of 1793.

WHERE TO SEE PONIATOWSKI'S WARSAW

The Łazienki Park and Palace complex, including the Old Orangerie *(see pp162–5)*, is a beautiful example of Neo-Classicism. Similar palaces can be seen on Krakowskie Przedmieście *(pp118–25)*, Długa Street *(p102)*, and Senatorska Street *(pp106–7)*.

Royal theater in the Old Orangerie

Each region had its own flag.

Theater on the Island
The fashion for antiquities led the king to construct a theater in Łazienki Park featuring Romantic ruins as a backdrop.

Tadeusz Rejtan
As a protest against the First Partition, in 1772, this member of Parliament barred the door to the Chamber of Deputies.

ROYAL ELECTION
Polish kings had been elected by the aristocracy since 1573. Bernardo Bellotto memorialized the election of Stanisław August Poniatowski in 1764.

Carriage of an 18th-century noble

1788 First session of the "Four-Year" Parliament

1789 Delegates from Polish cities stage the "Black Procession"

1791 Constitution ratified

1793 Second Partition of Poland

1794 Kościuszko's Insurrection

1795 Third Partition of Poland. King Stanisław August Poniatowski abdicates

1798 Stanisław August Poniatowski dies

1784 House numbers introduced

Jean-Pierre Norblin's Execution of Traitors

1790

1800

Warsaw During the Partitions

O NE OF THE MOST DIFFICULT periods in Warsaw's history was during the partition of Poland, among Austria, Prussia, and Russia, at the end of the 18th century. Hopes of regaining independence with Napoleon's support proved illusory. Moreover, insurrections resulted in tighter Russian control, with academic and cultural institutions being closed. It was a time, however, that saw rapid industrial growth.

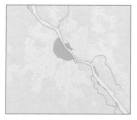

EXTENT OF THE CITY

| ▦ 1850 | ☐ Today |

Maria Walewska
This Polish aristocrat was Napoleon's mistress.

Napoleon Granting a Constitution to the Grand Duchy of Warsaw
Napoleon briefly inspired Polish hopes of regaining national independence.

Personification of Poland

Catherine the Great of Russia

POLAND PARTITIONED

Poland's three powerful neighbors – Russia, Prussia, and Austria – divided the Polish Commonwealth among them. In a contemporary caricature, Catherine the Great of Russia and Frederick Wilhelm II of Prussia quarrel over the spoils following the First Partition in 1772.

Piotr Wysocki
On November 29, 1830, he led fellow officer cadets in an attack on the residence of Grand Duke Constantine. This began the unsuccessful November Insurrection.

TIMELINE

	1800 Inaugural session of the Society of the Friends of Science in Warsaw		**1830** November Insurrection
1796 Prussian army enters Warsaw		**1815** Warsaw becomes capital of a Polish kingdom under the Russian tsar	**1832** In retaliation for the 1830 Insurrection, Russians begin building a citadel
1775	**1800**		**1825**
	1807 Grand Duchy of Warsaw created	**1816** Opening of the Royal University of Warsaw	**1825** Work commences on the Grand Theater
Soldiers of the Napoleonic era			**1845** First section of the Warsaw–Vienna railroad line opened

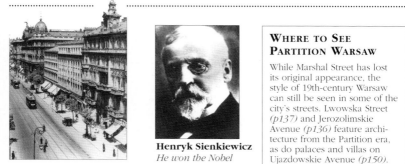

Marshal Street
This broad street, with its multistory buildings, was the principal thoroughfare of 19th-century Warsaw.

Henryk Sienkiewicz
He won the Nobel Prize in 1905 for his novel about ancient Rome, Quo Vadis. *However, his novels on Polish history are more popular.*

WHERE TO SEE PARTITION WARSAW

While Marshal Street has lost its original appearance, the style of 19th-century Warsaw can still be seen in some of the city's streets. Lwowska Street *(p137)* and Jerozolimskie Avenue *(p136)* feature architecture from the Partition era, as do palaces and villas on Ujazdowskie Avenue *(p150)*.

***Villa Sobański** is situated on Ujazdowskie Avenue.*

Advertisement for Okocim Beer
The original was painted by Wojciech Kossak, on tin.

King Frederick
Wilhelm II of Prussia

Frederic Chopin
This great pianist and composer left Warsaw in 1830, never to return.

Mourning Jewelry
Poland was in mourning after the Insurrection of 1863 failed. Women even wore special mourning jewelry.

Zachęta building

1863 January Insurrection begins

1881 Contract signed with Englishman William Lindley for the building of the city's sewer and water systems

1905 Poles support the laborers' insurrection in Russia

Warsaw streetcar

1908 Electric streetcars introduced

850	1875	1900

Grand Theater

1866 Warsaw's first horse-drawn streetcars

Insignia of the 1863 Insurrection

1900 Construction of the Philharmonic building begins

1915 Russian army withdraws from Warsaw

20th-Century Warsaw

Twenty years of independence ended when both the Nazis and the Soviets invaded Poland in 1939. Warsaw was then occupied by the Nazis for more than five years. The Jewish population suffered huge losses in the ghetto area and was exterminated in 1943 after the Ghetto Uprising; the next year, the Warsaw Uprising was also brutally suppressed. Eighty percent of the city had been destroyed, but massive reconstruction during the Communist era revived much of Warsaw's architectural character. Communist rule ended in 1989.

EXTENT OF THE CITY
◼ *1916*   ☐ *Today*

A Warsaw Coffeehouse
The colorful life of Warsaw between the wars, seen in a painting by Józef Rapacki.

Tanks on Puławska Street
The Communist government's reaction to the rise of Solidarity was to declare martial law in December 1981.

Józef Piłsudski
Marshal Piłsudski led the Polish army that liberated the country in 1918. He was subsequently proclaimed the first head of state of an independent Poland.

Warsaw Uprising
The Polish Home Army attempted to liberate the city from the Nazis in 1944.

TIMELINE

1918 Warsaw freed from German occupation

1920 Poland defeats Soviet Russia in the Battle of Warsaw in August

1939 The Nazis enter Warsaw on September 28

1944 On August 1, the Warsaw Uprising begins

1955 World Festival of Youth

The Airmen's Memorial

1915	1930	1945	19

1915 Warsaw University reopens

1926 Coup d'état by Marshal Piłsudski

1940 Jews are confined to the ghetto

1943 On April 19, the uprising begins in the Jewish Ghetto

1945 In January, Warsaw is liberated by the Red Army

1956 Władysław Gomułka seizes power after a rally Plac Defilad

Baśka Orwid
The 1930s film-star models an evening gown that won a prize at a society ball.

The Miner
As well as Socialism, the Communist era introduced a new style in the arts, Socialist Realism.

John Paul II's Visit (1987)
The Polish pope celebrated mass by the Palace of Culture and Science.

SOCIALIST REALISM

The principles of Socialist Realism developed in the Soviet Union under Stalin. This style was imposed on architecture, the visual arts, and literature in postwar Poland and lasted until the mid-1950s. The imagery often verged on self-caricature. Its heroes were Communist Party workers, hearty wenches, and muscular laborers, as in the painting below from the National Museum (pp154–7). Architectural examples of Socialist Realism (pp132–3) include the Palace of Culture (pp134–5), which combines monolithic architecture with sculptures and murals on the same colossal scale.

***Youth Brigade on Rebuilding Work** by Helena Krajewska*

WARSAW IN 1945
Scenes of massive devastation met the people of Warsaw when they returned after World War II.

Poster for the Fifth Chopin International Piano Competition
The Chopin Competition has been held in Warsaw every five years since 1927.

Church at Stegny
Modern churches are a hallmark of Polish avant-garde architecture.

Solidarity *emblem*

1968 In March, student demonstrations are held

1976 Workers' Defense Committee is organized

1981 Martial law is declared in Poland on December 13

1991 First democratic presidential elections

1975

1990

1989 Government holds round-table conference with Solidarity on Poland's future

1984 Communists murder opposition leader Father Jerzy Popiełuszko

1980 On November 10, the Solidarity trade union is legally registered in the Warsaw district court

Syrena car of the 1960s

WARSAW AT A GLANCE

ARSAW'S WIDE SELECTION of palaces, museums, monuments, and places of worship spans various periods and architectural movements. Gothic, Renaissance, Baroque, Rococo, Neo-Classical, Secession, and Socialist Realist are represented. Nearly 140 attractions are listed in the *Area by Area* section of this guide, most of which are easily reached within the city center. The following 18 pages summarize

Warsaw's leading sights, which convey the diverse character of the city. This ranges from ornate and romantic to grand and imposing, as well as modern and metropolitan. Each sight mentioned is cross-referenced to its own full entry elsewhere in the guide. This section also features some of Warsaw's most celebrated natives, who went on to achieve international acclaim. Some of the city's foremost attractions are illustrated below.

WARSAW'S TOP TEN TOURIST ATTRACTIONS

St. Anna's Church
See p116

Royal Castle
See pp70–73

National Museum
See pp154–7

St. John's Cathedral
See pp76–7

Old Town Market Square
See pp78–9

**Palace of Culture
and Science**
See pp134–5

**Monument to the
Ghetto Heroes**
See p142

Grand Theater
See pp110–11

Wilanów Palace and Park
See pp168–71

Łazienki Park and Palaces
See pp162–5

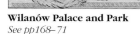
◁ **The Palace on the Water in Łazienki Park**

Famous Emigrés

WARSAW HAS BEEN HOME to many celebrated figures, including writers, musicians, and scientists. However, the 18th-century partitions, two world wars, and the Communist era created political situations hostile to the development of their talents. Many emigrated during these times and went on to attain international success, but the world has often been unaware of their origins.

Helena Modrzejewska (1840–1909)
Prior to her departure for the United States, she triumphed at the Variety Theater (Teatr Rozmaitości, see p111).

Isaac Bashevis Singer (1904–91)
This Polish Jewish writer lived for several years on Krochmalna Street. He won the 1978 Nobel Prize for Literature.

Ignacy Paderewski (1860–1941)
Composer, pianist, and politician, he led the Warsaw Philharmonic's first concert (see p131).

The Former Jewish Ghetto

Czesław Miłosz (b. 1911)
This poet, translator, and Nobel Prize winner for Literature lived in Warsaw from 1937–44. For the first two years, he worked for Polish Radio on Zielna Street.

Joseph Conrad (1857–1924)
Conrad was the nom de plume of novelist Teodor Józef Korzeniowski. Before settling in England in 1884, he lived at No. 47 Nowy Świat (see p124).

| 0 kilometers | 1 |
| 0 miles | 0.5 |

Roman Polański (b. 1933)
The actor and director was born in Paris and brought up in Poland. Best known for films such as Rosemary's Baby *and* Tess, *he has also staged* Amadeus *in Warsaw's Wola Theater.*

Maria Skłodowska-Curie (1867–1934)
Born in the New Town, she achieved international acclaim in Paris for her scientific discoveries and twice won the Nobel Prize (see p90).

Pola Negri (1896–1987)
A Hollywood star of the silent era, her real name was Apolonia Chałupiec. She lived at No. 11 Browarna Street.

Jan Kiepura (1902–66)
This famous tenor began his career in Warsaw's Grand Theater (see pp110–11).

New Town

Old Town

The Royal Route

Around Solidarity Avenue

Pope John Paul II (b. 1920)
Before leaving for Rome, where he was elected pope on October 16, 1978, John Paul II would stay with the Ursuline Sisters at No. 2 Wiślana Street whenever he was visiting Warsaw.

Tadeusz Kościuszko (1746–1817)
The leader of the 1794 insurrection conducted the defense of Warsaw, an event that was subsequently named in his honor. He was also a graduate of the Knights Academy (see p121).

Around Marshal Street

Around Łazienki Park

Frederic Chopin (1810–49)
One of the greatest composers and pianists, as a child he lived at No. 5 Krakowskie Przedmieście (see p121).

Artur Rubinstein (1886–1982)
This world-famous pianist studied at the Warsaw Conservatoire, before emigrating in 1906 (see p123).

Warsaw's Best: Museums and Galleries

Despite the devastations of World War II, Warsaw still enjoys a wide range of museums and art galleries. Their collections illustrate the city's history and explore the works of its writers, artists, and other historic figures. Many museum buildings are also of considerable architectural merit. The Modern Art Center (Centrum Sztuki Współczesnej), for instance, is housed in the 17th-century Ujazdowski Castle, while the Warsaw History Museum occupies several burghers' houses.

Warsaw History Museum
Various exhibits illustrate the history of the city together with its inhabitants.

Jewish History Institute Museum
The museum's collection details the cultural heritage of Poland's Jews.

Zachęta (National Contemporary Art Gallery)
This is Poland's premier modern art venue housed in an impressive Neo-Renaissance building, which dates from 1903.

The Former Jewish Ghetto

Ethnographic Museum
The folk arts and crafts of Poland and other lands are featured here.

Around Marshal Street

National Museum
Warsaw's largest museum has a collection of Polish and other art, including the famous painting by Józef Mehoffer, Strange Garden (1903).

Frederic Chopin Museum
The Chopin memorabilia includes personal possessions and the original manuscript for his Mazurka in F-minor, op. 68, no. 4.

Literature Museum
The museum displays memorabilia, manuscripts, and re-created room sets of Poland's most celebrated writers, including Melchior Wańkowicz's study.

New Town

Frederic Chopin Museum

Old Town

Polish Military Museum
Founded in 1920, at the instigation of Poland's head of state, Marshal Józef Piłsudski, the museum's collection of arms and memorabilia details the history of Poland's military forces, from their origins to the present day.

Around Solidarity Avenue

The Royal Route

Around Łazienki Park

Warsaw Archdiocese Museum
A limited, though interesting, collection of sacred art and crafts includes this cross, which dates from the early 16th century, with 17th-century appliqué.

0 kilometers 1

0 miles 0.5

Modern Art Center
In addition to exhibition space, the museum includes movie theaters, a library, and a modern art information center.

Exploring the Museums and Galleries

Ammonite

THE NATIONAL MUSEUM's extensive collection makes it the city's most interesting museum, though former royal residences such as the Royal Castle and smaller, more specialized museums also have fascinating collections.

POLISH PAINTING AND SCULPTURE

Józef Simmler's Death of Barbara Radziwiłł in the National Museum

THE LARGEST COLLECTION of Polish paintings and sculpture is on display in the **National Museum** (Muzeum Narodowe). This includes one of the most famous and popular Polish paintings, *The Battle of Grunwald* by Jan Matejko (1838–93), the country's finest historical painter. The modern and contemporary art gallery features work by such leading artists as Stanisław Wyspiański (1869–1907) and Jacek Malczewski (1854–1929).

The **Royal Castle** (Zamek Królewski) has a vast collection of furniture, decorative art, sculpture, and paintings, including works by Jan Matejko. The collection is growing all the time, thanks to donations from Polish émigrés.

A fascinating display of Polish fine arts, paintings, and sculpture can be seen in many of the buildings within **Łazienki Park**, particularly in the Palace on the Water (Pałac na Wodzie) and White House (Biały Dom). In the Old Orangerie, several Classical sculptures and plaster casts are evocatively set among the greenery.

Modern art can also be seen at the Neo-Classical Królikarnia Palace (a separate part of the National Museum). It houses the **Xawery Dunikowski Museum**, which is dedicated to the eponymous sculptor. Temporary modern art exhibitions take place at the

Modern Art Center (Centrum Sztuki Współczesnej) and **Zachęta**. The best modern art galleries include Test, Zapiecek, Foksal, and Kordegarda.

EUROPEAN PAINTING AND SCULPTURE

The Raising of Lazarus by Carel Fabritius in the National Museum

THE MOST comprehensive collection of European art in Warsaw can be seen at the **National Museum**. This includes works by various Flemish, Dutch, Italian, French, and German masters, such as Botticelli, Fabritius, and Greuze. The **Royal Castle** also has an extensive collection of European art. The Canaletto Room displays views of Warsaw by Bernardo Bellotto, pupil and nephew of Canaletto, who used his mentor's name.

Other nationalities represented include the Dutch painter Willem Claesz Heda, various French artists such as Claude Joseph Vernet and Elisabeth Vigée-Lebrun, while German artists include Hans Dürer,

Mask in the Ethnographic Museum

Joachim von Sandrart, and Angelika Kauffmann.

Various European masters can also be seen at **Wilanów** and **Łazienki** palaces. The **John Paul II Collection**, which includes Impressionist paintings, is housed in the former Bank of Poland and Stock Exchange building.

ARCHAEOLOGICAL COLLECTIONS

POLISH ARCHAEOLOGISTS have made significant contributions to archaeological discoveries around the world, and this is reflected in the wealth of the city's archaeological collections.

The **National Museum** has a wide range of ancient Egyptian, Greek, and Roman art. The museum's most extraordinary gallery, however, displays early medieval wall paintings from Faras in the Sudan. This is the only collection of its kind in Europe.

Archaeological discoveries made in Poland are exhibited at the **Archaeology Museum** (Muzeum Archeologiczne).

Portrait of St. Anna by an unknown artist in the National Museum

FOLK ART

FOLK ART can be seen at the **Ethnographic Museum** (Muzeum Etnograficzne). The extensive collection includes Polish folk costumes from different regions, together with various artifacts that illustrate folklore, rural life, and traditions. There are also works by internationally acclaimed Polish folk artists. Additionally, Asian and Pacific folk art forms part of the collection at the **Asia and Pacific Museum** (Muzeum Azji i Pacyfiku).

ARTS AND CRAFTS

ARTS AND CRAFTS, both Polish and international, are well represented in the **National Museum**. Meanwhile, a number of exhibits associated with handicrafts can be seen displayed at the **Warsaw History Museum** (Muzeum Historyczne m. st. Warszawy).

An interesting though limited collection can be seen in the **Handicraft and Precision Craft Museum** (Muzeum Rzemiosł Artystycznych i Precyzyjnych). Various leather objects and a selection of associated items are displayed in the **Guild of Leather Crafts Museum** (Muzeum Cechu Rzemiosł Skórzanych). There are other major exhibitions at the Palace on the Water in Łazienki Park, at the Royal Castle, and at Wilanów Palace.

The **Pod Blachą Palace**, within the Royal Castle complex, has Europe's most comprehensive collection of Eastern rugs.

In the gardens of Wilanów, the Orangerie houses an Arts and Crafts Gallery. Additionally, Wilanów's **Poster Museum** (Muzeum Plakatu) was the world's first museum of its kind, and is housed in a former stable. It contains posters by some of the finest artists of the 20th century, including Alphonse Mucha, Andy Warhol, and Pablo Picasso. The Poster Museum also organizes the Warsaw Poster Biennale.

The **Warsaw Archdiocese Museum** (Muzeum Archidiecezji Warszawskiej) features a selection of arts and crafts exhibits alongside its collection of religious art.

HISTORY AND HERITAGE

THE **Warsaw History Museum** illustrates the evolution of Warsaw, and the heritage of the city's people. The **Polish Military Museum** (Muzeum Wojska Polskiego) is housed in the National Museum. Its collection of military memorabilia spans centuries of the armed forces' history.

The **Jewish History Institute Museum** (Muzeum Żydowskiego Instytutu Historycznego) traces the history of Warsaw's Jews, including the events of the Holocaust.

The **Independence Museum** (Muzeum Niepodległości) has a collection of documents detailing Poland's struggle for independence over the past three centuries.

Warsaw has many other specialist museums. The **Literature Museum** (Muzeum Literatury) has exhibits detailing the life and work of the Romantic poet Adam Mickiewicz. The collection of manuscripts and first editions includes works by Juliusz Słowacki and Henryk Sienkiewicz. Museums have also been established in honor of Warsaw's famous inhabitants, such as Ignacy Paderewski (at Łazienki Park), Chopin (at Ostrogski Palace), and Maria Skłodowska-Curie.

Samovar, Warsaw History Museum

The history of Polish theater is exhibited at the **Theater Museum** (Muzeum Teatralne) within the Grand Theater.

SCIENCE AND TECHNOLOGY

THE DEVELOPMENT of science and technology is detailed in the **Museum of Technology** (Muzeum Techniki). A branch of this is the **Industry Museum** (Muzeum Przemysłu), housed in a former metalplating factory. Its collection includes vintage cars.

Natural history is covered by three museums. The **Museum of Evolution** (Muzeum Ewolucji) has dinosaur skeletons discovered in the Gobi Desert

Vintage cars on display in the Industry Museum

by Polish palaeontologists. The **Geology Museum** (Muzeum Geologiczne) features rock and mineral specimens collected from all over Poland. Meanwhile, the **Earth Sciences Museum** (Muzeum Ziemi) has an impressive collection of Polish amber.

Warsaw's Best: Sacred Buildings

POLAND HAS BEEN KNOWN HISTORICALLY for its religious tolerance. This is testified by Warsaw's magnificent range of sacred buildings, which form an important element of the city's character. While many of these buildings were destroyed during World War II, some survived intact, and retain their unique interiors and features. Others have been painstakingly restored in the postwar years.

Basilian Church of the Assumption of the Blessed Virgin Mary
This Byzantine-Ukrainian Orthodox church contains magnificent paintings by the 18th-century Polish artist Franciszek Smuglewicz.

The Former Jewish Ghetto

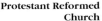

Protestant Reformed Church
This Neo-Gothic church, which was built in the 1860s, has an exquisite steeple.

Nożyk Synagogue
The only synagogue to survive World War II intact was founded from 1898–1902 by the Nożyk family.

Augsburg Protestant Community Church
This architectural masterpiece by Szymon Bogumił Zug is in early Neo-Classical style.

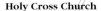

Holy Cross Church
Here you can see epitaphs to renowned Poles, and an urn containing Chopin's heart. This was placed here after his death in Paris, in accordance with his will.

Church of Our Lady Mary
The oldest church in the New Town has retained its Gothic character, despite being damaged in the war.

St. Mary Magdalene's Russian Orthodox Church
In 1969–70 restoration work was carried out on this principal Orthodox church. The conservation work restored Vinogradov's original 19th-century wall decorations.

New Town

Old Town

Around Solidarity Avenue

St. John's Cathedral
Many of the cathedral's monuments escaped wartime damage. Others were reconstructed, such as the tomb of the Speaker of the Sejm (Parliament), Stanislaw Malachowski, which was designed by Bertel Thorwaldsen.

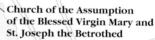

The Royal Route

Church of the Assumption of the Blessed Virgin Mary and St. Joseph the Betrothed
The late Baroque sculpture of Mary and Joseph's wedding is one of the finest of its kind.

Around Marshal Street

0 kilometers 1

0 miles 0.5

Around Lazienki Park

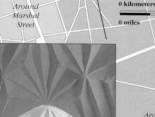

St. Anna's Church
Rebuilt after the war, St. Anna's stands adjacent to the Gothic vaulted Bernardine Monastery, which escaped wartime damage.

Exploring Warsaw's Sacred Buildings

Angel at St. Joseph the Guardian's Church

THE FIRST CHURCHES were built when Warsaw was founded in the 14th century. However, as a result of the devastation caused by the 1655 Swedish invasion, none of Warsaw's earliest churches have survived in their original form. The greatest era of religious building was the late Baroque, which remains the most typical style among Warsaw's churches.

Presbytery of St. Anna's Church

MEDIEVAL CHURCHES

WARSAW'S FIRST churches, built in the early 14th century, were wooden.

The city's oldest church is **St. John's Cathedral** (katedra św. Jana), which also dates from the 14th century. Originally a parish church built in the Gothic style, it underwent various alterations over the centuries. Following its destruction during World War II, the cathedral was restored to its original style, known as Mazovian Gothic.

Another example of Gothic is **Church of Our Lady Mary** (kościoł Panny Marii), which is in the New Town. It was founded in the 15th century by Anna, the wife of Duke Janusz I Starszy of Mazovia. The **Bernardine Monastery**,

by **St. Anna's Church** in Krakowskie Przedmieście, features an early Gothic presbytery, in addition to cloisters that are overarched with late Gothic vaulting.

RENAISSANCE AND MANNERIST CHURCHES

RENAISSANCE and Mannerist styles enjoyed only a brief popularity in Warsaw. Moreover, there are few examples of these styles because they were fashionable at virtually the same time as were late Gothic and early Baroque. The Bernardine Monastery,

Baroque façade of St. Martin's in the Old Town

for example, was built in a Gothic style in the 16th century and was almost contemporary with early Baroque alterations made to the Royal Castle (Zamek Królewski).

The finest example of Mannerism, albeit combined with Baroque, is the **Jesuit Church of Our Lady Mary the Merciful** (kościół Najświętszej Marii Panny Łaskawej, Jezuitów) in the Old Town. It has a Mannerist-Baroque façade, and an unusual elliptical dome above the presbytery.

BAROQUE CHURCHES

ALMOST ALL the city's early Baroque churches were destroyed during the Swedish invasion. However, one of the most interesting Baroque interiors to survive is in **St. Jacek's Church**. Its side aisles are an example of the Lublin style of ribbed vaulting.

Reconstruction following the Swedish invasion resulted in many new churches. Several designed by the architect Józef Szymon Bellotti feature wall-and-pillar aisles. These include the **Church of the Assumption of the Blessed Virgin Mary and St. Joseph the Betrothed** (kościół Wniebowzięcia NMP i św. Józefa Oblubieńca), **Holy Cross** (św. Krzyża), **St. Anthony of Padua Reformed Church** (św. Antoniego Padewskiego, Reformatów), and a re-created aisle of **St. Anna's Church**.

The Dutch architect Tylman of Gameren designed the **Bernardine Church of St. Anthony of Padua** (św. Antoniego Padewskiego, Bernardynów), built on

DOMES AND SPIRES

As in any city, church domes and spires provide good orientation points. They frame numerous perspectives from Warsaw's streets, and add variety to the panoramic view from the Vistula. A great number of churches were destroyed during World War II, but since then many have been rebuilt. Some were returned to their original form, which had been lost during previous refurbishments.

Gothic

Bell tower, Church of Our Lady Mary

Baroque

St. Casimir's

Neo-Classical

St. Alexander's Church

**Neo-Renaissance façade of
All Saints Church**

Czerniakowska Street, and **St. Casimir's** (św. Kazimierza).

The **Capuchin Church of the Transfiguration** (kościół Przemienienia Pańskiego, Kapucynów) is also a great Baroque masterpiece. The

Church of St. Andrew Bobola

most notable of the late Baroque churches are the **Church of the Holy Spirit** (św. Ducha) and **Holy Trinity** (Przenajświętszej Trójcy), but **St. Joseph the Guardian** (Opieki św. Józefa) is widely considered to be the most beautiful. The façades of existing churches, including those of **St. Martin's** and **Our Lady, Queen of Poland** (NMP Królowej Korony Polskiej), were carefully re-created in a late Baroque style.

NEO-CLASSICAL AND REVIVAL ARCHITECTURE

THERE ARE MANY outstanding examples of early Neo-Classical religious architecture in Warsaw. The **Augsburg Protestant Community Church** (kościół Ewangelicko-Augsburgski), on Królewska Street, was constructed by Szymon Bogumił Zug, in 1777–81. The **Basilian Church of the Assumption of the Blessed Virgin Mary** (kościół Wniebowzięcia NMP, Bazylianów) dates from the same period and was designed by Dominik Merlini.

Chrystian Piotr Aigner re-designed the façade of St. Anna's Church in a Neo-Classical style, modeling it on the Palladian façades of Venetian churches. Aigner also designed **St. Alexander's Church**, built in 1818–25.

Many churches were built during the 19th-century Revival period, when historic styles were back in fashion. Henryk Marconi specialized in the Neo-Renaissance, exemplified by **St. Charles Borromeo** (kościół Karola Boromeusza) on Chłodna Street, **All Saints** (Wszystkich Świętych) on Grzybowska, and **St. Anna's Church** in Wilanów.

The Neo-Gothic style was favored by Józef Pius Dzie-koński, who built the **Church of the Savior** (kościół Zbawiciela), **St. Florian's**, and **St. Stanisław the Bishop** in Wola. The **Protestant Reformed Church** in Leszno is also in the Neo-Gothic style.

Several Russian Orthodox churches were built in the 19th century, when Warsaw was under Russian rule.

They were usually built in the Byzantine-Russian style, though only four have survived; **St. Mary Magdalene's** is one of

St. Alexander's Neo-Classical altar

these. Most of the synagogues destroyed during World War II were from the 19th century. The only survivor is **Nożyk Synagogue**, built 1898–1902.

Revival

Eclectic

Modern

**Bell tower, St.
Anna's Church**

**Church of
the Savior**

**Our Lady Mary the
Merciful, in Stegny**

Exploring Warsaw's Cemeteries

Warsaw's oldest cemeteries were founded at the end of the 18th century. The majority of the city's cemeteries were spared the destruction of World War II, and even the Jewish cemetery survived unscathed. A walk around any of the Powązki cemeteries provides not only a historic, but also an artistic experience. These cemeteries feature mausoleums and tombs in various artistic styles, which were designed by master craftsmen for Warsaw's most distinguished citizens.

Muslim Tartar Cemetery
This was the only cemetery to be almost completely destroyed during World War II. Only a few tombstones have survived intact.

The Katyń Cross in the Communal Cemetery

Tombstone in the Tartar Cemetery

The Old Powązki Catacombs

Halpert family chapel in the Augsburg Protestant Cemetery

A maseba in the Jewish Cemetery

The Communal Cemetery in Powązki
Originally a military cemetery, it also features a symbolic cross commemorating the Katyń victims.

The Orthodox Church in Wolski Cemetery

The Protestant Reformed Cemetery

A grave in the Warsaw Uprising Cemetery

Warsaw Uprising Cemetery
This cemetery was established in 1945, as a resting place for the military and civilian victims of the 1944 Warsaw Uprising.

An obelisk in the Mausoleum Cemetery of the Red Army

Augsburg Protestant Cemetery
Splendid tombs of the city's former bourgeoisie can be seen at this cemetery.

Russian Orthodox Cemetery
One of Warsaw's two working Orthodox churches, St. Jan Klimak, is located here.

0 kilometers 5

0 miles 2

Bródno Cemetery
Founded in 1883 to serve Praga, it is now used by the entire city.

A wooden church in Bródno

Powązki Cemetery
Founded in 1790, almost 1 million people have been buried in this cemetery.

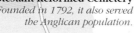

Jewish Cemetery
Many eminent Varsovian Jews are buried here, including Ludwik Zamenhof, the inventor of Esperanto. This is one of several cemeteries comprising the Powązki Cemetery.

Protestant Reformed Cemetery
Founded in 1792, it also served the Anglican population.

Mausoleum Cemetery of the Red Army
This monumental site is rich in architectural features and sculptures. It was designed by Jerzy Jarnuszkiewicz, with sculptures by Bohdan Lachert.

Exploring Warsaw's Cemeteries

Painting at Wolski Cemetery

THE GREATEST CONCENTRATION of cemeteries is in the Powązki district, where there are seven, bearing witness to Warsaw's multi-religious and multinational history. As well as its large-scale cemeteries, Warsaw has smaller, parish cemeteries, such as Wilanów, which are worth visiting.

Secessionist tomb by Wacław Szymanowski at Powązki Cemetery

ROMAN CATHOLIC CEMETERIES

POWĄZKI IS THE OLDEST of Warsaw's principal cemeteries. Since its establishment in 1790, approximately 1 million people have been buried here. The cemetery's tombs and mausoleums span the various artistic styles of the past 200 years.

Among the most historic sections of the cemetery are the Church of St. Charles Borromeo and the catacombs. By this section is the Aleja Zasłużonych (Avenue of Merit). Along this thoroughfare many celebrated Polish figures are buried, including the authors Władysław Reymont and Bolesław Prus, the opera singer Jan Kiepura, the composer Stanisław Moniuszko, and the film director Krzysztof Kieślowski, best known for his films *Red*, *White*, and *Blue*.

Many of the tombstones on this avenue were designed by outstanding architects and sculptors. The finest examples include works by Jakub Tatarkiewicz, Pius Weloński, and Wacław Szymanowski, whose Secessionist monument of Frederic Chopin stands in Łazienki Park.

Bródno is the largest cemetery in Poland. Originally it served the poorest inhabitants of the Praga district, but gradually the entire city and various social classes began to use it. By the 1920s even prominent citizens such as Roman Dmowski and Aleksander Cardinal Kakowski were buried here.

Roman Catholics were also served by a section of the **Communal Cemetery** (Cmentarz Komunalny) in Powązki, as well as the **Wolski Cemetery** and large, new municipal burial grounds on the outskirts of the city.

Some of Warsaw's most historic districts have retained their "rural" cemeteries. Even though they are now surrounded by modern buildings, their unique, intimate atmosphere has not been lost. Among these are cemeteries at **Wilanów, Tarchomin,** and **Służew**. At Służew Cemetery, by the chapel of St. Catherine (św. Katarzyny), lie the remains of political prisoners murdered during the Stalinist era.

MILITARY CEMETERIES

THE CEMETERY with the longest military tradition is the Communal Cemetery in Powązki. Originally established for Russian soldiers, it has been used since 1918 by the Polish Army. This includes servicemen who died during World War I and the Polish-Soviet War. There is also a section for victims of the January insurrection of 1863.

At the outbreak of World War II, the cemetery was initially used to bury soldiers killed during the first month of the war, followed by members of the resistance and victims of the Warsaw Uprising. From 1941 the cemetery was also used to bury Nazi soldiers. After the war, a symbolic tomb was established, dedicated to Polish officers murdered by the Red Army in Katyń.

Having been extended, the cemetery also incorporates Aleja Zasłużonych, where Polish politicians such as Bolesław Bierut and Władysław Gomułka are buried.

After the war, the ashes of Warsaw's resistance fighters were moved from the Communal Cemetery to the **Cemetery of the Warsaw Uprising** (Cmentarz Powstańcow Warszawy).

Powązki, the oldest of Warsaw's cemeteries

The Jewish Cemetery, in the Powązki district

This was founded in 1945, near the **Russian Orthodox Cemetery** (Cmentarz Prawosławny). The ashes of an estimated 40,000 Varsovians were exhumed and reburied in the Cemetery of the Warsaw Uprising, following the liberation of Warsaw. A separate tomb was established in memory of Jews murdered between 1940–43.

Warsaw also has military cemeteries that are dedicated to other nationalities. The **Italian Army Cemetery** (Cmentarz Żołnierzy Włoskich) on Pułkowa Street dates from 1927. Soldiers killed on Polish soil during World War I and the ashes of Italian prisoners of war killed by the Nazis were buried there.

Red Army soldiers killed during the liberation of Warsaw in 1944–5 are buried in a separate cemetery. Founded in 1949, it was the work of outstanding Polish architects, sculptors, and designers.

CEMETERIES SERVING OTHER RELIGIONS

ALMOST ALL RELIGIONS that have been practiced in Poland have also established their own cemeteries in Warsaw.

The **Jewish Cemetery** is in Powązki. Ludwik Zamenhof, the creator of the Esperanto language, is one of several eminent Jews who are buried here.

The **Augsburg Protestant Cemetery** holds the family tombs of Warsaw's great industrialists, including the Wedel family (whose chocolate confections are legendary), together with celebrated figures from the arts world. Among these are the painter Wojciech Gerson and Samuel Bogumił Linde, who compiled a renowned Polish dictionary. The **Protestant Reformed Cemetery** includes the biologist Marceli Nencki, the painter Józef Simmler, and the popular singer Anna German.

During World War II, a section of the Powązki Cemetery suffered considerable damage. However, the worst destruction was inflicted on two Muslim cemeteries, one of which is the **Tartar Cemetery**. These cemeteries include Russian soldiers, as well as merchants and diplomats.

Among those that escaped wartime destruction are the **Jewish Cemetery** in Bródno, and two in the Wola district.

Adamina Chołoniewska's ornate tombstone at Powązki Cemetery

They are the tiny **Karaite Cemetery** and a large **Russian Orthodox Cemetery**. In addition to Russians buried during the Partition of Poland (1772–1918), a number of Russian builders, accidentally killed during construction of the Palace of Culture and Science, are also buried in this cemetery.

Powązki Cemetery on All Souls' Day

Warsaw's Best: Palaces and Gardens

For centuries, warsaw's architectural style was dominated by the prevailing taste of the royal court and nobility. The Baroque era, from the late 16th to the early 18th century, saw many of Poland's wealthiest families establishing residences in Warsaw. The funds lavished on these private residences, which were designed by the finest architects, often exceeded the amounts spent on royal palaces. Their façades add an air of splendor to Warsaw's most prestigious streets, while many of the gardens that originally belonged to these houses are now attractive public parks.

Krasiński Gardens
Adjoining the Krasiński Palace, this park was laid out in the 17th century. After World War II, the park was extended to incorporate the former Nalewki Street and part of the destroyed Jewish Ghetto.

Saxon Gardens
Open to the public since 1727, the gardens were originally part of the so-called Saxon Axis, a Baroque town-planning scheme.

Botanical Gardens
These gardens were established in 1818, within the vicinity of Łazienki Park.

The Former Jewish Ghetto

Królikarnia
This small Neo-Classical palace was built in 1782–9 by royal architect Dominik Merlini, for the notorious gambler Karol de Valery Thomatis. The building now houses a museum dedicated to the Polish sculptor Xawery Dunikowski.

Wilanów Park
The gardens were laid out in two sections: the symmetrical French-style terraces, and the English-style landscaped garden, which runs along the lake.

Royal Castle
The ballroom, open to the public since 1988, was the final room to be reconstructed within the Royal Castle.

Ujazdowski Castle
Although the castle survived a fire during World War II, the ruins were demolished in 1954. Twenty years later, it was rebuilt in the original Baroque style, and now houses the Modern Art Center.

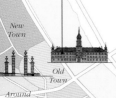

Łazienki Park
The park was established in the 17th century on the site of a former zoo. The palaces and pavilions were added later.

New Town

Old Town

Around Solidarity Avenue

The Royal Route

Around Marshal Street

Around Łazienki Park

Palace on the Water
A copy of the Belvedere Apollo adorns the ballroom's chimney-piece, which is supported by figures of Marsyas and Midas.

Wilanów Palace
The interiors of this palace, built as King Jan III Sobieski's summer residence, retain their original 17th-century style.

0 kilometers 1

0 miles 0.5

Exploring the Palaces and Gardens

N ONE OF WARSAW'S PALACES survived World War II intact, and those that escaped structural damage had their interiors looted. Major postwar reconstruction was often limited to the façades of the palaces, while the interiors were frequently adapted to other uses. The most beautiful palaces, however, did have their interiors restored, and most are now open to the public as museums. Other palaces serve as exhibition venues, government offices, and the headquarters of various organizations. Warsaw is also proud of its parks and gardens, and is one of Europe's greenest capitals.

Putti on the terrace at Wilanów

Ujazdowski Park

BAROQUE PALACES

W ARSAW'S OLDEST PALACE is the **Royal Castle** (Zamek Królewski), which includes fragments of the Mazovian dukes' original Gothic castle. Rebuilt for King Zygmunt III Waza (1587–1632), this is a unique early Baroque building, which was both a royal residence and the seat of the Polish Parliament. The **Ujazdowski Castle** (Zamek Ujazdowski) was also rebuilt in a Baroque style during the reign of Zygmunt III Waza. Other palaces from that period did not survive the 1655 Swedish invasion, and were rebuilt in later years.

The royal summer residence in **Wilanów** was built during the reign of Jan III Sobieski (1674–96). The royal architect, Tylman of Gameren, also designed other palaces for Warsaw's magnates. The most splendid are the **Krasiński Palace** (Pałac Krasińskich)

and the **Gniński-Ostrogski Palace** (Pałac Gnińskich-Ostrogskich), commonly called Ostrogski Palace, which contains the Frederic Chopin Museum.

The election of August II Mocny as king in 1697 led to architects from Dresden coming to Warsaw. They designed the Saxon Axis (Oś Saska) and Saxon Palace (Pałac Saski). New palaces were built, and existing ones restyled in Baroque and Rococo fashion. Among these are the **Kraków Bishops' Palace** (Pałac Biskupów Krakowskich), **Blue Palace** (Pałac Błękitny), and **Czapski Palace** (Pałac Czapskich).

The **Branicki Palace** on Miodowa Street, **Radziwiłł Palace** in Leszno, **Sapieha Palace** in the New Town, and **Potocki Palace** on Krakowskie Przedmieście were rebuilt after World War II.

NEO-CLASSICAL PALACES

D URING THE REIGN of King Stanisław August Poniatowski (1764–95), art and architecture continued to flourish. He commissioned new interiors for the Royal

The Baroque Ostrogski Palace

Castle and redesigned the **Łazienki Palace and Park**. Among the architects then working in Warsaw were Efraim Schroeger, Chrystian Piotr Aigner, Szymon Bogumił Zug, Jan Chrystian Kamsetzer, and Dominik Merlini. They designed and refurbished several Neo-Classical palaces, drawing their inspiration from antiquity and from the then fashionable Andrea Palladio (1508–80). Palladian style is evident in the **Primate's Palace** (Pałac Prymasowski) and the **Królikarnia** (Rabbit Warren) mansion, based on Andrea Palladio's Rotunda. The **Raczyński, Mostowski, Belweder, Lubomirski, Pac**, and **Tyszkiewicz** palaces are also Neo-Classical.

The exquisite Moorish Salon in the Neo-Classical Pac Palace

The Neo-Classical Tyszkiewicz Palace

The **Namiestnikowski Palace**, originally a 17th-century building, was restyled in the Neo-Classical manner by Chrystian Piotr Aigner, after Poland came under Russian rule in the early 19th century. First used as a residence for the tsar's governor, it is now the official residence of the president of Poland.

PARKS AND GARDENS

WARSAW'S first gardens were laid out for the grand palaces. The oldest examples are the **Krasiński** and **Saxon** gardens (Ogród Saski), with the Saxon Gardens the first to open to the public.

Centrally located and close to the Old Town, the Saxon Gardens provide an ideal haven while sightseeing. The largest of the former palace gardens are Łazienki Park and Wilanów Park, on the edge of the city. Fragments of the English landscaping style have also survived, such as Morskie Oko surrounding Szuster Palace, created in the 18th century for Princess Izabela Lubomirska. There are also several monastery gardens in Warsaw, situated on picturesque slopes. Among these are gardens that belong to the Order of the Blessed Sacrament and the Reformation Brethren in the New Town; the Nuns of the Visitation, on Krakowskie Przedmieście; and the St. Vincent de Paul Sisters of Mercy on Tamka Street. However, these gardens are not open to the public and can be seen only from a distance.

More parks were laid out in the 19th century, including the **Botanical Gardens** and the **Ujazdowski Park**. At the beginning of the 20th century, the extensive **Skaryszewski Park**, dedicated to Ignacy

Paderewski *(see p34)*, was created in the Praga district, which is located on the right bank of the River Vistula.

After Poland regained its independence in 1918, several parks were created on sites that were formerly occupied by fortifications. One example is **Traugutt Park**.

Following World War II, land was nationalized, which made it possible to transform several undeveloped and war-damaged demolition sites into parks and squares. This resulted in Podzamcze Párk, which is close to both the Old Town and New Town, and the vast Central Park of Culture (Centralny Park Kultury), in Powiśle. In 1992, the Park of Culture was dedicated to the prewar Polish leader, Marshal Edward Rydz-Śmigły.

The Botanical Gardens, laid out in the 19th century

The Palace on the Water in Łazienki Park, designed by Domenik Merlini

WARSAW THROUGH THE YEAR

W ARSAW has plenty to offer throughout the year, but is particularly enjoyable during spring and autumn, when the weather is sunny but mild, and there is a wealth of cultural and religious events. The summer means warmer weather and more visitors, as well as the annual Mozart Festival, among others. Music festivals continue in the autumn, with modern music celebrated in both the Warsaw Autumn and the Jazz Jamboree. The Chopin International Piano Competition is also held every five years. Winter is marked by Christmas preparations, followed by the carnival season. Details of festivals and continual events can be obtained from tourist information offices *(see p237)* and local publications *(see p245)*.

SPRING

T HE MAJOR religious festival in spring is Easter. It is as important for Poles as Christmas, and in Warsaw it dominates this time of the year. The season brings the first warm weather of the year; streets and parks come to life, and the sunshine hails the start of the tourist season. Consequently, museums extend their opening hours, and attractions such as the Botanical Gardens reopen their gates to visitors.

MARCH

Palm Sunday *(Sun before Easter)*. In the morning, people go to Mass to have their "palm" branches blessed. Traditionally, these branches are made as colorful as possible, using blossoming spring flowers, and the procession to church is a delightful sight.
Easter Saturday. Varsovians pack a basket with foodstuffs *(święconka)* such as rye bread, eggs, salt and pepper, and sausages, and take it to church to be blessed. Various churches display a symbolic

Easter palm

"Christ's Tomb," often beautifully decorated and carrying a social or political message.
Easter Monday. This public holiday is also known as *śmigus-dyngus*, after the tradition of sprinkling people with water. This rustic custom has also become an urban institution and source of much amusement.
Drowning of Marzanna *(Mar 21)*. Stemming from a pagan tradition, an effigy of Marzanna (a witch symbolizing winter) is "drowned" on the first day of spring to mark the death of winter. Children make a Marzanna figure out of straw and rags and carry her to the banks of the River Vistula. There, they throw her into the water, while singing folk songs.
International Poster Biennale. Held every two years, this exhibition of posters, gathered from sources around the world, is organized by the Poster Museum *(see p168)*.

APRIL

April Fools' Day *(Apr 1)*. People play practical jokes on one another. Newspapers,

Guard by the Tomb of the Unknown Soldier

and television and radio stations run bogus stories to trick the unwitting.

MAY

Labor Day *(May 1)*. This public holiday is in honor of the country's workers.
May 3 Constitution Day *(May 3)*. This public holiday marks the anniversary of the first Polish Constitution of 1791. Celebrations are in the Parliament and Royal Castle, and include arts events.
Warsaw International Book Fair *(third week of May)*. This fair for the publishing trade is held in the Palace of Culture and Science *(see pp134–5)*.
Festival of Latin American Culture. This week-long festival displays a range of art from the cultures of Central and South America.

Children throwing water on *śmigus-dyngus* (Easter Monday)

AVERAGE MONTHLY HOURS OF SUNSHINE

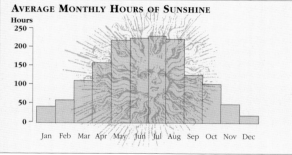

Hours
250
200
150
100
50
0

Jan Feb Mar Apr May Jun Jul Aug Sep Oct Nov Dec

Sunshine Chart
The largest number of sunny days in Warsaw is usually between the months of May and August. However, spring and autumn are also sunny and mild, particularly the months of April, September, and the first half of October. During the winter, Warsaw's skies are mostly clouded over.

Enjoying the sunshine by Chopin's monument in Łazienki Park

SUMMER

ALTHOUGH WARSAW is not as hot as some other European capitals, many people still leave the city and head for their *działka* (small chalet in the country), swimming pools, or the beach. In July and August, most theaters and the Philharmonic are closed, but the Chopin Music Society organizes regular performances through the summer. Plenty of seasonal cafés and beer houses open, offering live music and some food alfresco.

JUNE

Chopin Music Concerts
(Sundays in Jun). Concerts are held (weather permitting) in Łazienki Park, close to the Chopin Monument.
Garden Theater Festival
(early Jun–mid-Sep). Street theater troupes from across Europe perform in Warsaw's squares and the courtyard of the Dean's House.
Mozart Festival *(mid-Jun– end of Jul)*. Peformances of Mozart's music *(see right)*.

Midsummer's Eve *(Jun 23)*.
To celebrate the coming of summer, Varsovians set adrift on the River Vistula hundreds of wreaths bearing candles and then enjoy some tremendous fireworks displays.

JULY

Organ Music Festival
(Jul – end of the holidays).
This annual event is held in St. John's Cathedral.

Warsaw Summer Jazz Days
(Jul–end of Sep). This is an annual series of performances held at various venues, with performances by Polish jazz players as well as guest artists from around the world.

AUGUST

Anniversary of the 1944 Warsaw Uprising *(Aug 1)*.
The anniversary of this major event in Warsaw's 20th-century history is commemorated by all Varsovians.
Assumption of the Virgin Mary *(Aug 15)*. This is a public holiday, and an important religious festival, celebrated throughout Poland. The object of particular veneration is an icon of the Black Madonna, which is at Jasna Góra Monastery in Częstochowa, about 200 km (125 miles) southwest of Warsaw. Numerous pilgrims make the journey on foot from Warsaw and all over Poland to arrive in Częstochowa on this day.

MOZART FESTIVAL

This popular summer event provides a unique opportunity to hear all of Mozart's operas, including his early works, performed by the same group of artists. The festival is organized by the Warsaw Chamber Opera *(see p146)*, whose director is Stefan Sutkowski. Concerts of Mozart's music are also performed by symphony and chamber orchestras in the Philharmonic *(see p131)* and the opulent surroundings of some of Warsaw's palaces. Additionally, choral works, such as masses, are performed in several churches around the city.

Performance of *The Magic Flute* during the Mozart Festival

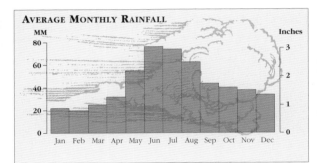

AVERAGE MONTHLY RAINFALL

Rainfall Chart
Warsaw has a continental climate, so its weather is often fickle. The city can suffer from heavy summer rain, which can go on for days, though during some years Warsaw has experienced drought. Snow falls every winter, which creates a beautiful white landscape.

AUTUMN

ONE OF THE BEST times to visit Warsaw is in the autumn, between September and early October. There are fewer tourists, generally the weather is good, and the parks are rich with autumnal tones.

The majority of Warsaw's cultural events take place in the autumn, the most important of which include the Warsaw Autumn, the Warsaw Film Festival, and the Jazz Jamboree. In addition, theaters and the National Philharmonic Orchestra reopen, following their summer break. Various ceremonies also mark the reopening of the universities.

Concert in the annual Jazz Jamboree festival

A park lane in autumn

SEPTEMBER

Warsaw Autumn *(third and fourth weeks of Sep)*. This ten-day festival of contemporary music brings together composers and performers from around the world.
Warsaw Autumn of Poetry *(throughout Sep)*. Poets give readings in several venues around the city. One of the most historic and popular of them is the Old Gunpowder Depository (Stara Prochownia, *see p89*).

OCTOBER

Warsaw Film Festival *(throughout Oct)*. An international festival of new and classic films, shown in several theaters around the city.
Jazz Jamboree *(Oct)*. One of the most important jazz festivals in Europe, held annually in Warsaw since 1958.
Festival of Early Music *(throughout Oct and Nov)*.
Focusing on Renaissance and Baroque music, performances are held in several venues. On Sundays, concerts take place in the Royal Castle.

NOVEMBER

All Saints' Day *(Nov 1)*. A public holiday, celebrated as the Feast of the Dead. Many people visit cemeteries, tidy up family graves, and decorate

CHOPIN INTERNATIONAL PIANO COMPETITION

One of the most important piano competitions in the world, this event has been held in October or November every five years since 1927. It is organized by the Frederic Chopin Society, and only music by this composer is performed. Concerts are held in the Philharmonic. The festival attracts the world's finest pianists and their peers, who sit on the competition jury or simply attend the competition to hear new performers. Among former winners of the competition, whose careers it has helped to launch, are Vladimir Ashkenazy, Maurizio Pollini, Garrick Ohlsson, and Krystian Zimerman.

Frederic Chopin

AVERAGE MONTHLY TEMPERATURE

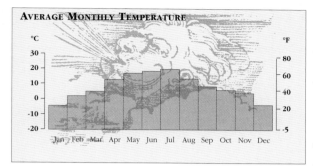

Temperature Chart
This chart shows the average temperatures for each month in Warsaw over the past 30 years. As the figures indicate, most summers are pleasantly warm, although sometimes there can be very hot spells. Winters are usually frosty, with temperatures frequently falling below freezing.

them with flowers and candles. At dusk, the cemeteries glow with candlelight.

Independence Day *(Nov 11).* This commemorates the end of the German occupation of Warsaw in 1918. It is regarded as the date when Poland finally regained independence, following the partitions that began in the late 18th century.

Candle illuminating a grave on All Saints' Day

WINTER

WARSAW'S WINTERS are usually very cold and snowy. Seeing the city shrouded in snow makes a lasting impression on visitors; among the most romantic areas to stroll in are Łazienki Park and the Old Town.

December is taken up with preparations for Christmas, which most people celebrate in a traditional manner. This means a 12-course meatless dinner (one course for each apostle) on Christmas Eve, which begins when the first star appears. After this dinner, Varsovians attend Midnight Mass, while Christmas carols are sung throughout the city.

New Year's Eve marks the beginning of the Carnival season of dances and parties, including masked balls. The

Carnival celebrations culminate with a bout of revelry on Shrove Tuesday.

DECEMBER

Christmas Fairs *(throughout Dec).* Defilad Square, in front of the Palace of Culture and Science, and Castle Square are occupied by stalls where you can buy Christmas trees, decorations, and various foodstuffs for the Christmas Eve dinner.

Christmas Eve *(Dec 24).* Festivities begin with a meatless dinner after nightfall.

Christmas *(Dec 25 and 26).* All churches hold special Masses on both days.

New Year's Eve *(Dec 31).* Celebrations go on in style, with grand balls and private parties. Crowds also gather in Castle Square under King Zygmunt's Column.

JANUARY

Warsaw Theater Meetings. Poland's most outstanding theater productions from the previous year are presented as an "encore" in January.

FEBRUARY

"Fat Thursday" *(end Feb).* In Poland, the last day of indulgence before the fasting of Lent is celebrated on the Thursday before Ash Wednesday. The traditional activity is to eat heartily, and patisseries and bakers sell more doughnuts than anything else on this day.

Shrovetide *(end Feb).* The last Saturday of the Carnival season before Ash Wednesday is a day of revelry, with balls and events, such as the Bill Haley Rock'n'Roll Competition.

PUBLIC HOLIDAYS

New Year's Day (Jan 1)
Easter Monday *
Labor Day (May 1)
Constitution Day (May 3)
Corpus Christi *
Assumption of the Virgin Mary (Aug 15)
All Saints' Day (Nov 1)
Independence Day (Nov 11)
Christmas (Dec 25 & 26)

* Dates change according to the church calendar.

A display of typical Christmas decorations

A RIVER VIEW OF WARSAW

THE RIVER VISTULA has always played an important role in Warsaw's history, particularly in developing the city's trade. As the Vistula is wide enough to provide 225 m (750 ft) of navigable waters, it was always the main waterway connecting Warsaw with other towns, such as Kraków and Sandomierz in the south, and Toruń, Płock, Włocławek, and Gdańsk in the north.

The first permanent bridge across the Vistula was built in the 16th century, but it lasted only about 30 years. It wasn't until the mid-19th century that the next permanent bridge was built, following the invention of caissons (watertight chambers used in underwater construction). Until that time, the river could be crossed all year round by boat, while pontoon bridges were

Detail of the Poniatowski Bridge showing Warsaw's mermaid

constructed in the summer. When the river froze during the winter, people also walked across the ice. Warsaw still has too few bridges. Currently there are only six road and two railroad bridges.

The problem of flooding was solved only in the 19th century when dams were built. At the same time, boulevards were constructed on the Left Bank, though only the central sections were completed.

Unlike other European capitals, Warsaw has managed to retain many undeveloped riverside sites, including Praga's marshy banks and several parks at the foot of the escarpment. Consequently, the river and riverbanks act as a viewing platform, providing wonderful panoramas of the city. Warsaw can be admired while strolling along the boulevards or on board a riverboat.

Warsaw panorama painted in 1770 by Bernardo Bellotto, Canaletto's nephew

The riverboat jetty by Poniatowski Bridge on Wybrzeże Kościuszkowskie

BOAT TRIPS ALONG THE VISTULA

Pleasure boats operate from May to September. Trips last 1 hour and there are five a day, departing at 9:20am, 11am, 1pm, 2:30pm, and 4pm. Boats leave from the jetty at Wybrzeże Kościuszkowskie by Poniatowski Bridge. For further information, group bookings, and private hire 620 76 00.

New Town

Old Town

The Former Jewish Ghetto

Around Solidarity Avenue

The Royal Route

Around Marshal Street

Around Łazienki Park

KEY

 Riverboat jetty

0 kilometers 5

0 miles 2

18th-century pontoon bridge across the Vistula

The River Dredgers
Dredging the Vistula increased its depth, making it far more navigable, while the sandy riverbed provided building material for the city. This painting (1887) by Aleksander Gierymski shows the "sand diggers" at work.

Old Town

The panorama of the old town (Stare Miasto) is dominated by the magnificent Royal Castle, with its Gothic and Baroque architecture. The Gothic St. John's Cathedral is also an imposing feature, together with the Jesuit Church of Our Lady Mary the Merciful. Burghers' houses form a backdrop to King Zygmunt's Column on Castle Square, while a cluster of steep, red roofs inset with skylights extends to the north.

St. Martin's Tower
This is visible at the end of a charming alleyway that connects Świętojańska Street with Piwna Street, opposite St. John's Cathedral (see p75).

Castle Square
Approached from Krakowskie Przedmieście, this square (Plac Zamkowy) is an impressive entrance to the Old Town (see p68).

Royal Castle
A feature of the castle is the late-16th-century Władysław Tower, which has an impressive stone portal (see p71).

Kubicki Arcades

Pod Blachą Palace
Originally built in the 1650s, its late Baroque façade dates from the 18th century. The tin roof added at the same time provided the name, which means "Under Tin" (see p69).

St. John's Cathedral
The Gothic façade, including this arched portal, was reconstructed after World War II and designed by Jan Zachwatowicz (see pp76–7).

Jesuit Church of Our Lady Mary the Merciful
This Mannerist-Baroque church dates from the 17th century (see p74).

No. 2 Old Town Market Square
Once owned by the Jesuits, this house features a plaque dedicated to the preacher Piotr Skarga (see pp78–9).

LOCATOR MAP
See Street Finder, maps 1–4

House "Under the Lion"
No. 13 in the Old Town Market Square, this house contains murals painted between 1928–9 by Zofia Stryjeńska (see p78).

Wąski Dunaj
This street owes its name (which means "narrow Danube") to a stream that flowed here during medieval times (see p82).

Kleinpoldt House
Part of the Warsaw History Museum, this house in the Old Town Market Square has the Old Town's only 18th-century painted ceiling (see p81).

Gnojna Góra
This was Warsaw's historic refuse dump (see p83).

Kamienne Schodki
Originally, this narrow and stepped street led up to a gate in the Old Town walls. The street's name means "Stone Steps" (see p83).

Old Town Market Square
The square includes Baroque, Gothic, and Neo-Classical buildings (see pp78–9).

New Town

SEEN FROM THE RIVER VISTULA, the New Town (Nowe Miasto) panorama features many church towers and spires, together with magnificent cloistered gardens along the river embankments. Remarkably unchanged despite almost 45 years of Communist rule, these tranquil gardens are still tended by monks and nuns, separated by only a wall from the bustle of the New Town. One of the most popular tourist attractions, the New Town's attractive streets are lined with churches, restaurants and shops.

St. Jacek's Church
This Baroque church was built by the Dominicans in the 17th century (see p88).

Barbican
Separating the Old Town and New Town, this gatehouse was built in the 16th century to a design by Venetian architect Giovanni Battista (see p83).

Freta Street
This charming, cobbled street is a favorite place for a promenade, with its many restaurants, cafés, and shops (see p90).

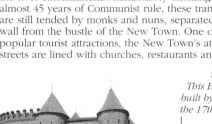

Mostowa Street

Old Gunpowder Depository

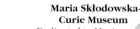

Maria Skłodowska-Curie Museum
Dedicated to Maria Skłodowska-Curie's life and work, the museum occupies her family home on Freta Street (see p89).

Church of the Holy Spirit
This Baroque church, originally built by the Pauline order in the early 18th century, was reconstructed from its wartime ruins (see p88).

18th-century Warsaw is seen in this panorama of the Old Town and New Town, depicting various landmarks that are still recognizable.

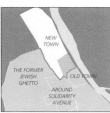

LOCATOR MAP
See Street Finder, maps 1–3

Nove Miasto Restaurant, one of several excellent restaurants in the New Town, is very popular with health food enthusiasts and vegetarians *(see p214)*. The restaurant's large terrace is ideal for alfresco dining during the summer.

Church of St. Benon
The church's Gothic sculpture of the Madonna was originally from Silesia (see p91).

New Town Market Square
This photograph, dating from 1917, shows St. Casimir's Church. To its left is the characteristic bell tower of Our Lady Mary's Church.

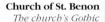

Our Lady Mary's Church
Reconstructed after World War II, this church retains its original Mazovian Gothic style (see p93).

St. Casimir's Church
The ornate tomb of Princess Marie Caroline de Bouillon, the last of the Sobieski line, is in this 17th-century church (see p90).

WARSAW
AREA BY AREA

OLD TOWN

THE OLD TOWN (Stare Miasto) is one of the most historic and fascinating parts of Warsaw. It was established at the end of the 13th century, around what is now the Royal Castle, originally the seat of the Mazovian dukes. The Old Town was designed as something of a geometric "chessboard" of streets, and the area has maintained its medieval town-planning scheme. The Old Town was completely destroyed by the Nazis during World War II.

Decorative portal of the "House Under the Ship"

The area was subsequently rebuilt from rubble with a fastidious eye for historical detail and is now listed by UNESCO as a World Heritage Site. The heart of the area is the Old Town Market Square (Rynek Starego Miasta), with its distinguished architecture, restaurants, cafés, shops, and museums. The surrounding streets also house museums and feature historic architecture, such as the City Walls, the Barbican, and St. John's Cathedral.

SIGHTS AT A GLANCE

Churches
Jesuit Church of Our Lady Mary the Merciful **10**
St. John's Cathedral **8**
St. Martin's Church **12**

Museums and Galleries
Guild of Leather Crafts Museum **23**
Handicraft and Precision Craft Museum **15**
Literature Museum Dedicated to Adam Mickiewicz **19**
Warsaw History Museum **20**

Historic Streets and Squares
Broad and Narrow Dunaj Streets **21**

Castle Square **2**
Gnojna Góra **28**
Kanonia **9**
Old Town Market Square **16**
Piekarska Street **14**
Piwna Street **11**
Stone Steps **27**
Zapiecek **13**

Historic Buildings and Monuments
The Barbican **25**
City Walls **24**
Fukier House **17**
The Mermaid **26**
Pelican House **6**
Pod Blachą Palace **7**
Royal Castle **1**

St. Anna's House **18**
Salvator House **22**
Zygmunt's Column **4**

Bridges
Gothic Bridge **5**

Communication Links
W–Z Route Tunnel **3**

GETTING THERE

While the Old Town is closed to traffic, there are bus stops in Castle Square for routes E-1, 116, 122, 174, 175, 179, 195, 495, and 503. Streetcar routes 4, 13, 26, and 32 stop by the W–Z Route Tunnel.

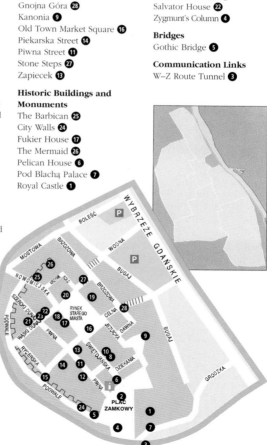

0 meters   300

0 yards   300

KEY

Street-by-Street map *pp66–7*

P Parking

i Tourist information

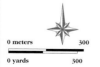

◁ **Summer crowds in the Old Town Market Square**

Street-by-Street: Old Town

THE OLD TOWN is one of Warsaw's most beautiful and fascinating areas. Varsovians as well as tourists enjoy strolling along its historic streets. The Old Town Market Square, with authentically re-created burgher's houses, offers a range of restaurants, cafés, galleries, shops, and museums. When the weather is warm, the square becomes full of café tables, various traders pitch their stalls, and street artists abound. The adjacent streets, particularly Piwna and Jezuicka, also feature an array of historic attractions, including monuments, churches, museums, and palaces.

St. Martin's Church
The lower floors of this church tower, a dominant feature of Piwna Street, are Gothic, while the top two floors are Baroque **12**

Piwna Street
Sculpted pigeons above the entrance to No. 6 commemorate a woman who fed the birds among the postwar ruins of the Old Town **11**

★ **Royal Castle**
This room, with magnificent interior features dating from 1777–81, currently serves as a venue for concerts and other important events **1**

Pod Blachą Palace
The extensive collection of Oriental rugs and textiles in the palace includes this 17th-century "dragon" design Armenian rug **7**

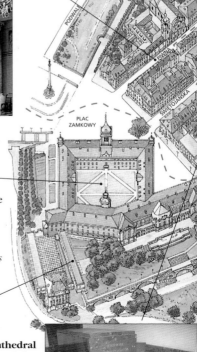

PODWALE

PLAC ZAMKOWY

PIWNA

ŚWIĘTOJAŃSKA

★ **St. John's Cathedral**
The vaults of this Gothic church house the tombs of celebrated Poles, including novelist Henryk Sienkiewicz **8**

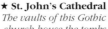

City Walls

In places, it is still possible to see the double ring of defensive walls that surrounded the Old Town. The walls are best preserved by the Barbican 24

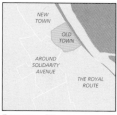

LOCATOR MAP
See Street Finder, maps 1, 4

Salvator House

Religious statues once stood atop the façade of this 17th-century house 22

PODWALE

RYNEK STAREGO MIASTA

This painting by Aleksander Gierymski, which was completed in 1883, depicts the portal of a house in the Old Town Market Square, as well as the dress styles of the time.

★ Old Town Market Square

Street artists are just one attraction in this beautiful and bustling square 16

KEY

— — Suggested route

0 meters 100

0 yards 100

Kanonia

A church bell dating from 1646 stands at the center of this small square, the site of houses that were originally built for the cathedral canons 9

STAR SIGHTS

★ Royal Castle

★ St. John's Cathedral

★ Old Town Market Square

Zygmunt's Column in the middle of Castle Square

Royal Castle **❶**
Zamek Królewski

See pp70–73.

Castle Square **❷**
Plac Zamkowy

Map 2 D4 & 4 D4. **▣** *E-1, 116, 122, 174, 175, 179, 195, 495, 503.*

Castle square dates from only 1818–21, when it was laid out according to a design by architect Jakub Kubicki. Before then, the area it covers was the outer courtyard, or bailey, of the castle. It was surrounded by houses and by sections of the city walls, including one of their most important gates, the Krakowska Gate. This was the town's main gateway to the south, giving access to the road to Kraków.

The eastern side of the square is fronted by the Royal Castle, while to the north and west it is framed by old houses. To the south, however, the square opens up into Krakowskie Przedmieście, which forms the initial part of Warsaw's "Royal Route" *(see pp112–25)*, leading from the castle to the royal summer residence of the Wilanów Palace and Park *(see pp168–71)*.

Castle Square is one of the emblems of Warsaw and symbolizes Poland's capital for the whole country. Crowds gather in the square for political demonstrations, and Varsovians greet the New Year here with the popping of champagne corks. This is also the favorite place in the city for lovers to arrange their rendezvous.

W–Z Route Tunnel **❸**
Tunel Trasy W–Z

Map 1 C2, 2 D2, 3 C5 & 4 D5. **▣** *4, 13, 26, 32.*

This tunnel is a section of the east–west (W–Z) route, running underneath Castle Square and Miodowa and Senatorska streets to take traffic between Solidarity Avenue and the Śląsko-Dąbrowski Bridge. The building of the tunnel in 1947–9 caused great concern among local people, as it was feared that the construction work was undermining the foundations of houses in the streets above. Escalators lead from Castle Square to the tunnel entrance. Since they were built at the height of the Communist era, the decor of these sections of the tunnel is in pure Socialist Realist style, reminiscent of the Metro stations in Moscow and St. Petersburg.

Figure of the king from Zygmunt's Column

Zygmunt's Column **❹**
Kolumna Zygmunta

Plac Zamkowy. **Map** 2 D2 & 4 D5.

The column standing in the center of Castle Square is the oldest secular memorial monument in Warsaw. It is dedicated to King Zygmunt III Waza, who transferred his residence to Warsaw in 1596 *(see pp20–21)*. The column was erected in 1644, on the orders of the king's son, King Władysław IV.

A drawing to show how Zygmunt's Column was erected

The granite main column rises from a tall plinth and supports a bronze figure of King Zygmunt holding a cross in one hand and a sword in the other. This impressive statue was the work of Clemente Molli, while the column and base were designed by two famous Italian architects who worked for many years for the kings of Poland: Agostino Locci the Elder and Constantino Tencalla.

The monument is 22 m (72 ft) high and virtually unique in Europe because, with its large cross, it glorifies the monarch in a manner that was usually reserved for saints. It has been damaged in war and restored many times over the centuries, but the bronze figure of the king has managed to escape destruction. The present column, however, is actually the third one that has been built to support the statue. Parts of the second one can be seen lying nearby.

A cheerful house in Warsaw's popular Castle Square

Gothic Bridge ❺
Most gotycki

Plac Zamkowy. **Map** 2 D2 & 4 D5.

ONLY A SECTION remains of this two-arched brick bridge, built at the end of the 15th century, but in use again today. It once spanned the moat in front of the Krakowska Gate, on the main route out of the city to the south. At its southern end, the bridge was protected by a fortified gatehouse. This, like the walls and main gate, was demolished in 1808, when the moat was filled in and the bridge buried. Its existence was forgotten for many years, and it was discovered only in 1977. After restoration, it was opened to pedestrians in 1983.

Pelican House ❻
Kamienica Pod Pelikanem

Plac Zamkowy 1/13. **Map** 2 D2 & 4 D4.

THE LARGE HOUSE that fills the corner where Piwna Street meets Castle Square was built in the late 17th century and completed in 1705. In the mid-18th century, this was the home of the royal architect, Karl Friedrich Pöppelmann. It is one of seven houses that originally stood on the north side of what was then Bernardyńska Street, one of the historic streets of Warsaw's Old Town. The south side of Bernardyńska Street was demolished when Castle Square was opened up in the early part of the 19th century. Since then, this and the other houses situated on the former north side of the street have faced onto the square. The "Pelican House" takes its name from the sculpture of a pelican that can be seen on one corner of the building. The house also has a wooden canopy that runs the length of the ground-floor windows. This is a characteristic feature of Warsaw houses that date from the 17th and 18th centuries.

The pelican on Pelican House

This house was destroyed in 1944, during World War II, as were others on this side of Castle Square. It was reconstructed in 1957, with new sgraffito by architect Edmund Burke. It now houses a tourist information center.

Pod Blachą Palace ❼
Pałac Pod Blachą

Plac Zamkowy 2. **Map** 2 D2 & 4 D4.
831 91 99, ext. 170. 🚌 116, 122, 175, 195, 503. 🚋 Plac Zamkowy. ⏰ 10am–4pm Tue–Sun. 🎟 included in Royal Castle, see pp70–73.

BAROQUE IN STYLE, this palace was last "modernized" in 1720, on the initiative of its owner, Jerzy Dominik Lubomirski. Its ornate walls conceal the remains of an older house that was constructed during the 17th century.

The palace frequently changed hands. Its owners included Poland's last king, Stanisław August Poniatowski, and his nephew, the famous hero of the Napoleonic Wars Prince Józef Poniatowski. Following many years of neglect, the building was partially restored in 1932. Several of the rooms in the north wing were redecorated using original paneling designed for the Royal Castle by the royal architect Dominik Merlini in 1778–80. Since 1988, the palace has formed part of the Royal Castle Museum and provided a home for a unique collection of Oriental rugs and textiles. The bequest of Teresa Sahakian, it is the world's largest and most valuable collection of Caucasian rugs.

At the rear of the palace, built into the escarpment above the River Vistula, there is a vault that in the 17th century belonged to a Masonic lodge. Statues of Greek deities stand along its walls.

The grand Baroque frontage of Pod Blachą Palace

Royal Castle ❶

THE ROYAL CASTLE (Zamek Królewski) is a magnificent example of Baroque architecture. A castle was built on this site by the Mazovian dukes in the 14th century. After Warsaw was chosen as the seat of the Sejm (Parliament) in 1569 and King Zygmunt III Waza moved his residence to this castle in 1596, Warsaw replaced Kraków as the capital of Poland. Between 1598 and 1619, the king commissioned Italian architects to restyle the castle into a polygon. In the 18th century, King Augustus III gave the east wing a Baroque style, while King Stanisław August Poniatowski added the Royal Library. In 1939, the castle was burned, and then blown up by the Nazis in 1944. Reconstruction funded by public donations lasted from 1971 to 1988. The castle is now a museum housing furniture, paintings, and numerous objets d'art.

Royal coat of arms on Władysław's Tower

Bacciarelli Annex
During the 18th century, this was a studio and school run by Marcello Bacciarelli. It is now a popular Registry Office.

★ Zygmunt's Tower
Also known as the clock tower, with a clock first installed in 1622, it was rebuilt and the clock restarted in 1974.

Great Court
Rebuilt in its original Gothic style, this was the residence of the Mazovian dukes during the 15th century.

TIMELINE

	1764 Stanisław August Poniatowski elected and crowned				**1988** Rebuilding completed	
1655–7 Castle looted by the Swedes during invasion			**1740–52** Saxon Wing added		**1971** Reconstruction of the castle begins	
Early 15th century Great Court built	**1598–1619** Royal Castle built in its present form				**1939** German artillery sets castle on fire	

1300	1400	1500	1600	1700	1800	1900

	1570–71 New residence built for Zygmunt August			**1775** Interiors designed by Dominik Merlini	**1926** Castle becomes residence of president of Poland	
Before 1339 Fortifications and watchtower built		**1596** Warsaw replaces Kraków as the capital city		**1791** Ratification of the Constitution of May 3		
				1944 Nazis blow up the castle		

★ Saxon Wing
Remodeled in a Baroque style during the reign of King August III in the 18th century, this wing faces east toward the River Vistula. Its statues were designed by Jan Jerzy Plersch.

VISITORS' CHECKLIST

Plac Zamkowy 4. **Map** 2 D2 & 4 D4. 657 21 70. **Ticket office** Świętojańska 2. 657 23 38 (9am–2pm Tue–Fri). E-1, 116, 122, 174, 175, 179, 195, 495, 503. 10am–4pm Tue–Sun.
Royal Apartments
Apr 15–Sep 30: 10am–6pm Tue–Sun. Jan 1, Easter, May 1, Corpus Christi, Nov 1, Dec 24–25, Dec 31. free Thu (except Royal Apartments).

The kitchen yard is the main entrance to the castle for visitors.

Władysław's Tower
Built in 1571, the tower was remodeled in 1637–43.

The Kubicki Arcade is a viewing terrace, supported by arcades, overlooking the re-created castle gardens.

Pod Blachą Palace
This palace became a part of the Royal Castle complex only in 1988. It now houses a collection of Middle Eastern rugs and textiles.

The Royal Library is an imposing Neo-Classical building used for exhibitions.

Grodzka Tower
The oldest part of the castle, this tower was built in the mid-14th century as a defensive feature.

STAR SIGHTS

★ **Zygmunt's Tower**

★ **Saxon Wing**

Exploring the Royal Castle

THE ROYAL CASTLE's fascinating interiors are the result of its dual role: being a royal residence as well as the seat of the Sejm (Parliament). Meticulously reconstructed after World War II, the castle features royal apartments, as well as the Chamber of Deputies and the Senate. Many of the furnishings and objets d'art are original, with statues, paintings, and even fragments of woodwork and stucco that were hidden from the Nazis. Among the paintings are works by Bernardo Bellotto and Marcello Bacciarelli.

Painted and inlaid tabletop (1777)

Lecture hall

★ Ballroom
Seventeen pairs of gilt columns support the ceiling of this grand room. The ceiling painting is a reproduction of Bacciarelli's Dissolution of Chaos.

Cel

Concert hall

Visitors' entrance

Ground floor

Prince's Apartments
Historical paintings by Jan Matejko adorn these rooms.

First floor

★ Senate Chamber
The Con-stitution of May 3 was ratified here in 1791 (see p26).

King Stanisław August Poniatow-ski's Apartment
The Rococo paneling, from the destroyed Tarnowski Palace, is thought to be by Juste-Aurèle Meissonier.

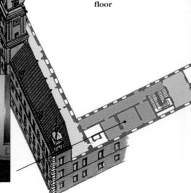

★ Marble Room
This room's lavish decor and furnishings date from the reign of King Władysław IV Waza in the 17th century. The portraits of Polish monarchs by Bacciarelli are 18th century.

The Former Chamber of Deputies housed the deputies of the Sejm's lower house during the 17th century.

Knight's Hall
A statue of Chronos by Jakub Monaldi dominates this beautifully appointed room.

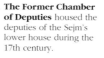

New Audience Room
In addition to its fine parquet floor, this room includes the original stuccowork.

KEY TO FLOOR PLAN

- [ ] Great apartment
- [ ] Royal apartments
- [ ] Courtyard rooms and the former Chamber of Deputies
- [ ] Sejm (Parliament)
- [ ] King Stanisław August Poniatowski's apartments
- [ ] Prince's apartments and galleries
- [ ] Permanent exhibitions
- [ ] Royal Library
- [ ] Nonexhibition areas

★ Canaletto Room
Bernardo Bellotto, who often used the name of his uncle Canaletto, painted the views of 18th-century Warsaw exhibited in this room.

STAR FEATURES

- ★ **Ballroom**
- ★ **Senate Chamber**
- ★ **Marble Room**
- ★ **Canaletto Room**

St. John's Cathedral ❽
Katedra św. Jana

See pp76–7.

Kanonia ❾

Map 2 D2. ⛟ *E-1, 116, 122, 174, 175, 179, 195, 195, 495, 503.*

THIS SMALL SQUARE (which is actually triangular in shape) is located behind St. John's Cathedral. It is lined with attractive houses, which were built for the cathedral clergy on the site of a former grave-yard. Originally dating from the 16th century, these houses were reconstructed in their present form after the war.

In the center of the square is a church bell, cast in 1646 by Daniel Tym. He also cast the original bronze figure of Zygmunt III Waza *(see p68).*

The covered footbridge originally connected the Royal Castle with the cathedral. It was built for royal use as a form of security, after Michał Piekarski attempted to kill Zygmunt III Waza (1587–1632) as he entered the cathedral.

Piekarski was tortured before being executed, and during his torture kept uttering non-sensical phrases. This resulted in a popular Polish saying: "muttering like Piekarski."

Between 1800 and 1823, the Society of the Friends of Science, established by the Enlightenment writer Stanisław Staszic, held its meetings in the square at Nos. 5 and 8.

One of Warsaw's most prominent poets, Artur Oppman (known as Or-Ot), lived at No. 8 from 1910 to 1925.

The Jesuit Church of Our Lady Mary the Merciful

Jesuit Church of Our Lady Mary the Merciful ❿
Kościół NMP Łaskawej

Świętojańska 10. **Map** 2 D2. 🚹 📷

BUILT TOGETHER with a monastery, in a style that mixes Mannerism and Baroque, this Jesuit church dates from 1621. After the dissolution of the monastery in 1773, the church remained largely unchanged until 1944, when it was almost completely destroyed. Fortunately, the original architectural records survived the war, which enabled this unique church to be accurately reconstructed. Occupying a particularly narrow site, the church has several interesting features. A lantern in the dome allows daylight to flood into the presbytery. The building's Gothic vaults were formed from the cellars of houses that were demolished when the church was built. Among the tomb-stones in the vaults is the magnificent monument to Jan Tarło, which was designed by the sculptor Jan Jerzy Plersch.

The entrance to the church features the figure of a bear, which formerly stood in the Piarist church on Długa Street.

Piwna Street ⓫
Ulica Piwna

Map 1 C2. ⛟ *E-1, 116, 122, 174, 175, 179, 195, 195, 495, 503.*

THE LONGEST STREET in the Old Town, Piwna Street connects Castle Square with Wąski Dunaj Street. Piwna Street was first mentioned in the 15th century, when it was

An illustration of Piwna Street in 1865

also known as St. Martin's (after the church on this street). Piwna Street was originally a fashionable address for aristocratic families, though it is now known for its fine restaurants.

St. Martin's Church ⓬
Kościół św. Marcina

Piwna 9/11. **Map** 1 C2. 🚹 📷

DATING FROM the 15th century, St. Martin's Church was built for the Augustinian Order, which came to Warsaw in 1352. Its present form is the

Kanonia's historic houses, with the church bell displayed in the square

Crucifix in St. Martin's Church

result of two Baroque-style refurbishments: between 1631 and 1636, and in the mid-18th century. The latter was supervised by the renowned architect Karol Bay, whose designs included a "wave-like" façade. Unfortunately, this restyling was destroyed during World War II.

Nevertheless, a modern interpretation of the Baroque interiors was re-created under the direction of Sister Anna Skrzydlewska. The only original artifact that remains is a partially burned crucifix, which has been hung on a pillar in the nave.

St. Martin's Church has long played an important role in the history of Warsaw. From the 16th century, it was used by the Mazovian gentry. In the 17th century, theological and philosophical debates were held at St. Martin's.

In 1950 the church was taken over by a Franciscan order of nuns, the Servants of the Holy Cross. Their mission is to care for the poor.

During the 1980s, members of Solidarity and other anti-Communist movements held clandestine meetings here.

Adjoining St. Martin's Church, there is a delightful cloistered courtyard, which is part of the nunnery.

Zapiecek ⑬

Map 2 D1. 🚌 E-1, 116, 122, 174, 175, 179, 195, 195, 495, 503.

Originally part of Piekarska Street, this small square is now classified as a thoroughfare in its own right.

During the 19th century, it was the venue for Warsaw's most important bird market. A comprehensive choice ranged from racing pigeons to more exotic songbirds.

The surrounding attractions currently include a contemporary art gallery. There are several restaurants in the square that provide alfresco tables during the summer months.

A plaque on one of the walls of the square commemorates the fact that Warsaw's Old Town has now been added to UNESCO's esteemed list of World Heritage Sites.

Piekarska Street ⑭
Ulica Piekarska

Map 2 D1. 🚌 E-1, 116, 122, 174, 175, 179, 195, 195, 495, 503.

This street was originally occupied by numerous bakers and millers, as its name suggests (*piekarz* is Polish for "baker").

Brick buildings were first constructed on this street in the 18th century. At the same time, a section of the Old Town's defensive walls was demolished to provide a direct link to Podwale Street.

At the junction of Piekarska and Rycerska streets, there used to be a small square called Piekiełko, meaning "little hell." During the 16th–17th centuries, executions were carried out in the square. These included the burning of witches and poisoners. Michał Piekarski, who attempted to kill King Zygmunt III Waza, was also executed here.

At the Podwale end of the street is the Jan Kiliński Monument *(see p101)*. He was a heroic leader of the 1794 Kościuszko Insurrection.

Handicraft and Precision Craft Museum ⑮
Muzeum Rzemiosł Artystycznych i Precyzyjnych

Piekarska 20. **Map** 2 D1. 📞 831 96 28. ⏰ 10am–1:30pm Mon–Fri. 📷

Housed in an 18th-century building, which was restored after World War II, the museum's collection includes watches and jewelry. The earliest exhibits date from the 16th century. Other objets d'art include the "masterworks" that had to be presented to a craft's guild by engravers

Clock at Handicraft Museum

and goldsmiths, before they were granted a license to work independently.

Old Town Market Square ⑯
Rynek Starego Miasta

See pp78–9.

Diners at one of the sidewalk restaurants on Zapiecek Square

St. John's Cathedral ❽

COMPLETED IN THE EARLY 15th century, St. John's Cathedral (katedra św. Jana) was originally a parish church. Gaining collegiate status in 1406, St. John's did not become a cathedral until 1798. Among the important events held here was the coronation of Stanisław August Poniatowski in 1764, and the swearing of an oath by the deputies of the Sejm (Parliament) to uphold the 1791 Constitution. After World War II, 19th-century additions were removed from the façade, and the cathedral was restored to its original Mazovian Gothic style. The cathedral's interiors feature ornate tombs and religious art.

Chalice
As the inscription states, this was made by King Zygmunt III Waza.

An Earlier Façade
This prewar photograph shows the cathedral's façade after it was refurbished in 1836–40 by the architect Adam Idžkowski.

★ Crypt of Gabriel Narutowicz
Poland's first president, assassinated two days after taking the presidential oath, is buried here, as is the Nobel Prize-winning novelist Henryk Sienkiewicz.

Main entrance

Tomb of the Mazovian Dukes
This marble tomb commemorates the last two Mazovian dukes, after whose death the dukedom became extinct and was incorporated into the Polish crown.

Bell tower

Adoration of the Magi
This is an early copy of a painting by Domenico Ghirlandaio.

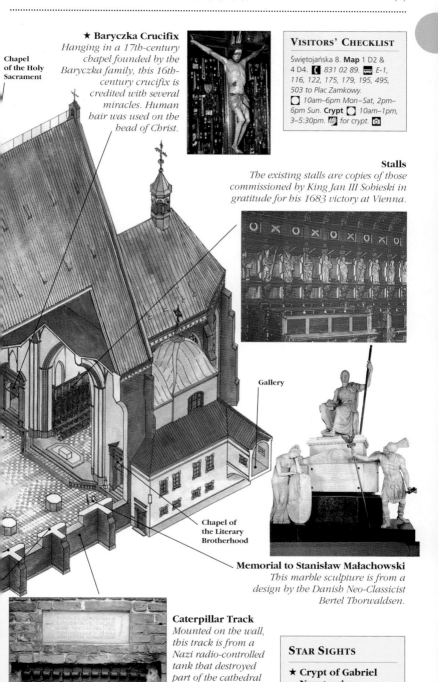

★ Baryczka Crucifix
Hanging in a 17th-century chapel founded by the Baryczka family, this 16th-century crucifix is credited with several miracles. Human hair was used on the head of Christ.

Chapel of the Holy Sacrament

VISITORS' CHECKLIST

Świętojańska 8. **Map** 1 D2 & 4 D4. 831 02 89. E-1, 116, 122, 175, 179, 195, 495, 503 to Plac Zamkowy. 10am–6pm Mon–Sat, 2pm–6pm Sun. **Crypt** 10am–1pm, 3–5:30pm. for crypt.

Stalls
The existing stalls are copies of those commissioned by King Jan III Sobieski in gratitude for his 1683 victory at Vienna.

Gallery

Chapel of the Literary Brotherhood

Memorial to Stanisław Małachowski
This marble sculpture is from a design by the Danish Neo-Classicist Bertel Thorwaldsen.

Caterpillar Track
Mounted on the wall, this track is from a Nazi radio-controlled tank that destroyed part of the cathedral during the Warsaw Uprising in 1944.

STAR SIGHTS

★ **Crypt of Gabriel Narutowicz**

★ **Baryczka Crucifix**

Old Town Market Square ⓰

UNTIL THE END OF THE 18TH CENTURY, the Old Town Market Square was the most important public square in Warsaw. Here, regular fairs and municipal festivities were held and, on rare occasions, executions were carried out. The Town Hall occupied the center until its demolition in 1817. The four sides of the 90 by 73 m (295 by 240 ft) square are named after prominent 18th-century parliamentarians. The houses that lend the square its unique character were built or restyled by wealthy merchant families in the 17th century.

Sign for Bazyliszek restaurant

Today, café tables and stalls line the square, and horse-drawn carriages *(dorożkas)* await those who wish to tour the narrow streets of the Old Town. The sound of barrel organs often echoes round its ancient walls.

OLD TOWN MARKET SQUARE

- ▢ Zakrzewski Side
- ▢ Barss Side
- ▢ Dekert Side
- ▢ Kołłątaj Side

ZAKRZEWSKI SIDE

Majeran House (No. 11)

Bazyliszek House (No. 5), with the bankers' sign of the mythical reptile

Gilded House
Stanisław Baryczka, mayor of the Old Town, lived here in the 17th century. His initials can be seen in the latticework of the transom window.

At the Lion
A painting by Zofia Stryjeńska (1928) decorates the façade of this house. There is also a lion in gilded relief on the corner.

BARSS SIDE

Troper House (No. 10)

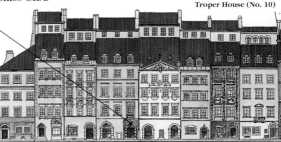

Orlemus House
This houses the Literature Museum (see p81). Here you will find first editions and memorabilia relating to Adam Mickiewicz, Poland's beloved Romantic poet.

Simonetti House
The plaque under the clock of this house commemorates the postwar reconstruction of the Old Town.

★ Fukier House
This once belonged to the Polish line of the medieval Fugger family. It now houses one of Warsaw's best restaurants (see p80).

Kołłątaj Side

Wilczek House
From the original medieval house on this side, only the Gothic portal remains.

★ Statue of St. Anna
A corner niche shows the figure of St. Anna holding the Virgin Mary and Child (see p80).

★ House of the "Little Black Boy"
This is named after the sculpture of a young boy on the façade.

Falkiewicz House
The parapet wall is crested with the figure of the Virgin Mary, flanked by Saints Elizabeth and Stanisław the Bishop.

Dekert Side

All the houses on this side are interconnected and form the Warsaw History Museum *(see p81)*.

Burbach House
(No. 2)

Baroque Ceilings
Ceilings on the third floor of No. 34, Kleinpoldt House, are painted in the Baroque style.

Star Sights

★ Statue of
   St. Anna

★ Fukier House

★ House of the
   "Little Black Boy"

Fukier House ⑰
Kamienica Fukierów

Rynek Starego Miasta 27. **Map** 2 D1 & 4 D4.

THE ORIGINS of this building, housing one of the city's most stylish restaurants, are

Fukier House, now transformed into a renowned restaurant

15th century. Its present Neo-Classical style is from 1782, when architect Szymon Bogu-mił Zug is thought to have been commissioned to make major alterations.

The house retains the name of the Fukier family, who ac-quired it in 1810. The Fukiers were the Polish branch of the Fuggers, a German family who for centuries were one of the most powerful banking families in Germany. Even German emperors were often in debt to them. The Fuggers were also merchants and the dominant force in Europe's spice trade.

While the Polish branch of the family did not achieve quite the same level of com-mercial success as their Ger-

man relatives, the Fukiers did amass a considerable fortune as wine merchants. Up until World War II, the Fukiers were particularly renowned for their stocks of Hungarian wine and Polish mead.

During World War II, only the ground floor and cellar of

Fukier House escaped de-struction. Having been pain-stakingly restored, the ornate, gilded façade now includes a frieze in the pattern of a gentleman's traditional dress sash. Above the portal is the Fukier family crest: two crossed lilies, together with the letter *F*.

The Fukier restaurant now occupies the ground floor, the cellar (which is original 15th century), and a charming cloistered courtyard. It is run by the Gessler family, who are established restaurateurs in the city. The menu offers modern interpretations of classic Po-lish cuisine (*see p214*).

The top floors of Fukier House are occupied by the Society of Art Historians.

St. Anna's House ⑱
Kamienica Pod św. Anną

Rynek Starego Miasta 31. **Map** 2 D1 & 4 D4. ⬤ *Entrance Hall only* *8am–4pm Mon–Fri.*

DATING FROM THE 15th cen-tury, this building has changed hands and been altered many times. However, the house has retained some of its earliest features. Gothic arches span the entrance hall, as well as the façade that faces Wąski Dunaj Street. The house also includes a statue of its namesake, St. Anna.

During the 18th century, the house served as a renowned restaurant, owned by a Frenchman called Quellus. In 1913, the house was bought by public subscription for the Historical Society of Warsaw. St. Anna's House is currently occupied by the Polish Academy of Science, which shares the premises with the Polish Historical Society.

Portal at St. Anna's House

PORTALS OF OLD TOWN BURGHER'S HOUSES
Among the Old Town's best preserved architectural features are its portals (doorways and other entrances). The portals are often highly decorative, and those in the Old Town Market Square exemplify a succession of architectural styles, ranging from Gothic to Renaissance, and from the Mannerist style to the Baroque.

Gothic

15th-century brick portals at No. 21 showing several stages of construction

Late Gothic

Elaborate Gothic portal at No. 31 exemplifies the genre

Julian Tuwim's study in the Literature Museum

Literature Museum Dedicated to Adam Mickiewicz 🔞

Muzeum Literatury im. A. Mickiewicza

Rynek Starego Miasta 18/20. **Map** 2 D1 & 4 D4. 📞 831 40 61. 🕐 10am–3pm Mon, Tue & Fri, 11am–6pm Wed, Thu, 11am–5pm Sun & public hols. 🎟 free on Thu.

THIS MUSEUM occupies two burgher's houses, Orlemus's and Balcer's, which date from the 15th century. Both houses have undergone changes over the centuries.

After World War II, they were reconstructed in a late Baroque style. However, the original Gothic arch and frescoes have been retained in the entrance hall of No. 20.

Ten of the museum's galleries are devoted to Poland's most renowned Romantic poet, Adam Mickiewicz *(see p117)*. On display can be seen his original manuscripts, first editions, and various memorabilia.

The lives and works of other Polish writers and poets – including Julian Tuwim, Leopold Staff, Melchior Wańkowicz, and Kazimierz Wierzyński – are explored in separate galleries. Additionally, the museum collects works of art relating to the periods in which these writers worked. The museum's vast collection can also be seen in frequent temporary exhibitions. The Literature Museum has a separate exhibition venue located at 40 Polna Street (in the vicinity of Łazienki Park). This branch of the museum celebrates the life and works of the Polish novelist Maria Dąbrowska.

Warsaw History Museum 🔟

Muzeum Historyczne m. st. Warszawy

Rynek Starego Miasta 28/42. **Map** 2 D1 & 4 D4. 📞 635 16 25. 🕐 noon–7pm Tue, Wed, 10am–3:30pm Thu, Fri, 10:30am–2:30pm Sat, Sun. 🎟 free on Sun.

THE WARSAW HISTORY Museum occupies all the houses on the Dekert side of the Old Town Market Square, as well as three in the adjacent Nowomiejska Street. Houses on the Dekert side were less damaged in World War II, some retaining their façades and one or two keeping their interiors, which can be viewed in the museum.

However, the museum's collection was totally destroyed during the war.

The existing collection is housed in 60 rooms, with Warsaw's history conveyed through paintings, drawings, illustrations, sculpture, arts and crafts, handicrafts, and archaeological finds.

Models are used to illustrate buildings that no longer exist. Additionally, a few galleries feature re-created room sets and artisans' studios, from various periods.

A vast collection of photographs and postcards spans historic and contemporary Warsaw, as does the museum's extensive library.

A film of the history of Warsaw, with commentary available in several languages, is shown in the museum theater. This includes footage shot by the Nazis, documenting their systematic destruction of Warsaw. The destruction had been ordered by Hitler in response to the Warsaw Uprising of 1944. The film also covers the city's massive postwar rebuilding program.

In the museum courtyard are fragments of historic stonemasonry and statuary. These were discovered during reconstruction work.

Printers' room reconstructed, Warsaw History Museum

Renaissance

Interior doorway in typical Renaissance style at No. 1

Mannerist

Ornate portal dating from the early 17th century at No. 36

Early Baroque

Reconstructed early period sandstone portal at No. 7

Baroque

Portal with pediment dating from 1663, at No. 38

Broad (Szeroki) Dunaj Street

Broad and Narrow Dunaj Streets ㉑
Szeroki i Wąski Dunaj

Map 1 C1.

WĄSKI (Narrow) Dunaj Street leads from the Old Town Market Square to the city walls, while adjoining it is Szeroki (Broad) Dunaj Street, which is effectively a small square. Both the names derive from the Dunaj stream, which originally had its source in this area.

During the Middle Ages, Wąski Dunaj Street was largely

Detail of portal at Salvator House

inhabited by Jews. Their place of worship was a synagogue on the corner of Wąski Dunaj Street and Żydowska (Jewish) Street. Neither the street nor the synagogue still exists.

Historically, both the Dunaj streets were commercial areas. In the 17th century, a fish market was held on Szeroki Dunaj Street; it became a vegetable and flower market in the 19th century.

The commercial importance of this area was underlined by the former Butcher's Gate (Brama Rzeźnicza), named after an abattoir by the city walls. Many cobblers also lived on Szeroki Dunaj Street, such as Jan Kiliński, who lived at No. 5. Esteemed in the trade, he was also a leader of the 1794 Kościuszko Insurrection.

Salvator House ㉒
Kamienica Salwator

Wąski Dunaj 8. **Map** 1 C1.

BUILT IN 1632 for Jakub Gianotti, Salvator House took its name from the figure of Jesus and bas-relief of St. Veronica that were above the façade.

The house has retained an early Baroque style, and the portal features the original owner's initials and monogram. However, the religious statues were omitted in the postwar Communist reconstruction and replaced by more secular images: an obelisk and a peddler girl.

Guild of Leather Crafts Museum ㉓
Muzeum Cechu Rzemiosł Skórzanych im. Kilińskiego

Wąski Dunaj 10. **Map** 1 C2. ☎ 831 97 92. ☐ 10am–3pm Thu–Sat. ☒

THE GUILD of Leather Crafts Museum is within a building that is known locally as the Shoemakers' House. It is a 16th-century building, reconstructed in an 18th-century style after World War II.

The museum's collection includes the reconstructed workshop of a shoemaker and also that of a saddler. Both feature examples of their respective crafts.

A Boy Insurgent

Exhibits also illustrate the life of Colonel Jan Kiliński, to whom the museum is dedicated. As well as a master of the guild, he was a hero of the 1794 Kościuszko Insurrection.

City Walls ㉔
Mury miejskie

Podwale. **Map** 1 C2.

WARSAW IS one of the world's few capital cities to have retained large sections of the original defensive walls. Constructed during the 14th and 15th centuries in the form of a double ring, they were additionally fortified by several towers, positioned at regular intervals. The Old Town was also protected by two main gates: Krakowska (Kraków), to the south, of which the only remaining feature is the Gothic bridge *(see p69)*, and Nowomiejska (as well as the Barbican), to the north of the Old Town.

Eventually, however, the brick walls became obsolete as a means of defending the city, and some sections were incorporated into houses that were subsequently built there.

In 1937–8, a major initiative was launched to excavate the city walls. During this period, buildings that had encroached on the city walls were demolished. This project continued after World War II, when more of the city walls were restored and certain fragments reconstructed.

Presently, the inner section of the city walls is far better

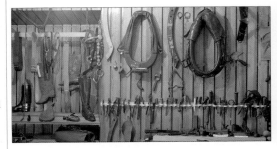

Saddlers' workshop in the Guild of Leather Crafts Museum

preserved than the outer walls, of which only mere fragments remain.

On Wąski Dunaj Street, the rectangular Knights Tower (Baszta Rycerska) has been reconstructed, and toward Nowomiejska Street there is the partly reconstructed Gunpowder Tower (Baszta Prochowa). On the remains of one of the turrets of this tower stands the famous statue *A Boy Insurgent*, designed by Jerzy Jarnuszkiewicz.

The Barbican, part of the Old Town's fortifications

The Barbican ㉕
Barbakan

Nowomiejska. **Map** 1 C1.

BUILT IN 1548 as the final part of the Old Town's fortifications, the Barbican was designed by the Venetian architect Giovanni Battista.

Constructed on the site of an earlier fortified building, the Barbican's principal role was to protect Nowomiejska Gate, to the north of the Old Town. The remains of Nowomiejska Gate are now marked by a low wall and variously colored flagstones.

The Mermaid ㉖
Pomnik Syrenki

Map 1 C1.

MERMAID IMAGES have been used as a symbol on the crest of Warsaw since the mid-14th century. Originally the Warsaw mermaid resembled a ferocious-looking monster, with overtones of a dragon, having claws and wings.

However, over the centuries, images of the mermaid gradually became more traditional (not to mention attractive) and took on the more recognizable form of the half-human and half-fish creature.

By the 19th century, artists such as the sculptor Konstanty Hegel also endowed the mermaid with great beauty. Nevertheless, she retained a ferocity, armed with a raised sword and shield. This image made her a perfect symbol for a city in which so many battles have been fought.

In 1855, Hegel's mermaid became the centerpiece of a fountain in the Old Town Market Square (on the site of the former Town Hall).

When the fountain was dismantled in 1929, the mermaid sculpture was initially transferred to the Solec sports club, and then, at a later date, to a park in Powiśle.

The mermaid finally returned to the Old Town in 1972, when it was decided to place the sculpture on the remains of the Marszałkowska Tower.

Stone Steps ㉗
Kamienne Schodki

Map 2 D1.

WIDELY REGARDED as the most picturesque street in the Old Town, Kamienne Schodki is effectively a series of steps. The steps run from the Old Town Market Square, cross Brzozowa Street, and continue on to Bugaj Street. Before Warsaw acquired a piped water supply, this route was used for carrying water from the River Vistula to supply the Old Town.

Enchanting views of the Vistula can be enjoyed from the top of Kamienne Schodki. It is a view that was much admired by Napoleon Bonaparte in the early 19th century, although he is said to have complained about the less enjoyable odors, which emanated from the hill of Gnojna Góra.

The mermaid

Stone Steps by the Market Square

Gnojna Góra ㉘

Celna. **Map** 2 D1.

LOCATED AT THE END of Celna Street, Gnojna Góra is an ideal vantage point from which

A 17th-century illustration of the mound of Gnojna Góra

to enjoy the panorama of the River Vistula and the views of Warsaw's Right Bank.

However, this site has a less picturesque heritage. Gnojna Góra, which translates as "Dung Mound," was used as a refuse dump by the Old Town for centuries.

Fragments of Gnojna Brama (Dung Gate), which provided access to the mound, can still be seen where it was attached to the house at the junction of Celna Street and Brzozowa Street. The gate is popularly abbreviated to Gnojna.

As strange as it may seem, Gnojna Góra was also thought to possess healing properties. Syphilis was one of many illnesses "treated" here, where the unfortunate patients were buried up to their necks in the mound. Regrettably, there is no record of how effective this treatment proved.

NEW TOWN

NOWE MIASTO (New Town) was originally known as New Warsaw. The area began to develop at the end of the 14th century, alongside a thoroughfare leading from the Old Town to the village of Zakroczym, on the banks of the River Vistula. In 1408 Duke Janusz the Elder granted Nowe Miasto its own separate status, outside the jurisdiction of the mayor of the Old Town. The New Town established its own council and a Town Hall on the Market Square, as well as several churches and monasteries. Unlike the Old Town with its barbican, the New Town was not fortified. The peak of the New Town's evolution was the end of the 18th century. However, the New Town lost its independent status in 1791, when it was incorporated into the city of Warsaw. It then became known as the district of Nowe Miasto. After World War II, the New Town was carefully re-created, and it is now one of Warsaw's most popular districts.

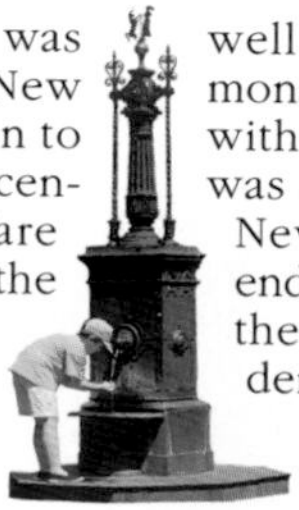

A historic well in the Market Square

SIGHTS AT A GLANCE

Churches
Church of Our Lady, Queen of Poland 14
Church Our Lady Mary 16
Church of St. Benon 11
Church of St. Francis 17
Church of St. John of God 18
Church of the Holy Spirit 2
St. Casimir's Church 10
St. Jacek's Church 1

Historic Buildings
Old Gunpowder Depository 7
Raczyński Palace 13
Royal Well 20
Sapieha Palace 12
Warsaw's Smallest House 5

Museums and Galleries
Asia and Pacific Museum 6
Citadel Museum 21
Maria Skłodowska-Curie Museum 3

Historic Roads and Districts
Freta Street 8
Mostowa Street 4
New Town Market Square 9

Parks and Gardens
Traugutt Park 19

Monuments
Memorial to the Heroes of the Warsaw Uprising 15

Residential Districts

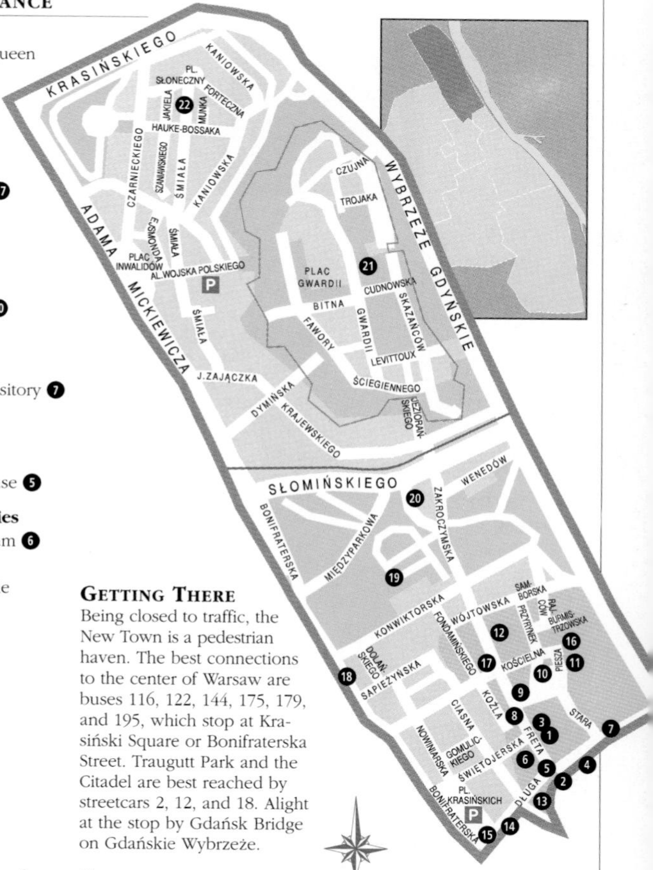

GETTING THERE

Being closed to traffic, the New Town is a pedestrian haven. The best connections to the center of Warsaw are buses 116, 122, 144, 175, 179, and 195, which stop at Krasiński Square or Bonifraterska Street. Traugutt Park and the Citadel are best reached by streetcars 2, 12, and 18. Alight at the stop by Gdańsk Bridge on Gdańskie Wybrzeże.

KEY

Street-by-Street map *pp86–7*

[P] Parking

◁ St. Casimir's Church

Street-by-Street: New Town

COLORFUL HOUSES AND CHURCHES, which were rebuilt from ruins after World War II, feature among the attractions of the New Town. Here you can take a stroll along the steepest street in Warsaw, Mostowa Street. This leads to a tower that, in the 16th century, guarded the entrance to one of Europe's longest bridges.

Freta
The strange name of the New Town's main street originally meant "uncultivated field" and subsequently came to denote a suburb **8**

★ **St. Jacek's Church**
The church's main feature – the magnificent 17th-century tomb of local burgher Adam Kotowski and his wife, Małgorzata – is the work of the celebrated Dutch architect Tylman of Gameren **1**

Maria Skłodowska-Curie
The house in which she was born in 1867 is now a museum **3**

Church of the Holy Spirit
Pilgrims travel from the steps of this Baroque church to the shrine of the Black Madonna at Częstochowa **2**

Old Gunpowder Depository
Once a bridge gate, later it became a gunpowder depository and then a prison; today it houses a theater company **7**

DŁUGA

ŚWIĘTOJERSKA

FRETA

MOSTOWA

STARA

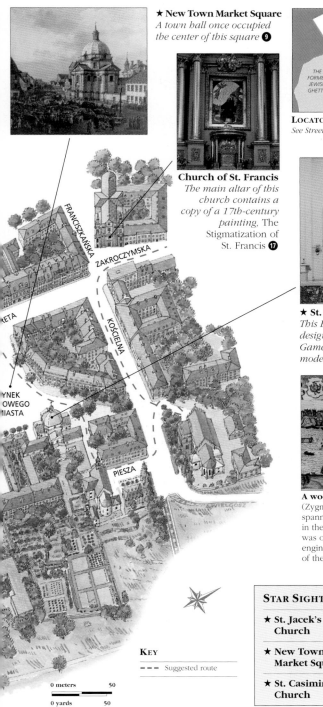

★ **New Town Market Square**
*A town hall once occupied
the center of this square* ❾

Church of St. Francis
*The main altar of this
church contains a
copy of a 17th-century
painting,* The
Stigmatization of
St. Francis ⓱

LOCATOR MAP
See Street Finder, maps 1, 3

Map labels:
FRANCISZKAŃSKA
ZAKROCZYMSKA
KOŚCIELNA
FRETA
YNEK
OWEGO
IIASTA
PIESZA

★ **St. Casimir's Church**
*This Baroque church,
designed by Tylman of
Gameren, now has a
modern interior* ❿

A wooden bridge
(Zygmunt August Bridge),
spanned the River Vistula
in the 16th century. It
was one of the greatest
engineering achievements
of the Renaissance.

KEY

- - - Suggested route

0 meters   50

0 yards   50

STAR SIGHTS

★ **St. Jacek's
Church**

★ **New Town
Market Square**

★ **St. Casimir's
Church**

St. Jacek's Church ❶
Kościół św. Jacka, Dominikanów

Freta 8/10. **Map** 1 C1. 116, 122, 174, 175, 179, 195.

AT THE BEGINNING of the 17th century, while the Jesuits were building a Baroque church in the Old Town, the Dominicans began to construct a Gothic presbytery at St. Jacek's Church. The reason for choosing the Gothic style for

St. Jacek's Church

their building may have been because of the order's conservative (even archaic) outlook. Alternatively, it may have been an attempt to underline the Dominicans' ancient history, even though the order was established in Warsaw only in 1603.

Construction of St. Jacek's Church was interrupted by a sudden outbreak of the plague in 1625. During this time, the Dominicans would hear confession and distribute Holy

The Kotowski tombs in St. Jacek's Church

Communion only through small holes that were specially made in the church doors. The church was finally completed in 1639, next to the city's largest monastery.

St. Jacek's has a side nave with a beautiful vaulted ceiling decorated in Lublin-style stuccowork. This nave also features the tombs of Anna Tarnowska and Katarzyna Ossolińska, who were the first of the four wives of Jerzy Ossoliński, the Voivode (lord lieutenant) of the Podlasie region.

The magnificent chapel of Adam and Małgorzata Kotowski, which includes their portraits painted on a tin surface, was built in 1690–94 to the designs of Tylman of Gameren (the renowned Dutch architect who was exalted in Poland). Their black marble tombs are in the crypt. Adam Kotowski was the son of a Silesian peasant who moved to Warsaw, acquired vast wealth, and became ennobled. Inscribed tablets within the church also commemorate Polish resistance leaders of World War II.

Pulpit in the Church of the Holy Spirit

Church of the Holy Spirit ❷
Kościół św. Ducha, Paulinów

Nowomiejska 23. **Map** 1 C1. 116, 122, 174, 175, 179, 195.

THE ORIGINAL wooden Church of the Holy Spirit was built during the 14th century. Subsequently extended, it was burned down in 1655 during the Swedish invasion. As the city lacked the necessary funds to rebuild the church, King Jan Kazimierz donated the site to the Pauline Order of Częstochowa. This monastic order was famous for defending the Jasna Góra monastery in Częstochowa (Poland's holiest shrine) against the Swedes. The church was rebuilt in the Baroque style, between 1707–17, by Józef Piola and Józef Szymon Bellotti.

The Pauline monks constructed defensive walls around the church and adjoining the monastery that were also integrated into the city's existing fortifications.

Since 1711, the church has served as a starting point for the annual pilgrimage to Jasna Góra monastery at Częstochowa, about 200 km (125 miles) south of Warsaw.

MARIA SKŁODOWSKA-CURIE (1867–1934)

Maria Skłodowska was 24 years old when she left Warsaw to study in Paris. Within seven years she had become internationally renowned as the co-founder of a new branch of science, radioactivity. Together with her French husband, Pierre Curie, she discovered two new radioactive elements: radium and polonium. In 1903 Marie Curie was the first woman to receive the Nobel Prize for physics. In 1911 she was awarded the Nobel Prize for chemistry. Marie Curie was also instrumental in establishing the Institute of Radiology in Paris. Following her death in 1934, she was interred in the family grave at Sceaux near Paris. In 1995 her remains were transferred to the Panthéon in Paris, which was a great tribute to Poland's foremost scientist.

The Church of the Holy Spirit seen from Mostowa Street

Maria Skłodowska-Curie Museum ❸

Muzeum Marii Skłodowskiej-Curie

Freta 16. **Map** 1 C1. ⬛ 831 80 92.
🚌 116, 122, 174, 175, 179, 195.
🕐 10am–4:30pm Tue–Sat,
10am–2:30pm Sun. ♿

THIS SMALL MUSEUM, estab-lished in the house where Maria Skłodowska-Curie was born, opened in 1967 on the centenary of her birth.

Various exhibits trace her successes and the challenges she faced. Films of Curie's life and the history of science can also be seen on request.

Mostowa Street ❹

Ulica Mostowa

Map 1 C1. 🚌 116, 122, 174, 175, 179, 195.

DESCENDING steeply toward the River Vistula, Mostowa Street (Bridge Street) is con-sidered one of the most picturesque in Warsaw.

The street led to a wooden bridge that from 1575–1603 connected the New Town with the nearby village of Praga. By the 18th century, Mostowa Street featured brick buildings, with various inns and shops, as well as accom-modation for craftsmen, shopkeepers, officials of the law courts, and the police. Policemen were employed

at the prison that was con-verted from the gate house by the bridge. Walking in the direction of the Vistula leads to the imposing Dominican church and monastery, which are situated adjacent to the junction with Freta Street.

Warsaw's Smallest House ❺

Najmniejszy Domek Warszawy

Długa 1. **Map** 1 C1. 🚌 116, 122, 174, 175, 179, 195.

THIS TINY HOUSE, which is attached to the Church of the Holy Spirit, is so small that it is now used merely as a

The kiosk that was originally Warsaw's smallest house

newspaper kiosk. The house was built toward the end of the 18th century, and is Neo-Classical in style.

It always had the distinction of being the smallest house in Warsaw, occupying a site that measures only a few square feet. However, in spite of its size, the house always had an individual street number.

Asia and Pacific Museum ❻

Muzeum Azji i Pacyfiku

Freta 5. **Map** 1 C1. ⬛ 635 28 11.
🚌 116, 122 174, 175, 195.
🕐 11am–5pm Tue–Sat. ♿

THE MUSEUM comprises two exhibition venues, one on Freta Street and the other on Nowogrodzka Street, leading to the Asian and Nusantara collections, respectively. Temporary exhibitions of Asian culture are also held in the museum.

Old Gunpowder Depository ❼

Stara Prochownia

Rybaki 2. **Map** 2 D1. 🚌 118.

ORIGINALLY this was a gate-house by the wooden bridge that crossed the Vistula from 1575 to 1603. Designed and built by Erazm Cziotko of Zakroczym, the bridge was financed by King Zygmunt August and his sister Anna.

Destroyed in 1603 by ice floes, some of the bridge's oak columns remained submerged in the river until salvaged in the mid-19th century. The Rus-sian field marshal Paskiewicz used them to make furniture for his palace in Belarus.

From 1646, the gatehouse was used to store gunpowder. In 1767 it became a prison. In-mates included the 18th-century schemer Maria Dogrum, who falsely accused the king's valet of trying to poison Duke Adam Kazimierz Czartoryski. In 1831 the prison was converted into rented accommodation.

Burned in World War II and rebuilt in 1961–5, the gate-house is now the headquarters of a theater company.

Triangular pediment on the façade of the Old Gunpowder Depository

Freta Street ❽
Ulica Freta

Map 3 C4 & 1 C1. 🚌 *116, 122, 174, 175, 179, 195.*

Now the main thoroughfare of Nowe Miasto, Freta Street was originally laid out as a section of road to link Warsaw with the nearby village of Zakroczym.

The first houses were built on Freta Street during the 14th century, though it wasn't until a century later that Freta Street was incorporated into the town of Nowe Miasto.

Before World War II, Freta Street's shops were principally occupied by milliners and makers of artificial flowers.

Baroque window in Pod Opatrznością house on Freta Street

Now the choice includes antique shops, restaurants, and cafés. Recommended are Pod Samsonem restaurant *(see p214)* and Pożegnanie z Afryką (Farewell to Africa) café, which serves some of the city's best coffee.

New Town Market Square ❾
Rynek Nowego Miasta

Map 3 C4 & 1 C1. 🚌 *116, 122, 174, 175, 179, 195.*

The market square is the heart of the New Town. It was formerly rectangular, but various redevelopments have produced an irregular

Snow and sunlight on New Town Market Square in winter

triangular shape. The Town Hall (Ratusz) stood in the center of the market square until 1818, when it was demolished. However, this also opened up a splendid view of St. Casimir's Church.

The market square was reconstructed after the war, but not very accurately, and the façades of several houses were covered by murals in the Socialist Realist style. Near the junction with Freta Street is a charming 19th-century well.

St. Casimir's Church ❿
Kościół św. Kazimierza

Rynek Nowego Miasta 2. **Map** 3 C4 & 1 C1. 🚌 *116, 122, 174, 175, 179, 195.* **Convent** *not open to public.*

The church and convent belonging to the French order of the Sisters of the Blessed Sacrament was founded in about 1688 by King Jan III Sobieski and Queen Maria Kazimiera.

The church was designed by Tylman of Gameren in a late Baroque style. The interior, which was originally decorated with frescoes, is now plain white. The most interesting feature is the tombstone for Princess Marie Caroline de Bouillon, the granddaughter of Jan III Sobieski. The tombstone was set in 1746 by Bishop Andrzej Załuski, along with Prince Michał Kazimierz Radziwiłł, a well-known rake, who was a former suitor of the princess. The broken shield and toppling crowns that decorate the tomb are taken from the Sobieski coat-of-arms, but also refer to the end of the Sobieski family line.

The green-domed roof of St. Casimir's Church

A splendid garden that lies behind the convent has remained unchanged since the 17th century. At its edge, terraces descend to the flowing waters of the River Vistula.

Church of St. Benon ⓫
Kościół św. Benona

Piesza 1. **Map** 1 C1. 🚌 116, 122, 174, 175, 179, 503.

THIS DIMINUTIVE CHURCH was founded in 1787 by King Stanisław August Poniatowski on behalf of Redemptorist monks. These monks were in

The New Town's 18th-century Church of St. Benon

the care of Abbot Clement Dworzak, a Moravian who was sent to Warsaw from Rome. He opened two orphanages, one for girls and one for boys, while also providing for the orphans' continued education.

In 1808, unfounded accusations that the monks were spying for the Austrians led the Napoleonic authorities to expel the abbot and 30 monks, and close the church. For the next 100 years, it was used to manufacture knives and kitchen utensils. The Redemptorists returned after the war to rebuild the church. The modern interiors also include original sculptures.

Sapieha Palace ⓬
Pałac Sapiehów

Zakroczymska 6. **Map** 3 C3. 📞 831 32 09. 🚌 175, 503. **Not open** to the public.

THIS VAST former palace originally belonged to the princely Sapieha family. It was built in 1731–46 for Jan Fryderyk Sapieha, who was the chancellor of the Grand Duchy of Lithuania. The powerful Polish-Lithuanian Commonwealth, which united the two countries, had been inaugurated in the 16th century, and by the mid-18th, it was Europe's largest empire.

The architect of the Sapieha Palace, Jan Zygmunt Deybel, was also an officer in the Saxon Corps of Engineers. Designed in the Rococo style, the palace has an impressive façade, which includes an ornamental triangular pediment, as well as urns, sculptures, and a balcony.

Magdalena Sapieha, née Lubomirska, who was married to one of the later owners of the palace, was a lively character and renowned as a society beauty, which made

The Rococo façade of Sapieha Palace

her the toast of 18th-century Warsaw. When Stanisław August Poniatowski was still young (and before he ascended the throne), he was in love with her.

The palace was converted for use as an army barracks in the 19th century, and its magnificent gardens were used, somewhat incongruously, for military exercises. The Fourth Polish Infantry regiment, which played an important and heroic role during the 1830–31 uprising, was stationed at the palace.

Having been burned by the Nazis in 1944, the façade was restored to its original style. The interiors were converted for use as a school.

St. Casimir's Church in New Town Market Square

Raczyński Palace ⓭
Pałac Raczyńskich

Długa 7. **Map** 1 C2. 🚌 *116, 122, 174, 175, 179, 195.*

THIS PALACE, which now serves as an archive for ancient documents, was completed in 1786. It was designed by the royal architect Jan Chrystian Kamsetzer.

An interesting feature of the palace is the reconstructed early Neo-Classical ballroom, which is decorated with stuccowork and allegorical paintings representing Justice. Ironically, the life and deeds of the original owner, Kazimierz Raczyński, the chief marshal of the crown, were at odds with these allegorical paintings. Public opinion branded him corrupt and a traitor to his country.

In the 19th century, the palace was the seat of the Administrative Commission of Justice, and during the interwar years, it housed the Ministry of Justice.

The palace witnessed several tragic events during World War II. One wall retains bullet marks from the public execution of 50 men who were stopped at random in the vicinity of the palace on January 24, 1944. On August 13, 1944, during the Warsaw Uprising, a German tank-trap loaded with ammunition

Anchor from the Church of Our Lady

exploded nearby, killing 80 resistance fighters. On September 2, 1944, when the palace was serving as a field hospital, the infamous SS arrived and murdered several hundred of the wounded.

Church of Our Lady, Queen of Poland ⓮
Kościół NMP Królowej Korony Polskiej

Długa 13/15. **Map** 1 C2. 🚌 *116, 122, 174, 175, 179, 195.*

DESIGNED BY Tytus Boratini, this Baroque church was built in 1660–82. A Palladian façade, designed by Jakub Fontana, was added in 1758–69.

The church features seven ornamental altars, with paintings by prominent artists of the time, including Szymon Czechowicz and Jan Bogumił Plersch. It also provided an office for Father Stanisław Konarski (1700–73) of the Piarist order. He was equally a politician, an educational reformer, and the founder of the Collegium Nobilium *(see p100)*.

In 1835, tsarist authorities commandeered

Church of Our Lady, Queen of Poland

the building, converting it into a Russian Orthodox church. The steeples were replaced by onion domes, which remained in place until Poland regained its independence in 1918. The church was then carefully restored to its original design.

Now serving as the cathedral church of the Polish armed forces, the walls are lined with plaques commemorating all the servicemen who fell during World War II.

Memorial to the Heroes of the Warsaw Uprising ⓯
Pomnik Bohaterom Powstania Warszawskiego

Plac Krasińskich. **Map** 1 C1 & 3 C4. 🚌 *116, 122, 175, 179, 195.*

UNVEILED IN 1989, this memorial was designed by Wincenty Kućma, within an architectural setting devised by Jacek Budyn. It consists of two bronze groups: soldiers defending a barricade and others descending into the sewers. Many sewers were used during the uprising as a means of communication between isolated combat groups. The manhole of one sewer entrance used during

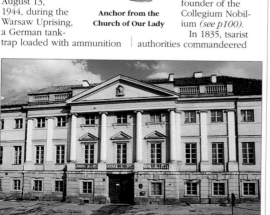

The dignified, Neo-Classical façade of the Raczyński Palace

the uprising has been preserved at the junction of Długa Street and Krasiński Square. During the 50th anniversary commemorations of the uprising in 1994, the German president Roman Herzog visited the memorial and apologized to the Polish nation for what it suffered during World War II, and for the bloody means the Nazis used to quell the uprising.

Church Our Lady Mary ⑯
Kościół Panny Marii

Przyrynek 2. **Map** 3 C3. 🚌 175, 503.

THE PARISH CHURCH of the Virgin Mary is the oldest church in Nowe Miasto. It was founded by Anna, the wife of Duke Janusz the Elder, at the beginning of the 15th century. According to tradition, the church was built on a site where pagan rituals had once been held.

During a series of 19th-century refurbishments, the church frequently changed its architectural style. Having been destroyed during World War II, the church was restored to its original 15th-century Gothic style. The presbytery was reconstructed using solely medieval methods, which precluded the use of precast building materials.

The churchyard also includes a memorial to Major Walerian Łukasiński (1786–1868), who founded the National Patriotic Association during the tsarist occupation. A terrace by the church provides wonderful views across the rooftops of the Old Town, the River Vistula, and the Praga district beyond.

Church of St. Francis ⑰
Kościół św. Franciszka, Franciszkanów

Zakroczymska 1. **Map** 3 C3. 🚌 175, 503.

FRANCISCANS first settled in Warsaw in 1645, and construction of the Church of St. Francis began in 1679.

A section of the Memorial to the Heroes of the Warsaw Uprising

However, completing the church was a slow process. While it was consecrated in 1737, the finishing touches to the façade weren't completed until 1788. Not surprisingly, several architects were involved in the design of the church. These included Jan Ceroni, Antoni Solari, Jakub and Józef Fontana, as well as Józef Boretti.

Subsequently, the nave retained a Baroque manner, while the façade was topped with obelisks that have lent it a Neo-Classical appearance.

The church is also significant for its religious relics. A glass coffin, for instance, contains the bones of the former Roman legionnaire who became St. Vitus. These bones were given to the Franciscans by Pope Benedict XIV in 1745.

Also worth seeing are the Baroque epitaphs of two of the church's benefactors, together with their portraits. One benefactor is depicted wearing Sarmatian armor; Sarmatia was an ancient province in southeastern Poland.

A painting of St. Anthony of Padua hangs in a side chapel. Painted in 1664 by a little-known artist named Mateusz, it is considered to be one of the most valuable examples of 17th-century Varsovian art.

The Church of St. Francis, with its dark, hard-edged towers

Church of St. John of God ⑱

Kościół św. Jana Bożego

Bonifraterska 12. **Map** 1 B1 & 3 C4. 🚌 116, 122, 174, 175, 179, 195, 503. 🚊 2, 15, 18, 31, 36.

THIS modest church, built in 1726

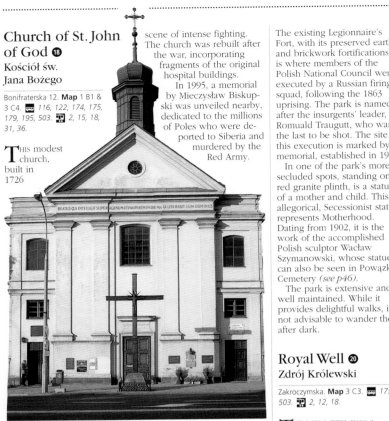

The modest façade of the Church of St. John of God

and designed by Józef Fontana and Antoni Solari, belonged to the Bonifraters' monastic order. The order was established in the 16th century with the aim of caring for the ill and infirm. Next to the church was a hospital, which was among the first to care for the mentally ill. Unfortunately, until about the mid-19th century, doctors were poorly equipped to deal with mentally ill patients. Treatments were limited to doses of castor oil, poppy seed potions, colonic irrigation, hot and cold baths, and bleeding the patients.

In 1760 the hospital was enlarged by the architect Jakub Fontana. At that time, it was customary to hold an annual open day during Whitsuntide, when Varsovians could visit the hospital.

During the 1944 Warsaw Uprising, the hospital was the scene of intense fighting. The church was rebuilt after the war, incorporating fragments of the original hospital buildings.

In 1995, a memorial by Mieczysław Biskupski was unveiled nearby, dedicated to the millions of Poles who were deported to Siberia and murdered by the Red Army.

Traugutt Park ⑲

Park Traugutta

Zakroczymska. **Map** 3 C3. 🚌 175, 503. 🚊 2, 12, 18.

THE TRAUGUTT PARK was laid out in 1925, on the site of historic fortifications that surrounded the city's 19th-century citadel.

The existing Legionnaire's Fort, with its preserved earth and brickwork fortifications, is where members of the Polish National Council were executed by a Russian firing squad, following the 1863 uprising. The park is named after the insurgents' leader, Romuald Traugutt, who was the last to be shot. The site of this execution is marked by a memorial, established in 1916.

In one of the park's more secluded spots, standing on a red granite plinth, is a statue of a mother and child. This allegorical, Secessionist statue represents Motherhood. Dating from 1902, it is the work of the accomplished Polish sculptor Wacław Szymanowski, whose statues can also be seen in Powązki Cemetery *(see p46)*.

The park is extensive and well maintained. While it provides delightful walks, it is not advisable to wander there after dark.

Royal Well ⑳

Zdrój Królewski

Zakroczymska. **Map** 3 C3. 🚌 175, 503. 🚊 2, 12, 18.

THE ROYAL WELL was a source of exceptionally pure and palatable water. It was originally enclosed by a small pavilion built in the early 18th century. The pavilion was then redesigned in 1771, at the request of King Stanisław August Poniatowski.

Records of workmen who were employed on the rebuilding project show that they received an extra payment to buy cudgels, which were intended to protect them against thieves on their way home at night.

In 1832, when the Russians were constructing the nearby citadel, they covered the Royal Well with soil. A few years later it was uncovered, and a Neo-Gothic pavilion was built around it, designed by the Polish architect Henryk Marconi.

Statue representing Motherhood in Traugutt Park

The Neo-Gothic pavilion that stands over the Royal Well

Warsaw Citadel and Independence Museum ㉑

Cytadela Warszawska i Muzeum Niepodległości

Museum, Pavilion X, Skazańców 25. **Map** 3 C2. ☎ 39 12 68. 🚌 118, 185. 🚊 2, 12, 18 (entails walking from Gdańsk bridge). ◯ 9am–4pm Wed–Fri, 10am–4pm Sat–Sun. 📷

THE CITADEL is an enormous fortress that was built by the Russians not to defend the city from outside attack, but to intimidate its inhabitants.

Construction of the citadel was ordered by Tsar Nicholas II in 1832, following the November 1830 insurrection. Based on a design by General Ivan Dehn, the citadel was built in stages and finally completed in 1887. This entailed destroying the barracks of the former Royal Guards, as well as the Piarist monastery and the residential area of Żoliborz.

The citizens of Warsaw had to bear the astronomical cost of building the citadel. Meanwhile, Russian officials and army officers made their fortunes by investing money in this development.

The brick and earth fortress, encircled by a moat and defensive brick wall, stands on a hill close to the River Vistula and dominates the surrounding area.

Four Neo-Classical gates lead to the interior, where a range of buildings include the so-called tenth pavilion. This was a high-security prison, used solely to house Polish political prisoners. Following World War II, this

pavilion was refurbished to provide an exhibition venue. Currently it houses a branch of the Independence Museum, tracing Polish history since the partitions, starting in the late 18th century. One of the museum's prized possessions is a *kibitka*, a specially constructed carriage that was used to transport Polish political prisoners to Siberia.

Some of the citadel's other buildings are occupied by the European Academy of Arts.

Former Officers' Quarters in Żoliborz ㉒

Żoliborz Oficerski

Between Mickiewicza, Krasiński, Plac Inwalidów, and Aleja Wojska Polskiego. **Map** 3 B2. 🚌 116, 122, 195. 🚊 15, 18, 31, 36.

A cannon on the citadel's ramparts

THIS AREA forms part of the large residential district of Żoliborz, developed between the wars. Much of Żoliborz incorporated the citadel's esplanade, an open area in front of the citadel that left any attackers exposed.

Redeveloped in the 1920s as a residential area for

military personnel, the quiet streets were lined with charming homes, designed in a traditional country-house style. The façades were typically ornamented with columns and porticoes, and distinctive stepped roofs.

Neighboring this area, which was then known as Officers' Żoliborz, was the Bureaucrats' Żoliborz, housing civil servants.

Following these developments, the Warsaw Housing Cooperative built apartment houses to provide comfortable but inexpensive accommodation for the city's workers. However, this district remained separate from its grander neighbors, divided by Krasiński Street. Construction of these housing developments gave architects the opportunity to draw upon avant-garde concepts.

The apartment buildings of particular interest are the so-called gallery apartments, built in an open arch along Suzin Street in 1932, and designed by Stanisław and Barbara Brukalski. They were separated by wide green spaces that were an innovation in Warsaw.

The apartment houses owned by the State Insurance Institution were constructed according to the highest standards. That at Nos. 34–36 Mickiewicz Street, designed by Juliusz Żórawski and built in the late 1930s, is an example of the influence of the renowned Modernist architect Le Corbusier.

A *kibitka* in the Independence Museum within the citadel

AROUND SOLIDARITY AVENUE

FROM THE END of the 18th to the mid-19th century, the area around today's Solidarity Avenue (Aleja Solidarności) and Plac Teatralny (Theater Square) was Warsaw's commercial and cultural center. The grand Neo-Classical buildings of the area, with their impressive colonnades, were constructed in the 1820s. These include the Grand Theater (Teatr Wielki), which is one of the largest buildings of its kind in Europe. The area also features several large parks. The Krasiński Gardens (adjoining Krasiński Palace) were first laid out in the late 17th cen-

Fountain near the Muranów movie theater

tury. The Saxon Gardens (Ogród Saski), designed in the Baroque style, were part of a town plan known as the Saxon Axis. The Saxon Gardens are all that remain of the former Royal Park, which encircled the residence of King August II Mocny in the 18th century. A 19th-century colonnade once divided the Saxon Gardens from Piłsudski Square, where official state functions are held. This is also the place where the Tomb of the Unknown Soldier, featuring a guard of honor and an eternal flame, was established in 1925.

SIGHTS AT A GLANCE

Churches and Monasteries
Basilian Church of the Assumption of the Blessed Virgin Mary **2**
Capuchin Church of the Transfiguration **6**
St. Anthony of Padua Reformed Church **25**

Historic Buildings
Arsenal **11**
Collegium Nobilium **1**
Former Bank of Poland **17**
Former State Bank **13**
Grand Theater **20**
Kings' House **14**

Landau Bank **23**
Mansions on Długa Street **10**
Town Hall **16**
Western & Discount Banks **19**

Palaces
Blue Palace **22**
Branicki Palace **3**
Krasiński Palace **8**
Morsztyn Palace **4**
Pac Palace **7**
Primate's Palace **26**
Przebendowski-Radziwiłł Palace **12**

Monuments
Jan Kiliński Monument **5**
St. John of Nepomuk Monument **24**

Squares
Bank Square **15**
Theater Square **21**

Historic Parks and Gardens
Krasiński Gardens **9**
Saxon Gardens **18**

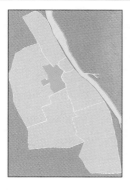

GETTING THERE
This area is adjacent to the city center, and is served by various streetcar and bus routes. Buses 107, 111, 166, 170, 171, and 180 and streetcars 2, 4, 13, 15, 18, 26, 31, 32, 34, and 36 stop in Bank Square (Plac Bankowy). If traveling from the direction of Krakowskie Przedmieście and the south-central area, buses 116, 122, 174, 175, 179, 195, and 503 can be taken from Nowy Świat and Krakowskie Przedmieście.

KEY
☐ Map *see pp98–9*
P Parking

0 meters 400
0 yards 400

◁ **The former Bank of Poland and Stock Exchange in Bank Square**

Street-by-Street: Miodowa

A S MIODOWA STREET lies just outside the Old Town, it is often overlooked by visitors. However, the attractions of this elegant street include three Baroque churches and several palaces, set behind spacious courtyards. One of these, the Borch Palace, is now the seat of the primate of Poland.

★ Capuchin Church of the Transfiguration
Founded in the 17th century by King Jan III Sob- ieski, it houses an urn containing his heart ❻

Borch Palace has been the seat of the primate of Poland since 1843. However, its history is less pious. Built in the 17th century for Count Piotr Ricourt, this was the city's most notorious haven for gamblers. In the 1780s, the palace was refurbished by Dominik Merlini for the deputy crown chancellor Jan Borch. The French-style garden has retained an exquisite pavilion.

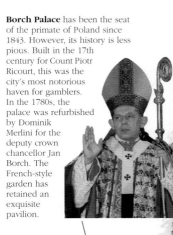

Kraków Bishops' Palace was built as a residence by Bishop Kajetan Sołtyk in 1760–62. Having been largely destroyed in World War II, the palace was painstak- ingly restored to its original form.

Two stones stand outside the entrance of the Kraków Bishops' Palace. The stones have unusual openings that were originally used to extinguish burning torches.

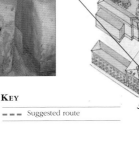

KEY

--- --- Suggested route

0 meters   100

0 yards   100

SCHILLERA

ALEJA SOLIDARNOŚCI

MIODOWA

SENATORSKA

Krasiński Palace

One of two Neo-Classical wellheads of 1823–4 standing in front of the palace **8**

LOCATOR MAP
See Street Finder, maps 1, 3

Collegium Nobilium

The 18th-century building of the Collegium Nobilium now houses the Academy of the Dramatic Arts **1**

Basilian Church of the Assumption of the Blessed Virgin Mary

This Ukrainian-Catholic church, which dates from the 18th century, boasts a grand and imposing façade **2**

★ Pac Palace

The palace's finest feature is a semicircular gateway, with Neo-Classical frieze by sculptor Ludwik Kaufmann **7**

Morsztyn Palace

This was once the Russian ambassador's residence, and was attacked during the 1794 insurrection **4**

Branicki Palace

The palace's Rococo façade is decorated with fine statues and sculptures **3**

STAR SIGHTS

★ Pac Palace

★ Capuchin Church of the Transfiguration

Collegium Nobilium ❶

Państwowa Wyższa Szkoła Teatralna
(Academy of the Dramatic Arts)

Miodowa 22/24. **Map** 1 C2 & 3 C4.
☎ 831 02 16. 🚌 116, 122, 174, 175, 179, 195. **Not open** to the public.

This 18th-century building originally housed the Collegium Nobilium, Poland's finest school for young nobles. It was established by Piarist monks, led by Father Stanisław Konarski, an academic and reformer during the Enlightenment. Built between 1743 and 1754 in a Rococo style, it was redesigned in 1786 in the Neo-Classical manner. The school occupied the building until 1807 and was closed by the Russians after the insurrection of 1830–31. The building now houses the Academy of the Dramatic Arts, and is dedicated to the great Polish actor Aleksander Zelwerowicz.

Basilian Church of the Assumption of the Blessed Virgin Mary ❷

Kościół Wniebowzięcia NMP, Bazylianów

Miodowa 16. **Map** 1 C2 & 3 C4.
🚌 116, 122, 174, 175, 179, 195.

The ornate Neo-Classical façade of this church looks as though it could adorn a royal palace. Built in 1782–4, it was designed by Dominik Merlini. The interior (which is a postwar reconstruction) includes paintings by the 18th-century Polish artist Franciszek Smuglewicz.

Branicki Palace ❸

Pałac Branickich

Miodowa 6. **Map** 1 C2 & 3 C4.
🚌 116, 122, 174, 175, 179, 195. **Not open** to the public.

Following almost complete destruction during World War II, this Rococo palace

Façade of the Basilian Church

was rebuilt between 1947 and 1953, using detailed historical research and 18th-century paintings for guidance.

Originally designed as a residence for the king's adviser Jan Klemens Branicki, construction of the palace was first undertaken in 1740, by the architects Jan Zygmunt Deybel and Jakub Fontana.

Branicki was a distinguished soldier, but also a connoisseur of fine art, especially from France. He therefore traveled to Paris to acquire silver, porcelain, furniture, and even marble fireplaces for his residences. His Warsaw palace was decorated with the advice and help of celebrated artists, such as the sculptor Jan Chryzostom Redler.

The palace faces Podwale Street, with the extensive forecourt entered through an ornamental gateway. Equally attractive is the façade overlooking Miodowa Street, which features Rococo sculptures. However, these are not original, having been fashioned in the 1950s.

Morsztyn Palace ❹

Pałac Morsztynów

Miodowa 10. **Map** 1 C2 & 3 C4.
🚌 116, 122, 174, 175, 179, 195. **Not open** to the public.

Originally completed at the end of the 17th century, subsequent rebuilding gave this palace a late Baroque façade and Neo-Classical out buildings. In the early 18th century it was owned by the Voivode (lord lieutenant) of the Sandomierz region, Stefan Bidziński. He was a fearless soldier, famous for donating a vast sum to release the noblemen of Sandomierz from their Muslim captors.

Subsequent owners of the palace included Ignacy

Attack on the Morsztyn Palace

Massalski, the bishop of Vilnius, a distinguished man of letters in the Enlightenment. But as he was also a gambler and a rake, and expropriated former Jesuit estates, he was hanged during the 1794 Kościuszko Insurrection. On April 17–18 1794, the palace (which had been the Russian ambassador's residence since 1790) was the scene of a fierce battle between Russian troops and Varsovians. Apparently, when the Russians finally ran out of shot, in desperation they used coins and buttons instead.

The façade of Branicki Palace from Miodowa Street

Jan Kiliński Monument ❺

Pomnik Jana Kilińskiego

Podwale. **Map** 1 C2 & 3 C4. 🚌 *116, 122, 174, 175, 179, 195.*

C OMPLETED IN 1936 by Stanisław Jackowski, this monument honors Jan Kiliński, a hero of the 1794 Kościuszko Insurrection. Originally a cobbler, Kiliński became a colonel in the army. During the insurrection he led a successful attack on Morsztyn Palace *(see p100)*, which was then the Russian ambassador's residence.

Originally erected in Krasiński Square, the monument was removed in 1942 by the Nazis and hidden in the vaults of the National Museum (Muzeum Narodowe). Graffiti soon appeared on a wall of the museum, painted by the scout master of the Szare Szeregi division of the Resistance,

Jan Kiliński Monument

saying: "People of Warsaw, I am in here, Jan Kiliński." Reconstructed in 1945, the monument was moved to its present site a few years later.

Capuchin Church of the Transfiguration ❻

Kościół Przemienienia Pańskiego, Kapucynów

Miodowa 13. **Map** 1 C2 & 3 C4. 🚌 *116, 174, 175, 179, 195.*

T HIS BAROQUE CHURCH, built by Izydor Affaita between 1683 and 1692, is thought to have been designed by Tylman of Gameren and Augustyn Locci, and completed by Karol Ceroni. Founded by King Jan III Sobieski, in gratitude for his victory over the Turks at Vienna in 1683, the modest church has a façade modeled on that of the Capuchin church in Rome. The somewhat ascetic interior features a number of unusual epitaphs.

The king's chapel contains a Rococo urn that holds the ashes of King August II Mocny, and a 19th-century sarcophagus containing the heart of King Jan III Sobieski. Another chapel houses an 18th-century marble urn, made by Jan Redler, dedicated to Anna (née Kolowrath), wife of Henryk Brühl, a hated minister at the court of King August II Mocny.

Since 1948 the church vaults have housed a nativity scene that, complete with moving figures, is always of particular interest to children.

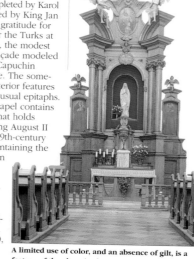

A limited use of color, and an absence of gilt, is a feature of the altars in the Capuchin Church, as monastic rules insist on the pursuance of poverty.

Pac Palace ❼

Pałac Paca

Miodowa 15. **Map** 1 C2 & 3 C4. 📞 *831 34 41.* 🚌 *116, 122, 174, 175, 179, 195.* ⬚ *by arrangement.*

O RIGINALLY A RESIDENCE of the Radziwiłł family, this Baroque palace was designed by Tylman of Gameren, and built between 1681 and 1697.

The palace was the scene of a historic event, on the night of November 3, 1771, when a rival royalist group kidnapped King Stanisław August Poniatowski in front of the palace gates. However, the plot was badly organized and soon failed, and by the following morning the king had returned to his castle.

Between the years of 1824 and 1828, the architect Henryk Marconi completely redesigned the palace inside and out, at the request of its new owner, Ludwik Pac. The interiors that resulted were a mixture of Gothic, Renaissance, Greek, and Moorish styles, while the façade was refashioned in a Palladian manner.

The impressive semi-circular gateway, which opens onto Miodowa Street, was modeled on a triumphal arch. The gateway's Neo-Classical reliefs depict the Roman counsel Fleminius, granting freedom to the Greek cities. This was the work of Ludwik Kaufmann, who was a pupil of the celebrated sculptor Antonio Canova. The building now houses the Ministry of Health.

Neo-Gothic style in Pac Palace

Krasiński Palace 8
Pałac Krasińskich

Plac Krasińskich 5. **Map** 1 C2 & 3 C4.
[] 635 62 09. [] 116, 122, 174,
175, 179, 195. [] by prior
arrangement.

THIS BAROQUE PALACE is
regarded as one of the
most beautiful buildings in
Warsaw. Constructed between
1687 and 1700, it was designed
by Tylman of Gameren for
the mayor of Warsaw, Jan
Dobrogost Krasiński.

A triangular pediment
features ornamental reliefs,
depicting the heroic deeds
of the legendary Roman
patrician Marcus Valerius
(known as Corvinus), an
ancestor of Jan Dobrogost
Krasiński. The reliefs are the
work of Andreas Schlüter, an
outstandingly gifted sculptor
and architect who later
designed the Arsenal and
Royal Castle in Berlin.

The Krasiński residence
was originally furnished with
great opulence. It included a
gallery featuring the works of
Rembrandt, Rubens, Dürer,
and Correggio. The palace
was owned by the Krasiński
family until 1765. Thereafter,
it housed the royal treasury,
followed by various legal
departments throughout the
19th century.

Rebuilt after World War II,
the Krasiński Palace now
houses a collection of antique
prints and manuscripts from
the National Library (Biblio-
teka Narodowa).

Krasiński Gardens 9
Ogród Krasińskich

Map 1 B2 & 3 C4. [] 116, 122,
174, 175, 179, 195.

TYLMAN of Gameren
designed the 17th-century
Krasiński Palace gardens and
the Baroque gateway, as well
as the palace itself. The gardens
have been open to the public
since 1776, when Krasiński
Palace was taken over by the
royal treasury.

The gardens were redesigned
several times during the 19th
century. From the end of that

Triangular pediment with ornamental reliefs at the Krasiński Palace

century until the beginning
of World War II, the gardens
were especially popular with
Jewish inhabitants from the
northern part of Warsaw,
which had few open spaces.

Summer in Krasiński Gardens

Since the war, the gardens
have been greatly enlarged,
and are now divided into
several sections by avenues.

Mansions on Długa Street 10
Pałacyki przy Długiej

Map 1 C2, 1 B2, 3 C4 & 3
C5. [] 116, 122, 174,
175, 179, 195.

DŁUGA STREET contains
several mansions, and
uniformly they each feature
a courtyard enclosed by
ornamental railings.

The façade of the 18th-
century house at No. 26,
formerly owned by Maria
Radziwiłł (née Lubomirska),
includes a triangular
pediment featuring
the Lubomirski
family crest.
Opposite, at
Nos. 23–25, is
a Neo-Classical

mansion, which has an un-
usual, irregular forecourt.

The most interesting building on Długa Street is the
Baroque Four Winds Palace
(Pałac Pod Czterema Wiatrami),
which is at Nos. 38–40. Its
ornamental gateway features
statues that personify the four
winds: Notus, Boreas, Eurus,
and Zephyrus.

Following their reconstruction after World War II, all
the buildings on Długa Street
now house a wide range of
public offices.

Arsenal 11
Arsenał

Długa 52. **Map** 1 B2 & 3 C5.
[] 831 15 37. [] 107, 111, 166,
171, 180. [] 2, 4, 15, 18, 31, 36.
[] 9am–4pm Mon–Fri (archaeological
exhibition 9am–6pm); 10am–4pm
Sun. [] free on Sun.

THIS EARLY BAROQUE arsenal
was built between
1638–47 on the orders of
King Władysław IV Waza.

One of Warsaw's
fortified buildings,
it now houses
the Museum of
Archaeology.
The exhibits have
been collected from
archaeological digs
within Poland's
prewar borders, as
well as the current
Polish Republic.
There are also exhibits
from other European
countries, Asia, the
Americas, and Africa.
The exhibition
of pre-
historic
Poland
is also

Statue at the Four Winds Palace

highly recommended. By prior arrangement, visitors can also make clay pots using prehistoric methods.

Przebendowski-Radziwiłł Palace 🕩
Pałac Przebendowskich-Radziwiłłów

Aleja Solidarności 62. **Map** 1 C2 & 3 C5. **[** 827 96 43, 826 90 91. **🚌** 107, 111, 166, 171, 180. **🚊** 2, 4, 15, 18, 31, 36. **Independence Museum** 🕐 *9am–4pm Tue–Fri, 9am–3pm Sat–Sun.* 🕮

O NE OF WARSAW'S most beautiful palaces, this was built in 1728 for Jan Jerzy Przebendowski, who was King August II's treasurer. The

Przebendowski-Radziwiłł Palace

design, by Jan Zygmunt Deybel, features mansard roofs (with two slopes on both sides and both ends), as well as a bow front.

From 1760, for two years the palace was occupied by the Spanish envoy, Count Pedro Aranda. A fierce opponent of the Spanish Inquisition, he founded the Spanish Masonic Lodge and instigated the banishment of Jesuits from Spain. During his stay in Poland, the count also dazzled Warsaw society with magnificent parties.

The palace's quiet location on a narrow shopping street changed after the East–West tunnel was constructed in

1948–9. That resulted in the palace being surrounded by a major traffic artery. After the war, the palace became the Lenin Museum. Since 1990 it has housed the Independence Museum (Muzeum Niepodległości), with a collection of documents relating Poland's history from the 18th-century partitions to the present day.

Former State Bank 🕭
Dawny Bank Państwa

Bielańska 16. **Map** 1 C2 & 3 C5. **🚌** 107, 111. **No admission** during *redevelopment*.

F ORMERLY occupied by the Russian State Bank, this building was built in 1906–11. Designed by the tsar's court architect from St. Petersburg, Leontij N Benois, it included yellow and red sandstone slabs.

For over 50 years, the building's battered walls bore witness to the battles of the Warsaw Uprising, when it was used as a military post defending access to the Old Town. The ruins have been included in the façade of a modern office building, which will also house the museum dedicated to the Warsaw Uprising.

Kings' House 🕮
Dom Pod Królami

Daniłowiczowska 14/Hipoteczna 2. **Map** 1 C2 & 3 C5. **[** 827 60 61. **🚌** 107, 111. 🕐 *8am–3:40pm.*

D ESPITE ITS NAME, this was never a royal residence. The building owes its name to the gallery of Polish monarchs on the façade. These range from Mieszko I to Stanisław August Poniatowski. These stone portraits were discovered during refurbishment carried out in 1821, and built into the façade 80 years later. The building, however, is much older; it was constructed from 1617–24 as a seat of Mikołaj Daniłowicz of Żurów.

Following its reconstruction, from 1740–7, this building housed the first public library in Poland, which was established in 1761 by the Załuski brothers. In 1795 the library's entire collection was moved to St. Petersburg, where it formed a foundation for the tsar's library. Part of the collection was retrieved in 1921, after Poland had regained independence. However, this important collection was burned during the 1944 Warsaw Uprising. The building currently houses the Polish Association of Authors (ZAIKS).

King Zygmunt III Waza

The ruined walls of the Former State Bank, now part of an office building

The grand, Neo-Classical buildings of Warsaw's Town Hall, rebuilt to the original plans of 1824

Bank Square 🅖
Plac Bankowy

Map 1 B3 & 3 C5. 🚌 *107, 111, 166, 171, 180, 512.* 🚊 *2, 4, 13, 15, 18, 26, 31, 32, 34, 36.*

WHILE THE WEST side of this square has retained an imposing Neo-Classical appearance, the rest of the square was completely altered during postwar reconstruction. It was originally triangular in shape and featured an ornamental

The Dzierżyński monument being pulled down in Bank Square

fountain and an arrangement of flower beds in the center.

After World War II, the square was extended and its name changed in honor of Feliks Dzierżyński, who established the Soviet security service. A statue of him was also erected. After the 1989 democratic elections, the square regained its former name. When the monument of the loathed Dzierżyński was pulled down it fell apart, and pieces were instantly snatched up by collectors.

Town Hall 🅖
Ratusz

Plac Bankowy. **Map** 1 B3 & 3 C5. 🚌 *107, 111, 166, 171, 180, 512.* 🚊 *2, 4, 13, 15, 18, 26, 31, 32, 34, 36.*

THIS GROUP of Neo-Classical buildings dates from 1824–30. Designed on a grand scale by Antonio Corazzi, they originally housed the Administrative Commission for Revenues and Treasury, ministerial palace of Duke Ksawery Drucki Lubecki, Bank of Poland, and Stock Exchange.

The buildings have impressive porticoes and arcades, with the former ministerial palace including a pediment by Paweł Maliński. It features Trade, Wisdom, and Industry (personified by Minerva, Jason, and Mercury), with allegories of the Vistula and Bug rivers. The ornamental borders and reliefs are the work of the sculptor Vincenti.

From 1829 to 1831, Juliusz Słowacki, a famous Romantic poet, was a clerk at the Administrative Commission for Revenues and Treasury.

The former ministerial palace was rebuilt in 1947, based on Corazzi's original drawings. It now houses the Town Hall (Ratusz).

Former Bank of Poland and Stock Exchange (John Paul II Collection) 🅖
Dawny Bank Polski i Giełda

Elektoralna 2. **Map** 1 B3 & 3 C5. 📞 *621 20 81, 620 27 25.* 🚌 *107, 111, 166, 171, 180, 512.* 🚊 *2, 4, 15, 18, 31, 36.* 🕐 *10am–4pm Tue–Sun.*

AN OUTSTANDING EXAMPLE of Polish Neo-Classicism, both the former Bank of Poland and the Stock Exchange were designed by Antonio Corazzi. Initially built from 1825–8, the building was extended as early as 1830, according to designs by Jan Jakub Gay.

The façades form two-story arcades, with a dome over the original trading room. The design includes minimally decorated spaces to underline its functional role.

Currently, the building houses a collection of European paintings, dedicated to Pope John Paul II, and donated by Janina and Zbigniew Porczyński. These include over 450 works that are arranged thematically: Mother and Child, the Bible and saints, mythology and allegory, still life, landscape, and Impressionism among others. The building also provides a venue for classical music concerts and poetry recitals.

The former Bank of Poland and Stock Exchange building, now housing an art gallery

Modernism in Warsaw

WHILE PLENTY of modern architecture appeared in Warsaw between 1960 and 1989, there are few examples of any note.

The design of various public buildings and apartment houses was generally uninspired. Unfortunately, they were often constructed using inferior materials and prefabricated elements, with rather shoddy results.

A rare exception is Supersam, a supermarket with a sophisticated design, an arched roof, and plenty of glass features. It was built in 1960–62, designed by Jerzy Hryniewiecki, together with Maciej and Ewa Krasiński. The largest

The Aktyn office building on Chmielna Street

architectural project of the 1960s was redeveloping the east side of Marszałkowska Street. This resulted in three apartment houses and pedestrian underpasses, followed by the Forum Hotel and four department stores.

The major developments of the 1970s were the Central Railroad Station (Dworzec Centralny) and the Łazienki Highway. There was little other construction during this decade, apart from a few hotels and office buildings built by foreign companies.

Two centrally located hotels were the major developments of the 1980s, bringing international style and standards to the capital.

The Holiday Inn, an example of late Modernism, was designed by Tadeusz Spychała. The towering Marriott Hotel, built in association with LOT Polish Airlines, was immediately established as a landmark building. Meanwhile, the residence of the French ambassador was constructed using imported French building materials.

Following the downfall of Communism after the 1989 democratic elections, an architectural and design revolution was initiated in Warsaw. Over the past few years, hundreds of interiors have been refurbished, and more than 50 public buildings constructed. While these buildings are hardly architectural wonders, they are at least on a par with current international standards.

The first section of Warsaw's subway system opened in 1995, after ten years of construction.

Meanwhile, high-rise late Modernist office buildings have appeared in Bank Square and on Grzybowska Street. They have also sprung up on John Paul II Avenue, where, between Grzybowska and Chłodna streets, the Atrium Business Center is under construction. This large complex is still being completed, and the first of the Atrium Center's four buildings was opened in 1995.

This building, featuring pink stone façades, also has

Patio within the Panorama shopping center

Warsaw's largest atrium. The city's most dramatic atrium, however, is in the Aktyn office building on Chmielna Street. It includes bridges, balustrades made from steel netting, and a skylight featuring tubes and pipes, which seem to have been inspired by 19th-century penal institutions.

One of the most elaborate modern interiors can be seen at the multistory Panorama shopping center in Mokotów. The center's patio includes marble from various parts of the world, as well as Afghanistan onyx, a waterfall and pool with a glass bridge, a scenic elevator, and mirrored walls.

The Jan III Sobieski Hotel, in Zawisza Square, is an example of Post-Modern architecture. With its green dome, the façades were inspired by the architecture of the Old Town.

One of the completed buildings at the Atrium Business Center

Saxon Gardens ⑱
Ogród Saski

See pp108–9.

Former Western and Discount Banks ⑲
Dawny Bank Zachodni i Dyskontowy

Fredro 6/8. **Map** 1 C3 & 3 C5.
📞 635 07 05. 🚌 *106, 107, 111, 506.* 🕐 *8am–7pm Mon–Fri, 8am–noon Sat.*

UNTIL the devastation that was wreaked by World War II, Fredro Street was a heavily built-up commercial neighborhood, the site of banks such as the Western and the Discount, shopping arcades, and hotels. One of the best known establishments was the Angielski (meaning "English") Hotel, which formerly stood at the junction of Fredro Street and Wierzbowa Street. It was at the Angielski Hotel that Napoleon Bonaparte stayed, during the time of his retreat from Moscow in 1812.

However, the former Western and Discount banks, dating

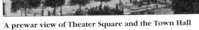
A prewar view of Theater Square and the Town Hall

from 1896, provide the area's only original architecture. The Western Bank, designed by Józef Pius Dziekoński, has a magnificent staircase and Neo-Rococo interiors on the first floor. A notable feature of the Discount Bank is the skylight crowning the original trading room. The building's upper floors, designed by Kazimierz Loewe, are also worth visiting, and currently house a music library.

Grand Theater ⑳
Teatr Wielki (Narodowy)

See pp110–11.

Theater Square ㉑
Plac Teatralny

Map 1 C3 & 3 C5.
🚌 *107, 111.*

THEATER SQUARE was the heart of Warsaw until the outbreak of World War II. It was laid out in the first half of the 19th century, when the Grand Theater was erected on the south side. The theater replaced a trading and hotel complex known as Marywil, which was established in the 17th century.

Surrounding Theater Square, there were once fashionable shops, arcades, and elegant restaurants. In 1848 the Russian composer Mikhail Glinka lived and worked in one of the square's neighboring houses, at No. 2 Niecała Street.

On the north side of the square, opposite the Grand Theater, stood the small Church of St. Andrew and the rambling Jabłonowski Palace. Between 1817–19 the palace was refashioned into the Town

Monument to the Heroes of Warsaw

Hall (Ratusz). Close by was Blank's Palace, a late Baroque building, which was owned by Piotr Blank, an 18th-century Warsaw banker. At the beginning of the Nazi occupation, Warsaw's mayor, Stefan Starzyński, was arrested in the palace. In 1944 during the Warsaw Uprising, the poet Krzysztof Kamil Baczyński died amid the ruins of the palace. After World War II, Blank's Palace was the only building to be reconstructed on the north side of Theater Square. However, the remainder of this side is currently being re-created. Period-style buildings will house various financial institutions.

The Monument to the Heroes of Warsaw 1939–45 (known as simply as "Nike"), which stands on the site of the former Town Hall, has been removed for the duration of the square's redevelopment.

Blue Palace ㉒
Pałac Błękitny

Senatorska 35/37. **Map** 1 C3 & 3 C5.
📞 826 82 11. 🚌 *107, 111, 166, 171, 180, 512.* 🚃 *2, 4, 15, 18, 31, 36.* **Not open** to the public.

THE BLUE PALACE, which dates from the 17th century, was acquired by King August II Mocny in 1726. The palace was intended as a Christmas present for the king's beloved daughter, Anna Orzelska. However, that entailed refurbishing it in a Rococo manner, as this was Anna Orzelska's favorite architectural style. The designers were Joachim Daniel Jauch, Jan Zygmunt Deybel, and Karol Fryderyk Pöppelmann. Moreover, as there wasn't much time before

Bernardo Bellotto's 18th-century painting of the Blue Palace

the Christmas in question, the alterations had to be completed in a great hurry. A total of 300 masons and craftsmen worked day and night for six weeks. Anna Orzelska subsequently named the palace after her favorite color.

In the late 18th century, the palace passed to the Czartoryski family. In 1811 it was acquired by the Zamoyskis, who refurbished it in a late Neo-Classical style, designed by Fryderyk A Lessel. The exquisitely furnished apartments were used to entertain royalty, such as the Saxon king Fryderyk August and Tsar Alexander I. Frederic Chopin also visited the palace and gave several concerts. The palace was reconstructed over two years, from 1948–50.

Landau Bank ㉓
Bank Landaua

Senatorska 42. **Map** 1 C3 & 3 C5. 📞 826 62 71. 🚌 *107, 111, 166, 171, 180, 512.* 🚊 *2, 4, 15, 18, 31, 36.* ⭕ *9am–6pm Mon–Fri.*

WHILE THE EXTERIOR of Landau Bank may not seem that impressive, having lost its original dome, the interiors are the best-preserved examples of Secessionism in Warsaw dating from the very end of the 19th century. The bank's former dealing room, for instance, is crowned by a particularly beautiful skylight.

Established by the renowned financier Wilhelm Landau, the bank was constructed over a two-year period from 1904–6. The bank was designed by two architects: Stanisław Grochowicz and Gustaw Landau-Gutenteger.

After World War II, the Landau Bank gained a new use as the Communist Party's Propaganda Center. Various political documents were stored in the bank's safe.

Currently, however, the Landau Bank building is home to several French cultural institutions.

The Primate's Palace, one of Poland's finest Neo-Classical buildings

St. John of Nepomuk Monument ㉔
Figura św. Jana Nepomucena

Senatorska. **Map** 1 C3 & 3 C5. 🚌 *107, 111, 166, 171, 180, 512.* 🚊 *2, 4, 15, 18, 31, 36.*

THIS ROCOCO FIGURE, by Giovanni Cievorotti, was commissioned in 1731 by the chief crown marshal Józef Wandalin Mniszech. The plinth depicts St. John's life (c.1345–93). He was murdered in Prague, when he opposed Wenceslas IV's attempt to disband an abbey.

St. Anthony of Padua Reformed Church ㉕
Kościół św. Antoniego Padewskiego Reformatow

Senatorska 31. **Map** 1 C3 & 3 C5. 🚌 *107, 111, 166, 171, 180, 512.* 🚊 *2, 4, 15, 18, 31, 36.*

KING ZYGMUNT III Waza founded this diminutive church in 1623, as a gesture of gratitude to God for the recapture of the town of Smolensk from Russia. The laying of the foundation stone was witnessed by the king and queen, as well as two future kings of Poland (Władysław IV and Jan Kazimierz), and the papal nuncio

St. John of Nepomuk monument

Emilio Altieri (who later became Pope Clement X).

Originally wooden, the church acquired its present form in 1671–81. The nave contains epitaphs to both wives of chief crown marshal Józef Wandalin Mniszech, dated 1747 and 1772.

The 19th-century cloisters bear commemorative plaques and epitaphs. One is dedicated to Jerzy Iwanow Szajnowicz, a British agent in World War II. Revered as a hero in Poland and Greece, he was executed by the Nazis in Athens in 1943.

Primate's Palace ㉖
Pałac Prymasowski

Senatorska 13/15. **Map** 1 C3 & 3 C5. 📞 620 02 31. 🚌 *116, 122, 144, 195, 503.* **Not open** to the public.

WHEN THE BISHOP of Płock, Wojciech Baranowski, became Poland's primate in 1601, he presented the palace to Warsaw's Cathedral Chapter (a committee of the city's bishops). This was in exchange for "the anniversaries," or daily prayers for the souls of the clergy. Nevertheless, the palace continued as the Warsaw residence of Poland's primates.

The palace was extended in 1777–84 for Primate Antoni Ostrowski: two semicircular wings, culminating in attractive pavilions, were added. The succeeding primate, Michał Poniatowski, also extended the palace, using designs by Szymon B Zug that recalled those of Andrea Palladio. Cited as the first Neo-Classical building in Poland, the palace was extensively rebuilt after being damaged during World War II.

Saxon Gardens ⓲

THE SAXON GARDENS were part of the Baroque town-planning project known as the Saxon Axis, which was undertaken by August II Mocny between 1713–33. The designers were Jan Krzysztof Naumann and Mateusz Daniel Pöppelmann. Adjoining the royal residence of Morsztyn Palace, the Saxon Gardens initially served as a royal garden, loosely based on those at Versailles. In 1727 the gardens became Warsaw's first public park, and nearly a century later, were redesigned by James Savage in the English style. Until World War II, the gardens served as an alfresco "summer salon" for Varsovian society. However, the park has since lost many of its original attractions, such as the wooden summer theater from 1870, which was destroyed at the outbreak of World War II.

The 19th-century water tower

Water Tower (Wodozbiór)
Set by the lake and modeled on the Temple of Vesta in Tivoli, this relic of Warsaw's first water-supply system was designed by Henryk Marconi.

★ **Garden Statuary**
This Baroque personification of Wisdom was carved in sandstone by Jan Jerzy Plersch in the 1730s. The gardens now contain 21 statues, a fraction of the original total. Many were removed to St. Petersburg by Marshal Suvorov. He recaptured Warsaw after the 1794 insurrection led by Tadeusz Kościuszko.

Fountain
Designed by Henryk Marconi in 1855, the fountain appears in a song inspired by a Viennese waltz: "In the Saxon Gardens, by a flowing fountain, a young man sat next to a fair maiden."

★ **Tomb of the Unknown Soldier**
A triple arch is all that remains of the Saxon Palace colonnade, destroyed in World War II. It houses the Tomb of the Unknown Soldier. On November 2, 1925, an unknown victim of the defense of Lvov (1918–19) was interred here.

Maria Konopnicka Monument
Designed by Stanisław Kulon, this monument was erected in 1965 to honor the Polish poet and writer Maria Konopnicka (1842–1910).

VISITORS' CHECKLIST

Map 1 C3. 106, 107, 111.
2, 4, 15, 18, 31, 36.

Lake
Wild ducks enjoy the lake, which originally held carp and turtles, and served as a skating rink in winter.

Alexander Nevski Orthodox Church
A symbol of Russian rule, this church was designed by Leontij N Benois. It stood for 30 years in Piłsudski Square, before being demolished in 1926.

Saxon Gardens
Before World War II, the gardens featured a 19th-century colonnade of the Saxon Palace.

Piłsudski Square was originally a courtyard of the Saxon Palace, though it has been used for various state ceremonies and parades since the early 19th century. It is named after Marshal Józef Piłsudski.

Józef Piłsudski Monument
Marshal Józef Piłsudski (1867–1935) was one of the most outstanding Polish statesmen of the 20th century (see p30).

STAR SIGHTS

★ **Tomb of the Unknown Soldier**

★ **Garden Statuary**

Grand Theater (National Theater) ❷⓿
Teatr Wielki (Narodowy)

ONE OF THE CITY'S LARGEST buildings before World War II, the Grand Theater was built in 1825–33, to a design by Antonio Corazzi and Ludwik Kozubowski. Renowned craftsmen also contributed to the sublime interiors. Initially the building was to be named the National Theater, but the defeat of the 1830 November Uprising forced a change of name. At one time, it was even planned to convert the building into an Orthodox church. Ravaged during World War II, the theater retained only its façade and several rooms. Greatly enlarged in the course of reconstruction, it also acquired modern interiors designed by Bohdan Pniewski. The theater currently houses the National Opera and Ballet.

National Theater
Since 1924, the National Theater has been housed in the building's west wing, which burned down for the third time in 1985, but was reopened in late 1996.

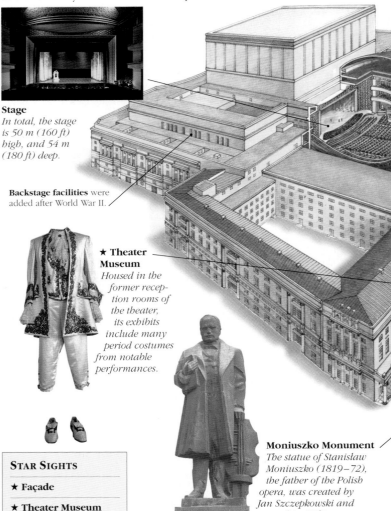

Stage
In total, the stage is 50 m (160 ft) high, and 54 m (180 ft) deep.

Backstage facilities were added after World War II.

★ Theater Museum
Housed in the former reception rooms of the theater, its exhibits include many period costumes from notable performances.

Moniuszko Monument
The statue of Stanisław Moniuszko (1819–72), the father of the Polish opera, was created by Jan Szczepkowski and erected in 1965.

STAR SIGHTS

★ Façade

★ Theater Museum

Triangular Pediment
The work of Tomaso Acciardi, this depicts the Muses crowning a bust of the ancient poet Anacreon with a wreath.

Emil Młynarski Auditorium

Bogusławski Monument
The father of the Polish national theater, and driving force behind the construction of the Grand Theater, Wojciech Bogusławski (1757–1829) was honored with this monument by Jan Szczepkowski in 1936. Destroyed during World War II, it was reconstructed in 1965. In front of the monument is a pillar dating from 1880. It marks Warsaw's latitude and longitude.

The foyer, which was inspired by the ballroom in the Royal Castle, was designed by Bohdan Pniewski as part of the theater's reconstruction after World War II.

★ Façade
A Neo-Classical covered market building, designed in 1819 by Chrystian Aigner, was incorporated into the façade of the theater. This is all that survives of the traditional market area of Marywil, established in the late 17th century and demolished when the theater was built.

Neo-Classical Frieze
Designed by Paweł Maliński, this frieze depicts Oedipus together with his entourage, returning home after competing at the Olympic Games.

THE ROYAL ROUTE

THE ROYAL ROUTE (Trakt Królewski) starts by Castle Square (Plac Zamkowy) and runs along Krakowskie Przedmieście and Nowy Świat. These thoroughfares originally developed in the late Middle Ages. Their rural setting, adjacent to the banks of the River Vistula, attracted Warsaw's wealthiest citizens, who built summer residences that were surrounded by gardens. Religious orders also established monasteries here. Although the

Railings at the Adam Mickiewicz Monument

area suffered enormously during the Swedish invasion in 1655, it was soon rebuilt. Krakowskie Przedmieście now features many buildings from the 17th and 18th centuries, particularly churches and palaces. The route extends into Nowy Świat (literally "New World"), which has buildings that are predominantly Neo-Classical in style. These include town houses and palaces, together with exclusive cafés, restaurants, stores, and fashionable boutiques.

SIGHTS AT A GLANCE

Churches
Church of the Assumption of the
Blessed Virgin Mary and St. Joseph
the Betrothed **8**
Holy Cross Church **18**
St. Anna's Church **2**
St. Joseph the
Guardian's Church **13**

Historic Buildings
Bristol Hotel **12**
Czapski Palace **17**
Dean's House **5**
Kossakowski Palace **26**
Namiestnikowski
Palace **10**
Polish Theater **22**
Potocki Palace **9**
Prażmowski House **1**
Staszic Palace **20**
Tyszkiewicz Palace **14**
Uruski Palace **15**
Warsaw University **16**
Zamoyski Palace **29**

Museums and Galleries
Caricature Museum **7**
Ostrogski Palace **23**

Historic Streets and Squares
Bednarska Street **3**
Chmielna Street **30**
Foksal **28**
Kozia Street **6**
Mariensztat **21**
Nowy Świat **25**

Monuments
Adam Mickiewicz
Monument **4**
Nicholas Copernicus
Monument **19**

Prince Józef Poniatowski
Monument **11**
Warsaw's Mermaid **24**

Shops
Blikle **27**

GETTING THERE
Buses 116, 122, 195, and 503
go to Nowy Świat and Krakowskie
Przedmieście. Streetcars 4, 13, 26, and 32 go to Plac
Zamkowy; 7, 22, 24, and 25 go to Rondo de Gaulle.

KEY
▓	Street-by-Street map pp114–15
Ⓟ	Parking
▬	Railroad line

◁ **Neo-Classical façade of St. Anna's Church**

Street-by-Street: Krakowskie Przedmieście

KRAKOWSKIE PRZEDMIEŚCIE is one of Warsaw's most historic and beautiful streets. Several imposing palaces stand back from the road, behind tree-lined squares and courtyards, alongside impressive town houses and some of the city's most interesting churches. Warsaw University's main building and the Fine Arts Academy are also located here, while monuments pay tribute to eminent Poles. A range of restaurants, cafés, and shops also make this street ideal for leisure.

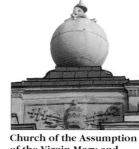

Church of the Assumption of the Virgin Mary and St. Joseph the Betrothed
This 17th-century Carmelite church has a splendid early Neo-Classical façade surmounted by an orb **8**

★ St. Anna's Church
Baroque murals by Walenty Żebrowski decorate the interior of this 16th-century church **2**

KAROWA

BEDNARSKA

TRASA W-Z

OSSOLIŃ

TREMBACKA

MIODOWA

KOZIA

Prażmowski House
This 17th-century house features a Rococo scroll supported by a cherub **1**

Prince Józef Poniatowski Monument
The figure of this early-19th-century military commander, dressed in Classical robes, stands in front of the President's Palace **11**

KEY

- - - Suggested route

Kordegarda houses a prestigious, though small, modern art gallery.

★ St. Joseph the Guardian's Church
One of the few churches in Warsaw to escape destruction, the interiors are original 18th century **⑬**

University Gate
Warsaw University is the country's largest university. Its buildings, on Krakowskie Przedmieście, house several departments **⑯**

LOCATOR MAP
See Street Finder, maps 1, 3.

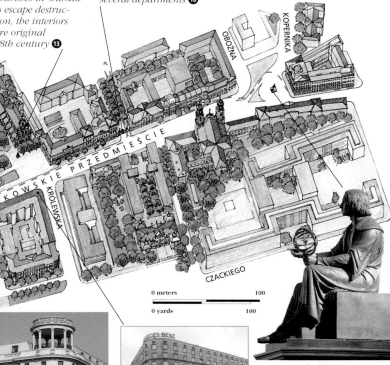

Nicholas Copernicus Monument
Created by Danish sculptor Bertel Thorwaldsen, and unveiled in 1830, this statue honors Poland's greatest astronomer (1473–1543) **⑲**

The Straight House (Dom bez Kantów) was built in 1933 by Czesław Przybylski. Its name is said to reflect not only the smooth, regular lines of the building, but also the honesty of the developers.

Bristol Hotel
Recently refurbished, this is Warsaw's most beautiful, luxurious, and expensive hotel. Its café and restaurants are excellent **⑫**

STAR SIGHTS

★ St. Anna's Church

★ St. Joseph the Guardian's Church

Prażmowski House ❶

Kamienica Prażmowskich

Krakowskie Przedmieście 87.
Map 2 D3 & 4 D5.

Prażmowski house was built in the second half of the 17th century for Dr. Pastorius, the royal physician. It is now considered one of Warsaw's most beautiful buildings, but, throughout its history, frequent changes of ownership have led to substantial changes in style.

The existing Rococo style of the house dates from 1754. The refurbishment was designed by Jakub Fontana on behalf of the Leszczyński family, whose monogram features on the grille above the main entrance.

When it was again restored, after the devastation of World War II, the house was given to the Polish Literary Society. It was a frequent venue for lively meetings, which decided the fate of many a Polish writer, if not the entire cannon of Polish literature. A bohemian atmosphere can still be enjoyed in the building's café.

Prażmowski House

St. Anna's Church ❷

Kościół św. Anny

Krakowskie Przedmieście 68.
Map 2 D3 & 4 D5.

This imposing Gothic church was founded by Anna, the widow of Duke Bolesław III, and built in the late 15th century, together with a Bernardine monastery. The church was extended

The organ at St. Anna's Church

between 1518 and 1533, but then destroyed during the Swedish invasion of 1655.

Following this turbulent period, St. Anna's was refurbished in the Baroque style. This was designed by Józef Szymon Bellotti, who preserved the original Gothic presbytery and façade. However, the façade was subsequently redesigned in the Neo-Classical style in the 18th century, by Chrystian Piotr Aigner and Stanisław Kostka Potocki.

The freestanding bell tower is another, though later, Neo-Classical feature, dating from the 1820s.

In 1864 St. Anna's became (and remains) the University Church. Additionally, the side chapel of St. Ładysław of Gielniów contains relics of this saint, who is also the patron saint of Warsaw.

The church has magnificent interiors, with several Rococo altars and frescoes by Walenty Żebrowski. Although the vaulted nave was destroyed during World War II, the Żebrowski frescoes have been restored.

St. Anna's is the most popular choice for wedding ceremonies among Warsaw's students. This is partly due to superstition, as it is said that any marriage celebrated at St. Anna's will be a happy one.

By the church are the remains of the 16th-century Bernardine monastery, which was closed in 1864. Cloisters in the monastery's east wing have retained their original

vaulted ceilings. Behind St. Anna's Church is an attractive Neo-Classical colonnade, called Odwach. This colonnade is the city's best location for second-hand booksellers and is an interesting place to browse.

Bednarska Street ❸

Ulica Bednarska

Map 2 D2 & 4 D5.

This steep, narrow street connecting Krakowskie Przedmieście with Powiśle was originally a dirt track, running alongside one of the numerous streams flowing into the River Vistula.

Between 1775 and 1864, the street was an important thoroughfare, as it led to a pontoon bridge that was the only road link with the district of Praga. Bednarska Street acquired a certain notoriety in

The cobbled Bednarska Street

the 18th century, after Kasztelanka, a bathhouse with an adjoining brothel, was built by a chatelain, Franciszek Jezierski.

The fine Neo-Classical houses along Bednarska Street were designed by architects such as Antonio Corazzi and Jan Jakub Gay. In 1832 Alfons Kropiwnicki built the Majewski Bathhouse at Nos. 2–4, near the river. This is currently a school building.

In 1840–41 Jan Jakub Gay built a house for the Warsaw Charitable Society, situated at the street's junction with

Krakowskie Przedmieście. During World War II, many houses suffered severe damage, but have been accurately rebuilt in keeping with the period character of this cobbled street.

Adam Mickiewicz Monument ❹
Pomnik Adama Mickiewicza

Krakowskie Przedmieście.
Map 2 D3 & 4 D5.

WARSAW'S MONUMENT to the country's greatest Romantic poet was un-veiled in 1898, on the centenary of his birth. As this anniversary took place during the Russian occupation of Poland, it was considered a great achievement by the Founding Committee, chaired by Michał Radziwiłł and Nobel Prize-winning author Henryk Sienkiewicz. The statue was designed by Cyprian Godebski, and the plinth was by Józef Pius Dziekoński and Władysław Marconi.

The Dean's House, with its elegant rounded niche

Adam Mickiewicz Monument

The monument occupies a square that was cleared in the mid-19th century. Only the Baroque statue of the Madonna of Passau remains from the original square. Completed in 1683 by Józef Szymon Bellotti, the statue was commissioned by King Jan III Sobieski, in gratitude to God for victory over the Turks at Vienna, and for saving his family from the plague.

Dean's House ❺
Dziekanka

Krakowskie Przedmieście 56.
Map 2 D3 & 4 D5.

DZIEKANKA, MEANING "the Dean's House," gained its name from the site it occupies. This was formerly owned by the deans of St. John's College. Built in 1770–84, this Neo-Classical building was converted into an inn during the 19th century. Having been restored after World War II, it became a student residence.

The façade features a large rounded niche, and the pictur-esque courtyard is surrounded by wooden balconies. In sum-mer, this is used for alfresco discos and theatrical performances.

Kozia Street ❻
Ulica Kozia

Map 2 D2 & 4 D5.

THIS NARROW, picturesque street connects Krakowskie Przedmieście with Miodowa Street. While the street dates

Kozia Street

from the 14th century, the existing buildings did not appear until the 17th century. Kozia Street acquired greater status in the 19th century,

due to the Saski Hotel and the Kawa u Brzezińskiej café, frequented by Frederic Chopin and various writers. Studio M café and gallery, which are at the junction of Kozia Street and Krakowskie Przedmieście, con-tinue this tradition.

On the adjacent Trembacka Street is the magnificent Rococo Saska Poczta (Saxon Post Office), which is also called Wessel Palace. Built in the mid-18th century for General Załuski, it became the main post office in 1780. It now houses the State Prosecutor's Office.

Caricature Museum ❼
Muzeum Karykatury

Kozia 11. **Map** 2 D4 & 4 D5. 827 88 95. 11am–5pm Tue–Sun.

FOUNDED IN 1978 at the urging of cartoonist Eryk Lipiński, this is the world's first museum of its kind. The museum is housed in the Gardener's House (Dom Ogrodnika), which is part of the Primate's Palace (see p107). The museum's collection includes satirical drawings, images, and maga-zines from all over the world. Two rooms house temporary exhibitions, which change every two to three months.

The Caricature Museum's sign

Neo-Classical façade of the Church of the Assumption of the Blessed Virgin Mary

Church of the Assumption of the Blessed Virgin Mary and St. Joseph the Betrothed ⑧
Kościół Wniebowzięcia NMP i św. Józefa Oblubieńca

Krakowskie Przedmieście 52/54. **Map** 2 D3 & 4 D5. 🚌 *116, 122, 175, 195, 503.* 🚊

ORIGINALLY BUILT for the Discalced (barefooted) Carmelite Friars between 1661–82, this late Baroque church is thought to have been designed by Józef Szymon Bellotti. However, the Neo-Classical façade was designed by Efraim Schroeger in 1782, which makes the church one of the earliest examples of Neo-Classicism in the country.

Despite the devastation inflicted during World War II, the church has retained many of its original features. These include an impressive transept with rows of interconnecting side chapels.

The beautiful main altar features a number of sculptures by Jan Jerzy Plersch. He also sculpted the Romantic grouping known as *Mary's Betrothal*, which stands in a side altar. This sculpture came from the Dominican Church of the Observants, which is no longer standing.

Other notable features of this church include Baroque altar paintings and two small canvases by Szymon Czechowicz in the side altars. The

friary buildings by the church were closed in 1864 and taken over by a theological seminary. Following recent refurbishment, they have become part of the Archdiocese Museum.

Potocki Palace ⑨
Pałac Potockich

Krakowskie Przedmieście 15. **Map** 2 D3 & 4 D5. 🚌 *116, 122, 175, 195, 503.* **Not open** to the public.

DATING FROM THE 1760s, this late Baroque palace is one of Warsaw's most imposing buildings. It was built for August Aleksander Czartoryski and his wife, Maria Zofia, on the site of a former 17th-century residence that was owned by the influential Denhoff family.

The palace was inherited by August Czartoryski's daughter Izabela, who was married to Stanisław Lubomirski. She

employed the prestigious architects Szymon Bogumił Zug and Jan Chrystian Kamsetzer to restyle the interiors in an extravagant manner.

Izabela Lubomirska was a renowned society figure, not only as the wife of the grand marshal, but also as a patron of the arts. Moreover, being something of a grande dame, she was actively involved in political life and intrigues during the reign of King Stanisław August Poniatowski. During the 19th century, the palace

fell into disrepair, and numerous rooms were sublet. A pavilion, erected in the courtyard, was used to exhibit notable 19th-century paintings, such as Jan Matejko's *Battle of Grunwald* and the *Prussian Oath of Allegiance*.

At the end of the 19th century, the palace regained some of its former splendor, due to restoration work undertaken by Władysław Marconi. Reconstructed after World War II, the palace is now part of the Ministry of Arts and Culture.

Namiestnikowski Palace ⑩
Pałac Namiestnikowski

Krakowskie Przedmieście 46/48. **Map** 2 D3 & 4 D5. 🚌 *116, 122, 175, 195, 503.* **Not open** to the public.

THE NEO-CLASSICAL style of this palace dates from Chrystian Piotr Aigner's refurbishment, carried out in 1818–19. Aigner restyled an existing palace

Entrance to the late Baroque Potocki Palace

that had been built during the mid-17th century.

The Namiestnikowski Palace has had a turbulent history, belonging to several important families, including the Koniecpolskis and Lubomirskis. From 1685 the palace was owned by the Radziwiłł family, who sold it in 1818 to the Russian government of Poland. Subsequently, the palace became the official residence of the tsar's governors in Warsaw. A flamboyant resident in the

Namiestnikowski Palace, the official presidential residence

19th century was the prima ballerina Mrs. Zająiczek. She maintained her staggering beauty into old age, and scandalized society with her romances. It was rumored that her vitality stemmed from a strict regime: bathing in icy water, sleeping in unheated rooms, and eating cold food.

After World War II, the palace became the Council of Ministers' Office, and was the setting for important political events. The Warsaw Pact was signed here in 1955, as was a treaty in 1970 to promote relations with Germany. The Round Table negotiations between the government and opposition groups were also held here in 1989.

Since 1994, the palace has been the official residence of the president of Poland.

Prince Józef Poniatowski Monument ⓫
Pomnik Księcia Józefa Poniatowskiego

Krakowskie Przedmieście.
Map 2 D3 & 4 D5.

Varsovians were not enthusiastic about this fine sculpture when it was first unveiled to the public. Instead of portraying the prince in his uniform, the Danish sculptor Bertel Thorwaldsen depicted him as a barefooted Classical hero, clad in a tunic. The prince, who was one of Napoleon Bonaparte's generals, perished in the River Elster in 1813 during the Battle of Leipzig, and quickly became a national

hero in Poland. The statue was commissioned in 1816 by the Monuments Founding Committee, but its official unveiling was interrupted by the insurrection of November

The Classical-style portrayal of Prince Józef Poniatowski

1830. The sculpture was transferred to the Modlin Fortress, and in 1840 was moved to a palace in Homel, Belarus. This palace was the private residence of Russian general Ivan Paskiewicz.

The monument was returned to Poland in 1922 and put in Saxon Square, but it was destroyed during World War II. A new casting from the original mold was presented to the city of Warsaw by the citizens of Copenhagen in 1965.

Bristol Hotel ⓬

Krakowskie Przedmieście 42/44.
Map 2 D3 & 4 D5. 📞 625 25 25.
🚌 116, 122, 175, 195, 503.

The Bristol was originally one of Europe's grandest hotels, although its construction was preceded by a scandal regarding the choice

of architect. A competition was held and prizes were duly awarded, but the prize-winning design was then abandoned in favor of a scheme by one of the judges, Władysław Marconi. He was an outstanding architect, and despite the resulting furor, Marconi's essentially Neo-Renaissance plans met with widespread approval.

The specially formed building consortium, which included Ignacy Paderewski *(see p34)* among its members, also commissioned Otto Wagner the Younger to design the Secessionist interiors.

The Bristol was quickly established as a society venue, hosting parties and receptions that were regarded as the most stylish in Warsaw. It was also used to celebrate special occasions, including Maria Skłodowska-Curie's Nobel Prize, and the triumphs of the renowned operetta singer Lucyna Messal. During the 1930s, the painter Wojciech Kossak kept a studio on the fifth floor. He offered his paintings as payment; they can still be seen in one of the hotel's restaurants.

After World War II, the hotel continued to receive notable guests, but fell into disrepair. Following refurbishment, the Bristol Hotel reopened in 1992, having regained all of its former style and prestige.

The refurbished Bristol Hotel

Tabernacle in St. Joseph the Guardian's Church

St. Joseph the Guardian's Church ⑬
Kościół Opieki św. Józefa

Krakowskie Przedmieście 34. **Map** 2 D3 & 4 D5. 🚊 *111, 116, 122, 175, 195, 503.*

CONSTRUCTION of the church began in 1654. However, it was soon abandoned, and building did not resume until the 18th century, under Karol Bay. The façade was completed in 1763, having been designed by Efraim Schroeger. Fortunately, the church has never been damaged and retains its original decor.

Among the church's most outstanding works of art are the Rococo pulpit, in the shape of a boat, and sculptures by the main altar. The ebony tabernacle, dating from 1654, was commissioned by Queen Ludwika Maria and is decorated with silver plaques by Herman Pothoff.

The church also features several renowned paintings: *The Visitation* by Tadeusz Kuntze-Konicz, *St. Luis Gonzaga* by Daniel Szulc, and *St. Francis of Sales* by Szymon Czechowicz.

In the church forecourt stands a monument to Stefan Cardinal Wyszyński,

erected in 1987. Adjacent to the church is the Baroque convent of the Nuns of the Visitation. This order was invited to settle in Poland by Queen Ludwika Maria. Behind the convent is a magnificent garden that is used by the nuns, but unfortunately is closed to visitors.

Tyszkiewicz Palace ⑭
Pałac Tyszkiewiczów

Krakowskie Przedmieście 32. **Map** 2 D3 & 4 D5. 🚊 *111, 116, 122, 175, 195, 503.*

REGARDED AS ONE of the city's most beautiful Neo-Classical residences, this palace was originally built for Ludwik Tyszkiewicz. Construction began in 1785,

The north elevation of Tyszkiewicz Palace

following a design by Stanislaw Zawadzki. However, the palace was completed by the architect Jan Chrystian Kamsetzer in 1792.

The relatively modest façade of the palace is decorated with some fine stuccowork, and the central balcony is supported by four elegant stone Atlantes *(see p51).*

In 1840 the palace was acquired by the Potocki family; their family crest now forms the central cartouche of the palace's façade.

The most flamboyant owner of the palace was Count August Potocki, who was fondly known in Warsaw's aristocratic circles as Count

Gucio. Renowned for his lavish lifestyle, he also figured in various scandals. However, this did not dispel his popularity, which he gained through his famous generosity and general *joie de vivre*.

The palace has been restored to its former glory, having been obliterated during World War II. It is currently part of Warsaw University, and houses an interesting collection of drawings and antique prints.

Uruski Palace ⑮
Pałac Uruskich

Krakowskie Przedmieście 30. **Map** 2 D3 & 4 D5. 🚊 *111, 116, 122, 175, 195, 503.*

THE LATE BAROQUE palace that originally occupied this site belonged to the father of Poland's last king. Moreover, it was in this palace that Stanisław August Poniatowski learned that he had been elected to the Polish throne in 1764. There is a monument in the courtyard that commemorates this event.

In 1844–7, the palace was restyled by Andrzej Gołoński for the new owner, Seweryn Uruski. Not only was Uruski considered nouveau riche, but he also had the brand-new title of count, granted by the Austrian authorities in 1844. This may explain why the family crest on the façade of the palace is so ostentatious. Restored after World War II, the palace also became part of Warsaw University, and it now houses the Geography Department.

Uruski family crest in a cartouche style

Warsaw University ⑯
Uniwersytet Warszawski

Krakowskie Przedmieście 26/28. **Map** 2 D3 & 4 D5. 🚊 *116, 175, 195, 503.*

THE PRESENT SITE of Warsaw University was originally occupied by a summer palace that belonged to the Waza

The Visitation by Tadeusz Kuntze-Konicz

Kazimierzowski Palace, part of the University of Warsaw

dynasty in the 17th century. This building, Kazimierzowski Palace, was used as the Knights School from 1765. In 1816 it became part of the newly established Warsaw University. The palace was rebuilt in the Neo-Classical style, and currently houses the rector's offices.

The university's other Neo-Classical buildings include two annexes: Porektorski and Poseminaryjny. Built in 1814–16, they were designed by Jakub Kubicki. The Main School building (Szkoła Główna), designed by Antonio Corazzi, was completed in 1841. Meanwhile, Michał Kado designed the main auditorium and the former Fine Arts Academy in 1818–22.

After the January Uprising of 1863, the university came under the direct control of the Russian authorities. Nevertheless, a new library was constructed, and opened in

1894. It was designed by Stefan Szyller and Antoni Jabłoński.

When Poland regained independence in 1918, the university acquired a new auditorium building, called the Audytorium Maximum.

Warsaw University is now Poland's largest academic institution and has expanded into a number of buildings around the city.

Czapski Palace ⑰
Pałac Czapskich

Krakowskie Przedmieście 5. **Map 2 D3 & 4 D5. Chopin family salon** 🕐 10am–2pm Mon–Fri. 🚌 111, 116, 122, 175, 195, 503.

THE CZAPSKI palace has a fascinating heritage, having been owned by several of the most distinguished Polish families, and been variously restyled by outstanding architects. The former owners of the palace include the Radziwiłł, Radziejowski, Sieniawski, and Czartoryski families, who commissioned a host of architects, such as Tylman of Gameren, Augustyn Locci, and Kaćper Bażanka. The current appearance of the palace is late Baroque,

Condottieri Monument in the courtyard of Czapski Palace

dating from 1752–65, when the palace became the seat of the Czapski family. In 1795 the architect Jan Chrystian Kamsetzer added Neo-Classical wings to the palace.

The south wing is notable for having been occupied by Frederic Chopin's family in 1826. Their former drawing room (salon) has been reconstructed, and is open to the public. The room features elegant period furniture and objets d'art, together with memorabilia of the composer.

By the end of the 19th century, the palace was owned by the Krasiński family, whose members included the Romantic poet Zygmunt Krasiński.

After substantial restoration following World War II, the palace was incorporated into the Fine Arts Academy.

The 18th-century Czapski Palace

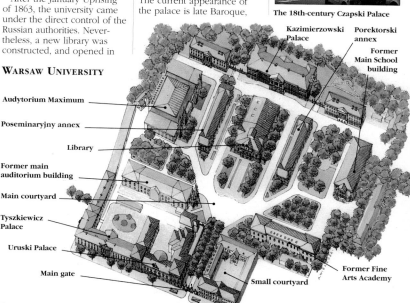

WARSAW UNIVERSITY

Kazimierzowski Palace

Porektorski annex

Former Main School building

Audytorium Maximum

Poseminaryjny annex

Library

Former main auditorium building

Main courtyard

Tyszkiewicz Palace

Uruski Palace

Main gate

Small courtyard

Former Fine Arts Academy

The magnificent twin towers of the Holy Cross Church

Nicholas Copernicus Monument ⑲
Pomnik Kopernika

Krakowskie Przedmieście. **Map** 2 D4.
🚌 *116, 122, 175, 195, 503.*

STATESMAN Stanisław Staszic began raising funds for a monument to Poland's greatest astronomer in 1810. Created by the Danish sculptor Bertel Thorwaldsen, it was unveiled in 1830. During World War II, the Nazis covered the monument's inscriptions with German plaques. They were removed by Alek Dawidowski, a member of the Szare Szeregi (Gray Ranks – a cryptonym of the Polish Scouts' Association during the war). The monument suffered much damage and was nearly dismantled for scrap in 1944. Fortunately, it was restored instead. A monument cast from the same mold can also be seen in Chicago.

Staszic Palace ⑳
Pałac Staszica

Nowy Świat 72. **Map** 2 D4.
📞 *826 99 45.* 🚌 *116, 122, 175, 195, 503.* ⬜ *by arrangement.*

A FOUNDATION established by the statesman Stanisław Staszic funded this Neo-Classical palace, which was designed by Antonio Corazzi in 1820–23 for the Royal Society of the Friends of Science. Taken over by the Russians after the defeat of the 1830 November Uprising, it was rebuilt in the Byzantine-Russian style in 1892–3.

The palace was returned to its original style in 1926, by the architect Marian Lalewicz.

Holy Cross Church ⑱
Kościół św. Krzyża

Krakowskie Przedmieście 3. **Map** 2 D4. 🚌 *116, 122, 175, 195, 503.*

THIS SUPERB example of late-17th-century Varsovian architecture was designed by Józef Szymon Bellotti. Built in 1679–96, the Holy Cross Church replaced an earlier church, destroyed during the 1655 Swedish invasion. The present building includes a wall-and-pillar basilica. The late Baroque façade and twin towers were completed in 1760 by Jakub Fontana.

An extraordinary aspect of the church is a "lower church" in the vaults, although its interior was largely destroyed, along with the main church, during World War II. Among the surviving features, the most interesting is

the altar in the south aisle, which was designed by Tylman of Gameren.

The church has served as a venue for many patriotic and religious ceremonies, including the funerals of statesman Stanisław Staszic, composer Karol Szymanowski, and painter Leon Wyczółkowski. The hearts of composer Frederic Chopin and Nobel Prize-winning novelist Władysław Reymont are in a side pillar of the nave. Mass is broadcast from the church each Sunday on national radio.

Façade of the Neo-Classical Staszic Palace

Mariensztat ㉑

Map 2 D2. 🚌 *128, 150.*

MARIENSZTAT is named after a street that formerly ran alongside the Bernardine monastery gardens, between Krakowskie Przedmieście and Dobra Street. This area also housed

Mariensztat's postwar buildings, influenced by 18th-century architecture

the Powiśle market, destroyed during World War II.

The Powiśle site was redeveloped in 1948–9. It was intended to act as a "showpiece" of Socialist housing. Designed by Zygmunt Stępiński, in a style based on 18th-century Varsovian architecture, the complex was named Mariensztat.

The project was extolled in various songs and was even featured in the film *Przygoda na Mariensztacie (Adventure in Mariensztat)*. Ironically, this necessitated building a mock-up of the complex, as it had not been completed.

The Polish Theater, resembling the Empire architectural style

Polish Theater 22
Teatr Polski

Karasia 2. **Map** 2 D4. 827 79 92.
116, 122, 175, 195, 503.

WHEN the Polish Theater was built in 1912, it was the country's most modern theater, featuring a revolving stage and an iron safety curtain. Designed by Czesław Przybylski, in a contemporary version of Empire style, the project was initiated by Arnold Szyfman, who became the theater's first director. His opening production was *Irydion*, by Zygmunt Krasiński.

Szyfman reopened the theater after World War II,

when Juliusz Słowacki's *Lilla Weneda* was staged by the legendary director Juliusz Osterwa. The Polish Theater remains one of the city's most popular theatrical venues.

Ostrogski Palace 23
Pałac Gnińskich-Ostrogskich

Okólnik 1. **Map** 2 E4. 827 54 71. 10am–5pm Mon, Wed & Fri, noon–6pm Thu, 10am–2pm Sat & Sun. for concerts.

OSTROGSKI PALACE was built in about 1681, as a pavilion to a much grander, but never completed project by Tylman of Gameren. The pavilion was erected close to the Vistula, on an elevated terrace above a cellar. According to legend, this cellar was inhabited by a golden duck that stood guard over a treasure trove. The palace was frequently refurbished, but is now a postwar re-creation of its late-18th-century form.

In 1859 the palace became the home of the Warsaw Conservatoire, and its musical connections were preserved when it was chosen as the

The Frederic Chopin Museum in Ostrogski Palace

headquarters of the International Frederic Chopin Society after World War II.

A Chopin Museum has since been established in the palace. The collection includes portraits, letters, and manuscripts, as well as the grand piano on which Chopin composed during the last two years of his life.

The palace has a concert hall, where regular performances of Chopin's music are organized by the society.

Warsaw's Mermaid 24
Pomnik Syreny

Wybrzeże Kościuszkowskie. **Map** 2 F3. 162, 195.

THIS IS the second monument devoted to Warsaw's mermaid – a mythical half-woman, half-fish – which was believed to protect the city. The mermaid has appeared in the city of Warsaw's crest since the 14th century.

Warsaw's Mermaid

Erected in 1939, this monument was designed by Ludwika Nitsch. The mermaid was modeled on Krystyna Krahelska, a famous poet who composed the march that was sung by the Polish Resistance during the Warsaw Uprising of 1944: "Hej chłopcy, bagnet na broń" ("Hey lads, put a bayonet on your weapon"). Krahelska was killed during the uprising.

The mermaid figure was originally designed to be 20 m (62 ft) high and made of glass. Moreover, the intention was to place the figure on a pillar fixed in the bed of the River Vistula. It was later decided to cast the mermaid in bronze at 2 m (6 ft) high and erect the monument on Wybrzeże Kościuszkowskie, along the banks of the Vistula.

Warsaw's other mermaid monument is situated in the Old Town (see p83).

Nowy Świat, painted in 1892 by Władysław Podkowiński

Nowy Świat ㉕

Map 2 D4 & 6 D1. 🚌 *116, 122, 195, 503.*

Cᴏɴᴛɪɴᴜɪɴɢ ᴏɴ from Krakowskie Przedmieście, Nowy Świat (meaning "New World") is the next stage of the Royal Route. The street's origins are medieval, when it became established as the main route to the towns of Czersk and Kraków.

It wasn't until the end of the 18th century that the first stone buildings were built on Nowy Świat. They were Neo-Classical palaces, with several late Neo-Classical town houses added in the early 19th century. At the end of that century, Nowy Świat was renowned for expensive restaurants, cafés, shops, theaters, and hotels.

After World War II, the Neo-Classical buildings were authentically reconstructed, with the remaining buildings also restyled in the Neo-Classical manner, to create uniformity.

This is still one of Warsaw's most elegant streets, with its cafés and chic boutiques.

Kossakowski Palace ㉖
Pałac Kossakowskich

Nowy Świat 19. **Map** 2 D5 & 6 D1. 🚌 *116, 122, 195, 503.*

Tʜɪs ᴘᴀʟᴀᴄᴇ was originally built at the end of the 18th century for Izaak Ollier, who was a wealthy merchant. However, the present Italian

Kossakowski Palace

Renaissance style dates from a refurbishment in 1849–51, when the new owner, Władysław Pusłowski, commissioned the famous architect Henryk Marconi to renovate and restyle the building.

The palace was subsequently acquired by Count Kossakowski. He established it as one of the city's most fashionable venues, with glamorous balls and a literary salon every Friday, attended by the intellectual elite. Guests also had the opportunity to admire the count's art collection. It was one of the finest private collections in Poland, including works by many foreign artists.

In 1892 the palace's belvedere (summer house) was used as a studio by the painter Władysław Podkowiński, who painted some outstanding views of Nowy Świat.

Blikle ㉗

Nowy Świat 33. **Map** 2 D5 & 6 D1. 🚌 *116, 122, 195, 503.*

Aɴᴛᴏɴɪ Kᴀᴢɪᴍɪᴇʀᴢ Bʟɪᴋʟᴇ established his eponymous patisserie in 1869, when he opened a shop and café in Nowy Świat. Until World War II, the Blikle Café was a popular meeting place for actors and artists. During the war, actresses were employed here as waitresses.

During the Communist era, the Blikle family managed to retain ownership of the patisserie (but not the café), which produced the finest doughnuts in Warsaw. Since the democratic elections in 1989, the current owner, Andrzej Blikle, has opened other shops in Warsaw. In 1993 he also opened a café next to the patisserie on Nowy Świat.

Foksal ㉘

Map 2 E5 & 6 D1. 🚌 *116, 122, 195, 503.*

Fᴏᴋsᴀʟ sᴛʀᴇᴇᴛ was named after the pleasure garden that was established in this area during the 18th century. Modeled on the Vauxhall Pleasure Gardens in London, it was laid out at the urging

Apartments on Foksal Street

Zamoyski Palace 🟢
Pałac Zamoyskich

Foksal 1/2/4. **Map** 2 E5 & 6 D1.
📞 827 87 12. 🚌 116, 122, 195, 503.

Set in a magnificent landscaped park, this palace was built in 1878–9. It was designed by Leandro Marconi, who was from a family of distinguished architects. He created Baroque-style interiors, while ensuring that the palace was comfortable as a private residence. Its façade exemplified the fashionable "French Costume" manner (inspired by the Renaissance style of Henry IV and Louis XIII).

Entrance to Zamoyski Palace

The palace was occupied by the Zamoyski family until World War II. One of their distinguished guests was, in 1923, the French World War I hero Marshal Ferdinand Foch.

After World War II, the palace was taken over by the state and given to the Society of Polish Architects. Since 1965, the left wing has housed Foksal Gallery, an interesting modern art collection.

Musicians on Chmielna Street

Chmielna Street 🟢
Ulica Chmielna

Map 2 D5 & 6 D1. 🚌 179, 180, 522. 🚋 2, 4, 15, 18, 31, 35, 36.

This street is interesting more for events that have happened here, than for its architecture. Before World War II, Chmielna Street was renowned for its range of shops, street theater, and cafés.

During the Communist era, the street was renamed Henryk Rutkowski Street and became a center for private enterprise and retailing. It was here that Varsovians came to order outfits for weddings and other special occasions, and to buy accessories such as gloves and shoes. Second-hand shops offered what were known

Shops and cafés on Chmielna Street

locally as "things from foreign parcels," meaning goods sent by relatives from the West. These included fragrances, clothes, and other items, such as Barbie dolls, that were impossible to buy in state-run stores in Poland.

Chmielna Street's fame has declined since its heyday, but it remains a charming pedestrian shopping street with numerous cafés.

of a banker, Fryderyk Kabryt. The attractions of the garden included the first balloons ever seen in Warsaw.

During the mid-19th century, when the pleasure garden was redeveloped, one of its lanes was converted into a cul-de-sac that connected with Nowy Świat, and this became Foksal Street. Some palaces and apartment houses were then built along the road, as well as the magnificent building for the Warsaw Rowing Society, which can be seen at No. 19.

At No. 6 Foksal Street stands the elegant Prze-ździecki Palace, which was designed by Marceli Berent. It was built in 1878–9 and was originally owned by the Przeździecki family. The palace now houses the Diplomatic Club of the Polish Ministry of Foreign Affairs.

The delicate columns of Przeździecki Palace on Foksal Street

AROUND MARSHAL STREET

DURING THE MID-19th century the commercial center of Warsaw began to move away from the area around Krakowskie Przedmieście and Theater Square, and toward Marshal Street (Marszałkowska). This was prompted by a new railroad station serving the Warsaw–Vienna line, which opened in 1845 by the junction of Jerozolimskie Avenue

Plaque bearing the date of the Palace of Culture and Science

and Marshal Street. The following decades saw Marshal Street established as the city's principal shopping area. Despite being destroyed during World War II, and subsequently redeveloped, Marshal Street has maintained its traditional status. However, the city's commercial center has continued moving westward, toward the Central Railroad Station.

SIGHTS AT A GLANCE

Churches
Augsburg Protestant
   Community Church **2**
Church of the Savior **15**

Historic Buildings and Streets
Central Railroad Station **11**
Engineers' Society **4**
Filtering Plant **14**
Former Bracia Jabłkowsky
   Department Store **8**
Historic Buildings on
   Jerozolimskie Avenue **10**
Lwowska Street **13**
Palace of Culture and Science **9**
Philharmonic **7**
PKO S.A. Bank **5**
Technical University of
   Warsaw **12**
Warszawa Hotel **6**

Museums and Galleries
Ethnographic Museum **3**
Zachęta (Fine Art Society) **1**

GETTING THERE

As Marshal Street lies in the center of Warsaw, the area is well served by bus and streetcar routes, which also provide connections with the rest of the city. Additionally, an underground train service operates between Polytechnic Station and the districts of Mokotów, Ursynów, and Natolin.

KEY

▨	Street-by-Street map *pp128–9*
P	Parking
M	Metro station

0 meters 500
0 yards 500

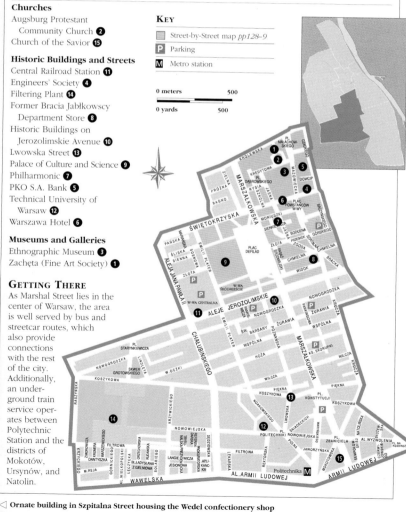

◁ **Ornate building in Szpitalna Street housing the Wedel confectionery shop**

Street-by-Street: Marshal Street

Stained-glass window at Jabłkowscy's store

Marszałkowska (Marshal Street) is one of the city's main locations for banks, hotels, and stores. The 1950s saw construction on a major scale in this street, including Warsaw's tallest building, the Palace of Culture and Science. However, there are also some impressive turn-of-the-century buildings featuring ornate interiors.

Zachęta (Fine Art Society)
Designed by Stefan Szyller and built from 1899–1903, it has recently been greatly extended ❶

★ Augsburg Protestant Community Church
This 18th-century church is famous for its excellent acoustics ❷

Philharmonic
This hall is the venue for the renowned Chopin Piano Competition, held every five years ❼

★ Palace of Culture and Science
Statues of the astronomer Nicholas Copernicus (left) and the poet Adam Mickiewicz are distinctive features of the main entrance. The façade also includes other sculptures in the Socialist Realist style ❾

KEY

--- Suggested route

0 meters   200

0 yards   200

Ethnographic Museum
Traditional Polish folk costumes are a highlight of the collection ❸

LOCATOR MAP
See Street Finder, maps 1, 2

The Bank Under the Eagles takes its name from the stone eagles by Zygmunt Otto that surmount the roof. A contemporary art historian described the eagles as "looking like victims sacrificed on the altar of Polish style." Designed by Jan Heurich, Jr., and built in 1912–17, the bank is an example of Poland's early Modernist architecture.

The Wedel Patisserie on Szpitalna Street has retained its ornate turn-of-the-century decor. It is home to the famous confectionery company Emil Wedel.

★ **Former Bracia Jabłkowscy Department Store**
Built in 1913–14, this is the city's oldest department store; it has recently been restored ❽

Central Arcades, a pedestrian area with a few small stores, was built in the 1960s, behind the city's main department stores.

STAR SIGHTS

★ **Augsburg Protestant Community Church**

★ **Palace of Culture**

★ **Bracia Jabłkowscy Department Store**

Zachęta ❶

Plac Małachowskiego. **Map** 2 D4.
☎ 827 58 54. **🚌** 106, 160, 175,
179. **🕐** 10am–6pm Tue–Sun.
🎟 free on Fri.

THIS MONUMENTAL building
was constructed between
1899–1903, on behalf of the
Society for the Promotion of
Fine Art (Towarzystwo
Zachęty Sztuk Pięknych,
though usually it is simply
abbreviated to Zachęta).

The Neo-Renaissance design
was by Stefan Szyller, the leading architect of Warsaw's
Revival period. His design
included an imposing central
staircase, a glass-roofed inner
courtyard, and plans for four
wings. However, these wings
were completed only as
recently as 1995.

The aim of Zachęta was to
promote contemporary Polish
art. This included organizing
exhibitions, competitions, and
annual salons. The society
also purchased works of art
for its own collection.

In 1922, Zachęta was the
scene of a major political
assassination. At an exhibition
opening, the first president
of the newly independent
Republic of Poland, Gabriel
Narutowicz, was shot dead.

**Ornate façade of the Neo-
Renaissance Zachęta building**

His assassin was a Polish
painter and art critic, named
Eligiusz Niewiadomski.

More recently, the Zachęta
collection has been transferred
to the National Museum, or
Muzeum Narodowe as it is
known in Warsaw *(see pp154–
7)*. The building currently
serves as a venue for temporary exhibitions of modern
and contemporary Polish art.

**Portico of the Augsburg
Protestant Community Church**

Augsburg Protestant Community Church ❷

Kościoł Ewangelicko-Augsburski (Zbór
św. Trójcy)

Plac Małachowskiego 1. **Map** 2 D4.
🚌 106, 160, 175, 179.

REGARDED AS ONE of the most
outstanding examples of
Neo-Classical architecture in
Poland, this church was built
especially for the Lutheran
community of Warsaw, in
1777–91. It also bears witness
to the country's religious
tolerance during the reign of
Stanisław August Poniatowski,
Poland's last king.

Designed by the architect
Szymon Bogumił Zug, the
church is reminiscent of the
Pantheon in Rome, which
the Romans built as "a temple
of all the gods." However,
this source of inspiration was
merely a starting point, from
which Zug developed a unique
architectural design.

There is an impressive Doric
portico, which emphasizes
the severity of the façade. It
is crowned by a 58-m (189-ft)
high dome. This feature originally made the church the
tallest building in Warsaw.

The interior of the church
features a vast cylindrical nave
with rectangular transepts,
and two-tier galleries supported by columns. It is renowned
for its excellent acoustics and
is frequently used for concerts by church choirs of
various denominations.

Ethnographic Museum ❸

Muzeum Etnograficzne

Kredytowa 1. **Map** 1 C4. **☎** 827 76
41. **🚌** 106, 160, 175, 179.
🕐 9am–4pm Tue, Thu & Fri,
11am–6pm Wed, 10am–5pm Sat &
Sun. **🎟** free on Wed.

ONE OF THE CITY'S most
beautiful 19th-century
buildings, this museum was
built in a Neo-Renaissance
style, partly inspired by the
Libreria Sansoviniana in
Venice. It was originally built
as the head office of the Land
Credit Union, in 1854–8, and
designed by Henryk Marconi,
an Italian settled in Warsaw.

Within the Ethnographic
Museum's collection, there
are permanent displays of

Ethnographic Museum

Polish folk costumes, folklore,
and arts and crafts. Also, the
museum has a collection of
ethnic and tribal art from
around the world, including
Africa, Australia, the Pacific,
and Latin America.

Temporary exhibitions are
also put on, and the museum
shop has a varied choice of
items. Near the museum on
Mazowiecka Street is the
Artist's House (Dom Artysty),
which contains a modern art
gallery and a well-stocked
bookshop on the first floor.

**Triangular pediment at the
Engineers' Society**

Engineers' Society ❹
Dom Stowarzyszenia Techników

Czackiego 3/5. **Map** 2 D4.
📞 826 74 61. 🚌 150, 174, 179.
🕙 8am–4pm daily.

THIS BUILDING's lavish Neo-Baroque façade was designed by Jan Fijałkowski in 1903. It is embellished with allegorical figures by Zygmunt Otto, together with sculptures and other decorative details by Józef Gardecki.

The inscription on the portico is *Artibus Technicis* (Art and Engineering). Below this are two figures: one is Archimedes holding a lever, and the other a "modern" woman, bearing luminous radium in her hand.

PKO S.A. Bank ❺
Bank PKO S.A.

Czackiego 21/23. **Map** 2 D4.
📞 661 27 18. 🚌 150, 174, 179.
🕙 8am–6pm Mon–Fri, 8am–3pm occasionally on Sat.

Head office of the PKO S.A. Bank

THE BUILDING's eclectic design was the work of Julian Ankiewicz. It was constructed in stages between 1878–94, and was later extended by Władysław Marconi in 1909–11. He added a triangular pediment above the portico that was decorated with an allegory of Prosperity by Pius Weloński.

Formerly housing the Urban Credit Union, the building now serves as the head office of

the PKO S.A. bank. The main hall, which is decorated with scenes of 18th-century Warsaw, has a fine skylight.

Warszawa Hotel ❻

Plac Powstańców Warszawy 9.
Map 2 D4. 📞 826 94 21. 🚌 150, 174, 166, 171, 179, 180. 🚊 2, 4, 15, 18, 31, 36.

UNTIL THE Palace of Culture and Science was completed in 1955, this was the tallest building in Warsaw.

Built in 1934 on behalf of Prudential, the insurance company, it was in the heart of the city's prewar banking district. The designers were Marcin Weinfeld and the mathematician Stefan Bryła. The latter was responsible for the steel frame, which enabled the building to withstand heavy shelling during the Warsaw Uprising in 1944.

Rebuilt in the Socialist Realist style during the postwar period, the building was then converted into a hotel.

Philharmonic ❼
Filharmonia

Jasna 5. **Map** 1 C4. 📞 826 72 81.
🚌 179. **Box office** 🕙 noon–6pm Mon–Sat. ⏰ 3–3:30pm.

THE ORIGINAL style of the Philharmonic building was one of the city's most eclectic. Embellished with allegorical figures and statues of great composers, it was designed by the firm of Kozłowski and Pianka, and financed by private subscription. It was also built in record time. Construction began in 1900, with the inaugural concert held on

Stained glass in Bracia Jabłkowscy store

The Philharmonic at the beginning of the century

Warszawa Hotel, rebuilt after the war in the Socialist Realist style

November 5, 1901, led by Ignacy Paderewski *(see p34)*.

Rebuilt in the Socialist Realist style after World War II, the Philharmonic bears only a vague resemblance to its original form. The Chopin Piano Competition has been held here since 1927.

Former Bracia Jabłkowscy Department Store ❽
Dawny Dom Towarowy Bracia Jabłkowscy

Bracka 25. **Map** 2 D5.
📞 827 60 21. 🚌 101, 117, 128, 159, 166, 175. 🚊 7, 22, 24, 25.
🕙 10am–8pm Mon–Fri, 10am–5pm Sat, 10am–6pm Sun.

ORIGINALLY WARSAW's largest department store, this early Modernist building is considered to be one of the best examples of early-20th-century Polish architecture.

Designed by Franciszek Lilpop and Karol Jankowski, it was built in 1913–14 around a reinforced-concrete framework. Nationalized after World War II, it initially traded as the Central Department Store (Centralny Dom Towarowy), before becoming the city's principal shoe shop (Dom Obuwia). The building fell into disrepair, but was restored recently and now houses chic boutiques. The ornate lobby features a Post-Secessionist stained-glass window (the largest in Warsaw), and humorous reliefs by Edmund Bartłomiejczyk.

Socialist Realism in Warsaw

THE REBUILDING OF WARSAW coincided with the emergence of Socialist Realism. This style of architecture presented an idealized version of reality, championing the achievements of Communism and its growing power with buildings and developments constructed on a monumental scale. Marshal Street Residential Area (Marszałkowska Dzielnica Mieszkaniowa) is a symbol of this Socialist Realist era, inspiring the praise of writers and poets. Known as MDM, it was built in 1950–52, and replaced the partially destroyed houses on Marshal Street. The focal point of the development was at Constitution Square (Plac Konstytucji). While the façades of the buildings do show architectural merit, they are not as original as proclaimed in the propaganda of the day. Ironically, some

A Socialist Realist-style lamppost

recall the 1913 building originally owned by Count Krasiński in Małachowski Square. And houses on Wyzwolenia Avenue resemble those fronting the Place Vendôme in Paris. During Stalin's regime, architects were banned from visiting Paris, so this was a way of enjoying a "small fragment" of that city in Warsaw.

The distinctive office building at No. 36 Krucza Street

KRUCZA STREET

AT THE END OF the 1940s and beginning of the 1950s, plans were drawn up to develop an office district in the area around Krucza, Wspólna, and Żurawia streets. Large buildings with stone façades were subsequently constructed on the sites of burned down 19th-century tenement buildings. They were used to house government ministries, offices, and industrial organizations.

Some buildings were also given unusual façades. The ministry building at No. 36 Krucza Street is reminiscent of a turn-of-the-century Chicago-style office building. The ten-story Grand Hotel at No. 28 Krucza Street has a flat roof, intended to serve

The mainly glass façade of Smyk Department Store

SMYK ("THE BRAT")

BUILT OF GLASS and reinforced concrete, the materials associated with Modernism, this department store was officially condemned as "ideologically alien, cosmopolitan" architecture, when it was completed in 1952.

During the 1950s, the press frequently pictured the building's interiors and former café as the meeting place of Warsaw's "decadent youth."

The store suffered a major fire in 1977, but has since been rebuilt.

The monumental colonnade of the Ministry of Agriculture

as a helicopter landing pad. Near the hotel, on Three Crosses Square (Plac Trzech Krzyży), stands a group of buildings, originally housing the State Planning Committee, and featuring a large dome-covered conference hall.

THE MINISTRY OF AGRICULTURE

BUILT IN THE Socialist Realist style, between 1951–5, the Ministry of Agriculture features Warsaw's tallest colonnade (on the Wspólna Street side), which is several floors high. In the 1950s, plans were also drawn up to establish a large square situated opposite the ministry. This was intended to feature a cultivated field, where state-farm workers who were visiting the ministry could be acquainted with the best farming methods.

OFFICE BUILDING ON WSPÓLNA STREET

IN THE 1950s, the architect of this office building, Marek Leykam, was at the forefront of a particular architectural "resistance movement." While other architects were drawing up designs in accordance with the Socialist Realist "gospel," he was working in the International Style, creating buildings that were known as "razor blades," which were characterized by façades composed of repeated, prefabricated elements.

Among the examples of this style are the Budimex building at No. 82 Marshal Street, and the Mining Institute at No. 4 Rakowiecka Street.

In the first few years of the 1950s, Leykam planned to build a multistory "razor-blade" building at No. 62 Wspólna Street. However, the authorities rejected his design, which prompted him to create a building on this site whose architectural style is actually a veiled parody of Socialist Realist principles.

The façades are variations on the theme of a 15th-century Florentine banker's palace, while the interior

A dome-covered courtyard of the office building at No. 62 Wspólna Street.

features a huge circular courtyard, covered by a concrete dome and surrounded by several tiers of open galleries.

THE BANKING AND FINANCE CENTER

THIS BUILDING, essentially influenced by Modernism, but with detailing in the style of Socialist Realism, was built in 1948–51 to a design by Wacław Kłyszewski, Jerzy Mokrzyński, and Eugeniusz Wierzbicki. It was originally the seat of the ruling Communist Party Central Office.

It now serves as the Banking and Finance Center and houses the Stock Exchange (Eastern Europe's largest).

HOUSING PROJECTS

MANY OF WARSAW's housing projects dating from the 1940s and 1950s display Socialist Realist architecture.

Among these, the oldest is the small and very attractive complex at Mariensztat *(see pp122–3)*.

Larger projects were built on the site of the former Jewish Ghetto. One of them is Muranów, designed by Bohdan Lachert. Its buildings were constructed on mounds of rubble, created from the postwar ruins of the district, which had been destroyed by the Nazis. The complex is full of tranquil squares and colonnades, as well as arched gateways leading to courtyards.

More monumental is the architecture of a housing complex built along General Anders Avenue and John Paul II Avenue, between Elektoralna Street and Solidarity Avenue. The basement of No. 36 John Paul II Avenue houses the Time Shop, which retains well-preserved 1950s decor.

The Banking and Finance Center, housing Poland's Stock Exchange

Palace of Culture and Science ❾

T HIS MONOLITHIC BUILDING was a "gift" from the Soviet Union to the people of Warsaw and was intended as a monument to "the inventive spirit and social progress." Built between 1952 and 1955 to the design of a Russian architect, Lev Rudniev, it resembles Moscow's Socialist Realist high-rises. Although the palace has only 30 stories, it was Europe's second tallest building when completed. Measuring just over 230 m (750 ft), including the spire, the structure contains 40 million bricks. The interiors are said to feature many architectural and decorative elements that were removed from stately homes after World War II. Although the palace is nearly half a century old, it still inspires extreme emotions among Varsovians, ranging from great admiration to demands for its demolition. With the recent end of Soviet domination, the building's role has changed, and it now provides a considerable amount of office space. However, the palace has remained a cultural center as well, with its two theaters, movie house, puppet theater, and excellent bookshop.

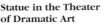

Statue in the Theater of Dramatic Art
There are 28 such figures around the building. As Socialist Realist allegories, they represent themes such as Science, Art, and the Collective Economy.

The Youth Palace contains a swimming pool, gymnasiums, and a winter garden.

Lampposts, forming a semicircle in front of the palace, are almost identical to their Muscovite prototypes.

★ **Congress Hall**
This is where Communist Party Congresses were held. The hall continues to serve as a venue for various conferences, concerts, and festivals. The best known festival is the Jazz Jamboree, at which such jazz legends as Louis Armstrong, Ray Charles, and Miles Davis have performed.

The Museum Technology's main attraction are a planetarium and the Glass Girl, wh is a model of human body.

PLAC DEFILAD

Almost 1 million people gathered here on October 24, 1956, to celebrate more enlightened government policies and the appointment of Władysław Gomułka as first secretary of the Polish Communist Party. The next great occasion here was the mass celebrated by Pope John Paul II in 1987, attended by hundreds of thousands of people.

The Viewing Terrace provides magnificent panoramas across the city.

Renaissance Attics

In Renaissance architecture, an ornamental wall above a cornice is known as an attic. The attics here were inspired by those on buildings in Kraków, Baranów, and Krasiczyn.

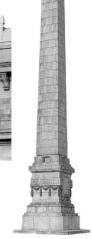

Stone obelisk in front of the palace

The Theater of Dramatic Art is one of Poland's finest theaters.

Wiedza Movie Theater was a popular venue for classic films. Other movie theaters have become the BAS Department Store.

Dolphin Fountains

In the squares surrounding the palace are four cast-iron fountains featuring dolphins. Nearby there are also three large stone fountains and two smaller fountains.

Marble Interiors

Marble corridors and staircases link the Congress Hall with the first-floor reception rooms.

STAR SIGHT

★ **Congress Hall**

Historic Buildings on Jerozolimskie Avenue ⑩

Kamienice w Alejach Jerozolimskich

Map 5 C1 & 5 C2.

THE AREA ENCLOSED by Jerozolimskie Avenue and the neighboring Nowogrodzka, Poznańska, and Emilii Plater streets features several outstanding buildings that date from the turn of the century.

The Polonia Hotel, at No. 45 Jerozolimskie Avenue, has a Parisian Beaux-Arts façade. Built between 1909 and 1913, it was commissioned by Count Konstanty Przeździecki. The hotel's flamboyant dining

Buildings on Jerozolimskie Avenue

room has also retained its original Louis XVI style.

The adjacent building, at No. 47, has Secessionist interiors. There is also an impressive dome on one corner of the building. The eclectic façade of No. 51 was designed for the Hoser Brothers, a renowned landscape-gardening firm.

Through the main entrances of Nos. 49 and 51, there are two consecutive courtyards, known locally as "well shafts." These adjoining courtyards are typical of building in prewar Warsaw. Another example of this kind is at No. 53, where the connected courtyards have been converted into a glass-encased atrium, with galleries and glass-fronted elevators.

Nearby, in Nowogrodzka Street, there is a huge building that was the headquarters of the former Agricultural Bank. The architect was Marian Lalewicz, a Pole who returned to Warsaw after having worked in St. Petersburg. Consequently, the building's Neo-Classical style resembles that of

numerous buildings erected in St. Petersburg before the Russian Revolution. The entrance hall was subsequently refurbished with various colorful Art Deco features.

Central Railroad Station

Central Railroad Station ⑪

Dworzec Centralny

Aleje Jerozolimskie 54. **Map** 5 C1.
📞 25 50 00. 🚌 102, 105, 109, 128, 158, 160, 175. 🚊 7, 10, 16, 17, 19, 22, 24, 29, 33.
♿ 🚇 ℹ️

BUILT BETWEEN 1972 and 1976 to the design of Arseniusz Romanowicz, this is the principal railroad station in Warsaw. Most trains passing through the city stop here, arriving at the station's underground platforms via a tunnel under Jerozolimskie Avenue. The platforms are joined by several passageways, which run beneath the main concourse. In recent years, these passages have gained a great number of shops, effectively becoming shopping arcades.

Technical University of Warsaw ⑫

Politechnika Warszawska

Plac Politechniki. **Map** 5 C3.
📞 66 02 13. Ⓜ️ Politechnika.
🚌 114, 130, 174. 🚊 14, 15, 19.
🕐 7am–9pm daily.

THE TECHNICAL UNIVERSITY is a complex of six buildings, built in record time between 1899 and 1901. Stefan Szyller worked with Bronisław Brochwicz-Rogóyski on five of the buildings, but the main building he designed alone. He used a unique concept: a pentagonal layout arranged around a four-story galleried courtyard, known as the "Aula" (Assembly Hall). This spacious, glass-covered courtyard is a bright and popular venue.

The glass-roofed Assembly Hall at the Technical University of Warsaw

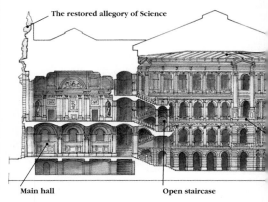
The restored allegory of Science

Main hall   **Open staircase**

Lwowska Street ⓭
Ulica Lwowska

Map 6 D2 & 6 D3. Ⓜ *Politechnika.*
🚌 *114.* 🚃 *14, 15, 19.*

AN ATMOSPHERE of turn-of-the-century Warsaw can best be enjoyed on Lwowska Street. This is the only street from that period in the city center to escape the destruction of World War II.

A picturesque example of early Modernism, inspired by Scandinavian architecture, can be seen at Nos. 15–17. This building was designed in 1910 by Artur Górney.

The courtyard of No. 13 even features a small palace, which was built in 1912. The vast Secessionist-Modernist building on the corner of Lwowska and Koszykowa

Buildings at the corner of Lwowska and Koszykowa streets

streets was originally the Russian high school, but it now houses the Technical University's Architecture Department.

Filtering Plant ⓮
Stacja Filtrów

Koszykowa 81. **Map** 5 B2 & 5 B3.
📞 *628 80 61.* 🚌 *159.*
⬜ *by arrangement.*

THE WATER-FILTERING PLANT, which occupies a large site in central Warsaw, is one

Part of the Filtering Plant

of the city's most important examples of 19th-century industrial architecture.

In the 1880s, Warsaw was the first city in the former Russian Empire to acquire a modern water and sewer system, thanks to the initiative of the city's president, General Sokrates Starynkiewicz.

However, the project had many opponents, particularly among landlords, who did not want to bear the expense of a sewage plant. One argument they cited was that the new system would damage agriculture in the surrounding region, by depriving farmers of the city's natural fertilizer.

The principal designers of the system were from England: William Lindley and his son William H Lindley, who had designed water-supply systems for other European cities. River

and canal pumping stations were also built at various points in Warsaw.

The Filtering Plant's most interesting features are within its underground structure. There, water filters consisting of interconnected, vaulted brick chambers can be seen. They are supported by large granite pillars.

The former engine room now includes a small museum, which demonstrates the process of the Filtering Plant and illustrates the history of the project to build this water and sewer system.

Church of the Savior ⓯
Kościół Zbawiciela

Marszałkowska 37.
Map 6 D3. Ⓜ *Politechnika.*
🚌 *117, 180.* 🚃 *4, 14, 15, 18, 19, 31, 35, 36.*

Church of the Savior

BUILT IN 1901–11, the overall design of this church was based on a medieval cathedral. However, the façade and interiors were also inspired by Polish Renaissance and Baroque styles. The side chapels were modeled on the Zygmunt Chapel in Kraków's Wawel Castle, the royal residence until 1596.

The architects of this church, which is one of the city's largest, were Józef Pius Dziekoński, Ludwik Panczakiewicz, and Władysław Żychiewicz.

MAIN BUILDING OF THE TECHNICAL UNIVERSITY

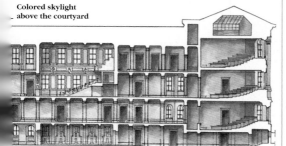

Colored skylight above the courtyard

Galleries surrounding the courtyard

| 0 meters | 500 |
| 0 yards | 500 |

GETTING THERE
The former Jewish Ghetto
area is a sprawling district that
is located near the city center
and served by an extensive network of public transportation.
When traveling from the center
you can take any streetcar running along John Paul II Avenue
or Marshal and Andersa streets
heading toward Żoliborz.

◁ **Monument to the Ghetto Heroes**

THE FORMER JEWISH GHETTO

BEFORE THE OUTBREAK of World War II, the northwestern part of Warsaw's city center was a large and mainly Jewish district known as Nalewki. Warsaw's Jewish population was then about 400,000, which was almost one-third of the city's total and the largest Jewish population after that of New York. Jews in Nalewki had economic and cultural links with the rest of the city and were free to settle in any district. Nalewki was densely built up with

Chanukah menorah

apartment houses and had virtually no green spaces within it. The languages spoken in the area were Yiddish, Hebrew, and also Russian, used by Jews who had fled Russia and settled in Warsaw.

During World War II Nalewki was turned into the Jewish Ghetto by the Germans. The ghetto was then systematically destroyed between 1942 and 1943, and almost all the inhabitants were either killed immediately or transported to death camps. Following the Ghetto Uprising in 1943, Nalewki was completely razed by the Nazis. In the postwar years, redevelopment transformed the area into housing projects.

However, traces of the original Jewish community remain. In addition to Warsaw's monuments and memorials to the Jews who perished, there are the Jewish History Institute Museum, as well as the Jewish National Theater and Nożyk Synagogue – the only synagogue in Warsaw to have survived the war intact.

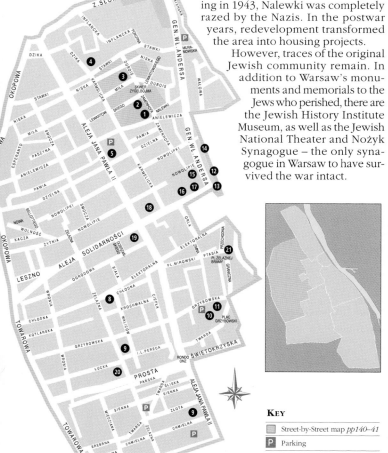

KEY

▨	Street-by-Street map *pp140–41*
🅿	Parking

Path of Remembrance

THE NAZIS CREATED the Jewish Ghetto on November 16, 1940, by driving the Jewish inhabitants of Warsaw and surrounding villages, as well as local Gypsies, into an area in the northwest of the city center. The ghetto was divided into two areas, joined by a bridge that crossed Chłodna Street.

The ghetto initially housed 450,000 people, with up to 10 people living in each room. Officially it had an administration, in the form of the Jewish Council (Judenrat), led by Adam Czerniaków. This was a sham, however, as only Nazi orders were carried out. The Nazis hoped to exterminate the ghetto's inhabitants by conducting a reign of terror and creating appalling living conditions. They took over Jewish factories and introduced slave labor, and in March 1942 began to actively destroy the population, transporting over 300,000 to gas chambers at Treblinka. By July 1942, an additional 100,000 people had died inside the ghetto.

The Ghetto Uprising, instigated by the Jewish Fighters Organization, began on April 19, 1943, with the aim to defy the Nazis and die with honor. Following the suppression of the uprising, the Nazis razed the ghetto to the ground and used the area to execute prisoners from Pawiak *(see p143)*.

The locations of significant events in the ghetto, and the courage of its inhabitants, are marked by a series of monuments along the Path of Remembrance.

Bunker Monument
This marks the site of the bunker from which Mordechaj Anielewicz of the Jewish Fighters Organization commanded the Ghetto Uprising ❸

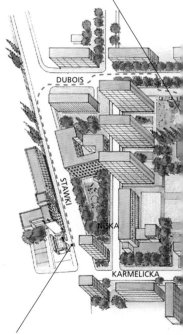

DUBOIS

STAWKI

NISKA

KARMELICKA

Borders of the Warsaw Ghetto in 1940

The Jewish Ghetto was formed in the northwestern quarter of the city center. Initially, the Nazis built a heavily guarded barbedwire fence to define the area, before replacing the border with brick walls. When it was created in 1940, the ghetto occupied an area of 307 ha (760 acres). It was steadily reduced, and by the end of 1941, many streets were no longer within the ghetto.

★ **Umschlagplatz Monument**
From this spot, the Nazis deported some 300,000 Jews to the death camps. The monument's design recalls the cattle cars used for transportation ❹

KEY

--- Path of Remembrance

★ **Path of Remembrance**
This series of granite blocks was erected in the late 1980s. Each is dedicated to an event or a hero of the ghetto, with an inscription in Polish and Hebrew ❷

LOCATOR MAP
See Street Finder, maps 1, 3

ZAMENHOFA

LEWARTOWSKIEGO

MORDECHAJA ANIELEWICZA

A. WIELGOSZ

| 0 meters | 50 |
| 0 yards | 50 |

El-Mole-Rachim
Bronisław Linke's painting, in the National Museum, expresses the despair of the Jewish people.

Janusz Korczak
Commemorated on the Path of Remembrance, Korczak was a teacher who chose to go with the children from his orphanage to the death camps (see p179).

★ **Monument to the Ghetto Heroes**
Erected in 1948, this powerful sculpture commemorates the Ghetto Uprising. The large square it overlooks was at the center of the former Jewish Ghetto ❶

STAR SIGHTS

★ **Umschlagplatz Monument**

★ **Path of Remembrance**

★ **Monument to the Ghetto Heroes**

Detail of the Monument to the Ghetto Heroes

Monument to the Ghetto Heroes ❶
Pomnik Bohaterów Getta

Zamenhofa. **Map** 1 A1, 3 B4.
🚌 *107, 111, 180.*

Erected in 1948 when the city of Warsaw still lay in ruins, this monument was created by the sculptor Natan Rapaport and the architect Marek Suzin. The work symbolizes the heroic defiance of the Ghetto Uprising in 1943, which was planned not as a bid for liberty, but as an honorable way to die.

Reliefs on the monument depict men, women, and children struggling to flee the burning ghetto, together with a procession of Jews being driven to death camps under the threat of Nazi bayonets.

The monument was created from labradorite stone, quarried in Sweden. It is the stone that the Nazis intended to use for victory monuments in countries they conquered.

The flattened area of the Warsaw Ghetto after its destruction in 1944

Path of Remembrance ❷
Trakt Męczeństwa i Walki Żydów

Zamenhofa, Stawki. **Map** 1 A1, 3 B4.
🚌 *109, 111, 180.*

The path of Remembrance is a route laid out between the Monument to the Ghetto Heroes and the Umschlag-platz Monument. It is marked by 16 granite blocks, commemorating the 450,000 Jews who were murdered in the Warsaw Ghetto and the heroes of the 1943 uprising

One of the granite blocks on the Path of Remembrance

(see pp140–41). Among those named on the blocks are Szmul Zygielbojm (1895–1943), a member of the Polish National Council in London, who committed suicide as an act of protest against the liquidation of the Warsaw Ghetto; and Emanuel Ringelblum (1900–44), who founded the ghetto archives. Each of the granite blocks is engraved with inscriptions in Polish, Hebrew, and Yiddish, together with the dates 1940–43.

Bunker Monument ❸
Pomnik Bunkra

Dzielna. **Map** 1 A2, 3 B5.
🚌 *109, 111, 180.*

Between the streets of Miła and Niska, there is a small mound, topped with a boulder, commemorating the location of the bunker from which Morde-chaj Anielewicz (1917–43) led the Ghetto Uprising in 1943. He blew up the bunker, and thereby committed suicide.

Marble wall of the Umschlagplatz Monument

Umschlagplatz Monument **4**
Pomnik Umschlagplatz

Stawki. **Map** 1 A1, 3 B4. 109, 111, 157, 180.

THE UMSCHLAGPLATZ Monument was completed in 1988, on the site of a former railroad siding (called Umschlagplatz) by Dzika Street.

It was from this point that an estimated 300,000 Jews, from the Warsaw Ghetto and elsewhere, were loaded into cattle cars and dispatched to almost certain death in the concentration camps.

The monument is composed of black and white marble blocks, and was a collaboration between the architect Hanna Szmalenberg and the sculptor Władysław Klamerus.

The names of hundreds of people from the ghetto, who passed through Umschlagplatz, are inscribed on the surface of the monument, including Janusz Korczak and his group of Jewish orphans *(see p141)*.

Pawiak Prison **5**

Dzielna 24/26. **Map** 1 A2, 3 A5. 831 13 17. 148. 12, 17, 19, 29, 33. 9am–5pm Wed & Fri, 9am–4pm Thu & Sat, 10am–4pm Sun.

PAWIAK WAS BUILT as a prison by the Russians in 1830–35, following a design by Henryk Marconi, a member of a renowned family of architects.

The building became notorious during World War II, when it was used to imprison Poles

and Jews arrested by the Nazis. Now in ruins, Pawiak serves as a museum. By the entrance gates stands a "silent witness," in the form of a long-dead tree covered with obituary notices for prisoners who died here during the war.

Obituaries on a tree at Pawiak

Jewish Cemetery on Okopowa Street **6**
Cmentarz Żydowski Przy Okopowej

See pp178–9.

Detail of the façade of Nożyk Synagogue *(see p144)*

Monument to 300 Victims **7**
Pomnik 300 Pomordowanych

Gibalskiego 21. 111, 180. 22.

DURING BUILDING WORKS in 1988, the remains of 300 people were unearthed near the Jewish Cemetery. The victims had been murdered by Nazis on the playing fields of the Skra Sports Club.

This site now serves as a small cemetery and is marked by a symbolic monument that takes the form of a funeral pyre. The monument was designed and built by two of Warsaw's most famous architects, Tadeusz Szumielewicz and Marek Martens.

The Monument to 300 Victims, designed as a symbolic funeral pyre

Wooden footbridge over Chłodna Street, connecting both parts
of the Warsaw Ghetto during the Nazi occupation

Chłodna Street **8**
Ulica Chłodna

Map 5 A1. ▣ *148, 155, 500, 510, 511.* ▣ *12, 17, 19, 29, 33.*

BEFORE WORLD WAR II, this was one of Warsaw's busiest streets. Its apartment houses included numerous shops, as well as several movie theaters. However, the only remnants of the street's original character are sections of streetcar rails and a few houses that survived the war.

Among these is the Neo-Baroque house at No. 20, known as the "House Under the Clock" (dom Pod Zegarem). Designed by Wacław Heppen and Józef Napoleon Czerwiński, it was built in 1912. During the Nazi occupation, the house was within the ghetto area and was inhabited by Adam Czerniaków, chairman of the Judenrat (Jewish Council within the ghetto). Through his diaries, Czerniaków related the tragedy of Poland's Jews.

Remains of the Ghetto Wall **9**
Fragmenty murów getta

Sienna 55, Waliców. **Map** 5 A2. ▣ *155, 174.* ▣ *10, 12, 17, 19, 29, 33.*

THE JEWISH GHETTO was created by the Nazis in 1940. The area demarcated for the ghetto was initially surrounded by a 3 m (10 ft) wall, with an additional 1 m (3 ft) of barbed wire subsequently added. The boundary of the ghetto originally

incorporated the walls of exisiting buildings. However, when the boundaries were redrawn in 1941, to reduce the size of the ghetto, additional walls had to be constructed. Many of them were built down the middle of the area's streets.

The wall also ran along both sides of Chłodna Street, so that this important road link could be kept open for the Nazis, while preventing it from being used by Jews. This effectively separated the ghetto area into two parts, which were connected by a wooden pedestrian bridge across Chłodna Street. A replica of the bridge can be seen in the Holocaust Museum in Washington.

The ghetto wall initially had 22 guarded entrances, but in order to tighten security the number was reduced to 15. Unauthorized crossing of the wall was punishable by death. Nevertheless, many tunnels and concealed holes were dug out and used to smuggle people and goods into and out of the ghetto.

Only a few fragments of the ghetto wall have survived. A section can be seen in the courtyard at No. 55 Sienna Street, where there is a memorial plaque. Another fragment stands at the junction of Pereca and Waliców streets.

Fragment of the ghetto wall

Nożyk Synagogue **10**
Synagoga Nożyków

Twarda 6. **Map** 1 B4. ▣ *106, 160, 506.*

THE FOUNDERS of this synagogue were Zelman and Ryfka Nożyk, who in 1893 donated the land on which it was built and left half of their estate to the Orthodox Jewish community. Building work lasted from 1898–1902, with the synagogue effectively concealed within a courtyard that was surrounded by

The façade of Nożyk Synagogue

apartment houses. The synagogue was closed during World War II and used by the Nazis as a warehouse. It was reopened in 1945 and is currently the only active synagogue in Warsaw.

From 1977–83, the synagogue was renovated to restore it to its original condition. However, few of the apartments that surrounded the synagogue survive.

The synagogue has an impressive portico crowned by a metal dome bearing the Star of David. The interior features the ark, the cabinet that contains the Torah scrolls. The Pentateuch (the first five books of the Bible) is written on these scrolls, portions of which are read consecutively during the year from a pulpit, or *bimah*, in the nave. The galleries that surround the nave were intended for the seating of women.

Jewish National Theater ⓫
Państwowy Teatr Żydowski

Plac Grzybowski 12/16. **Map** 1 B4.
☎ 620 70 25. 🚍 106, 160, 506.
🕐 10am–7pm Mon, 10am–6pm Tue–Fri, noon–7pm Sat, 4pm–6pm Sun.

Performing plays steeped in Jewish traditions, the Jewish National Theater was founded in Łódź in 1949, when that city's theater company merged with another Jewish theater company from Lower Silesia. The company moved to Warsaw in 1955, and its present building dates from 1970. Performances are given in Yiddish, with translations into Polish. The theater also runs a Mime Theater and an actors' studio.

A scene from a performance by the Jewish National Theater

Jewish History Institute ⓬
Żydowski Instytut Historyczny

Tłomackie 3/5. **Map** 3 C5. ☎ 827 92 21. 🚍 107, 111, 166, 171, 180, 512. 🚊 2, 4, 15, 18, 31, 36.

A Torah shield, displayed at the Jewish History Institute

Although the Jewish History Institute's Neo-Classical building appears to be much older, it was actually completed as recently as 1936. The architect, Edward Eber, was renowned for his modern, luxurious buildings. However, when designing this building, he aimed to harmonize the institute's façade with that of the neighboring Great Synagogue (which was destroyed by the Nazis seven years later). The building served as both the Judaic Library and the Judaic History Institute. One of the Judaic History Institute's lecturers was the outstanding historian Dr. Majer Bałaban.

Restored after World War II, the building became the Jewish History Institute, housing archives, a library, and a museum. The museum includes relics from Jewish ghettos and Nazi death camps, as well as German collections of Judaica. Paintings by Jewish artists include the works of Leopold Gottlieb, Eliasz Kanarek, and Jan Gotard.

Blue Tower ⓭
Błękitny Wieżowiec

Plac Bankowy 2. **Map** 1 B3, 3 C5.
☎ 637 27 16. 🚍 107, 166, 171, 180. 🚊 2, 4, 15, 18, 31, 36.
🕐 7:30am–7pm Mon–Sat.

With its shimmering, aquamarine glass walls, this high-rise is considered to be one of the city's most attractive modern buildings.

It was completed in the early 1990s, by converting a high-rise that had stood unfinished for over 25 years. The partially built façades featured gold-colored aluminum, resulting in the building being known as "the golden tooth of Warsaw." Moreover, it was rumored to be cursed, as it had been built on the site of the Great Synagogue, once the largest Jewish temple in Warsaw. On May 16, 1943, the synagogue was blown up on the orders of the "butcher of the ghetto," General Jürgen Stroop, marking the final liquidation of the Jewish quarter. Only a fragment of a stone column and a cloakroom ticket survived its destruction. These two items can now be seen in the Jewish History Institute Museum.

Blue Tower

The Great Synagogue before it was destroyed by the Nazis

Bohaterów Ghetta Street ⓮
Ulica Bohaterów Ghetta

Formerly Nalewki Street.
Map 3 C5. 🚌 *107, 166, 171, 180.* 🚊 *2, 4, 15, 18, 31, 36.*

BEFORE WORLD WAR II, this was the area's main commercial street and was occupied principally by Jews. Among numerous shops and offices, the largest was Simons Arcade, at the junction with Długa Street. Several stories high, it was built of glass and reinforced concrete over a four-year period from 1900 to 1904. The arcade housed stores, a hotel, small Jewish theaters, and the Makabi Sports Club.

Nalewki Street was completely destroyed during World War II, and it is difficult to envision its former appearance. However, part of the original street runs through Krasiński Gardens. There are bullet marks on fragments of remaining walls and sections of streetcar rails among the cobbles.

Mostowski Palace ⓯
Pałac Mostowskich

Andersa 15. **Map** 1 B2 & 3 B5. 🚌 *107, 166, 171, 180.* 🚊 *2, 4, 15, 18, 31, 36.*

THIS BEAUTIFUL Neo-Classical building was originally a Baroque palace that belonged to the *voivode* of Minsk, one

Jan Hilzen. From 1823, the palace housed the Administrative Commission for Internal Affairs. The Minister of the Interior, Tadeusz Mostowski, commissioned architect Antonio Corazzi to redesign the palace. The building's ornamental façade includes Neo-Classical reliefs that were created by Paweł Maliński and Jan Norblin.

Following the Russian suppression of the November Uprising of 1830, the palace was converted into barracks for use by the Russian army.

After World War II, the building was greatly extended and served as the headquarters for the city's militia. For years, rumors circulated that the cellars were crowded with political prisoners. The palace now houses the Warsaw police headquarters.

Warsaw Chamber Opera ⓰
Warszawska Opera Kameralna

Aleja Solidarności 76b. **Map** 1 B3 & 3 B5. 📞 *831 22 40.* 🚌 *107, 166, 171, 180.* 🚊 *2, 4, 15, 18, 31, 36.*
Box office ⏰ *Sep–Jul: 10am–2pm, 4–7pm.*

ORIGINALLY BUILT as a Protestant church between 1770–80, this building now houses the Warsaw Chamber Opera. It is also the venue for an annual Mozart Festival, held at the end of June and beginning of July.

Warsaw Chamber Opera building

Designed by Szymon Bogumił Zug, the church was founded by the inhabitants of Leszno, a small town established and owned by the aristocratic Leszczyński family. Leszno was home to settlers from Germany, who assimilated into Polish life but also maintained their Protestant faith.

The tall, Neo-Gothic spire of the Protestant Reformed Church

Protestant Reformed Church ⓱
Kościół Ewangelicko-Reformowany

Aleja Solidarności 76. **Map** 1 B3 & 3 B5. 📞 *831 45 22.* 🚌 *107, 166, 171, 180.* 🚊 *2, 4, 15, 18, 31, 36.*

DESIGNED BY Adolf Adam Loewe, this Neo-Gothic church, with its distinctive openwork tower, was built between 1866 and 1882.

Unlike churches of other Christian denominations, the Protestant Reformed Church does not feature a main altar. In its place is a pulpit from which lessons are read.

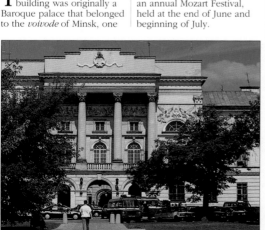
The imposing Neo-Classical façade of Mostowski Palace

The Baroque Church of the Nativity of the Virgin Mary

Church of the Nativity of the Virgin Mary ⑱
Kościół Narodzenia NMP

Aleja Solidarności 80 (formerly Leszno Street). **Map** 1 A3 & 3 B5. 🚌 *148, 166, 171.* 🚊 *12, 17, 19, 29, 33.*

BUILT OVER A long period of time from 1638 to 1731, this modest Baroque church includes a courtyard that originally held a pillory. This was used to punish "promiscuous youths, notorious rogues, and thieves."

During the partitions of Poland *(see pp28–9)*, the church was used as a prison for political activists.

Under the Nazi occupation, the church was within the boundaries of the Warsaw Ghetto and acted as a help center for Jews. It is said that tunnels running from the crypt were used to smuggle Jews out of the ghetto.

After World War II, when Leszno Street was widened to make way for the W–Z Route, the church was stranded in the middle of the new traffic system. As a consequence, the entire building was moved by 20 m (65 ft) in 1962, using what was then state-of-the-art technology.

Courts of Justice ⑲
Gmach Sądów

Aleja Solidarności 127. **Map** 1 A3 & 3 B5. 📞 *620 03 71.* ⏰ *8:30am–3:30pm.* 🚌 *148, 166, 171.* 🚊 *12, 17, 19, 29, 33.*

THIS MONUMENTAL building, designed by Bohdan Pniewski, was constructed between 1935–9. A notable feature, extending across the full width of the façade, is the inscription "Justice is the foundation of the strength and stability of the Republic."

During the Nazi occupation, Polish Jews and Christians used this building to smuggle themselves into and out of the Warsaw Ghetto.

After World War II, show trials of clergymen and political opponents of Communism were held here. However, in 1980 the Solidarity Trade Union was officially registered in the building, which was an unprecedented act in Communist bloc countries.

Steps up to the Courts of Justice

Norblin Factory ⑳
Fabryka Norblina

Żelazna 51/53. **Map** 1 A3 & 5 B1. 📞 *620 47 92.* 🚌 *105, 109.* 🚊 *10.* **Industry Museum** ⏰ *10am–2pm Tue–Sat (factory halls Apr–Oct only).*

CURRENTLY HOUSING the Industry Museum, part of the Museum of Technology *(see p134)*, this was formerly the Norblin, Buch Bros. & T Werner Joint Stock Co., which was renowned for producing silver and silver-plated items, sheet metal, and wire.

The museum comprises the original production halls, complete with equipment used there, such as stamping presses and forging machines.

Additional temporary exhibitions illustrate the history of the Norblin plant and the evolution of the motorcycle. This includes a prewar Sokół (Falcon) motorcycle, which connoisseurs put on a par with the Harley-Davidson.

Lubomirski Palace ㉑
Pałac Lubomirskich

Plac Żelaznej Bramy. **Map** 1 B4. 🚌 *107, 166, 171, 180.* 🚊 *2, 4, 15, 18, 31, 36.* **Not open** to the public.

THE MOST extraordinary event in the history of this 17th-century palace occurred in 1970, when the entire building was turned 78 degrees. The façade now completes the Saxon Axis (a Baroque town-planning scheme).

Originally Baroque, the palace was rebuilt and updated to the Rococo style. It also acquired Neo-Classical features, including a colonnade, in 1791–3. The architect was Jakub Hempel, commissioned by Prince Aleksander Lubomirski, whose wife, Aleksandra, was one of the few Poles guillotined during the French Revolution. Legend has it that Aleksandra was killed for having rejected the advances of the revolutionary leader Maximilien Robespierre.

The monumental colonnade of the Lubomirski Palace

Getting There

Various buses to Ujazdowskie
Avenue, Ujazdowski Park, and
Łazienki Park pass along the
Royal Route. Buses and streetcars
run along Jerozolimskie Avenue
passing the National Museum
and Polish Military Museum. By
these museums is the suburban
railroad station, Powiśle.

Key

　▢　Street-by-Street map *pp150–51*

　Ⓟ　Parking

◁ **A pretty corner in Ujazdowski P**

AROUND ŁAZIENKI PARK

THIS PART of Warsaw includes parks, palaces and other historic buildings, museums, and government offices. Extending south from Three Crosses Square (Plac Trzech Krzyży), the main thoroughfare is Ujazdowskie Avenue, along which the former residences of Polish aristocrats and the city's wealthy merchant families can be seen. In addition to several government departments, the two chambers of the Polish Parliament occupy a large complex on adjacent Wiejska Street.

Statue of a satyr in Łazienki Park

At the far end of Ujazdowskie Avenue is Belweder Palace, until 1994 the residence of Poland's president. A number of foreign legations are also on Ujazdowskie Avenue, including the embassies of Spain, the UK, Canada, and the US.

However, Łazienki Park is the most popular attraction. This romantic, landscaped park includes the Palace on the Water, together with various other palaces, pavilions, an amphitheater, and two orangeries.

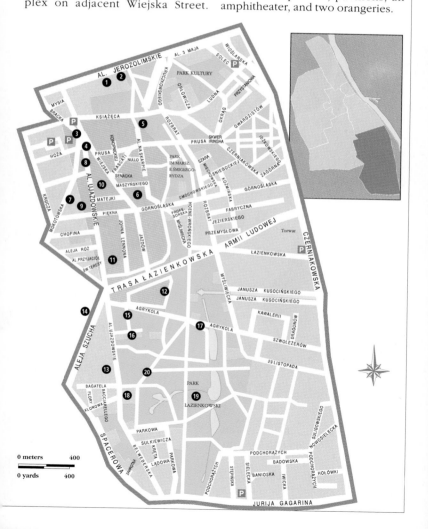

Street-by-Street: Along Ujazdowskie Avenue

THE AREA AROUND Ujazdowskie Avenue and Three Crosses Square is Warsaw's political and diplomatic district. It includes Belweder Palace, which was occupied by the head of state Józef Piłsudski *(see p30)* before World War II, and by Lech Wałęsa until 1994. In the last year of his presidency, he transferred the official residence to Namiestnikowski Palace *(see pp118–19)*.

Stanisław Wyspiański's self-portrait in the National Museum

Parliament
Both parliamentary chambers are on Wiejska Street. The mace represents the office of the Speaker of the Lower Chamber **6**

Polish Military Museum

Polish Military Museum
This museum traces the 1,000-year history of the Polish army **2**

Three Crosses Square
Small 18th-century houses and St. Alexander's Church can be found alongside multistory 20th-century buildings **3**

The Road to Calvary crosses
are two gilt crosses, dating from the 18th century, on the top of columns. They formed part of the Calvary Road, which continued in the direction of Jazdów.

St. Alexander's Church
This Neo-Classical 18th-century church was greatly enlarged between 1886 and 1895. Rebuilt after being destroyed during World War II, the church was also restored to its 18th-century form **4**

KEY

--- Suggested route

0 meters   200

0 yards   200

★ Modern Art Center
*Ujazdowski Castle, rebuilt after World War II in its
original early Baroque style, now houses the
Modern Art Center* **12**

LOCATOR MAP
See Street Finder, maps 2, 6

★ Łazienki Park
*One of the city's most
beautiful parks, it was
laid out in the second half
of the 18th century* **19**

Łazienki
Park

Botanical Gardens
*These gardens, which were
established in 1818, feature
specialized plots, such as
for medicinal plants, as
well as an observatory* **15**

Villas on Ujazdowskie Avenue
*Villa Rau, like several other period
buildings on this street, is occupied
by a foreign legation* **9**

STAR SIGHTS

★ Modern Art Center

★ Łazienki Park

National Museum ❶
Muzeum Narodowe

See pp154–7.

Polish Military Museum ❷
Muzeum Wojska Polskiego

Aleja Jerozolimskie 3. **Map** 2 E5 &
6 E1. 🛈 629 52 71. 🚌 *102, 111,
117.* 🚋 *7, 22.* 🚉 *Powiśle.*
🕐 *noon–6pm Wed, 11am–4pm
Thu–Sat, 10:30am–5pm Sun.*
🎟 *free on Fri. Exhibition in park open
until dusk, admission free.*

Established by the statesman
and military leader Marshal
Józef Piłsudski *(see p30)*, the
Polish Military Museum was
opened in 1920. The museum
has occupied its present site
since 1933, and is Warsaw's
second largest museum.

The collection illustrates the
history of Polish firearms and
armor over the last thousand
years, focusing particularly on

18th-century cavalryman's cartridge box

the period from the early
Middle Ages to the 18th
century. This includes full
tournament armors and an
extremely rare gilded helmet,
which belonged to a Polish
chieftain in the early Christian
era (Poland became a Christian country in 966).

The collection of hussars'
armor is unique in Europe,
and there is also a fine life-
size mounted figure of a
hussar on display. During the
17th century, Polish hussars
were acknowledged as the
finest heavy cavalry in Europe,
and their ultimate victory was
at Vienna in 1683, when their
charge broke the Turkish
army. A splendid Turkish
officer's tent was part of the
booty taken by the hussars.

Weapons, tanks, and aircraft
from World War II can also be
seen in the museum's park.

Three Crosses Square ❸
Plac Trzech Krzyży

Map 6 E1. 🚌 *108, 114,
116, 119, 122, 166, 171,
195, 501, 503.*

The name of this
square does not
quite tally with the
fact that there are only
two columns topped
with gilded crosses
in the square.
These crosses
were erected in
1731 by Joachim
Daniel Jauch, on the order of
King August II Mocny, and
they marked the beginning of
Calvary Road (Stations of the
Cross).

However, a third cross is
held by the figure of St. John
of Nepomuk. This monument
was erected in the square in
1752, founded by the Grand
Court Marshal Franciszek
Bieliński, to commemorate
the completion of Warsaw's
street-paving project. A fourth
cross can be seen
on the dome of
nearby St. Alex-
ander's Church.

The square was
originally called
the Crossroads of
the Golden Cross-
es, and subse-
quently it was renamed St.
Alexander's Square.

The two oldest houses on
the square date from the 18th
century. The house on the
corner of Nowy Świat Street
has a very attractive early
Neo-Classical façade, while
the house located at No. 2
in the square is part of a

Figure of St. John of Nepomuk

complex belonging to the
Institute for the Deaf and
Blind, founded in 1817
by the parish priest
Father Jakub Falkowski.
The institute's main
office occupies a Neo-
Renaissance house that
was built in the mid-
19th century.

The area around the
Wincenty Witos Monu-
ment (Witos was Po-
land's prime
minister in the
early 1920s) is
now a favorite
haunt of young
skateboarders.

St. Alexander's Church ❹
Kościół św. Aleksandra

Plac Trzech Krzyży. **Map** 6 E1.
🚌 *108, 114, 116, 122, 144, 166,
171, 195, 503.*

Chrystian Piotr Aigner designed this church, which
was built between 1818–25.
While the church was mod-
eled on Rome's Pantheon, it
is far more modest in size.

The most remarkable
features of the church are two
monumental porticoes, set
in an otherwise plain façade.
The church was given the
name of St. Alexander to
commemorate Alexander I,
the tsar of Russia who
became king of Poland in
1815, following the partitions
of Poland *(see pp28–9)*.

Enlarged during the 19th
century, according to a design
by Józef Pius Dziekoński, the
church was restored to its
original early-19th-century
form after World War II.

St. Alexander's Church, modeled on the Pantheon in Rome

Earth Sciences Museum ❺
Muzeum Ziemi

Na Skarpie 20/26 & 27. **Map** 6 E1.
📞 629 74 97. 🚌 108, 114, 116,
122, 144, 166, 171, 195, 503.
🕐 Apr–Sep: 9am–4pm Mon–Fri
(6pm Thu), 10am–5pm Sun; Oct–
Mar: 9am–4pm Mon–Fri, 10am–4pm
Sun. 🛗 🎫 free on Sun.

Tʜɪs ᴍᴜsᴇᴜᴍ's collection
comprises some 150,000
exhibits, including rocks,
precious stones, and fossils,
while the amber collection is
one of the world's finest.

The interiors also feature a
marble slab that is stained
with the blood of a soldier
who died during the 1944
Warsaw Uprising.

The museum occupies two
buildings on the crest of an
escarpment that descends
toward the River Vistula, on
the site of the former Na
Górze (On the Hill) Park.

This park, together with a
palace and various other

**Minerals in the Earth Science
Museum's vast collection**

buildings, was designed in
the 18th century by Szymon
Bogumił Zug, on behalf of
Prince Kazimierz Poniatowski,
who was the brother of
Poland's last king, Stanisław
August Poniatowski.

However, very little is left
of the original houses or the
Poniatowski Palace. More-
over, in 1935, the renowned
Polish architect Bohdan
Pniewski built his own Modernist villa on this site; it
incorporated the remaining
Doric columns of the palace.
He subsequently bequeathed
the villa to the museum.
Pniewski's work also includes
the foyer at the Grand Theater (see p111) and the Courts
of Justice (see p147).

The Chamber of Deputies of the Polish Parliament in session

Parliament ❻
Sejm

Wiejska 2/4/6. **Map** 6 E2. 📞 694
25 00. 🚌 108, 116, 119, 122, 159,
179, 195.

Pᴏʟᴀɴᴅ's parliamentary
tradition reaches back
to the 15th century, before
Warsaw became the seat of
the Sejm in 1569.

The partition of Poland at
the end of the 18th century
(see pp28–9) interrupted the
parliamentary process, which
was restored only when Poland
regained independence after
World War I in 1918. Since
there was no suitable building
available at that time, parliamentary sessions were held
in the rooms of a former girls'
finishing school.

These initial rooms were
subsequently rebuilt and
extended, and a semicircular
hall to house the Chamber of
Deputies was built in 1928,
designed by the architect
Kazimierz Skórewicz. This
hall was decorated with Art
Deco bas-reliefs by Jan
Szczepkowski. Among the
various elements represented
in the bas-reliefs are science,
justice, commerce, the air
force, and the merchant navy.

After World War II, additional parliamentary buildings
were constructed, designed
in the prevalent style of
Socialist Realism.

Following the democratic
elections in 1989 (Poland's
first such elections since
1939), the Senate was formally
reinstated. The Senate had
been abolished by the
Communists after the war.

Mokotowska Street ❼
Ulica Mokotowska

Map 6 D2. 🚌 114, 116, 119, 122,
171, 195.

Mᴏᴋᴏᴛᴏᴡsᴋᴀ sᴛʀᴇᴇᴛ is one
of the best preserved
thoroughfares that composed
the city's central district.

Among the period houses
on Mokotowska Street, one
of the most outstanding is at
No. 57. Dating from around
1900, the house was designed
by the architect Zygmunt
Binduchowski. Its original
features include figures of a
Krakovian and a góral (Polish
highlander), both of which
support bay windows. The
original wood-block paving
at the entrance has also
survived. Additionally, the
open courtyard at Nos. 51–53
was specially designed by the
architect Marian Lalewicz to
avoid having an enclosed,
shadowy courtyard.

**Polish highlander on the façade
of No. 57 Mokotowska Street**

National Museum ❶

ORIGINALLY ESTABLISHED in 1862 as the Fine Art Museum, this became the National Museum (Muzeum Narodowe) in 1916. The museum's present Modernist building was designed by Tadeusz Tołwiński. The collections include archaeological artifacts, medieval art, and Polish paintings, while the east wing houses the Polish Military Museum *(see p152)*.

The Kiss
by Wacław
Szymanowski

★ **Madonna and Child**
One of the finest paintings in the collection, this is the only work by Sandro Botticelli (1445–1510) in a Polish museum.

★ **The Battle of Grunwald (detail)**
The work of Jan Matejko (1838–93), this is one of the most highly regarded of all Polish paintings. The vast canvas shows the combined Polish and Lithuanian armies defeating the Teutonic Knights in 1410.

First floor

Second floor

Polish Hamlet
The portrait of Aleksander Wielopolski, painted by Jacek Malczewski in 1903, belongs to the school of Polish Symbolists.

Court Dress, 1764
This was worn by Anna Rostkowska at the coronation of Stanisław August Poniatowski. It is in the decorative arts department, together with jewelry, glass, and furniture.

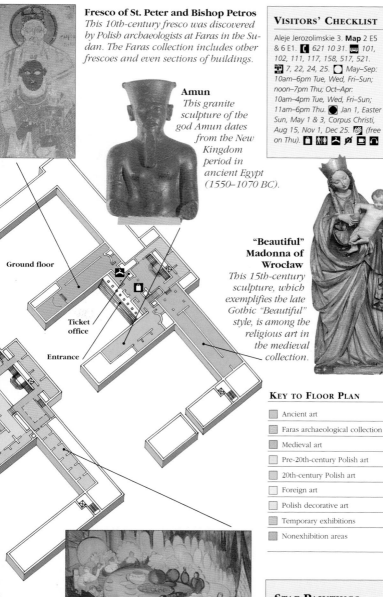

Fresco of St. Peter and Bishop Petros
This 10th-century fresco was discovered by Polish archaeologists at Faras in the Sudan. The Faras collection includes other frescoes and even sections of buildings.

Amun
This granite sculpture of the god Amun dates from the New Kingdom period in ancient Egypt (1550–1070 BC).

Ground floor

Ticket office

Entrance

"Beautiful" Madonna of Wrocław
This 15th-century sculpture, which exemplifies the late Gothic "Beautiful" style, is among the religious art in the medieval collection.

VISITORS' CHECKLIST

Aleje Jerozolimskie 3. **Map** 2 E5 & 6 E1. 621 10 31. 101, 102, 111, 117, 158, 517, 521. 7, 22, 24, 25. May–Sep: 10am–6pm Tue, Wed, Fri–Sun; noon–7pm Thu; Oct–Apr: 10am–4pm Tue, Wed, Fri–Sun; 11am–6pm Thu. Jan 1, Easter Sun, May 1 & 3, Corpus Christi, Aug 15, Nov 1, Dec 25. (free on Thu.)

KEY TO FLOOR PLAN

- Ancient art
- Faras archaeological collection
- Medieval art
- Pre-20th-century Polish art
- 20th-century Polish art
- Foreign art
- Polish decorative art
- Temporary exhibitions
- Nonexhibition areas

The Feast
In this painting, the artist and mathematician Leon Chwistek demonstrated his theory of stratification: the picture divides into areas dominated by shapes and colors.

STAR PAINTINGS

★ **The Battle of Grunwald by Jan Matejko**

★ **Madonna and Child by Sandro Botticelli**

Exploring the National Museum's Collection

T HE MUSEUM'S VAST COLLECTION was started in 1862 with an initial purchase of 36 paintings. Subsequent acquisitions have since turned the museum into one of the city's finest. Despite losses suffered during World War II, the wide-ranging collection spans several centuries, from ancient artifacts to modern works. It includes Polish art and archaeological finds from Faras in present-day Sudan. As space is limited, some collections can be seen only as part of special exhibitions.

ANCIENT ART

T HIS GALLERY exhibits the discoveries of Polish archaeologists working in Egypt, Sudan, Cyprus, and the Crimea (part of Ukraine).

In the Egyptian rooms, there are displays of mummies, sarcophagi, and papyri. Among the papyi *The Book of the Dead,* from the New Kingdom period of ancient Egyptian history, is particularly interesting.

Ancient Greece is represented by pottery from various periods. There are also later Roman copies of ancient Greek sculptures. The sections devoted to Roman and Etruscan art are strong in statues, urns, and bronze artifacts.

Greek vase

FARAS ARCHAEOLOGICAL COLLECTION

T HE FARAS COLLECTION was brought together in 1972, and consists of items discovered by Polish archaeologists working in Nubia (a part of present-day Sudan) during the early 1960s.

The majority of the finds originate from the cathedral of Faras, which was the seat of the Nubian bishops between the 7th and 14th centuries AD.

The collection includes a large number of frescoes and architectural fragments, ranging from details of carvings to entire columns and capitals.

The earliest frescoes date from the 8th century, and include depictions of St. Peter and St. Paul in majestic poses, as well as of St. Anna *(see p38).*

The magnificent portraits of Nubian bishops dating from the 10th century were commissioned by Bishop Petros.

MEDIEVAL ART

G OTHIC PAINTING and sculpture are the main focus of the medieval gallery. Many of the religious artifacts are from Polish churches that no longer exist. The most important of these are altarpieces, such as the painting from St. Barbara's altar, dating from 1447. Other altarpieces include one taken from Grudziądz, created in about 1380. It is decorated with scenes from the lives of Jesus Christ and the Virgin Mary.

From the Church of St. Elizabeth (św. Elżbieta) in Wrocław comes a sculpted altarpiece representing the Annunciation. It is thought to have been created in about 1480. A 16th-century triptych from Pławno illustrates the legend of St. Stanisław. Its panels are thought to have been painted by the artist Hans Süss of Kulmbach.

Among other religious artworks, the most notable are a splendid pietà from Lubiąż, dating from about 1370, and the so-called Beautiful Madonna from Wrocław, dating from 1410.

Detail of St. Barbara's altar

Also from Wrocław is a retable – an ornamental screen situated behind an altar and used as the setting for a religious painting or sculpture. The one on display was carved by Jacob Beinhart in about 1400. It is decorated with a bas-relief of St. Luke painting the Virgin Mary.

PRE-20TH-CENTURY POLISH ART

B Y FAR THE LARGEST department in the National Museum is the collection of Polish painting, sculpture, and other works of art created between the 16th century and the outbreak of World War II.

The largest number of historic paintings are portraits, while the so-called golden age of the Enlightenment is represented by superb artists such as Bernardo Bellotto, who often used the name of his uncle and mentor, Canaletto. Among Bellotto's detailed paintings is a view of Warsaw in 1773, looking from the terrace of the Royal Castle. The series of 18th-century portraits by Marcello Bacciarelli includes a portrait of King Stanisław August Poniatowski that is full of symbolism, showing the king with an hourglass.

Highlights of the section devoted to the Romantics are two paintings by Piotr Michałowski: one of his

Gossamer (1875) by Józef Chełmoński

daughter on horseback, and the other of Napoleon Bonaparte, also on horseback. Other Romantic painters whose works are represented in the collection include Józef Simmler and Henryk Rodakowski. The former is famous for his painting *The Death of Barbara Radziwiłł*.

Leading the collection of paintings of historical subjects is Jan Matejko's great work *The Battle of Grunwald*. Among his other works are *The Sermon by Skarga* and *Stańczyk*, which depicts the famous Polish court jester.

The Academic style can be seen in Henryk Siemiradzki's, work, particularly *Christian Dirce*, with Realism represented by the Gierymski brothers and Józef Chełmoński.

The collection of Impressionist paintings includes works by the renowned Leon Wyczółkowski, Władysław Podkowiński, and Józef Pankiewicz.

Symbolism and Modernism are represented by artists such as Jacek Malczewski and Józef Mehoffer, who painted *The Strange Garden*, as well as through Stanisław Wyspiański's pastel works.

20TH-CENTURY POLISH ART

BETWEEN 1918–39, Polish art reflected all the main schools and genres of European art, with numerous examples among the National Museum's collection.

Important works include a number by Gauguin's disciple Władysław Ślewiński, and a large collection by the Cubist artist Tadeusz Makowski.

Expressionist painters whose works can be seen in the museum's collection include Tytus Czyżewski, Leon Chwistek, and Bolesław Cybis.

Works by Abstract painters such as Władysław Strzemiński and Henryk Stażewski, who were members of the "Blok" and "Praesens" artistic circles, are also exhibited in the National Museum.

More traditional styles of painting were followed by a number of Polish artists who were working in Paris, such

***Primavera* (1936) by Polish artist Bolesław Cybis**

as Jan Cybis and Józef Czapski, as well as Tamara Łempicka, who became internationally renowned, especially for her striking portraits.

There is also an interesting and varied selection of works by modern Polish sculptors. These include examples by Bolesław Biegas and the renowned Xawery Dunikowski *(see p172).*

***The Guitar Player* (1757) by Jean-Baptiste Greuze**

FOREIGN ART

THE FOREIGN ART collection embraces a wide range of artistic styles and schools, including works by Italian, French, Dutch, German, and Flemish masters.

In the Italian collection, the most significant canvas is undoubtedly Sandro Botticelli's *Madonna and Child*. Other masterpieces include *Jesus Teaching in the Temple* by Cima de Conegliano and the splendid *Venus and Amor* by Paris Bordone.

Baroque art is represented by several painters such as Crespi and Tiepolo, together with some outstanding works by Bernardo Bellotto.

A comparatively modest French collection includes *The Guitar Player* by Jean-Baptiste Greuze, as well as works by Natier and Largillière.

The German and Dutch collections include a polyptych of St. Reinold by Joos van Cleve, a triptych known as *Ecce Homo* by Maerten van Heemskerck, and a painting entitled *Beautiful Princess*, the work of Lucas Cranach.

Other Flemish and Dutch artists exhibited in the gallery include Jan Brueghel, Jacob Jordaens, Jan Steen, and Hendrick Terbrugghen. However, the most impressive painting from the Flemish and Dutch school is the *Resurrection of Lazarus* by Carel Fabritius.

The museum contains relatively few modern paintings by non-Polish artists. However, included among the small collection are several works by Gustave Courbet, Maurice Vlaminck, and Paul Signac, dating from the late 19th and early 20th centuries.

POLISH DECORATIVE ART

THE SECOND FLOOR of the National Museum houses Polish arts and crafts. One gallery displays embroideries and a selection of other textiles together with some Gobelin tapestries. Another gallery features glass, porcelain, faïence, and gold artifacts from the workshops maintained by Polish aristocrats.

There are also displays of furniture of the 19th and 20th centuries, fashion, and many other objects of applied art.

Beds, cabinets, and a wardrobe (1909) by Karol Tichy

"Under the Artichoke" villa on Ujazdowskie Avenue

Ujazdowskie Avenue ❽

Aleje Ujazdowskie

Map 6 E2 & 6 E3. 🚌 114, 116, 119, 122, 195, 501, 503.

THIS TREE-LINED STREET is one of Warsaw's most beautiful, attracting crowds of people during the summer months.

The street was originally known as Calvary Road (referring to the Stations of the Cross). It was designed by Joachim Daniel Jauch for King August II Mocny, and laid out on land belonging to Ujazdów village. In the late 18th century, Ujazdów became part of an urban development and the street was lined with lime trees. On the west side stand elegant villas and houses, built for Warsaw's ruling classes, while the eastern side is bordered by parks and gardens running from Piękna Street to Belweder Palace.

Villas on Ujazdowskie Avenue ❾

Pałacyki w Alejach Ujazdowskich

Map 6 E2.

AMONG the avenue's most interesting villas is one that stands at No. 12/14. It was built in the 19th century and owned by the Marconi family. Restyled in 1869 by Leandro Marconi, it is known as "Under the Artichoke" after the decorative artichoke on its façade. At No. 27 is the Neo-Renaissance Rau villa, which was also designed by Marconi.

Town Houses on Ujazdowskie Avenue ❿

Kamienice w Alejach Ujazdowskich

Map 6 E2. 🚌 114, 119, 116, 122, 195, 503. **Not open** to the public.

GILT STUCCOWORK, marble walls, and roof gardens were typical features of Ujazdowskie Avenue's chic houses. Nos. 17 and 19, designed by Stanisław Grochowicz, have survived in their original form. The eclectic No. 17 was built in 1904 for the caviar importer Nicholas Szelechow. No. 19 was built in 1912 for Henryk Kołobrzeg-Kolberg, who produced optical instruments. Among the magnificent interiors were gilded balcony balustrades and Rococo-style bedrooms, complete with white marble fireplaces imported from Paris.

Ujazdowski Park ⓫

Park Ujazdowski

Aleje Ujazdowskie. **Map** 6 E2. 🚌 114, 119, 122, 195, 501, 503. ⏰ dawn–dusk.

ONE HUNDRED years ago, this area was a venue for folk dancing and other types of popular entertainment. The most famous celebration held here was in 1829, when Tsar Nicholas I was crowned king of Poland. Crowds drank mead from special fountains, while beer and wine flowed from "natural springs."

The park's present form, with a lake, a waterfall, bridges, and various trees, was laid out in 1896, following a design by Franciszek Szanior. Two bronze statues can be found in the park: *Gladiator* by Pius Weloński (1892) and *Eve* by Edward Wittig. A set of scales for public use dates from 1912.

Modern Art Center ⓬

Centrum Sztuki Współczesnej

Aleje Ujazdowskie 6. **Map** 6 E3. 📞 628 12 71. 🚌 116, 119, 122, 195, 501, 503. ⏰ 11am–5pm Tue–Sun (until 9pm Fri). 📷

Gladiator by Pius Weloński in Ujazdowski Park

UJAZDOWSKI CASTLE, which now houses the Modern Art Center, was built at the beginning of the 17th century for King Zygmunt III Waza and his son Władysław IV. The castle featured a courtyard, four towers, and richly decorated interiors. Its splendor, however, was not long-lived, as the castle was looted by Swedish soldiers during the invasion of 1655. Between 1809 and 1944, it was used as a military hospital. Burned out after the war, the ruins were detonated by the Communists in 1953.

The castle was reconstructed in the 1970s, and it currently houses a major collection of works by many of the world's greatest 20th-century artists. The Qchnia Artystyczna restaurant is also situated here and offers the opportunity to enjoy wonderful views over the Royal Canal from its windows.

Ujazdowskie Avenue's wide, shaded walkways

Ujazdowski Castle, reconstructed in the 1970s and home to the Modern Art Center

Cabinet Office ⑬
Urząd Rady Ministrów

Aleje Ujazdowskie 1. **Map** 6 E3.
🚌 116, 119, 122, 195. **Not open**
to the public.

THE POLISH CABINET holds its regular meetings in this imposing office, situated on Ujazdowskie Avenue.

The building was constructed in 1900, following a design by architects Wiktor Junosza Piotrowski and Henryk Gay, and originally it served as the barracks for the Suvorov Cadet School. The Infantry Officers' School was also housed here until 1926, after which the building became the headquarters of the Inspector General of the Polish Armed Forces.

During the interwar years, one wing was used to house the Military Library and the Rapperswil Museum collection. Both the library and the museum collection were destroyed in 1939 by a fire that was caused by Nazi bombardment.

Between 1984 and 1990, part of the building was occupied by the Communist Party's Academy of Social Sciences, which was commonly called "The First of May Academy."

These days the Cabinet Office is often the scene of antigovernment demonstrations. Protesting miners have been known to spread heaps of coal outside the main entrance. Similarly, farmers have followed the miners' example by dumping mounds of potatoes.

The impressive main entrance to the Cabinet Office

Ministry of Education ⑭
Ministerstwo Edukacji Narodowej

Aleja Szucha 25. **Map** 6 E3. 📞 628
04 61, 629 49 19. 🚌 114, 119, 116,
122, 195, 501, 503.
**Museum of Struggle and
Martyrdom** ☐ 9am–5pm Wed,
9am–4pm Thu, 10am–5pm Fri,
9am–4pm Sat, 10am–4pm Sun.

THE DESIGN of this building, which was constructed in 1925–30, is notable for the striking contrast between its façade and the interiors.

The Modernist façade, with its impressive Neo-Classical columns, was designed by the architect Zdzisław Mączeński. The Art Deco interiors were completed by Wojciech Jastrzębowski. The monumental proportions of this building must have pleased the Nazis, who used it as the Gestapo headquarters. The building's cellars were turned into torture chambers, and thousands of Poles died here during World War II.

Since then, the cellars have been transformed into the Museum of Struggle and Martyrdom (Mauzoleum Walki i Męczeństwa). Within this museum, one of the cells, which the prisoners called "the tramcar," has been preserved exactly as it was left by the Nazis. Prisoners waiting to be tortured had to sit behind one another, as in a streetcar, with their backs to the door. There they remained, motionless and silent, awaiting their fate.

Botanical Gardens ⑮
Ogród Botaniczny

Aleje Ujazdowskie 4. **Map** 6 E3.
📞 *628 75 14.* 🚌 *116, 119, 195, 503.* ⭕ *May–Oct: 9am–8pm Mon–Fri, 10am–7pm Sat & Sun.* 📷

WARSAW'S first botanical gardens were laid out in 1811 behind Kazimierzowski Palace for the Medical School, which five years later became part of Warsaw University (*see pp120–21*). The present gardens were laid out in 1818, when Tsar Alexander I endowed the University of Warsaw with a 22-hectare (54-acre) site in Łazienki Park. The gardens' director, Michał Szubert, published the first catalogue of plants growing in the gardens in 1824, listing more than 10,000 species, and at the time it was thought to be Europe's finest botanical garden.

Following the November Uprising of 1830, Russian acts of reprisal included reducing the size of the gardens by around two-thirds.

Ironically, Varsovians did not initially have much respect for the gardens. Even as late as the 1850s, it was well known that society ladies used to arrive in horse-drawn carriages and steal specimens from the cacti collection.

During the same period, the gardens were also used as a rendezvous for clandestine patriotic meetings. On this site in 1792, foundations were laid for the Temple of Providence to commemorate the May

A quiet section of the historic Botanical Gardens

Constitution of 1791. Although the temple was never completed, traces of the foundations can still be seen in the gardens.

Azaleas and roses

Flower beds

Medicinal herbs

New rock garden

Creepers

Edible plants

Water plants

Fountain and pools

Tulips blooming in the spring

The Observatory

The Observatory ⑯
Obserwatorium Astronomiczne

Aleje Ujazdowskie 4. **Map** 6 E3.
📞 *629 40 11.* 🚌 *116, 119, 195, 503.*

THE OBSERVATORY was built for the University of Warsaw in 1824, according to a design by Michał Kado and Hilary Szpilowski, and under the supervision of the renowned architect Chrystian Piotr Aigner.

In the 19th century, the society ladies of Warsaw used to gather on the Observatory's terrace to view the Botanical Gardens and various alternative entertainments held in Ujazdowski Square. During the 1944 Warsaw Uprising, the Observatory was burned, but was subsequently rebuilt following the war.

Jan III Sobieski Monument ⑰
Pomnik Jana III Sobieskiego

Agrykola. **Map** 6 E3. 🚌 *107, 108, 114, 116, 119, 195, 503.*

THIS MONUMENT was erected by Poland's last king, Stanisław August Poniatowski, in 1788. It stands on the

Jan III Sobieski Monument

BOTANICAL GARDENS

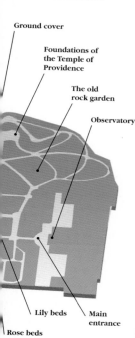

Ground cover

Foundations of
the Temple of
Providence

The old
rock garden

Observatory

Lily beds

Main
entrance

Rose beds

One of the wide variety of plants in the Botanical Gardens

Agrykola Bridge and can be seen from the Palace on the Water, across the lake.

The monument was probably designed by André le Brun, and sculpted by Francis Pinck. The king is wearing Roman-style armor, according to the artistic conventions of the time, and his horse is trampling a Turk.

Apart from honoring Jan III Sobieski for defeating the Turks at Vienna in 1683, the monument also had a political motive. King Stanisław August Poniatowski aimed to incite anti-Turkish feelings, before joining a Russo-Austrian coalition in the war against the Ottoman Empire.

Belweder Palace ⑱
Pałac Belweder

Belwederska 52. **Map** 6 E3. 49 18 39. 116, 119, 195. 10am–3pm Tue–Sat.

ALTHOUGH THIS palace dates from the 17th century, it acquired a certain notoriety in

1818, when it became the residence of Warsaw's Russian viceroy, Grand Duke Constantine (the loathed brother of Tsar Alexander I).

The palace was refurbished and extended before the grand duke and his wife (a Polish aristocrat) took up residence, with the grounds also laid out to provide a landscaped park. Several Romantic pavilions in Greek, Egyptian, and Gothic styles were set around a pool and canals. These grounds are now part of Łazienki Park.

On November 29, 1830, an initial action of the November Insurrection saw a detachment of cadet officers, together with a number of students, attacking Belweder Palace. However, the grand duke managed to escape.

Since 1918, the palace has belonged to the state. Marshal Józef Piłsudski *(see p30)* occupied it from 1926 to 1935. It was again the president's residence in 1945–52 and 1989–94. The beautiful

Neo-Classical palace is best viewed from the foot of the escarpment.

Łazienki Park ⑲

See pp162–3.

Magnolias in Łazienki Park

Palace on the Water ⑳
Pałac Na Wodzie

See pp164–5.

The elegant portal and columns at the entrance of Belweder Palace

Łazienki Park and Palaces ⓳
Łazienki Królewskie

The ŁAZIENKI PARK dates from the Middle Ages, when it belonged to the Mazovian dukes. By the early 17th century, it belonged to the Polish crown and housed a royal menagerie. In 1674 the Grand Crown Marshal Stanisław Herakliusz Lubomirski acquired the park, and Tylman of Gameren designed its hermitage and bathing pavilion. The pavilion gave the park its name, as *łazienki* means "baths." In the 18th century, the park was owned by King Stanisław August Poniatowski, who commissioned Karol Agrykola, Karol Schultz, and Jan Schuch to lay it out as a formal garden. Dominik Merlini redesigned the pavilion as a residence. The Łazienki Palace is now a museum.

Peacock in Łazienki Pa[rk]

★ Old Orangerie

In 1788 Dominik Merlini created a theater in the east wing of this building. It is now one of the few remaining 18th-century court theaters.

★ Chopin Monument

This Secessionist monument to Frederic Chopin was sculpted in 1908 by Wacław Szymanowski, but not unveiled until 1926. Positioned at the side of a lake, it depicts Poland's most celebrated composer sitting under a willow tree, seeking inspiration from nature.

0 meters 200

0 yards 200

Sibyl's Temple

This Neo-Classical building, inspired by an ancient Greek temple, was constructed in the 1820s.

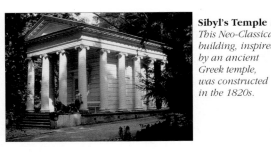

Water Tower

Built in 1778 to a design by Dominik Merlini, this water tower was restyled in 1827 by Chrystian Piotr Aigner.

Hermitage

Designed by Tylman of Gameren as a retreat for Stanisław Herakliusz Lubomirski, it was completed in 1690. During the reign of Stanisław August Poniatowski, Henrietta Lhullier, a soothsayer and the king's confidante, lived here.

**...ieski
...nument**

Palace on the Water

Officer's School

It was from this building that officer cadets marched to attack the Belweder

Palace (see p161). This incident started the 1830 Insurrection, on November 29.

Myślewicki Palace

Dominik Merlini designed this Neo-Classical palace in 1784 for Stanisław August Poniatowski's nephew, Prince Józef Poniatowski.

★ Theater on the Island

A moat separates the auditorium from the stage, which has the form of a ruined temple in Baalbek.

★ White House

Designed by Dominik Merlini in 1774–7, it was used by Stanisław August Poniatowski for romantic rendezvous. In 1801 it was occupied by the future King Louis XVIII of France, then in exile.

New Orangerie

Constructed in 1861 using cast iron and glass, the new orangerie was designed by Józef Orłowski and Adam Loewe.

STAR SIGHTS

- ★ Theater on the Island
- ★ White House
- ★ Old Orangerie
- ★ Chopin Monument

Palace on the Water ⓲

THIS PALACE is one of the finest examples of Neo-Classical architecture in Poland. King Stanisław August Poniatowski commissioned Dominik Merlini to refashion an existing 17th-century bathing pavilion into a royal summer residence. The task was completed between 1772–93. Unfortunately, the king was able to enjoy the palace for only a few years. After the Third Partition of Poland, he was forced to abdicate, and left Warsaw on January 7, 1795, watched by tearful crowds. He died three years later in St. Petersburg. The Nazis planned to blow up the palace but, lacking time during their withdrawal from Warsaw, set fire to it instead. Rebuilding was completed in 1965.

Personifications of the Four Elements by André le Brun

18th-century jardinière

Bridge with a pillared gallery

Terrace

Detail of Hercules in the Ballroom
Figures of Hercules, a centaur, and Cerberus (the dog that guarded Hades) support the ballroom chimneypiece, symbolizing man's triumph over the forces of darkness.

★ **Bas-reliefs in the Bathing Room**
17th-century bas-reliefs from the original bathing pavilion depict scenes from Ovid's Metamorphosis.

★ **Ballroom**
The highly decorated ballroom was designed by Jan Chrystian Kamsetzer.

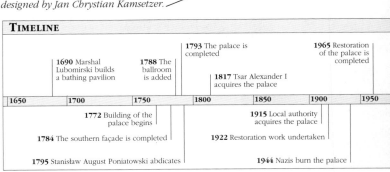

TIMELINE

	1690 Marshal Lubomirski builds a bathing pavilion	**1788** The ballroom is added	**1793** The palace is completed		**1965** Restoration of the palace is completed		
				1817 Tsar Alexander I acquires the palace			
1650	**1700**	**1750**	**1800**	**1850**	**1900**	**1950**	
	1772 Building of the palace begins			**1915** Local authority acquires the palace			
	1784 The southern façade is completed		**1922** Restoration work undertaken				
	1795 Stanisław August Poniatowski abdicates			**1944** Nazis burn the palace			

THURSDAY DINNERS

The king invited artists, writers, and intellectuals to dinner every Thursday. During the summer, these dinners were held in the Palace on the Water, and in the Marble Room of the Royal Castle during the winter. A frequent guest was the poet Bishop Ignacy Krasicki. The men-only dinners served as an artistic and political forum. But this did not prevent a tradition of "dessert poetry" – the writing of indecent verses during dessert that diners left under their dessert plates. The end of the meal was indicated by the serving of a dish of plums.

Bishop Ignacy Krasicki

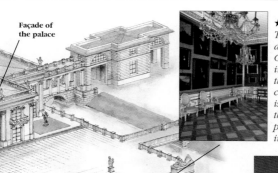

Façade of the palace

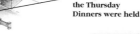

Dining hall where the Thursday Dinners were held

★ Picture Gallery
The gallery was designed by Jan Chrystian Kamsetzer in 1793, to exhibit the king's extensive collection. Each wall is hung with up to three rows of pictures, creating an impressive effect.

Francis Bacon
This portrait by Frans Pourbus is in the picture gallery.

Solomon's Hall
This was the main reception room. The ceiling was originally painted by Marcello Bacciarelli; destroyed in World War II, it has since been re-created.

Rotunda
This circular room was designed by Dominik Merlini as an equivalent of the Pantheon, for Poland's great monarchs. It includes sculptures of kings such as Kazimierz Wielki, Zygmunt Stary, Stefan Batory, and Jan III Sobieski.

STEPHANUS BATOREUS

STAR SIGHTS

★ Ballroom

★ Bas-reliefs in the Bathing Room

★ Picture Gallery

FARTHER AFIELD

HILE CENTRAL Warsaw's most historic buildings were generally reconstructed after the devastation of World War II, other parts of the city feature many historic buildings that survived the war intact. Along the escarpment on the Left Bank of the River Vistula, for example, are several delightful residences set in their own parks. Most of these can easily be reached by public transportation or even on foot. On the outskirts of the city is Wilanów Palace and Park,

Airmen's Memorial by Wawelska Street

originally the residence of King Jan III Sobieski. There is also the church and former Camaldolese hermitage, both situated in Bielański Forest. For leisurely day trips beyond the city boundaries, there are several options, including the romantically landscaped Arkadia Park and the neighboring Nieborów Palace. There is also Żelazowa Wola, birthplace of Frederic Chopin and now a museum, as well as a scattering of historic towns, such as Łowicz, Pułtusk, and Płock.

SIGHTS AT A GLANCE

Palaces and Gardens
Królikarnia Palace ❸
Natolin Palace ❺
Powsin Botanical Gardens ❼
Rozkosz Palace ❹
Szuster Palace ❷
Wilanów Palace
  and Park ❶
Zoological Garden ⓫

Churches
Church of St. Stanisław
  Kostka ⓭

St. Anthony of Padua
  Church ❻
St. Mary Magdalene's Russian
  Orthodox Church ❾

Cemeteries
Augsburg Protestant
  Cemetery ⓰
Jewish Cemetery on
  Okopowa Street ⓯
Powązki Catholic Cemetery ⓮
Protestant Reformed
  Cemetery ⓱

Woodlands and Parks
Bielański Forest ⓬
Kabacki Forest ❽

Markets
Różycki Market ❿

KEY

▢	City center
▬	Main road
✈	Airport

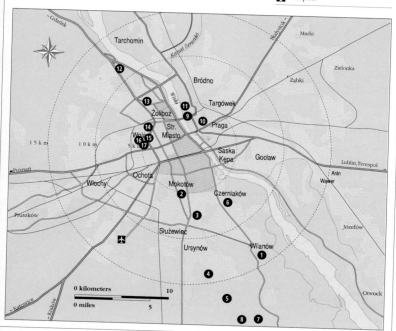

◁ **The Neo-Classical entrance gates to Wilanów Palace and Park**

Wilanów Palace and Park ❶

ALTHOUGH IT WAS a royal residence, Wilanów Palace was actually designed as a private retreat for King Jan III Sobieski, who valued family life above material splendor. The original property, known as Villa Nova, was purchased in 1677 and within two years had been rebuilt into a mansion, designed by royal architect Augustyn Locci. Subsequently, two wings, towers, and a first-floor banqueting hall were added, with the interiors decorated by some of Europe's finest craftsmen. Sculptures on the façades are by Andreas Schlüter, while a series of murals includes work by the 17th- and 18th-century artists Michelangelo Palloni, Claude Callot, and Jerzy Eleuter Szymonowicz-Siemiginowski.

Detail of putti

Orangerie
This currently serves as a venue for arts and crafts exhibitions.

Tomb of Stanisław Kostka Potocki
Ironically, Poland's foremost Classical expert lies under a Neo-Gothic, rather than a Neo-Classical, canopy, just outside the main gate.

0 meters	50
0 yards	50

Main Gateway
Dating from the 17th century, this impressive entrance features two allegorical figures representing War and Peace.

★ Poster Museum
Wilanów's former riding school now houses the fascinating Poster Museum.

Gazebo

This Chinese gazebo is situated in the English-style garden, laid out during the 19th century, on the north side of the palace.

VISITORS' CHECKLIST

Wiertnicza 1. **☎** 42 81 01, 42 25 09. 🚌 130, 139, 164, 165, 188, 410, 522, 710, 728, E-2. **Palace** ◯ Feb–Dec: 9:30am– 2:45pm Wed–Mon. **Park** ◯ 9:30am–dusk.

★ Baroque Park

The most historic section of Wilanów's grounds, laid out in the Baroque style, are behind the palace.

Palace Façade

The gardens were laid out to provide open perspectives, with this façade visible across the park and even across the adjoining fields of Morysin.

Stucco Pediment

Symbolizing King Jan III Sobieski's courage, this pediment is on the façade above an entrance to the park.

★ Wilanów Palace

This was King Jan III Sobieski's favorite "retreat."

STAR SIGHTS

★ **Wilanów Palace**

★ **Poster Museum**

★ **Baroque Park**

Exploring Wilanów Palace

The most interesting apartments, originally occupied by King Jan III Sobieski and his wife, Marysieńka, are on the ground floor of Wilanów's main building, which has retained many of its original 17th-century features. The north wing has 19th-century rooms. They were formerly used to house the Potocki family's art collection, while also serving as living quarters for subsequent owners. The south wing houses the late Baroque Great Dining Room, designed for King August II Mocny, as well as Princess Izabela Lubomirska's apartments, which include a bathroom dating from 1775. The nursery and governesses' rooms are situated on the first floor, together with a fascinating portrait gallery.

Decorative detail from the façade

Florentine Bureau
This magnificent 17th-century bureau is in the king's antechamber.

Great Crimson Room
Taking its name from the colored fabric that covers the walls, this room contains a giant table and serves as a venue for entertaining VIPs.

Sobieski Family Portrait
The marriage of King Jan III Sobieski and Marysieńka was a genuine love match, which was then rare among royal couples.

TIMELINE

1692 Great Dining Room completed	**1775** Bathroom built for Izabela Lubomirska	**1805** Stanisław Kostka Potocki creates a museum
1667 Building of Wilanów begins	**1723** Work commences on the wings	**1855–6** Chapel furnished

1600	1650	1700	1750	1800	1850	1900

1681 Towers and galleries added	**1730** King August II Mocny takes a lease on Wilanów	**1850** North wing extended and new pavilions built
1696 King Jan III Sobieski dies	**1720** Palace acquired by Elżbieta Sieniawska	**1945** Wilanów becomes a museum

North Gallery
This gallery includes a portrait of Stanisław Kostka Potocki, painted by the French artist Jacques-Louis David (1748–1825).

Queen's Antechamber
The walls are still covered with the original Baroque fabric, dating from the 17th century, when Queen Marysieńka was in residence.

★ Great Hall
Szymon Bogumił Zug's Neo-Classical redesign retained some Baroque details, such as the Allegory of the Four Elements.

★ King's Bedchamber
The canopy over the bed is of 17th-century Turkish fabric.

Chapel
This bas-relief is above the door to the mid-19th-century chapel, designed by Henryk Marconi and Franciszek Maria Lanci.

The Great Dining Room, completed between 1730–33, was designed by Jan Zygmunt Deybel for King August II Mocny, who held a lease on Wilanów at that time.

KEY TO FLOOR PLAN

- ▢ Queen's apartments
- ▢ King's apartments
- ▢ Great Dining Room
- ▢ Princess Lubomirska's apartments
- ▢ Other rooms open to the public

STAR SIGHTS

- **★ King's Bedchamber**
- **★ Great Hall**

Szuster Palace ❷
Pałacyk Szustra

Szuster Palace

Puławska 55. **Map** 6 E5. 📞 *49 68 56.*
🚌 *130, 144, 505, 514, 515.*
🚊 *4, 18, 19, 35, 36.*

E FRAIM SCHROEGER originally
designed this small palace
as a "picturesque villa" for
Princess Izabela Lubomirska
(née Czartoryska). Built in
1774 and set in a landscaped
park, the palace occupies an
enchanting site, standing on
an escarpment in Mokotów,
an area on the outskirts of
Warsaw. The park, which is
known as Morskie Oko, was
laid out in 1776–8 by Szymon
Bogumił Zug, who went on
to redesign Szuster Palace
during the 1780s.
In 1820 the palace was
acquired by Anna Wąsowicz-
Potocka (née Tyszkiewicz).
She commissioned Henryk
Marconi to refurbish it in a
Neo-Gothic style, which was
undertaken between 1822–5.
The German scientist Alexander von Humboldt was
received here in 1830. He
described the palace and
park as "richly adorned with
flowers, marbles, and ancient
Greek artifacts." This was,
however, a disappointment
for Anna Potocka, who was
used to more effusive praise.
Moreover, hurt by this remark
she is reputed to have said:
"I try talking to him about
many interesting things and
all he does is drone on about
some Siberian grasses. A typically dense Prussian!"
From 1845 (for almost the
next 100 years) the palace
was owned by the Szuster
family. After a fire in 1944, it
was rebuilt as the headquarters
of the Warsaw Music Society.
The park, which was recently

restored, includes a Moorish
house, a dovecote, a late-18th-
century gateway designed by
Szymon Bogumił Zug, and
the Szuster family mausoleum.

Królikarnia Palace ❸
Pałacyk Królikarnia

Puławska 113a. 📞 *43 15 86.*
🚌 *144, 505, 508.* 🚊 *4, 18, 19,
31, 36.* ⏰ *10am–3:30pm daily.*
🎫 *free on Thu.*

T HE UNUSUAL name of
this exquisite palace
(literally meaning "rabbit
hutch") stems from
the fact that it occu-
pies the site of a
rabbit farm and
hunting grounds that
belonged to King
August II Mocny in
the 18th century.
Designed in the
Neo-Classical style
by Dominik Merlini,
the square shape
and dome recall
Andrea Palladio's
masterpiece –
the Villa
Rotonda, near
Vicenza.
The palace
was built be-
tween 1782
and 1786 for Karol de Valery
Thomatis, who was director
of King Stanisław August
Poniatowski's Royal Theater.
Set within a park in Mokotów, the palace houses the
Xawery Dunikowski Museum,
containing works by this
famous Polish sculptor.

*Falum by Xawery Dunikowski
in Królikarnia Palace*

Rozkosz Palace ❹
Pałac Rozkosz

Nowoursynowska 166. 🚌 *182, 515.*

B UILT BETWEEN 1775 and 1780
for Izabela Lubomirska,
the wife of the renowned
marshal, this palace is idyl-
lically set on an escarpment
in Ursynów, by the River
Vistula. The name of the palace
literally means "delight." Ten
years after being built, it was
greatly refurbished, according
to a joint design by Chrystian
Piotr Aigner and Stanisław
Kostka-Potocki (the sub-
sequent owner).
Between 1822 and
1831, the palace be-
longed to the politi-
cian and writer Julian
Ursyn Niemcewicz,
who served as aide-
de-camp to Tadeusz
Kościuszko, the leader
of the 1794 Insurrection.
In 1858, the palace's
new owner, Ludwik
Krasiński, commis-
sioned Zygmunt
Rospendowski to
redesign Rozkosz
in a Neo-Classical
style. The façade
was then deco-
rated with busts
of military com-
manders, includ-
ing Stefan Czarniecki, Paweł
Sanguszko, Władysław Koniec-
polski, and Jan Tarnowski.
There were also busts of
several Polish queens, such
as Barbara and Jadwiga.
Nowadays, Rozkosz Palace
houses the offices of the Agricultural College.

Neo-Classical façade of Rozkosz Palace in the snow

Natolin Palace, set in an ornate landscaped park

Natolin Palace **5**
Pałac w Natolinie

Nowoursynowska. 108, 312.
M *Natolin.* **Not open** to the public.

Decorated ceiling by Vincenzo Brenna in Natolin Palace

WHEN THIS Neo-Classical residence was built in 1780–82, Natolin was several kilometers outside Warsaw's southern boundary. Today, however, urban housing projects encroach on the palace grounds.

Natolin's architect, Szymon Bogumił Zug, was recommended to its owners by Prince August Czartoryski and his daughter Izabela Lubomirska, who owned the neighboring palace and estate of Wilanów *(see pp168–71)*.

Natolin Palace has several notable features, including ornate wall and ceiling paintings by Vincenzo Brenna, an Italian architect and painter. The palace was significantly

modified in 1808 by Chrystian Piotr Aigner, who added the distinctive dome and an unusual summer drawing room, which opens onto the garden.

The palace is set in a landscaped park, which extends along an escarpment. The park has a great many buildings and decorative features, among them a bridge, a Doric temple, an aqueduct, and a Moorish gateway.

As neither the palace nor the gardens are open to the public, the only feature that can be readily admired is a remarkable oak tree, named Mieszko (as were several of the early Polish kings), which is situated by the palace on Nowoursynowska Street. This is the oldest tree in the whole of Warsaw. It is also thought that it is the sole surviving tree of the Mazovian Forest, which at one time covered the entire area.

St. Anthony of Padua Church **6**
Kościół św. Antoniego Padewskiego

Czerniakowska 2/4. 131, 159, 179, 180, 185, 187.

THIS BAROQUE CHURCH, built between 1687 and 1693 by the Bernardine order, was designed by the renowned architect Tylman of Gameren. The church stands on the site of the former village of Czerniaków, which belonged to Stanisław Herakliusz Lubomirski, the crown marshal.

The relatively plain façade of this church belies its highly ornate interior. This includes stuccowork and murals illustrating the life of St. Anthony of Padua that were principally painted by Antonio Giorgioli.

The altars include Baroque designs by the famous German architect and sculptor Andreas Schlüter (1664–1714). Additionally, the main altar features a glass coffin that contains the relics of St. Boniface (a 5th-century pope). These sacred relics were given to Stanisław Herakliusz Lubomirski in 1687 by Pope Innocent XI.

Powsin Botanical Gardens **7**
Ogród Botaniczny w Powsinie

Prawdziwka 2. 42 79 01. 519. Jun 13–Oct 20: 10am–6pm Tue–Sun.

POWSIN BOTANICAL GARDENS were established by the Polish Academy of Science in 1974 as a research and educational establishment. Since 1990, the gardens have been open to the public.

The 16-hectare (40-acre) site, located by the River Vistula, includes an arboretum, a collection of rare and endangered plants and trees, various medicinal plants, and spices. There are also greenhouses that contain decorative plants.

Various pot plants, flowers, and seedlings are for sale here, while fairs are held throughout the winter months.

The green-domed Baroque St. Anthony of Padua Church

Walking in the Kabacki Forest, to the south of Warsaw

Kabacki Forest ❽
Las Kabacki

Ⓜ *Kabaty.* 🚌 *139, 519.*

THE KABACKI FOREST, near the Botanical Gardens, on Prawdziwka Street, is a favorite with Varsovians for day trips. Comprising 920 ha (2,275 acres), the forest offers a wide variety of deciduous species, such as its oak trees, while other areas consist mainly of evergreen pines.

Before the outbreak of World War II, the forest was saved from developers by Stefan Starzyński, the mayor of Warsaw. He purchased the forest from its owners, on behalf of the City Council.

In the vicinity of Powsin, on the southeastern edge of the forest, is a vacation center set among trees. The center contains a swimming pool and other sports facilities, as well as cabins.

St. Mary Magdalene's Russian Orthodox Church ❾
Cerkiew św. Marii Magdaleny

Aleja Solidarności. **Map** 4 E3. 🚌 *101, 160, 192, 460, 512.* 🚊 *4.*

SITUATED in the district of Praga, St. Mary Magdalene's Church was built in 1868–9. The work of Russian architect Nikolai Sychev, his plans were influenced by Byzantine-Russian churches, and the building is topped with distinctive onion-shaped domes.

The interiors feature murals by several Russian artists and an interesting iconostasis. This elaborate screen, which includes doors and icons arranged in tiers, divides the nave from the sanctuary. The church is not usually open to

Domes of St. Mary Magdalene's Russian Orthodox Church

the public, apart from during services. One of the best times to visit is on Orthodox feast days, when you can also listen to the superb church choirs.

Różycki Market ❿
Bazar Różyckiego

Targowa 54. **Map** 4 F4. 🚌 *101.* 🚊 *13, 26.* ⏰ *6am–6pm Mon–Fri.*

AS A LONG ESTABLISHED institution, the Różycki market is an ideal example of "old Warsaw." The market is located in the heart of Praga, to the south of St. Mary Magdalene's Russian Orthodox Church.

However, with ongoing economic reforms and the redevelopment of Praga, the market has lost its position as

Warsaw's most important shopping spot. Nevertheless, it has maintained its traditional and highly individual atmosphere.

The market was established at the turn of the century by a Warsaw chemist, A Różycki, on the site of an even older market. Squeezed between dilapidated tenement buildings, the market has hundreds of wooden stalls, selling mainly clothing and food. A local specialty is a hot tripe dish called *flaki*, which is eagerly recommended by street vendors.

The market has always been a haunt for pickpockets, and visitors should be attentive and guard valuables carefully.

The streets directly behind the market, Ząbkowska and Brzeska, are lined with old brick tenements, whose walls are still scarred with bullet marks dating from World War II. Brzeska Street was, until recently, one of the best places to obtain illicit drink. It is still considered relatively unsafe and is best avoided, especially at night or if you are alone.

Zoological Garden ⓫
Ogród Zoologiczny

Ratuszowa 1/3. **Map** 4 D3 & 4 D4. 🅲 *619 40 41.* 🚌 *160, 179, 512.* ⏰ *9am–dusk daily.* 🅿

WARSAW'S ZOO, located on the Right Bank of the River Vistula, opened in 1928. However, the city has a much longer zoological tradition, dating back to the 17th century, when wealthy magnates established private zoos.

The original Warsaw zoo, established in the Praski Garden, was continually

Mother and baby baboon in the Zoological Garden

expanding until the outbreak of World War II. During the first few weeks of the war, much of the zoo was destroyed; some animals died, and the remainder were slaughtered by the invading Nazis.

The zoo was reestablished after the war, in 1948, and currently occupies about 40 ha (100 acres), which is largely open-air. The zoo has about 3,000 animals in total, including 91 species of mammals, 87 species of birds, 49 of reptiles, and about the same number of fish species.

The Small Zoo (Małe Zoo) is a section where animals can be fed and petted. Additionally, there is a bear run, surrounded by a moat, that is located a few minutes' walk from the main zoo on Solidarity Avenue.

Father Jerzy Popiełuszko's tomb at the Church of St. Stanisław Kostka

Bielański Forest ⓬
Las Bielański

Dewajtis. *121, 181, 511.*
15, 17, 27.

Sﾞ ITUATED on the banks of the River Vistula, to the north of the city, the Bielański Forest occupies an area of 150 ha (370 acres). This is all that remains of the prehistoric Mazovian Forest. The Bielański Forest includes a wide range of plant-life and trees, such as its 700-year-old oaks.

The forest is now a protected national park, although even as recently as a few decades ago, it was a popular site for fairs and picnics, with people arriving in their thousands in pleasure boats.

The highest point of the forest is Pólkowska Hill, where the Church of the Immaculate Conception can be seen, by the banks of a river. This church was built by the Camaldolese monks between 1669 and 1710, and features an oval-shaped nave with Rococo-style stuccowork. The monastery's benefactors included the Polish royal family and various other wealthy patrons. Their family crests can still be seen on the portals of the hermitages, at the rear of the church. These tiny dwellings were inhabited by monks until 1904. In the

adjoining cemetery is the tomb of Stanisław Staszic (1755–1822), a famous political writer, philosopher, and scientist, who co-founded the Royal Society of the Friends of Science.

Close to the church is the Catholic Theological Academy and the Warsaw Seminary. Both of these buildings were constructed in the 1980s.

On Pułkowa Street, at the edge of the Bielański Forest, there is a small military cemetery for Italian soldiers. It was established in 1927 and designed by the Chief Technical Commissioner for Military Cemeteries, in Rome.

Buried here are the remains of Italian soldiers who were killed on Polish soil during World War I. Also buried are approximately 1,200 prisoners of war, who were murdered by the Nazis during World War II. The gateway to the cemetery is shaped in the form of a triumphal arch. The railings are lavishly decorated with laurel leaves and Roman shield motifs.

Church of St. Stanisław Kostka ⓭
Kościół św. Stanisława Kostki

Hozjusza 1. **Map** 3 A2. *116, 122, 195.* *15, 31, 36.*

Tﾞ HIS MODERNIST CHURCH, featuring an openwork twin tower, is a center for Polish pilgrims, who come to visit the tomb of the late Father Jerzy Popiełuszko. He was renowned for his courageous sermons in defense of Poland's freedom during the Communist era. He was eventually murdered in 1984 by Communist security agents.

The Church of St. Stanisław Kostka is set among the villas of Żoliborz.

Powązki Cemetery ⓮
Katolicki Cmentarz Powązkowski

See pp176–7.

Candles and flowers decorating Powązki Cemetery on All Saints' Day

Powązki Catholic Cemetery ⑭
Katolicki Cmentarz Powązkowski

THIS IS WARSAW'S OLDEST and most beautiful cemetery. It forms part of a vast complex divided into separate areas, according to religious denominations, which includes Jewish and Protestant sections (*see pp178–9*). Before the Catholic cemetery was established in 1790, the neighboring site was occupied by Izabela Czartoryska's Rococo palace, modeled on the Trianon at Versailles and set in a romantic park. Close to the cemetery are streets with names such as Spokojna (quiet) and Smętna (sad). However, as the cemetery expanded, the system of indexing plots became ever more complicated. Locating specific tombs usually requires patience and a good map. By the main entrance (St. Honorata Gate) is the church of St. Charles Borromeo. Originally founded in the 18th century by King Stanisław August Poniatowski and his brother Michał, primate of Poland, this church was refurbished in 1891–8.

Lilpop Family Tomb
This Neo-Gothic cast-iron spire, designed by Józef Manzel in 1866, rises above the tomb of the Lilpop family (plot B), who were co-owners of a large metalworks.

Wacław Szymanowski
Szymanowski (1821–86) was a journalist and editor-in-chief of the Kurier Warszawski *newspaper. His tomb (plot 40) was carved by his son Wacław, Jr., in 1905, and is an outstanding example of Secessionist style.*

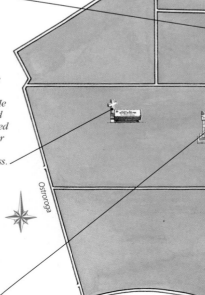

Edward Rydz-Śmigły
The Polish army's supreme commander during the September 1939 campaign, Rydz-Śmigły subsequently left the country and was interned in Romania. He escaped to Hungary and then returned to occupied Warsaw, where he died. He was buried under the pseudonym Adam Zawisza, in a modest grave (plot 139) marked by a white birch cross.

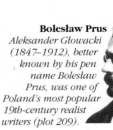

Bolesław Prus
Aleksander Głowacki (1847–1912), better known by his pen name Bolesław Prus, was one of Poland's most popular 19th-century realist writers (plot 209).

Frederic Chopin's Parents and Stanisław Moniuszko

Resting in adjoining tombs (plot 9) are Stanisław Moniuszko, composer and creator of the Polish national opera, and Justyna and Mikołaj Chopin.

Lusia Raciborowska

Dating from 1900, this poignant statue (plot 3) was sculpted from white marble in the Milan workshop of Donato Barcaglio.

Stanisław Wojciechowski (1869–1953), the second president of independent Poland, was dismissed in May 1926 during Marshal Józef Piłsudski's coup d'état. He is buried in plot 12.

The Church of St. Charles Borromeo was built to an eclectic design by Józef Pius Dziekoński.

St. Honorata Gate

Powązkowska

The Avenue of Merit was created in 1925. On its south side lie some of the city's most prominent artists, scientists, and politicians.

Jan Kiepura

The "boy from Sosnowiec" was a celebrated operatic tenor who also appeared in numerous films with his wife, Martha Eggerth. His funeral in 1966 attracted tens of thousands of admirers.

Władysław Reymont

Reymont, whose tomb is on the Avenue of Merit, was one of Poland's most outstanding writers. In 1924, a year before he died, Reymont received the Nobel Prize for his novel Chłopi *(The Peasants).*

Jan Szczepkowski

This statue of an angel guards the tomb of Jan Szczepkowski (1878–1964), who was a leading Art Deco sculptor.

Catacombs

Built in 1792 and enlarged in 1851, the catacombs became the burial place for King Stanisław August Poniatowski's family and other renowned Poles.

Other Cemeteries at Powązki: Jewish Cemetery ⑮
Cmentarz Żydowski

THE JEWISH CEMETERY on Okopowa Street was established between 1799 and 1806. Now deserted, it is a very poignant area, with its trees and thick undergrowth among tombstones making it difficult even to reach certain sections. Religious dictates ban human forms from appearing on tombstones, so they are decorated mainly with symbols and ornaments. Most tombs are marked by simple stones (*masebas*). However, there are also more elaborate features, such as marble obelisks, sarcophagi, and chapels bearing memorial plaques (*oheles*).

Wedel Family Mausoleum
This tomb of the renowned chocolate producers (Ave A, No. 31) is adorned with a bronze statue of Christ made in 1931 by Stanisław R Lewandowski.

Halpert Chapel
This large Empire-style chapel (Ave E) was commissioned by Maria Halpert and dedicated to the memory of her husband, Salomon, who died in 1832.

Braeunig Chapel
The oldest cast-iron chapel in Warsaw, this was constructed in 1821. It can be found on Ave D, No. 55a.

Jenike Family Tomb
Made of red sandstone, this Secessionist tomb (Ave 54) was designed by Zygmunt Otto in 1903.

PROTESTANT REFORMED CEMETERY ⑰
The Lutheran and Protestant Reformed communities originally shared a cemetery on Mylna Street. Since it moved to this well-maintained cemetery (Cmentarz Ewangelicko-Reformowany), their respective burial grounds have been separated by a wall.

Mlynarska

Augsł Prote Ceme

Protestant Reformed Cemetery

Laskowicki Family Tomb
This tomb (plot B) is crowned with the sculpture of an angel with a torch, designed by Bolesław Jeziorański.

Żytnia

Stefan Żeromski
Żeromski was one of the best-loved early-20th-century Polish writers, author of many short stories and novels such as Ludzie Bezdomni (Homeless People). His tomb is situated in plot F.

Estera Rachela Kamińska
This stage and film actress was known as the "mother of Jewish theater." In 1915 she founded the Warsaw Jewish Theater dedicated to her husband, Abraham Kamiński. Her tombstone (plot 39) was designed by Feliks Rubinlicht.

Janusz Korczak Monument
This monument (in plot 72) stands over a symbolic grave of Janusz Korczak (1878–1942). It depicts him accompanying the Jewish orphans who were under his care to a Nazi death camp.

Jewish Cemetery

Samuel Orgelbrand (1810–66) was a bookseller and publisher who also owned a printing house. His tombstone is in plot 20.

Ludwik Zamenhof
Although an ophthalmologist by training, Zamenhof (1859–1917) achieved renown by devising the language of Esperanto in 1887. He is buried in plot 10.

Okopowa

Augsberg Protestant Cemetery ⑯
Since 1792, this small burial ground (Cmentarz Ewangelicko-Augsburski) on Młynarska Street has served as the resting place for various distinguished people. The cemetery was designed by Szymon Bogumił Zug, who was buried here in 1807.

Wojciech Gerson (1831–1901) was a popular 19th-century painter from Warsaw. His tomb can be found on Ave 19.

Anna German
This great performer (1936–82) had a wonderful voice and was one of Poland's most popular stars.

Symbols on Tombstones
The *masebas* at the Jewish Cemetery are decorated with symbols representing the family, the surname, or the profession of the deceased.

Day Trips from Warsaw

WARSAW IS SURROUNDED by the flat plains of Mazovia, which are varied by extensive forests and the Vistula, the only European river that still follows its natural, unregulated course. There are several historic towns and attractions that provide a leisurely day trip from Warsaw. These include the ruined medieval castle in Czersk; Jabłonna Palace, which is set in a beautiful park; and Żelazowa Wola, the manor house where Chopin was born. Some travel agents also offer organized tours *(see p237)* to these places.

Niobe from the Nieborów collection

KEY

▢	Central Warsaw
▢	Greater Warsaw
▰	Major road
✈	Airport

25 km = 16 miles

Łowicz costume

Czersk ❶

39 km (24 miles) S of Warsaw.
🚌 *from Mokotów station, junction of Puławska and Nowoursynowska streets.*

THE VILLAGE of Czersk was originally the capital of the Mazovian region. In 1413 Czersk was succeeded by Warsaw as the Mazovian capital, when the route of the River Vistula apparently turned away from Czersk.

The village includes the ruins of a medieval castle, approached via a Gothic bridge spanning a moat. The visible ruins date from the 14th–16th centuries, and three towers enlarged in the 16th century are still standing.

In the 13th century, Prince Konrad Mazowiecki, who brought the Teutonic Knights to Poland in 1226, imprisoned the infant princes Bolesław Wstydliwy (future prince of Kraków), and Henryk Brodaty, the prince of Wrocław, in the south tower.

Jabłonna ❷

20 km (12 miles) N of Warsaw.
☎ 628 16 75. 🚌 723.
Park ☐ 6am–10pm daily.

SINCE THE 15TH CENTURY, there has been a palace on this site. Following the death of King Władysław IV Waza in 1648, the original palace

became Karol Ferdynand Waza's headquarters when he contested the Polish throne.

The present Neo-Classical style dates from 1775–9 and is the result of Dominik Merlini's design for the Polish primate, Michał Poniatowski.

In 1837 the palace was refurbished by Henryk Marconi. One significant change to the façade was the addition of a tower that has an unusual spherical roof.

The palace is set in a park, designed by Szymon Bogumił Zug in the 18th century.

During the summer, concerts and various other events are held in the park and the palace.

Nieborów ❸

81 km (50 miles) W of Warsaw.
☎ 046 38 56 20, 046 38 56 23.
🚌 *to Łowicz, then by local bus.*
☐ 10am–3:30pm Tue–Fri; 10am–5:30pm Sat & Sun. 🎫

DESIGNED in the Baroque style by Tylman of Gameren, Nieborów was built in 1690–96 and was set in a symmetrical garden. The palace was commissioned by the archbishop of Gniezno,

Michał S Radziejowski, who was an aesthete and a generous patron of the arts.

Around 1766 a subsequent owner, Prince Michał K Ogiński, had the pediment decorated in the Rococo style. It featured a dancing figure of Bacchus, crowned with a laurel wreath and holding a bunch of grapes. Ogiński is famous for establishing the canal system that connected

The Baroque Nieborów Palace

the Black Sea with the Baltic via a network of rivers.

Between 1771 and 1945, Nieborów belonged to the aristocratic Radziwiłł family. Their magnificent furnishings and extensive collection of art can be seen throughout the palace's rooms and corridors.

The collection includes Antoine Pesne's portrait of Anna Orzelska, the daughter of August II Mocny, who was renowned for her beauty *(see p25)*. The antique head of Niobe, carved in white marble, is a Roman copy of

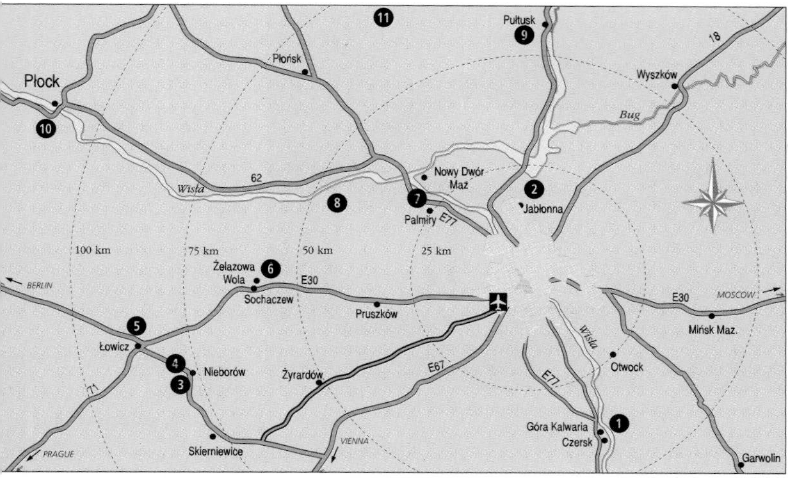

he Greek original, which lates from the 4th century BC. The head was extolled by the poet Konstanty Ildefons Gałczyński, and was presented to Princess Helena Radziwiłł by Empress Catherine II.

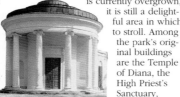

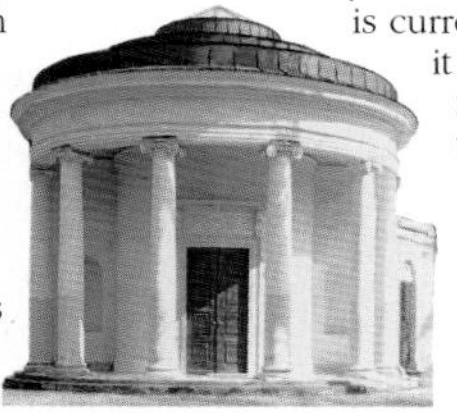
Temple of Diana, Arkadia Park

Arkadia ❹

35 km (53 miles) W of Warsaw. 🚆 *from Śródmieście Station to Mysłaków.* 🕒 *May–Oct: 10am–6pm daily.* ♿

ROMANTIC Arkadia Park, situated between the towns of Nieborów and Łowicz, was established in 1778 by Princess Helena Radziwiłł.

The intention was to create an idyllic landscape of trees and lakes, together with picturesque buildings. Several pavilions were designed by Szymon Bogumił Zug and Henryk Ittar. While the park is currently overgrown, it is still a delightful area in which to stroll. Among the park's original buildings are the Temple of Diana, the High Priest's Sanctuary, Bugrave House with its stone arch, the Gothic House, the Sybil Grotto, and the aqueduct. Some of the park walls incorporate fragments of the original sculptures and stonework from the Renaissance bishop's palace that once stood in the town of Łowicz.

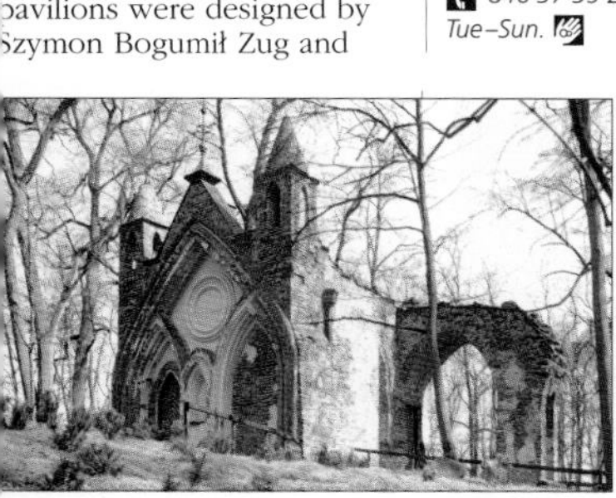
Remains of a Gothic building in Arkadia Park

Łowicz ❺

81 km (50 miles) W of Warsaw. 🚆 *from Śródmieście or Central Station.* **Łowicz Regional Museum** ☎ *846 37 39 28.* 🕒 *10am–4pm Tue–Sun.* ♿

THIS SMALL town dates from the 13th century and was originally the center of one of the oldest Polish castellanies (counties). For several centuries, Łowicz was the residence of the archbishops of Gniezno, who were also the primates of Poland. Their legacy includes several ecclesiastical buildings.

The most outstanding among these is the medieval **Collegiate Church**, which was reconstructed in the 17th century. The church is filled with magnificent works of art and tombs. A notable tomb is that of Jakub Uchański, the primate of Poland, who died in 1581. It is in a chapel rebuilt in 1782–3 in an early Neo-Classical style to a design by Efraim Schroeger. The tomb features a 16th-century alabaster statue by Jan Michałowicz of Urzędów.

It is worth visiting Łowicz on the feast of Corpus Christi (which is in either late May or early June) to see the ceremonial procession in which many of the women wear traditional folk costumes.

By the market square is a series of buildings, including a former monastery and the Seminary for Missionaries, which houses the **Łowicz Regional Museum**. The museum has a collection of folk art, and in the vaults of the former chapel (designed by Tylman of Gameren in 1689–1701) is an exhibition of Baroque art and murals by Michelangelo Palloni. A small *skansen* (open-air museum) behind the chapel features two period farmhouses with original furnishings.

Żelazowa Wola, the birthplace of Frederic Chopin

Żelazowa Wola 6

52 km (32 miles) W of Warsaw.
0494 223 00. from Zachodni
Station. 9am–4pm Tue–Sun.

Poland's most famous composer, Frederic Chopin, was born in this manor house on March 1, 1810. At that time, the house was a thatched cottage, occupied by Chopin's parents, Mikołaj and Justyna (née Krzyżanowska).

The house was opened as a museum in 1931, under the administration of the Chopin Society in Warsaw. The society rebuilt the house, furnishing it in the original 19th-century manner. It assembled a collection of memorabilia associated with the composer to form the museum's exhibits. The surrounding park was planted with a wide range of trees and shrubs, donated by various Polish regions.

During World War II, many artifacts were looted by the Nazis. They also banned performances of Chopin's music and even destroyed portraits of the composer.

Following refurbishment, the house was reopened to the public in 1949, on the 100th anniversary of the composer's death.

Chopin concerts are held on the terrace at the side of the house, on most weekends between May and October.

About 11 km (7 miles) northwest of Żelazowa Wola is Brochów, a village on the edge of Kampinos National

Park. The village contains a Renaissance church, in which Chopin's parents were married. Frederic Chopin was later baptized at this church.

Palmiry 7

25 km (16 miles) NW of Warsaw.
from Marymont and Zachodni
stations.

Situated in Kampinos National Park, Palmiry Cemetery is a resting place for over 2,200 victims of Nazi executions that were carried out here and in other forests within the Warsaw area.

By the entrance to the cemetery is an inscription bearing the words of an unknown prisoner of the Gestapo: "It is easy to talk

Graves at Palmiry cemetery

about Poland, more difficult to work for her, even harder to die for her, but the hardest of all is to suffer for her."

Between December 1939 and July 1944, prisoners were brought here regularly and shot. These mass-grave sites were subsequently planted with trees. Many well-known Varsovians were killed here, including Janusz Kusociński, the 10,000-meter gold medal winner at the 1932 Los Angeles Olympic Games.

Kampinos National Park 8
Puszcza Kampinoska

On the NW borders of Warsaw.
municipal and suburban, from
Marymont and Zachodni stations.
The best starting point is Dziekanów
Leśny, Truskaw, Zaborów, or Kampinos

Kampinos National Park

Established in 1959, the Kampinos National Park comprises 35,500 ha (88,000 acres) of a large forest to the northwest of Warsaw.

Although the forest consists mainly of pine, the area also includes about 1,000 species of trees, shrubs, and other plants. The indigenous wildlife features beavers, elks, cranes, and rare black storks. Until recently, there were even lynxes. One of the park's most unusual features is its tree-covered inland dunes.

Several marked trails provide very enjoyable day-long rambles through the park.

Interior of the Gothic-Renaissance Collegiate Church in Pułtusk

Pułtusk ❾

60 km (37 miles) N of Warsaw. 🚌 from Zachodni Station.

PUŁTUSK'S SETTING on the River Narew is one of the loveliest to be found in Mazovia. Its Old Town occupies a large island and features an ornate town hall with a brick tower and one of the largest market squares *(rynek)* in Europe. At the northern end of the market square is the Gothic-Renaissance Collegiate Church of the Virgin Mary. The main nave's arched vaulting is the work of one of Venice's greatest architects, Giovanni Battista.

On the opposite side of the market square is the castle. Originally Gothic, the castle was subsequently destroyed and rebuilt several times. Following its reconstruction during the 1980s, the castle is now home to the Polish Expatriates House (Dom Polonii). The house is used mainly by Polish émigrés, but is open to everyone. It provides elegant rooms for overnight accommodation, and its restaurant serves traditional cuisine that is highly recommended. There are also sports facilities.

Epitaph in Pułtusk's Collegiate Church

Płock ❿

110 km (68 miles) NW of Warsaw. 🚌 from Zachodni Station.
Mazovian Museum
📞 024 62 44 91.
🕐 9am–5pm Sun. 📷
Diocesan Museum
📞 024 62 26 23.
🕐 Apr–Oct: 10am–1pm Wed–Sat, 11am–2pm Sun; Sep: 10am–3pm Tue–Sat, 11am–4pm Sun. 📷

THE FOCAL POINT of this city is its cathedral hill, where most of the historic sights are located. Płock has been the seat of the Mazovian bishops since 1075, and for a few hundred years after 1138 it was also the residence of the Mazovian and Płock princes.

The city's principal attraction is the Mazovian Museum (Muzeum Mazowieckie), which has the finest collection of Secessionist artifacts in Poland. These include several rooms that are furnished exactly as they would have been during the Secessionist era.

The Renaissance cathedral was built in the 16th century, by Giovanni Cini and Bernardino Zanobi de Gianotis, on the site of an earlier Romanesque church. The cathedral was subsequently refurbished by the Venetian architect Giovanni Battista. The richly decorated interiors contain several Renaissance and Baroque tombs. There are also a number of Secessionist-style frescoes.

Close to the cathedral is the Diocesan Museum (Muzeum Diecezjalne), which has a wide range of religious exhibits.

Opinogóra ⓫

100 km (62 miles) N of Warsaw.
📞 023 71 70 25. 🚌 from Zachodni Station to Ciechanowa, then by local bus. 🕐 10am–4pm Tue–Sun. 📷

OPINOGÓRA is a small Neo-Gothic palace that is set within a Romantic, landscaped park. The palace was built in 1843, when it was given as a wedding present to Count Zygmunt Krasiński (1812–59). Krasiński is one of Poland's greatest Romantic poets, alongside Adam Mickiewicz and Juliusz Słowacki.

The design of the palace has been attributed to the eminent French architect Eugène Emmanuel Viollet-le-Duc. In the 19th century, he was also responsible for the restoration of Notre-Dame in Paris.

The palace is home to the Museum of Romanticism (Muzeum Romantyzmu), which includes restored interiors and various items that once belonged to Zygmunt Krasiński. Additional exhibits can be seen in a neighboring building.

The park, which is also worth a visit, contains the parish church. Built between 1874 and 1885 in a Neo-Classical style, the church was designed by Wincenty Rakiewicz. The vaults of the church contain the Krasiński family mausoleum, where Zygmunt Krasiński was laid to rest.

Main entrance to Płock Cathedral

THREE GUIDED WALKS

WARSAW is an ideal city to explore on foot, as the major attractions in the city center are within a short walk of one another. In addition, the entire Old Town and New Town are closed to traffic, and several more parks, squares and arcades, and the River Vistula are within easy reach.

One attractive walking itinerary is the Royal Route, along which you will find historic palaces, churches, and monuments. This runs south from the Old Town, roughly parallel to the Left Bank of

Urn on the terrace of the Ostrogski Palace

the Vistula (see pp112–25). Or, if you have time, try one of the three walks described on the following six pages. The first takes you through the districts between the Royal Route and the Left Bank. The second leads through parks near the river in the Powiśle district, while the third takes you through the Saska Kępa district, on the Right Bank of the Vistula. This includes Skaryszewski Park and residential areas with striking modern architecture from the 1920s and 1930s.

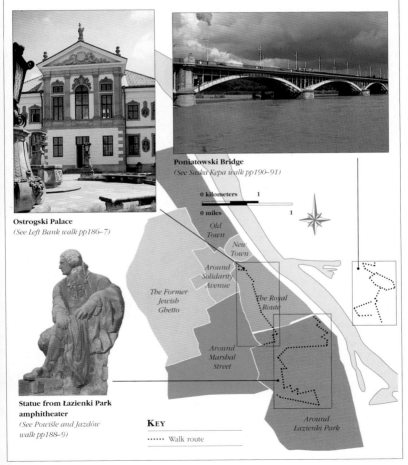

Ostrogski Palace
(See Left Bank walk pp186–7)

Poniatowski Bridge
(See Saska Kępa walk pp190–91)

0 kilometers 1
0 miles 1

Old Town
New Town
Around Solidarity Avenue
The Former Jewish Ghetto
The Royal Route
Around Marshal Street
Around Łazienki Park

Statue from Łazienki Park amphitheater
(See Powiśle and Jazdów walk pp188–9)

KEY

····· Walk route

◁ **Skaryszewski Park, on the Saska Kępa walk**

A Walk Along the Left Bank

THIS WALK WILL TAKE you along the crest of the escarpment, parallel to the River Vistula, along its Left Bank. It leads through the gardens of several palaces and monasteries, across the Military Museum's grounds, and through the Frascati district, ending at Three Crosses Square. A short distance farther on is Łazienki Park.

View from Mariensztat Square ②

Kazimierzowski Palace ⑤

From Castle Square to Kazimierzowski Palace

Start your walk at Castle Square. From here, turn toward the River Vistula and descend the steps by the bell tower of St. Anna's Church ① to the Mariensztat district. At the end of a narrow passage you will reach Sowia Street. Alternatively, after descending the steps, you can walk across Mariensztat Square ②. Sowia Street leads into Furmańska. Continue along this street, taking time to notice the former Carmelite gardens and park, at the rear of Namiestnikowski Palace ③.

The next right turn takes you onto Karowa Street. Climb halfway up the steps to the level of a spiral road, and pass under the arches of the 19th-century viaduct, with its statue of the mermaid of Warsaw ④. Then take the path that runs along the crest, at the rear of the university. The green expanse of Kazimierzowski Park ⑤ stretches below this point.

From Kazimierzowski Park to Powiśle Station

Walk through Kazimierzowski Park and cross Oboźna Street; then follow the escarpment. From this vantage point, you will be able to see Dynasy Park. Continue walking and you will join Bartoszewicza Street. At the end of this street, there is a flight of steps that takes you down to a footbridge over Tamka Street. This brings you to the back of Ostrogski Palace ⑥, which is now the home of the Frederic Chopin Museum. If you look down from the footbridge, you will see a square with a fountain at its center. This marks the location of an underground pool, in which the legendary golden duck of Warsaw *(see p19)* guarded a hoard of treasure. The treasure was hidden in dungeons under Ostrogski Palace, and according to the legend, its finder would be allowed to keep it after fulfilling a condition imposed by the golden duck. The condition was to spend 1,000 ducats, entirely for the finder's benefit and within 24 hours. The legend tells that one man succeeded in finding the treasure. He amused himself with his wealth, according to the condition, until he was down to the last ducat. At the final moment of his allotted

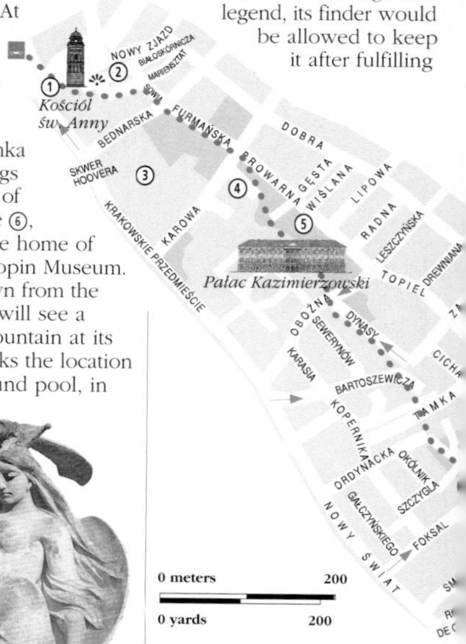

Mermaid of Warsaw statue ④ on top of the 19th-century viaduct

Bust from Ostrogski Palace ⑥

24 hours, he gave this single ducat to a beggar and so was denied the remaining hoard.

Once you have passed Ostrogski Palace, climb the steps to the park at the rear of the Academy of Music ⑦. Many years ago, a circus stood here that was famous for its wrestling competitions. In 1966, the present Academy of Music was built in its place. Continue by following the wall on the left, behind which lie the gardens of the Sisters of Charity ⑧. From the crest of the escarpment, you can observe the nuns tending their gardens, remote and totally shielded from the noise of nearby city life. On your right, behind the iron railings, you should be able to see

Pałac Ostrogskich
⑧
amoyskich

the pink and white edifice of Zamoyski Palace ⑨. Dating from 1877, the palace is surrounded by attractive gardens. Interestingly situated in the left wing of the palace is the Foksal Gallery, which exhibits contemporary art. Pick up the route again, and continue until you reach Jerozolimskie Avenue and Powiśle Station.

From Powiśle Station to Three Crosses Square
Before resuming the walk, music lovers might like to turn right and make a detour to visit a shop called Digital ⑩, the best place to buy records in central Warsaw.

Zamoyski Palace, viewed from the escarpment ⑨

Walk under the viaduct of Poniatowski Bridge ⑪, which is flanked by towers built in a Polish Renaissance style. It is the work of architects Stefan Szyller and Mieczysław Marszewski, and when built in 1914, was Europe's longest reinforced-concrete construction. From the underpass, you emerge onto the grounds of the Polish Military Museum ⑫, where many weapons and vehicles from World War II

are exhibited. Leave by the southern gate, and walk through Na Książęcem Park until you cross the footbridge over Książęca Street. To your left stretches an 18th-century park with its original pavilions. Continue along the escarpment, passing the house of the architect Bohdan Pniewski *(see pp110–11),* which he had built for his family. It is a fine example of modern, functional architecture. Currently it houses a branch of the Earth Sciences Museum ⑬.

From this point, the path along the escarpment becomes Na Skarpie Street. Walk on until you reach the right turn onto Bolesława Prusa Street. Here you will see the YMCA, which houses the Theater Buffo ⑭. Continue past the Sheraton Hotel, and turn right into Three Crosses Square ⑮.

KEY

• • • Walk route

✺ Viewing point

🚌 Bus stop

Insect in Baltic amber from the Earth Sciences Museum ⑬

TIPS FOR WALKERS

Starting point: Castle Square.
Length: 3 km (2 miles).
Getting there: Take buses 116, 122, 175, 195, 495, and 503 to Castle Square (Plac Zamkowy).
Stopping-off points: Cafés and restaurants at the Sheraton (Prusa Street), Tsubame (Foksal Street), and Literacka (Castle Square).

A Walk in Powiśle and Jazdów

MOST OF THIS WALK passes through the parks and attractive greenery of Jazdów and Powiśle. Before World War II, Powiśle was an industrial district; after the war, the large Rydz-Śmigły Park was created from the ruins. Continuing past the Polish Parliament (Sejm), the walk takes in the 19th-century Ujazdowski Park. The final stretch of the walk passes the entrance to Łazienki Park *(see pp162–3)* and the Botanical Gardens *(see p160)*, both just to the south of Agrykola.

From Poniatowski Bridge to Rydz-Śmigły Park

Holy Trinity Church ②

This walk begins at the western end of Poniatowski Bridge. From the streetcar stop at Wisłostradą, walk down the steps on the south side of the bridge to reach Wioślarska Street. As you walk along this street, with the River Vistula to your left, you will pass (on the right) the Neo-Classical pavilion that was erected in the mid-19th century as an abattoir. It now houses the office of the Asia and Pacific Museum ① *(see p89)*.

By the museum turn right onto Ludna Street, walk as far as the next junction, and then turn left onto Solec Street. At the end of this street, you will see Holy Trinity Church ②. This small Baroque church was built between 1699–1726. The interiors were largely destroyed in World War II and have been restored. But the 17th-century figure of Christ miraculously survived destruction and is an object of special veneration. A monastery was also built here for the Trinitarian Order, which was dissolved in 1795. These former monastery buildings are now home to the Warsaw Archdiocese Museum ③.

From the church, turn right down Gwardzistów Street and take the first left into the park. Continue through the park until you reach Bolesław Prus Avenue, a wide tree-lined road that links the district's green spaces. On this avenue stands the dramatic Military Engineers' Memorial ④, which takes the form of concrete pillars "shooting" into the air. It was designed by Stanisław Kulon in 1975.

Continue along the same avenue toward the top of the escarpment and Rydz-Śmigły Park. In the middle of this park is a viewing terrace ⑤ built in a Socialist Realist style in the Communist era. It provides delightful views of the Vistula and the city below.

Military Engineers' Memorial ④

From Rydz-Śmigły Park to Ujazdowski Park

From the viewing terrace, you can choose between two routes to continue the walk, one that takes you along the district's streets, and one that continues through parks.

To take the street route, walk downhill away from the terrace along Frascati Street. No. 2 on this street is an imposing modern building, completed in 1939 for the Chamber of Industry and Commerce and designed by Zdzisław Mączeński. It is now the Foreign Ministry ⑦. Turning left at the end of Frascati Street takes you onto Wiejska Street, featuring the Parliament buildings and the site of the 19th-century Ujazdowski Hospital, which was destroyed in World War II ⑨.

To take the park route from the Rydz-Śmigły viewing terrace, turn left onto Na Skarpie Street. The houses that

line this street were built for prominent Communist Party officials. Then continue along the rear of the buildings that house both chambers of Parliament, the Sejm and the Senate ⑥. On the left are prefabricated timber houses *(domki fińskie)* ⑧. These

The Senate in session ⑥

Prefabricated Russian-built house on Na Skarpie Street ⑧

were "presented" to Warsaw by the Soviet Union in 1945–6, during a severe shortage of housing in the city. Only a few of the original 350 houses remain. At the end of Na Skarpie, cross Górnośląska Street using the footbridge, turn right, and walk

Jazdów Street, and then past John Lennon Street, to reach the gate at the northern entrance to Ujazdowski Park.

Ujazdowski Park to Agrykola

Turn left through the park's Piękna Street gate. Statues in the park include Pius Weloński's *The Gladiator* ⑩, *Eve* by Edward Wittig ⑪, and the

the path along Piaseczyński Canal to reach Myśliwiecka Street. Turn right to come to Agrykola Street and the former guardhouse at the entrance

Ujazdowski Castle ⑬

to Łazienki Park ⑭ *(see pp162–3)*. From here you can enter the park or continue along Agrykola to the King Jan III Sobieski Monument ⑮ *(see p160)*. Beyond, past the

The plain façade of the former guardhouse in Łazienki Park ⑭

Paderewski Memorial ⑫. At the southern gate of the park, turn left and walk to the footbridge to cross Trasa Łazienkowska. On the far side is Ujazdowski Castle ⑬, which now houses the Modern Art Center *(see p159)*. The castle was built above a stronghold that predates the founding of Warsaw's Old Town. Take the steps behind the castle and

along Górnośląska Street to its intersection with Wiejska and Piękna streets. Here you join the street route. The two routes are linked midway by a path from Wiejska Street under the bridge that connects the Sejm with an office building. Continue along Piękna Street, and go past

entrance to the Botanical Gardens, is Na Rozdrożu Square, the end of this walk, where buses return to the city center.

KEY

••• Walk route

☀ Viewing point

🚌 Main bus route

TIPS FOR WALKERS

Starting point: Poniatowski Bridge.
Length: 4 km (2.5 miles).
Getting there: Buses 101, 102, 111, 117, 158, 517, and 521. Streetcar lines 7, 22, 24, and 25 alighting at the Wisłostrada stop.
Stopping-off point: Qchnia Artystyczna restaurant in Ujazdowski Castle.

Eve by Edward Wittig ⑪

(map labels) Św. Trójcy · SOLEC · Pomnik Sapera · KA ZAGÓRNA · NOŚLĄSKA · CZERNIAKOWSKA · ŁAZIENKOWSKA · ZA KUSOCIŃSKIEGO · KAWALERII · DRAGONÓW · SZWOLEŻERÓW · 29 LISTOPADA

0 meters 200
0 yards 200

A Two-Hour Walk in Saska Kępa

Saska Kępa is one of Warsaw's most attractive districts. It is divided from the Praga-Północ district by Kamionkowskie Lake and Skaryszewski Park, and from central Warsaw by the River Vistula. Historically, the river was even wider than its current 500 m (1,600 ft), and frequent floods converted Saska Kępa into an island *(kępa)*. August III (elector of Saxony and king of Poland) used this "island" from time to time as a picnic spot, and it is from this that it derived the name Saska (Saxon).

The Neo-Classical Tollhouse ①

Kamionek District

Beginning at the Neo-Classical Tollhouse ① on Grochowska Street, walk south toward the Church of Our Lady of Victories ②, which is immediately visible in the distance. Although construction of this church began in 1929, it is still not finished. The parish of Kamionek, created in the 13th century, is the oldest parish on this side of the Vistula. The first election of a Polish king was held here in 1572, when Henryk Walezjusz was elected.

The Three Days' Battle against the Swedes was fought here in 1656. This, and numerous later battles, are commemorated by a stone monument that is dedicated to the soldiers of various nationalities and creeds who were buried in the former graveyards surrounding the church.

From the church, walk in the direction of Kamionkowskie Lake ③, originally a tributary of the Vistula. Following the curve of the lake leads to Zieleniecka Street.

Skaryszewski Park

Walking around the lake and continuing south along Zieleniecka Street leads to Skaryszewski Park ④, which is also known as Paderewski Park. Designed by Franciszek Szanior and laid out between 1905 and 1922 in a Secessionist and early Modernist style, this is one of the most beautiful parks in Warsaw.

Following the edge of the lake – a favorite place for anglers – you will reach a memorial ⑤ to the crew of the *British Liberator 961*, from 178 Squadron RAF. This plane was shot down over the city during the Warsaw Uprising in 1944, while dropping supplies to the Home Army (Armia Krajowa). The memorial was unveiled in 1988 by Margaret Thatcher (then British prime minister).

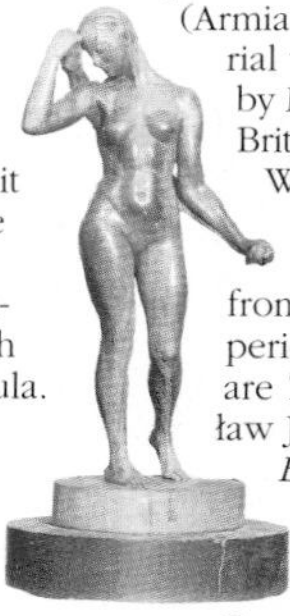

***The Bather* ⑦**

Within the park you can also see several sculptures dating from the 1918–39 interwar period. Among the finest are *The Dancer* by Stanisław Jackowski ⑥, *The Bather* by Olga Niewska ⑦, and Henryk Kuna's *Rhythm*. There is also a statue of Colonel Edward House ⑧, adviser to President Woodrow Wilson during World War I and a staunch supporter of Poland. This monument was recently recast, as the original was destroyed by the Communists. First unveiled in 1932, it was funded by the pianist and statesman Ignacy Paderewski. A bust of Paderewski stands by the path near the park gate leading onto Rondo Waszyngtona ⑨. Across this large square is a bust of the first president of the US, George Washington ⑩, unveiled in 1989.

Washington memorial ⑩

Saska Kępa

Continue south from Rondo Waszyngtona along Francuska Street, which is the main shopping thoroughfare of Saska Kępa. This street and the surrounding district were almost entirely developed between 1918 and 1939.

The street's Modernist-style houses ⑪ are generally only a few stories high and are set among green shrubbery.

At the corner of Obrońców Street, you can take a detour from the route by turning left past spacious villas from the 1930s. Take the third street on the left, Nobla, and turn right at the end of the street to reach the Church of Our Lady of Perpetual Succor ⑫.

This church was built over a long period between 1938 and 1956, and was designed by Piotr Lubiński, Józef Łowiński, and Jan Bogusławski. The appearance of its façade was influenced by the style of provincial churches of the Middle Ages. The nave is surprisingly high, while the ceiling is supported by concrete columns and arches.

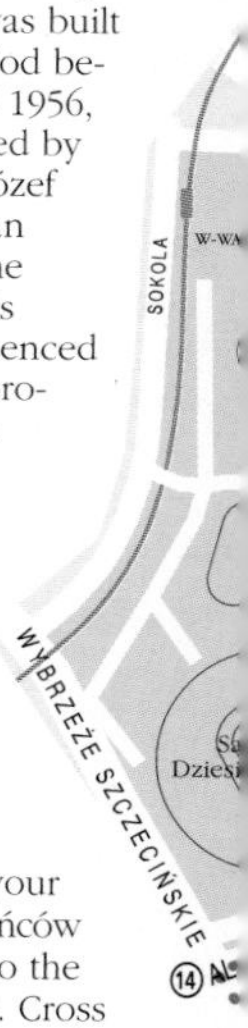

Leaving the church, retrace your steps along Obrońców Street to return to the main walk route. Cross Francuska Street, and then turn right onto narrow Katowicka Street. This street features several avant-garde villas that date from the late 1920s and the 1930s.

One particularly interesting house is at No. 7a Katowicka Street. Built in 1938 for the Avenarius family, it was designed by Jerzy Szanajca, Stanisław Barylski, and Bohdan Lachert. The house boasts a glass-fronted concrete staircase, which is covered with a flat, perforated concrete roof.

established by the renowned 20th-century Modernist architect Le Corbusier.

Other buildings that line this street boast interesting decorative features dating from the 1940s. Several of the villas currently belong to the German Embassy.

When you come to the end of Katowicka Street, at the corner of Walecznych Street, turn left and continue along this street until you come to the Miedzeszyński Embankment, which runs alongside the River Vistula. From here, there is a good view across the river, including buildings in the low-lying Powiśle district and, beyond, the rooftops and spires that dominate central Warsaw.

Interior of the Church of Our Lady of Perpetual Succor ⑫

The avant-garde Villa Lachert in Katowicka Street ⑬

disrepair, but after 1989 a new role emerged for it: the stadium became Eastern Europe's largest open-air market, known as the "Saxon Fair." Traders from across the whole of Europe and even from Asia traveled to the market to buy and sell a wide range of merchandise. Continuing past the stadium, you will come to the Socialist Realist statue entitled *The Relay* ⑯. From here, it is a short walk back to Rondo Waszyngtona, where there are numerous bus and streetcar connections running to central Warsaw.

The Relay ⑯

Tenth Anniversary Stadium

Turn right when you come to the eastern end of Poniatowski Bridge ⑭ and, from there, continue back toward Saska Kępa, heading away from the river. The twin towers of the Poniatowski Bridge were rebuilt in 1988, following the original, turn-of-the-century design, which was by Stefan Szyller.

Passing underneath the bridge, you will be faced by the massive Tenth Anniversary Stadium ⑮. The stadium was built in 1954–5 to mark the tenth anniversary of the end of World War II and the first decade of Communist rule. The architects were Jerzy Hryniewiecki, Marek Leykam, and Czesław Rajewski. Rubble from the wartime destruction of the city's buildings was used to construct the foundations of this new stadium.

Soon after the stadium was completed in 1955, it was used to stage the opening ceremony of the World Festival of Youth. After years of isolation imposed by Communism, it was the first opportunity for Poles to meet people from all over the world, and these visitors appeared highly exotic to local citizens. In later years, the stadium gradually fell into

At No. 11 Katowicka Street stands the two-story Villa Lachert ⑬, which Bohdan Lachert designed as his private residence. Constructed in 1929, it is based on the design principles that were

KEY

• • • Walk route

🚌 Main bus stops

TIPS FOR WALKERS

Starting point: Zamoyski Street by the toolhouses and the Church of Our Lady of Victories in Kamionek.
Length: 5 km (3 miles).
Getting there: Streetcar no. 6 arrives at the beginning of the walk, while no. 25 has a stop within 100 m (100 yards). Return from Rondo Waszyngtona by streetcars 7, 9, 22, 24, and 25 or buses 101, 102, 111, 117, and 158.
Stopping-off points: During the summer, a café is open in Skaryszewski Park, which also has plenty of benches and delightful spots in which to sit. Otherwise, there are numerous cafés and bars in Rondo Waszyngtona and along Francuska Street.

TRAVELERS'
NEEDS

WHERE TO STAY

UNTIL QUITE RECENTLY, it was difficult to find accommodations in Warsaw, and hotel standards were far behind those of Western Europe. Many new hotels have opened since 1989, but these are mostly deluxe and very expensive. They also tend to be part of international chains and therefore do not reflect local tradition. With a few exceptions, mid-price hotels are fairly anonymous but comfortable, and are at least centrally located. A growing range of budget-priced options, typically converted from workers' hostels, office buildings, barracks, and student residence halls, are located mainly in the suburbs, and there is still a shortage of inexpensive accommodations in the city center. The hotel listings on pages 200–203 cover a range of options, with hotels listed by area and in order of price. Accommodations can also be arranged in private houses *(see p197)*, many of which are centrally located. Some booking agencies also handle property rentals.

Youth hostels and campsites provide other inexpensive options *(see pp196–7)*. The facilities are often limited, and locations are not always very convenient.

Porter at the exclusive Bristol Hotel

The elegantly restored reception area at the Bristol Hotel

WHERE TO LOOK

WARSAW IS A sprawling city, so the city center (*śródmieście*), close to the main tourist attractions and the best stores and restaurants, is the most convenient place to stay. Although this part of town has a large number of hotels, they are not concentrated in any particular areas. An ideal location is around Krakowskie Przedmieście and Plac Piłsudskiego (Piłsudski Square). This is Warsaw's most historic part, and is only a short walk from the Old Town (Stare Miasto).

Accommodations in this area are provided mainly by international chain hotels of varying standards, or by large, plain hotels that are aimed at foreign traveling salesmen, often from the ex-Soviet countries, who come to trade in Warsaw's markets. There are only a few hotels in the city that still have original interiors and their own unique atmosphere. A prime example of one that does possess these qualities is the exclusive Bristol Hotel, which has beautifully restored Secessionist-style interiors. There are much cheaper hotels in the same area, but they usually need modernization. Small roadside hotels and motels in the suburbs have a friendly atmosphere and are often set in pleasant gardens. However, staying in the suburbs involves a time-consuming journey to reach the center of Warsaw.

BOOKING AHEAD

IN PLANNING A VISIT to Warsaw, it is advisable to book your hotel in advance. Finding accommodations on arrival may be difficult, especially in June and July, from September to November, and during religious holidays. During these periods, hotel reservations should be made several weeks ahead.

The grand and stately setting of the restaurant at the Polonia Hotel

The modern hotel lobby of the Mercure

FACILITIES

Hotel rooms in poland tend to be rather small as a rule, though those that have been refurbished and modernized usually have en suite showers or bathrooms. Most of these hotels are equipped with televisions in each room, and some also have VCRs. There is generally a laundry service at most hotels.

The more expensive hotels also offer 24-hour room service and have a minibar in each room. Some hotels are able to accommodate pets, should you be taking them on your visit to Warsaw.

Guests are usually asked to vacate their rooms by midday when checking out. But if you are departing later, you may leave luggage with the hotel's concierge. The majority of hotel staff in Warsaw speak English or German.

DISCOUNTS

Prices in all of Warsaw's more comfortable hotels are quite high, and are quoted in US dollars. Hence in the hotel listings (see pp200–203), the price categories are given in dollars. However, many hotels, including the more exclusive ones, offer weekend discount packages and special rates for children. Various discounts are also offered by hotels belonging to international chains, such as the Intercontinental and

Forum. Sometimes discounts can be negotiated in advance with the hotel, especially if visiting outside the peak seasons of summer and autumn. Prices are charged per room, and discounts are rarely offered for single occupancy of a double room – and in Warsaw there are relatively few single rooms available.

HIDDEN EXTRAS

Most hotels quote prices that include both VAT (which is currently fluctuating between 7 and 22 percent) and service. In Poland it is not customary to tip staff, except in the capital's more exclusive hotels.

A choice of set breakfast menus and Swedish-style buffets are a standard feature of most hotels. Some hotels charge extra for breakfast, whether served in the room or in the hotel restaurant – check this when you book in.

Most hotels have direct-dial telephones in the rooms for the use of guests. Bear in mind, however, that international calls from hotels usually prove expensive, as they incur a high surcharge.

Public telephones are significantly cheaper, and also offer international direct dialing. Public phones are easily found throughout the city center and work using phone cards (see p242), which are readily available from newsstands and kiosks.

DISABLED VISITORS

Only a few of Warsaw's hotels provide adapted rooms and facilities for aiding the disabled visitor. Detailed information on hotels that offer wheelchair access can be found on page 244.

The National Council for the Disabled (Krajowa Rada Osób Niepełnosprawnych) can also be contacted for further advice on hotels, as well as specific information on sightseeing in Warsaw and throughout Poland (see p244).

TRAVELING WITH CHILDREN

Warsaw is generally a child-friendly city (see pp232–3), and most hotels welcome children warmly.

Many offer a reduced price for children, while some hotels provide free accommodations for children up to the age of three. In a few cases this even extends up to the age of 14, as long as the child is traveling with its parents. It is best to inquire about any discounts that are available when making the reservation.

It is also common for children to share their parents' room, often for no extra charge. Hotels are used to this, and will generally provide a

An opulent, if slightly faded, room in the Europejski Hotel

folding bed for this purpose. Many hotel restaurants are very accommodating, though they may not offer a special children's menu, and highchairs are relatively rare. The biggest problem, however, is that it tends to be quite difficult to find a baby-sitter.

DIRECTORY

USEFUL ADDRESSES

American Travel Abroad
250 West 57 Street.
New York,
NY 10107.
((212) 586-5230.

LOT Polish Airlines
500 Fifth Ave.
New York,
NY 10036.
((800) 223-0593 .

Orbis Polish Travel Bureau
342 Madison Ave.
New York,
NY 10173.
((212) 867-5011.

Polish Consulate
233 Madison Ave.
New York,
NY 10016.
((212) 889-8360.
1530 North Lake Shore Drive.
Chicago, IL 60610.
((312) 337-8166.
12400 Wilshire Blvd.
Los Angeles, CA 90025.
((310) 442-8500.

Polish Embassy
2640 16 Street. NW.
Washington,
DC 20009.
((202) 234-3800.

Polish National Tourist Office
275 Madison Ave.
New York,
NY 10016.
((212) 338-9412.

ACCOMMODATIONS AGENCIES

Almatur
Kopernika 23.
Map 2 E4.
(826 26 39.
◯ Jun–Sep.

Gromada Tours
Plac Powstańców.
Map 2 D4.
(827 92 51.

Mazurkas Travel
Nowogrodzka 24/26.
Map 6 D1.
(629 12 49.

Długa 8/14.
Map 1 C2.
(635 51 82.

Orbis
Marszałkowska 142.
Map 1 C4.
(827 80 31.

Syrena Unilevel
(accommodation in private properties)
Krucza 17.
Map 6 D2.
(628 75 40.

Warsaw and National Accommodation Agency (Warszawska i Krajowa Agencja Noclegowa)
(telephone inquiries only)
(641 53 66.
◯ 10am–5pm Mon–Fri.
(662 64 89.
◯ 5–11pm Mon–Fri, 10am–5pm Sat–Sun.

Warsaw Tourist Information Center (Warszawskie Centrum Informacji Turystycznej)
Plac Zamkowy 1/13.
Map 2 D2.
(635 18 81.
◯ 9am–6pm Mon–Fri, 10am–6pm Sat, 11am–6pm Sun.

APARTMENTS AND ROOMS TO RENT

These agents deal with leases that are usually of at least several months' duration.

Agencja Kaczmarczyk
Aleje Jerozolimskie 31.
Map 6 D1.
(625 20 20.

Drągowski Properties (Drągowski Nieruchomości)
Jasna 10.
Map 1 C4.
(827 30 02.

Marszałkowska 93.
Map 6 D3.
(622 30 33.

Tamka 37.
Map 2 E4.
(826 58 80.

Śliska 3.
Map 1 B5.
(624 88 56.

Małolepszy Agency (Agencja Małolepszy)
Krucza 16/22.
Map 6 D2.
(622 25 62.

Nobil House Agency (Agencja Nobil House)
Aleje Ujazdowskie 20
Floor 10.
Map 6 E2.
(625 40 59.

Piotrowski Agency (Agencja Piotrowski)
Zurawia 24.
Map 6 D2.
(621 47 46.

Strzelczyk Brothers (Bracia Strzelczyk)
Plac Konstytucji 4.
Map 6 D2.
(620 37 39.

Unikat
Krucza 16/22.
Map 6 D2.
(628 70 95.

Marszałkowska 83.
Map 6 D2.
(628 90 56.

STUDENT HALLS AND BOARDING HOUSES

Duet Medical Academy Students' Hall No. 1 (Dom Studenta Duet nr 1 Akademii Medycznej)
Batalionu "Pięść" 9.
(36 03 71.

Grosik Students' Hall (Dom Studenta Grosik)
Madalińskiego 31/33.
(49 23 02.

Hermes Students' Hall (Dom Studenta Hermes)
Madalińskiego 6/8.
(49 67 22.

No. 9 Coeducational Boarding House (Bursa Koedukacyjna nr 9)
Rzymowskiego 36.
(43 19 95.

Oasis Students' Hall (Dom Studenta Oaza)
Madalińskiego 39/43.
(49 24 01.

YOUTH HOSTELS

Karolkowa 53A.
(632 88 29.
◯ all year.

Międzyparkowa 4/6.
(831 17 66.
◯ Apr–mid-Nov.

Smolna 30.
(827 89 52.
◯ all year.

Wał Miedzeszyński 397.
(617 88 51.
◯ Apr 15–Oct 15.

CAMPSITES

Bitwy Warszawskiej 1920 r.
(23 27 48.
◯ all year.

Grochowska 1.
(610 63 66.
◯ all year.

Powsin.
(42 10 91.
◯ late Apr–early Oct.

Żwirki i Wigury 3/5.
(25 43 91.
◯ May–Sep.

Apartments and Rooms to Rent

The number of rooms available to rent in Warsaw has risen considerably in the past few years. They offer an inexpensive and popular option, particularly when located near the city center. An average price for a night in a private house or apartment is $10 for one person, and $15 for two. However, these prices do not include extras such as breakfast.

Agencies usually offer a wide choice of accommodation, and some offer longer term rents. When making a reservation, specify the range of facilities you require and the preferred district. Praga-Północ (Praga-North) and other large housing projects in outlying areas are not recommended. One exception is Ursynów Natolin, which is linked to the city center (*śródmieście*) by Warsaw's metro service.

Agencies expect to be paid in cash and issue a receipt that is then presented to the landlord. Bank transfers can be arranged, but only for longer term rentals.

Accommodation in student halls is sometimes available in the summer, coordinated by the **Almatur** agency.

Youth Hostels

Warsaw has two youth hostels that are open all year, with another two open only during the peak season. They are all relatively clean, and mainly offer dormitory-style accommodation. Bookings should be made two or three days prior to arrival. The busiest periods are Fridays and Saturdays, but also during spring and autumn, when hostels are taken over by school trips. Hostels close between 10am and 4pm. You should check in before 10pm, as arriving any later may be problematic. Prices are below $10 a night for a bed in a communal room. Hostels offer discounts if you have an **IYHF** (International Youth Hostel Federation) card.

Campsites

Most campsites are located on the outskirts of Warsaw; the only exception is the site at Żwirki i Wigury. Facilities are fairly standard, though in addition to space to pitch a tent, or park a trailer or camper, they provide cabin accommodation. Campsites are usually open from May to October. One campsite that is open for tents throughout the year is at Grochowska Street. This is near the Warsaw to Moscow trunk road, 8 km (5 miles) east of the city center. The city's most attractive campsite is Powsin. Open only for the main tourist season, Powsin is set in a forest, close to the Botanical Gardens. Information on Warsaw's campsites, and their facilities, is available from the **Warsaw Tourist Information Center (Waszawskie Centrum Informacji Turystycznej)**.

uite of rooms at the Karat Hotel, near Łazienki Park

Using the Listings

The hotels included on pages 201–203 are listed in order of price, from the cheapest to the most expensive. The symbols summarize the facilities at each hotel:

🚿 rooms with shower and/or bathroom

[1] single room

👪 rooms for more than two persons or with space for an additional bed

[24] 24-hour room service

[TV] TV in every room

🚭 rooms for nonsmokers

🏞 rooms with a scenic view

❄ all rooms air-conditioned

🏋 gymnasium

🏊 swimming pool

💼 business facilities: including information service, fax, desk, and telephone in the room; conference room

👶 facilities for children; cots available

♿ wheelchair access

⇅ elevator

[P] parking

🌳 garden or terrace

🍸 bar

🍴 restaurant

ℹ tourist information

💳 credit cards welcome

AE American Express

DC Diners Club

MC MasterCard

V VISA

JCB Japanese Credit Bureau

Price categories for a double with bathroom or shower per night, including breakfast, service, and 7 percent VAT:

[$] up to $35

[$][$] $35–70

[$][$][$] $70–105

[$][$][$][$] $105–140

[$][$][$][$][$] over $140

Warsaw's Best: Hotels

THE NUMBER OF HOTELS in Warsaw has increased
considerably over the past few years. New
luxury hotels have been built, while many older
establishments have also been refurbished and
modernized. The standards of service and range
of facilities have generally improved, although
there are still exceptions. The selection of hotels
on these two pages (all of which have been
reviewed in the listings section) offer a very
enjoyable, albeit expensive, stay in Warsaw.

Mercure-Fryderyk Chopin
*This contemporary hotel offers
French cuisine in Le Balzac
restaurant, and an international
menu in Le Stanislaus (see p203).*

*The Former
Jewish Ghetto*

Holiday Inn
*Having opened in 1989,
this was Warsaw's first
international standard
hotel (see p202).*

Marriott
*Various restaurants,
as well as business and
sports facilities, have helped
establish this deluxe hotel
as one of the most popular
(see pp202–3).*

Jan III Sobieski
*This hotel features a modern
interpretation of traditional
Varsovian architecture (see p202).*

Europejski
With a mid-19th-century façade, this is the city's oldest hotel. The restaurant and patisserie are also well established (see p202).

Bristol
Following extensive renovation, this is Warsaw's most luxurious hotel, combining modern facilities with beautiful Secessionist interiors (see p202).

Sheraton
This deluxe venue is the latest international chain hotel to open in Warsaw (see p203).

Old Town

The Royal Route

Around Łazienki Park

Around Marshal Street

0 kilometers 1

0 miles 1

Victoria
With its renowned restaurant, the Victoria also has attractive modern interiors (see p203).

Choosing a Hotel

THIS CHART is a quick reference guide to the hotels that we have reviewed on the following pages. They are a selection of the best hotels in and around Warsaw, in terms of value, location, facilities, and service. The selection takes in a wide range of hotels right across the price spectrum, and there should be a choice to suit all needs. For information on other types of accommodations see pages 194–7.

	Price	Number of Rooms	Double Rooms Available	Business Facilities	Facilities for Children	Recommended Restaurants	Shops Nearby	Quiet Location	24-Hour Room Service
CITY CENTER *(see pp201–3)*									
Belfer	$	216							
Garnizonowy No. 1	$	48					●		
Harenda	$	40					●		
Saski	$	105					●		
Dom Chłopa	$$	236					●		●
Grand	$$	319		●	●		●		●
Karat	$$	39	●					●	
Maria	$$	24	●		●				●
MDM	$$	111		●		●	●		
Metropol	$$	192		●			●		●
Polonia	$$	234					●		●
Warszawa	$$	144					●		
Parkowa	$$$	44			●			●	
Solec	$$$	147		●	●				●
Europejski	$$$$	220	●	●	●	●	●		●
Forum	$$$$	733		●	●		●		●
Bristol	$$$$$	206	●	●	●	●	●		●
Holiday Inn	$$$$$	336	●	●	●		●		●
Jan III Sobieski	$$$$$	414	●	●	●	●	●		●
Marriott	$$$$$	521	●	●	●	●	●		●
Mercure–Fryderyk Chopin	$$$$$	250	●	●	●	●	●		●
Sheraton	$$$$$	350		●	●		●	●	●
Victoria Intercontinental	$$$$$	365	●	●	●	●	●		●
FARTHER AFIELD *(see p203)*									
Agra	$	40						●	
Felix	$$	257							●
Gromada	$$$	127							●
Novotel	$$$	144			●	●			●
Vera	$$$	155				●			●
Zajazd Napoleoński	$$$	24							
BEYOND WARSAW *(see p203)*									
Eden	$$	46							
Konstancja	$$	44				●			

Price categories for a double room with bathroom or shower, including breakfast, service, and 7 percent VAT. Hotel prices in Warsaw are quoted in US dollars:

$ under $35
$$ $35–$70
$$$ $70–$105
$$$$ $105–$140
$$$$$ over $140

BUSINESS FACILITIES
Including a telephone in the room, plus information service, fax, and conference facilities.

FACILITIES FOR CHILDREN
Including cots or folding beds in the rooms.

RECOMMENDED RESTAURANTS
Restaurants near the hotel that have excellent reputations for their cuisine and unusual or historic settings.

CITY CENTER

Belfer

Wybrzeże Kościuszkowski 31/33.
Map 2 E3. **(** 625 05 71. **FAX** 625
26 00. **TX** 81 64 20. **Rooms:** 216.
⬛ 72. **①** **⊞** **↻** **▮▮** **▮** **$**

The dilapidated rooms of this former teachers' hostel do not create a very good first impression. However, the hotel is conveniently located, near the city center and the Old Town, and rooms on the upper floors have good views along the Vistula and its scenic banks. Not all bathrooms are *en suite*, and rooms on the east side of the building can be noisy.

Garnizonowy No. 1

Mazowiecka 10. **Map** 2 D4.
(683 35 65. **Rooms:** 48. **TV** **↻**
Y **▮▮** **$**

Originally a garrison hotel, this has been open to the general public for the last few years, but has not really developed beyond its military origins. The staff still cultivates manners that are reminiscent of army barracks, with a receptionist who deigns to smile on only rare occasions. Smells from the kitchen hit you as soon as you cross the threshold. The rooms are not very clean and lack private bathrooms, which are instead situated along the corridors. On the other hand, the hotel has competitive rates and is conveniently located, close to the city center.

Harenda

Krakowskie Przedmieście 4/6. **Map** 2
D4. **(** 826 00 71, 826 00 72, 826 00
73. **FAX** 826 26 25. **Rooms:** 40. **⬛** 15.
① **Y** **▮▮** **▮** **$** AE, DC, MC, V, JCB. **$**

Located above an antique shop and auction house, this small hotel is on the second floor of the former Tourist Hostel (Dom Turysty). There is no elevator, but the location is excellent, as Krakowskie Przedmieście is adjacent to the Old Town, and also happens to be one of the most beautiful streets in Warsaw's historic center. Only a few rooms have a private bathroom, and even these are modest. Meanwhile, double rooms are quite small and can barely contain beds, a table, and chairs. Another option the Harenda offers is dormitory-style accommodation, without a private bathroom. However, the conditions are more reminiscent of a campsite than a hotel. The Harenda does feature a restaurant, which has a good reputation; an English-style pub; and, if you are truly desperate for Western food, a Burger King.

Saski

Plac Bankowy 1. **Map** 3 C5. **(** 620
46 11. **FAX** 620 11 15. **Rooms:** 105.
⬛ 6. **①** **▮▮** **Y** **▮▮** **▮** AE. **$**

While the hotel occupies an attractive building from the mid-19th century, it is currently awaiting much-needed refurbishment. The main attractions of the Saski are inexpensive prices and its location, by the Saxon Gardens (Ogród Saski) and the Old Town.

Dom Chłopa

Plac Powstańców Warszawy 2. **Map** 2
D3. **(** 827 92 51. **FAX** 625 21 40.
Rooms: 236. **⬛** 128. **①** **⊞** **Y**
Y **▮▮** **▮** **$** AE, DC, MC, JCB. **$$**

The antiquated name ("Peasants' House") stems from the Communist era, when the government tried to forge better relations between industrial workers and peasants. The hotel still retains some of that character, as it continues to attract Polish country folk visiting the capital. Designed by Bohdan Pniewski, an outstanding architect of the mid-20th century *(see pp210–11)*, this is one of the more interesting examples of late 1950s design. However, the large lobby is quite gloomy, and the restaurant is still haunted by ghosts of the late Polish People's Republic. Fortunately, rooms are currently undergoing modernization.

Grand

Krucza 28. **Map** 2 D3. **(** 629 40
51. **FAX** 621 97 24. **TX** 81 34 22.
Rooms: 319. **⬛** **①** **⊞** **TV** **↻** **≋** **Y**
▮▮ **▮** **◪** **▮** **▮▮** **▮** **$** AE,
DC, MC, V. **$$**

This is something of a misnomer, as not much grandeur is offered in this large-scale building, which dates from the late 1950s. Originally the roof was to include a helicopter landing pad, which fortunately was never constructed. The rooms are indifferently decorated, with those on the top floors providing the most interesting views. The main attraction, for gamblers at least, is the extensive gaming club in the Grand.

Karat

Słoneczna 37. **Map** 6 E4. **(** 601 44
11, 49 84 54. **FAX** 49 52 94. **Rooms:**
39. **⬛** **①** **⊞** **TV** **↻** **Y** **▮▮** **$** **$**

This is a newly renovated hotel located on a residential street lined with picturesque villas, by the banks of the Vistula, and close to Łazienki Park. Rooms are larger than average for Warsaw hotels, and prices are relatively low. Stylish white bathrooms are immaculately maintained.

Maria

Aleja Jana Pawła II 71. **Map** 3 A3.
(38 40 62. **FAX** 38 38 40. **TX** 81
77 57. **Rooms:** 22. **⬛** **①** **⊞** **24**
TV **✿** **P** **Y** **▮▮** **$** AE, DC, MC,
V, JCB. **$$**

This small hotel, set at the northern edge of the town center, has a homey atmosphere. The rooms are large and tastefully furnished, as well as being clean.

MDM

Plac Konstytucji 1. **Map** 6 D2. **(**
621 62 11. **FAX** 621 41 73. **TX** 81 48
71. **Rooms:** 111. **⬛** **①** **⊞** **TV** **▤**
◪ **✿** **↻** **Y** **▮▮** **▮** **◪** **▮** AE, DC,
MC, V, JCB. **$$**

The MDM is a good example of Socialist Realism *(see p31)* and is located in Plac Konstytucji, which is midway between Łazienki Park and the Central Railroad Station (Dworzec Centralny). Following thorough modernization, all rooms now have sparkling clean bathrooms *en suite* and pleasant, but modest, furnishings. A small lobby leads to a large restaurant, the Ugarit, with interiors inspired by Syrian architecture. The hotel is surrounded by a range of good stores and the most interesting urban development of the 1950s, the Marshal Street Residential Area (Marszałkowska Dzielnica Mieszkaniowa), which gave the hotel its name *(see p132)*.

Metropol

Marszałkowska 99a. **Map** 6 D2.
(628 72 41. **FAX** 628 66 22. **TX** 81
48 74. **Rooms:** 192. **⬛** **①** **⊞** **24**
TV **≋** **◪** **✿** **P** **Y** **▮▮** **▮** **◪**
▮ AE, DC, MC, V, JCB. **$$**

The Metropol is situated in the heart of Warsaw, just a few minutes' walk from the Central Railroad Station (Dworzec Centralny). Built in the 1960s, the Metropol is an architectural monstrosity but, by way of compensation, it does have clean rooms with decent bathrooms and prices are modest. The company that owns the Metropol also owns the Hotel Polonia, which is nearby.

Polonia

Aleje Jerozolimskie 45. **Map** 2 E5.
(628 72 41. **FAX** 628 66 22. **TX** 81
36 27. **Rooms:** 234. **⬛** 147. **⊞** **24**
Y **▮▮** **▮** **◪** AE, DC, MC, V, JCB. **$$**

Built between 1909 and 1913 in a distinctive Beaux-Arts style *(see p136)*, the Polonia features some opulent interiors, particularly in the lobby and in its restaurant. During the immediate postwar period, the hotel provided accommodations for several embassies and other diplomatic agencies.

For key to symbols, *see p197*

Unfortunately, refurbishment that took place during the 1960s deprived the rooms of much of their character. However, the building is now due for further renovation, which may improve matters. The Polonia is in a central location, by the Palace of Culture and Science (Pałac Kultury i Nauki) and next to the 1960s Metropol Hotel.

Warszawa

Plac Powstańców Warszawy 9. **Map** 6 D1. ☎ *826 94 21.* [FAX] *827 18 73.* [TX] *81 38 57.* ***Rooms:*** *144.* 🛁 *88.* [1] ⊞ ❄ ⇅ 🍸 🍴 💳 *AE, DC, MC, V, JCB.* [$][$]

Dating from 1934, this was once the tallest building in Poland *(see p131)* but was overtaken by the towering Palace of Culture and Science (Pałac Kultury i Nauki). Following postwar reconstruction, the building was converted into a hotel, but not all rooms include private bathrooms. The currency-exchange counter offers some of the city's best rates.

Parkowa

Belwederska 46/50. **Map** 6 E4. ☎ *694 80 00, 41 60 21.* [FAX] *41 60 29.* ***Rooms:*** *44.* 🛁 [1] ⊞ [TV] ❄ ☰ 🏢 ⇅ [P] 🍴 🌿 💳 *AE, DC, MC, V, JCB.* [$][$][$]

In its previous incarnation, the Parkowa was a garrison hotel and was regarded as luxurious by officers of the former Warsaw Pact countries. It is now open to the general public, having undergone thorough modernization, even though the staff continues the unhelpful attitudes fostered during the years of Communism. However, the hotel's location does make up for its shortcomings. Rooms on the upper floors provide some magnificent views over the Russian Embassy gardens, as well as the Ministry of Defense grounds and Łazienki Park *(see pp162–3).*

Solec

Zagórna 1. **Map** 6 F2. ☎ *625 44 00.* [FAX] *625 44 24.* [TX] *81 46 76.* ***Rooms:*** *147.* 🛁 [1] ⊞ [24] ☰ 🚭 🏋 🚸 ⇅ 🌿 🍸 🍴 [i] 💳 *AE, DC, MC, V, JCB.* [$][$][$]

Next to a park and the River Vistula, this two-story hotel was built in the 1970s. The hotel's facilities include a shopping arcade with a restaurant, a bar, and a few stores. Rooms are relatively modern, but somewhat sterile. This is also one of the very few hotels in central Warsaw with its own garden. Although the garden is quite small and is situated by the busy and noisy Wisłostrada trunk road, it provides a restful oasis.

Europejski

Krakowskie Przedmieście 13. **Map** 2 D3. ☎ *826 20 51.* [FAX] *826 11 11.* [TX] *81 36 15.* ***Rooms:*** *220.* 🛁 [1] ⊞ [TV] 🚭 🌿 ❄ 🏋 🚸 ⇅ 🍸 🍴 [i] 💳 *AE, DC, MC, V, JCB.* [$][$][$][$]

With its Neo-Renaissance façade, this is Warsaw's oldest hotel, built in stages between 1855 and 1877. In 1939 it provided a refuge for King Zog of Albania, after he was overthrown by the Italians. However, having been rebuilt from its wartime ruins, the interiors lost their former character. Rooms can be quite small, though all have minibars. The hotel has fallen into a somewhat dilapidated state in recent years and is now due for modernization. The restaurant has a good reputation, and the ground-floor café serves pastries made on the premises, renowned as some of Warsaw's finest. Another coffee bar in the hotel, facing Krakowskie Przedmieście, also offers these famous pastries.

Forum

Nowogrodzka 24/26. **Map** 5 B2. ☎ *23 03 64, 621 02 71.* [FAX] *625 04 76.* [TX] *81 47 04.* ***Rooms:*** *733.* 🛁 [1] [24] [TV] 🚭 ❄ ☰ 🏢 🏊 🏋 🚸 ♿ ⇅ [P] 🍸 🍴 [i] 💳 *AE, DC, MC, V, JCB.* [$][$][$][$]

This is Warsaw's largest hotel, and was built by a Swedish company in the mid-1970s. Unfortunately, rooms are small, with rather uninteresting furniture dating from the Polish People's Republic. Some rooms do have minibars, and the newly refurbished bathrooms are very good. There is a large lobby on the ground floor, with cafés, restaurants, travel agents, and other shops. Rooms situated above the 20th floor offer superb views of central Warsaw.

Bristol

Krakowskie Przedmieście 42/44. **Map** 2 D3. ☎ *625 25 25.* [FAX] *625 25 77.* ***Rooms:*** *206.* 🛁 [24] [TV] 🚭 ☰ 🏢 🏊 🏋 🚸 ♿ ⇅ ❄ 🍸 🍴 [i] 🌿 💳 *AE, DC, MC, V, JCB.* [$][$][$][$][$]

The most exclusive hotel in Warsaw is listed as a national monument. Its beautiful Secession-style architecture was designed by the Viennese architect Otto Wagner the Younger. Since first opening in 1900, the hotel has received a great many celebrities, including Marlene Dietrich, Douglas Fairbanks, Jr., Edvard Grieg, Richard Strauss, and Enrico Caruso. The restaurant has hosted former French president Charles de Gaulle and the shah of Iran, Reza Pahlavi. Following extensive restoration, the Bristol was officially reopened in December 1992 by Margaret Thatcher. Prices are very high at this hotel, but it does offer a superlative experience. The Malinowa restaurant provides exemplary Polish and French cuisine, and Italian food is served in the Marconi restaurant. The Bristol has an ideal location, close to the Old Town, and even pets are welcome.

Holiday Inn

Złota 48/54. **Map** 5 B1. ☎ *620 65 34, 620 03 41.* [FAX] *830 05 69.* [TX] *81 74 18.* ***Rooms:*** *336.* 🛁 [1] [24] [TV] 🚭 ☰ 🏢 🏋 🚸 ♿ ⇅ [P] 🍸 🍴 [i] 💳 *AE, DC, MC, V, JCB.* [$][$][$][$][$]

Opened in 1989, the Holiday Inn was Warsaw's first Western-standard hotel and features a glasss-enclosed lobby full of greenery, as well as restaurants, cafés, and stores. Some rooms offer extra space, gained from triangular bay windows. The hotel is by the Central Railroad Station and the Palace of Culture and Science.

Jan III Sobieski

Plac Zawiszy 1. **Map** 5 B2. ☎ *658 44 44.* [FAX] *659 88 28.* [TX] *81 57 65.* ***Rooms:*** *413.* 🛁 [1] ⊞ [24] [TV] 🚭 ☰ 🏢 🏋 🚸 ♿ ⇅ [P] 🍸 🍴 [i] 🌿 💳 *AE, DC, MC, JCB.* [$][$][$][$][$]

Postmodern façades, mixed with avant-garde interiors (at least by Polish standards), made this hotel a controversial subject when it opened in 1992 *(see p105).* However, the building was soon accepted by locals and has also blended into the city landscape. A spacious lobby is decorated with pink marble and colorful mosaics, and an open-plan restaurant includes an atrium and a water feature. The hotel commemorates its namesake, King Jan III Sobieski *(see pp22–3),* with a marble statue, together with a selection of old paintings and framed copies of 17th-century drawings. Rooms are decorated with wicker, cherry wood, and marble furniture. It is worth requesting a room overlooking the roof garden, where a café operates in the summer. The hotel also has a business center.

Marriott

Aleje Jerozolimskie 65/79. **Map** 2 E5. ☎ *630 63 06.* [FAX] *830 03 11.* [TX] *81 65 15.* ***Rooms:*** *521.* 🛁 [1] ⊞ [24] [TV] 🚭 ❄ ☰ 🏢 🏊 🏋 🚸 ♿ ⇅ [P] 🍸 🍴 [i] 💳 *AE, DC, MC, V, JCB.* [$][$][$][$][$]

The Marriott is a deluxe 40-floor tower, with spacious, elegantly furnished rooms on the 20 topmost floors. A grand lobby, extending from the ground floor to a mezzanine level, has marble, chrome, and crystal glass features. Various restaurants span Polish, Italian, American, and international cuisine, with cafés, a casino, and several bars providing alternative options. The Panorama Bar, which is situated 140 m (460 ft) above ground level, offers amazing views of the city. Various function and conference rooms are available; the hotel complex also houses the downtown office of LOT Polish Airlines *(see p246)*.

Mercure–Fryderyk Chopin

Aleja Jana Pawła II 22. **Map** 3 A3. ☎ *620 02 01.* FAX *620 87 79.* TX *81 58 79.* ***Rooms:*** *250.* 🛁 [1] ⊞ [24] [TV] 🚭 ❄ 🏋 🍼 💼 ♿ ⇅ [P] 🍸 🍴 [i] 💳 *AE, DC, MC, V, JCB.* $$$$$

This recently built luxury hotel is part of the French Mercure chain. Rooms are furnished with elegant, modern furniture. The choice of restaurants comprises Le Balzac, specializing in French cuisine, and Le Stanislaus, which boasts an international menu. There is also a charming café-patisserie. The hotel is located by the Central Railroad Station (Dworzec Centralny).

Sheraton

Prusa 2. **Map** 6 E2. ☎ *657 61 00.* FAX *657 62 00.* ***Rooms:*** *350.* 🛁 [1] 🚭 ❄ ⊞ [24] 💼 🍼 [TV] 🏋 ♿ ⇅ [P] 🍸 🍴 [i] 💳 *AE, DC, MC, V.* $$$$$

This is the city's most recently built deluxe hotel. Behind an impressive Postmodern façade, it has strikingly opulent interiors in an international style. An excellent location is combined with every amenity to make a stay more enjoyable, including a jazz bar that is renowned in Warsaw. The hotel is mainly geared to visiting VIPs and businesspeople. The even more luxurious "Towers" section, which occupies the top floors, functions almost as a separate hotel, with superb suites and service.

Victoria Intercontinental

Królewska 11. **Map** 4 D5. ☎ *657 80 11.* FAX *657 80 57.* TX *81 25 16.* ***Rooms:*** *365.* 🛁 [1] [24] [TV] 🚭 🌿 ❄ 🏊 🍼 💼 ♿ ⇅ [P] 🍸 🍴 [i] 🌳 💳 *AE, DC, MC, V, JCB.* $$$$$

In the late 1970s, this was Warsaw's most exclusive hotel. However, since the 1989 democratic elections, several luxurious hotels have opened up, leaving the Victoria lower down the ladder. Nevertheless, all rooms are equipped with minibars and modern bathrooms, and are furnished in a mid-1970s style. Amenities include pleasant restaurants, a café, and a spacious lobby, overlooking Piłsudski Square. This is one of the largest squares in Warsaw, named after Marshal Piłsudski *(see p30)* and bordered by the National Theater (Teatr Wielki Narodowy) and Saxon Gardens (Ogród Saski).

FARTHER AFIELD

Agra

Falęcka 9/11. **Map** 6 D5. ☎ *49 38 81.* ***Rooms:*** *40.* 🛁 ⊞ 🍸 💳 *AE.* $

Inexpensive rates are the main advantage of this hotel, formerly a student residence hall belonging to the Agricultural Academy (Szkoła Główna Gospodarstwa Wiejskiego). In line with student hostels, bathrooms are shared by two rooms. There is a cellar bar, and local dining options include Fuks, a vegetarian restaurant, close by on Madalińskiego Street.

Felix

Omulewska 24. ☎ *10 97 72, 10 06 91.* FAX *13 02 55.* ***Rooms:*** *257.* 🛁 [1] ⊞ [24] [TV] 🏋 ⇅ [P] 🍸 🍴 $$

The Felix has been virtually monopolized by traveling salesmen from former Soviet countries. Converted from what was once a workers' hostel, modest rooms are reflected in equally modest prices.

Gromada

17 Stycznia 32a. ☎ *846 58 22.* FAX *846 15 80.* ***Rooms:*** *127.* 🛁 [1] [24] [TV] ⇅ [P] 🍸 🍴 💳 *AE, DC, MC, JCB.* $$$

This is a new hotel belonging to the Gromada Company, which also owns Dom Chłopa *(see p201)*. Situated near Okęcie Airport, the hotel is only a 30-minute bus ride from the city center. The rooms are clean, and each has a private bathroom and television. Adjacent to the hotel is a large, less expensive motel, offering brick bungalows, wooden chalets, and carports.

Novotel

11 Sierpnia. ☎ *846 40 51.* FAX *846 36 86.* TX *81 25 25.* ***Rooms:*** *144.* 🛁 [1] [24] [TV] 🚭 🏊 *in summer.* 🍼 💼 ♿ ⇅ [P] 🍸 🍴 [i] 🌳 💳 *AE, DC, MC, V, JCB.* $$$

Situated on a tree-lined avenue leading to Okęcie Airport, this is one of several chain hotels built in Poland during the 1970s, by the eponymous French company. The hotel's size and design are similar to those of the Vera and Solec hotels. The garden features a swimming pool, which is open during the summer. Pets are also welcome here.

Vera

Bitwy Warszawskiej 1920 roku 16. ☎ *22 74 21.* FAX *23 62 56.* TX *81 61 84.* ***Rooms:*** *155.* 🛁 [1] [24] [TV] 🚭 💼 ♿ ⇅ [P] 🍸 🍴 🌳 💳 *AE, DC, MC, V, JCB.* $$$

Built in 1980 by a Yugoslav consortium, the hotel's architectural style, standards, and prices are similar to those of the Novotel and Solec. Located by Warsaw's Western Railroad Station (Dworzec Zachodni), the hotel is a 15-minute bus ride from the center of Warsaw.

Zajazd Napoleoński

Płowiecka 83. ☎ *15 30 68.* FAX *15 22 16.* TX *81 63 62.* ***Rooms:*** *24.* 🛁 [1] [TV] 🍼 [P] 🍸 🍴 🌳 💳 *AE, DC, MC, V.* $$$

Although Napoleon Bonaparte was never actually a resident in this building, he must at least have passed by the area when making his doomed march on Moscow with his Great Army. The Napoleonic legacy is reflected in the hotel's interiors, which are modeled on a Polish manor house and are Neo-Classical in style.

BEYOND WARSAW

Eden

Raszyn, Mszczonowska 43. ☎ *756 05 22.* ***Rooms:*** *46.* 🛁 [1] ⊞ [P] 🍸 🍴 💳 *AE, DC, MC, V, JCB.* $$

The Eden is a small hotel with a pleasant, homey atmosphere and a popular restaurant. It is situated on the main road to Katowice, near a large shopping center in Janki.

Konstancja

Konstancin Jeziorna, Źródlana 6/8. ☎ *756 43 25, 756 46 74.* FAX *756 43 67.* ***Rooms:*** *44.* 🛁 [1] [24] [TV] ❄ 💼 ♿ [P] 🍸 🍴 🌳 💳 *AE, DC, MC, V, JCB.* $$

Located about 20 km (12 miles) from Warsaw, the Konstancja is situated in the spa town of Konstancin-Jeziorna. The hotel is surrounded by a park, featuring the spa's twin saline water towers, which create a unique microclimate. Additional amenities, such as barbecues and horseback riding, are also available from the hotel.

RESTAURANTS, CAFÉS, AND BARS

THE RESTAURANT SCENE has flourished in Warsaw ever since the return of private ownership, following the 1989 democratic elections. While the quality of the city's restaurants continues to improve, just as the number continues to grow, Warsaw already has a surprisingly wide choice of international cuisines. This ranges from French, Italian, Spanish, British, and Greek, to Japanese, Chinese, Vietnamese, and Mexican – not to mention vegetarian. Naturally, there are many restaurants

Vegetarian platter

serving traditional Polish food, while modern Polish cuisine, featuring imaginative updates of traditional dishes, is also becoming popular. Although prices are generally rising, eating out in Warsaw still represents an excellent value for Western tourists, with the city also providing a good choice of inexpensive eateries. Meanwhile, cafés and bars are booming, with an ever wider selection. These pages provide guidelines on deciding where to eat and drink in Warsaw, with individual listings on pages 214–19.

Chopin restaurant in the Jan III Sobieski Hotel *(see p219)*

RESTAURANTS

WHILE A LARGE selection of international cuisine – spanning Mediterranean, Asian, and South American – can easily be enjoyed in Warsaw, hotel restaurants tend to serve traditional Polish food. This ranges from the hearty and rustic, to the more sophisticated. Modern Polish (classics updated with a range of international techniques and ingredients) is the forté of more expensive restaurants, such as Fukier, the Malinowa in the Bristol Hotel, and the Chopin in the Jan III Sobieski Hotel.

Various restaurants also provide highly atmospheric interiors. In the Old Town, for instance, Bazyliszek resembles an 18th-century hunting lodge, while Świętoszek is

housed in an intimate, brick-vaulted cellar.

The city's restaurants usually stay open from 11am or noon until 11pm, and often later. Booking in advance is recommended.

CAFÉS, BARS, AND PUBS

WARSAW has a great choice of cafés and patisseries, offering tempting cakes served with specialty coffees, hot chocolate, or lemon tea.

Particular favorites include the Krokodyl café in

the Old Town Market Square, Café Blikle, Wedel's café, the Hotel Europejski's patisserie, and Café Bristol, which has beautiful Secession-style interiors. In the summer, café tables spill out onto numerous squares and sidewalks throughout the city.

Bars and pubs are ideal for sampling vodka, especially as Poland produces the world's largest range of clear and flavored vodkas, including lemon, pepper, honey, and cherry styles. English- and Irish-style pubs are also to be found in the city, offering an impressive range of beers.

Alfresco terrace of Nove Miasto restaurant

Fast Food and Snacks

The city center has an abundance of self-service cafeterias as well as fast-food outlets. These span the usual range of McDonald's, Burger King, and Pizza Hut, as well as inexpensive Chinese, Vietnamese, and Polish food. Many delicatessens and grocery stores also sell sandwiches. During the summer, ice-cream vans operate throughout the city.

Vegetarian Food

A few restaurants, such as Fuks, specialize in vegetarian food, while salad bars are also appearing. Additionally, many eateries offer meatless dishes. Some classic Polish dishes, like *pierogi* (ravioli) and *mizeria* (cucumber and sour cream salad), are ideal vegetarian choices. Asian and Italian restaurants also offer a wide selection of vegetable-based dishes.

Ugarit restaurant, which specializes in Middle Eastern food *(see p216)*

Prices and Tips

Prices can vary enormously in the city's restaurants. The least expensive three-course meal (without drinks) usually costs around 20 złotys ($8) per person. However, in a luxurious restaurant, the bill can easily reach ten times as much. Another consideration is that prices do not always include VAT, which may be stated separately on the menu. If a dish is not priced, then the cost should be established before you order (though this may also mean that the dish is temporarily unavailable). Many restaurants offer fixed-price menus or buffets, which are often a good value.

Because imported wines and spirits can be very expensive (and they are always more than Polish drinks), it is worth checking the price before you order. Even soft drinks can drastically increase the bill.

Credit cards are usually accepted in more expensive restaurants, but they can rarely be used in bars, pubs, cafés, and the cheaper eateries. It is customary in Warsaw to leave a 10 percent tip.

Montmartre restaurant on Nowy Świat Street *(see p218)*

The candlelit interior of the Restauracja Polska *(see p215)*

Using the Listings

Key to symbols in the listings on pages 214–19.

[V] vegetarian dishes

♫ live music

🍴 outdoor eating

🍷 good wine list

★ highly recommended

💳 credit cards accepted

[$] under $7

[$][$] $7–$14

[$][$][$] $14–$25

[$][$][$][$] over $25

Warsaw's Best: Restaurants and Cafés

THE CITY'S comprehensive range of restaurants and cafés spans traditional and modern Polish food and drink, as well as the pick of the world's most interesting cuisines. Numerous restaurants and cafés in central Warsaw also provide historic and beautiful settings, such as a vaulted cellar, a burgher's house, or even Secessionist splendor and elegance.

Pożegnanie z Afryką
Out of Africa is a café serving some of the city's finest coffee (see p214).

The Former Jewish Ghetto

Café Bristol
As well as excellent coffee and cakes, this café offers light lunches. The Secessionist interiors create a delightful Viennese atmosphere (see p215).

Café Blikle
Having been carefully restored, this historic café is one of the city's most fashionable meeting places, offering a selection of mouth-watering pastries (see p214).

Casa Valdemar
A magnificent clay oven, used to prepare Castilian roasts, is a feature of this celebrated Spanish restaurant (see p218).

0 kilometers | 1
0 miles | 0.5

Fuks
Among Warsaw's growing number of vegetarian restaurants, this is one of the most popular (see p219)

Fukier

An exquisite burgher's house in the Old Town Market Square provides an idyllic setting for modern Polish dishes, served in a traditional atmosphere (see p214).

Malinowa

This elegant Secessionist dining room has received many distinguished guests and is now highly regarded for its modern interpretations of classic Polish cuisine (see p215).

Tsubame

Having provided the city with its first sushi bar, Tsubame is also one of the finest Asian restaurants, serving elegant Japanese dishes (see p215).

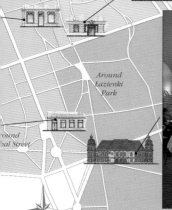

Old Town

ity e

The Royal Route

Around Lazienki Park

ound al Street

Qchnia Artystyczna

This Post-Modern restaurant in the Modern Art Center, where concerts as well as exhibitions are held, offers delightfully eccentric interiors and an interesting menu (see p217).

Belvedere

With its sublime location, a historic orangerie in the Łazienki Park, this restaurant offers superb modern Polish and French cuisine (see p218).

What to Eat in Warsaw

POLISH CUISINE, which has Slav origins, was also influenced by the foods of neighboring countries, such as Russia, Lithuania, Belarus, Ukraine, and Germany. Similarly, the Jewish population added various dishes, while French and Italian princesses who married Polish kings introduced their own native specialties. Under Communism, when shortages were a fact of daily life, Polish cuisine regressed. However, Warsaw's finest chefs are now reviving and updating traditional dishes. Meals often begin with soup, followed by a meat dish (beef, pork, poultry, or game), served with potatoes, buckwheat *(kasza)*, or dumplings, and vegetables such as wild mushrooms, beets, and cabbage. Typical desserts include stewed fruit and cheesecake.

Flaki (Tripe)
The only local dish to be found on most restaurant menus, tripe Warsaw-style is usually accompanied by hearty meatballs.

Hors d'Oeuvres and Garnishes
Pickled dill cucumbers and various types of pickled mushrooms are popular hors d'oeuvres (zakąski), accompanied by Polish vodka. They also provide a typical garnish for main dishes (particularly meat).

Dill cucumbers

Pickled mushrooms

Cèpe Mushrooms in Cream
While this dish is a great favorite during the mushroom season, it can be prepared year-round using preserved mushrooms.

Roast Duck with Apples
Game is very popular in Poland, and this is one of the most typical duck dishes. It is usually served with roast potatoes.

Bigos (Hunter's Stew)
This classic Polish dish is cooked slowly, in order to blend the flavors of the meats, including Polish sausage, and both sauerkraut and fresh cabbage.

Carp Jewish-style

Herring Japanese-style

Smoked eel

Cold Snacks
Popular as snacks or sometimes appetizers, these include the traditional carp Jewish-style (with ginger sauce) and smoked eel, as well as the more international herrings Japanese-style.

Borscht (barszcz)

Żurek with white sausage

Lithuanian borscht

Soups

Borscht (beet soup) is served hot, with Lithuanian borscht a cold variation, and żurek a fermented "sour" soup with white sausage.

Suckling Pig in Bison Grass

Bison grass, an aromatic herb, and suckling pig are two Polish specialties that are brought together in this innovative dish.

Perch Polish-style

This is poached and garnished with melted butter, lemon wedges, and chopped hard-boiled egg.

Beef Roulades

These rolled beef slices are stuffed with bacon and onion, and served with either small dumplings or buckwheat.

Roast Pork with Prunes

Pork loin is a popular cut and a great favorite when stuffed with prunes to make this classic "Old Polish" dish.

Yeast cake   Apple Charlotte

Cream puff   Fruit tart

Poppy-seed pastry

Rum baba   Éclair   Doughnut

Poppy-seed cake

Desserts

Among the most popular desserts are cakes and pastries, including doughnuts filled with rose petal jam, poppy-seed cake (especially at Easter and Christmas), and ginger cake made from a traditional medieval recipe.

What to Drink in Warsaw

Logo of Polish vodka distilleries

POLISH VODKA is internationally renowned for its excellent quality. The vast range available includes clear vodkas, generally distilled from rye, with flavored varieties ranging from dry to sweet, and from fruity to herbal and spicy. Imported drinks – such as Cognac, Scotch whisky, gin, and wine – carry much higher duties than Polish drinks, so prices can be astronomical. Beer is also enjoying a boom in popularity, with English- and Irish-style pubs opening throughout Warsaw. Meanwhile, the range and quality of Polish beer have improved dramatically over the past few years and are now on a par with those of imported brands. Among soft drinks, Poland excels in fruit juices such as blackcurrant, rasp-berry, and cherry, while several brands of mineral water are sourced from Polish spa towns.

Żywiec, one of Poland's most historic and popular beer brands

POLISH VODKA

VODKA HAS long been estab-lished as Poland's national drink, and there are hundreds of brands of vodka on the market. Unlike neutral-tasting "international" vodka, Polish vodka has a distinct character. It should be served chilled, and sipped to appreciate the depth of flavors.

Vodkas are divided into clear and flavored varieties. Among clear vodkas, the most famous is Wyborowa. It has a rye flavor and subtle sweetness that are derived entirely from the distillation process, not from the use of additives. Kosher vodkas are also produced, in accordance with kosher regulations. Deluxe vodka brands have appeared

over the past few years, including Chopin, which features a portrait of the composer on the label. Belvedere is another such brand and is named after the palace in Warsaw.

Label on Żubrówka bottle

Flavored vodkas are infusions of fruit, herbs, and various other ingredients. One of the most original is Żubrówka, flavored with an herb called

bison grass. This grass, which grows only in the Białowieża National Park in eastern Poland, is a favorite foodstuff of the European bison, which are still to be found roaming there.

Another unique Polish vodka is Goldwasser, which includes flakes of gold leaf, in accor-dance with the original 16th-century recipe. It is usually drunk as a *digestif*, after a meal.

Vodka is rarely served with-out food. Before a meal, it will be accompanied by a range of hors d'oeuvres (referred to as *zakąski*), such as salt herring fillets, pickled mushrooms, dill cucumbers, Polish sausage, and rye bread. Their salty, spicy flavors balance that of the vodka, while encouraging the next round.

Clear vodkas   **Flavored vodkas**

Premium Vodka, distilled in Poznań

Wyborowa, the most famous export brand

Żubrówka, flavored with bison grass

Goldwasser, which includes gold leaf

BEER

Brok

Żywiec

EB

Okocim

BREWERIES were among the first businesses to take advantage of Poland's transformation into a free-market economy in 1989. The result has been a dramatic improvement in the quality of Polish beers, which are predominantly lagers. The choice of brands has also become much wider, with the establishment of various regional and "boutique" breweries.

Among the most popular beer brands are Żywiec, Brok, Heweliusz, EB, and Okocim.

Okocim label

Żywiec label

The bar of a typical Warsaw pub

Polish beer now competes successfully in terms of quality with imported beers, including Irish, German, Dutch, Danish, and Czech brands, which are readily available.

The recent emergence of themed pubs, as well as various new bars, has also helped to boost beer's popularity (see pp214–19).

MEAD

ONE OF POLAND'S most historic drinks, mead is still prepared according to traditional recipes. Mead is created from fermented honey, diluted with water and flavored with spices and hops, though precise recipes are usually shrouded in secrecy.

The strength of mead usually ranges from 9–18 percent alcohol by volume, with the strength and character of the mead determined by the ratio of honey to water. Different ratios have their own official terminology. *Połtorak* (meaning "two-thirds") indicates a ratio of 2 parts honey to 1 part water. This style of mead, the strongest and the sweetest, is also widely considered to be the finest quality. *Dwójniak* is equal parts honey and water, *trójniak* is 1 part honey to 2 parts water, while *czwórniak* refers to 1 part honey to 3 parts water.

— Alcoholic strength

— Strength of extract

— The "best consumed before" date

Deciphering an Okocim beer label

***Trójniak*-strength mead**

Choosing a Restaurant

THE RESTAURANTS AND CAFES in this guide have been chosen primarily for their fine food, although some may get a mention for their great value or their ambience. This chart highlights some factors that may influence your decision when choosing a restaurant, while full reviews appear on pages 214–19. Establishments are listed by area of the city, and alphabetically within each price category.

		Attractive Location	Tables Outside	Polish Specialties	Late Opening	Vegetarian Specialties
OLD TOWN (see p214)						
Maharaja-Thai	$$	●	■		■	●
Rycerska	$$$	●	■	●	■	
Dom Restauracyjny Gessler	$$$$	●	■	●	■	
Fukier ★	$$$$	●	■	●	■	●
NEW TOWN (see p214)						
Pożegnanie z Afryką ★	$	●				
Pod Samsonem	$$	●	■	●		
Nove Miasto	$$$$	●	■	●		●
AROUND SOLIDARITY AVENUE (see p214)						
Bel Ami	$$$	●	■	●	■	
Elefant Pub	$$$	●			■	●
Pekin	$$$				■	●
THE ROYAL ROUTE (see pp214–15)						
Europejska	$	●	■			
Harenda	$		■		■	
Pod Baryłką	$		■		■	
Café Blikle ★	$$	●				●
Literacka	$$	●	■			
Przy Koperniku	$$		■			
Café Bristol ★	$$$	●				●
Tsubame ★	$$$				■	●
Da Pietro	$$$$	●	■		■	
Malinowa ★	$$$$	●		●	■	●
Nowy Świat	$$$$	●	■		■	
Restauracja Polska	$$$$					●
AROUND MARSHAL STREET (see pp216–17)						
Batida	$					●
Krokiecik	$					●
Café Brama	$$				■	
Ha Long	$$	●			■	●
Akwarium	$$$				■	
Dong Nam	$$$					●
O'Hare Pub	$$$	●			■	
Maharaja	$$$				■	●
Mekong	$$$				■	●
Metromilano	$$$					●
Ugarit	$$$				■	
U Szwejka	$$$	●			■	
Chicago Grill	$$$$				■	
Kahlenberg	$$$$	●		●	■	

Price categories refer to a three-course meal for one, half a bottle of house wine; and all unavoidable extra charges such as service tax (in US dollars).

$ under $7
$$ $7–14
$$$ $14–25
$$$$ over $25

★ Means highly recommended

ATTRACTIVE LOCATION
Restaurants in unusual or historic settings, or with an outstanding view

TABLES OUTSIDE
Food is served outdoors in fine weather.

POLISH SPECIALTIES
Restaurants that have a good selection of traditional dishes.

LATE OPENING
Last orders accepted at or after 11:30pm.

VEGETARIAN SPECIALTIES
Restaurants that have a good selection of vegetarian dishes.

	Attractive Location	Tables Outside	Polish Specialties	Late Opening	Vegetarian Specialties
Le Balzac	$$$$				●	
Lila Weneda	$$$$			●	●	●
Parmiggiano	$$$$				●	●
THE FORMER JEWISH GHETTO (see p217)					
Valencia	$$$				●	●
Malibu	$$$$		●			●
AROUND ŁAZIENKI PARK (see pp217–18)					
Czytelnik	$	●				
Zielona Budka	$					
Adler	$$		●			
Da Elio	$$					●
Qchnia Artystyczna ★	$$	●	●		●	●
Klub Aktora	$$$	●			●	
London Steak House	$$$	●	●		●	
Belvedere ★	$$$$	●	●	●	●	●
Casa Valdemar ★	$$$$	●	●		●	●
Montmartre	$$$$				●	
OTHER DISTRICTS (see pp218–19)					
B-40	$	●	●		●	
Boston Port	$$		●			
Fuks ★	$$				●	●
Positano	$$		●			●
Zielona Gęś	$$		●		●	
Zorba	$$		●			●
ALAMO Steak House	$$$		●		●	
Blue Cactus	$$$		●			
Ciao Maurizio	$$$				●	●
Flik	$$$	●	●	●	●	
Mibella	$$$		●		●	
Rong Vang	$$$					●
Santorini	$$$		●			●
Chopin	$$$$		●	●		
Shogun	$$$$				●	
Zajazd Napoleoński	$$$$		●	●	●	
FARTHER AFIELD (see p219)					
Pod Złotym Linem	$$	●	●	●		

The photographs and descriptions on pages 208–9 illustrate some of Poland's most popular dishes.

Old Town

Maharaja-Thai

Szeroki Dunaj 13. **Map** 1 C1 & 3 C4. ☎ *635 25 01.* 🕒 *noon–midnight daily.* [V] 🍴 🍸 💳 $$

This was the first Thai restaurant in Poland. It has an interesting interior and somewhat passive service, but the food is very good indeed. The chef has, out of necessity, substituted the usual Thai coconut milk with cow's milk and straw mushrooms with oyster mushrooms but, thanks to a skillful and inventive use of ginger, garlic, lemon, peppers, herbs, and various types of curry, the resulting dishes have a truly Thai flavor. The best among them are lemon-flavored chicken soup, green curry chicken, fried fish, Thai chopped pork omelette, and stuffed chicken wings, with the bones artfully removed.

Rycerska

Szeroki Dunaj 9/11. **Map** 1 C1 & 3 C4. ☎ *831 36 68.* 🕒 *11am–11pm daily.* [V] 🍴 💳 $$$

While the restaurant and the menu have remained in the style of the early 1970s, the food is rather good, and the atmosphere is very pleasant. Rycerska serves an interesting, old-fashioned Polish white borscht, known as *żurek*, as well as tasty herrings, rustic dishes like suckling pig roasted in beer, and turkey in mulled-wine sauce. Among the fish dishes, look for the appetizing boiled carp in lemon sauce.

Dom Restauracyjny Gessler

Rynek Starego Miasta 21. **Map** 4 D4 & 6 D1. ☎ *831 16 61.* 🕒 *11am–until the last guest leaves daily.* 🎵 🍴 💳 $$$$

The food is not the best in Warsaw, but the interior never fails to impress, particularly the cellar, built in the style of an 18th-century country inn, supposedly brought over from a small village called Wojtkowice Stare. It is full of arts and crafts, and the effect is enchanting. Many traditional Polish dishes are served.

Fukier

Rynek Starego Miasta 27. **Map** 4 D4 & 6 D1. ☎ *831 10 13.* 🕒 *noon–until the last guest leaves daily.* [V] 🎵 🍴 🍸 💳 $$$$ ★

Here you will find excellent cuisine served in one of Warsaw's most beautiful surroundings. The oak floors and tables, together with the aroma of herbs, candles, and flowers, create a wonderful atmosphere. Fukier serves mainly Polish cuisine at its most creative, enriched with French and other European influences. The menu includes such dishes as pig's feet in aspic, carpaccio of cèpes, *żurek* (fermented soup) with cèpes and white sausage, calf's liver with balsamic vinegar, asparagus, carp baked in cream with cèpes and haunch of venison. Among the desserts are wonderful poppy-seed cake, lemon sorbet with vodka, and delightfully fluffy cheesecake.

New Town

Pożegnanie z Afryką

Freta 4/6. **Map** 1 C1 & 3 C4. 🕒 *11am–8pm daily.* $ ★

The most delectable aromas in town emanate from this tiny café. It is connected with a shop, and both offer a huge selection of excellent coffees. Only coffee is sold here, unless you count wafer cakes, but there is neither space nor need for anything else. The quality of coffee served outclasses anything else you may get in town; a visit here is an adventure in itself.

Pod Samsonem

Freta 3/5. **Map** 1 C1 & 3 C4. ☎ *831 17 88.* 🕒 *10am–10pm daily.* [V] 🍴 💳 $$

Recommended for anyone on a budget, this is a favorite meeting place for cost-conscious, though outstanding representatives of Warsaw intelligentsia. The restaurant offers unpretentious service, clean surroundings, and a combination of Polish and Jewish cuisine. Their specialties include chopped liver, stuffed carp, and escalopes. For dessert, the cardinal peaches come highly recommended.

Nove Miasto

Rynek Nowego Miasta 13. **Map** 1 C1 & 3 C4. ☎ *831 43 79.* 🕒 *10am–midnight daily.* [V] 🍴 💳 $$$$

Set on the New Town Market Square, this mostly vegetarian restaurant is decorated in bright colors and is comfortably furnished. The extensive menu features a range of unusual salads, vegetarian *pierogi*, and, for fish eaters, pasta with tuna and crab. All the dishes are subtly flavored with herbs and spices, and are presented with flair. Enjoy the live music indoors, or dine outside when the weather is fine.

Around Solidarity Avenue

Bel Ami

Senatorska 14. **Map** 1 C2 & 4 D5. ☎ *826 67 71.* 🕒 *noon–midnight daily.* 🍴 🍸 💳 $$$

Bel Ami consists of several cozy rooms, set in an underground maze of corridors. Aimed at businesspeople, it offers sophisticated dishes that are carefully prepared and well presented. Prices are high, but not outrageous. Bel Ami's specialties include bliny (buckwheat pancakes) with herring, Russian-style mushroom soup, rose-sauce duckling, and veal shank with vegetables.

Elefant Pub

Plac Bankowy 1. **Map** 1 B3 & 3 C5. ☎ *620 46 11.* 🕒 *10:30am–1:30am daily.* 💳 $$$

The Elefant offers some of the best pub food in town, as well as a terrific atmosphere, and Irish and German beers. Grilled meat, such as steaks, kabobs, large spicy hamburgers *(pleskawica)*, and sausage, are all served with fries. There are also tasty hot mussels served with cold sauces and deep-fried Camembert with cranberries.

Pekin

Senatorska 27. **Map** 1 C2 & 4 D5. ☎ *827 48 04.* 🕒 *noon–11pm daily.* [V] 💳 $$$

Pekin offers some of the best Asian dishes in town. While it is not very expensive, the service can be poor. Chinese music is piped into the restaurant, and an excellent choice of fish is offered, along with several types of shrimps, tasty duck, and a variety of vegetarian dishes. For dessert, the banana fritters are unrivaled. The range of beer and spirits is reasonably priced.

The Royal Route

Europejska

Europejski Hotel, Krakowskie Przedmieście 13. **Map** 2 D3 & 4 D5. ☎ *826 50 51, ext 565.* 🕒 *10am–10pm (midnight in summer) daily.* 🎵 🍴 🍸 💳 $

This large café offers an engaging atmosphere. Once a favorite meeting place in Warsaw, it has retained many loyal patrons, particularly for breakfast.

Harenda

Krakowskie Przedmieście 4/6. **Map** 2 D3 & 4 D5. ☎ *826 29 00.* ♫ 🪑 💳 $

Large, fashionable, and always buzzing, this is the favorite spot for Warsaw's liberals, foreigners, and better-off students. You can have a three-course meal here, but the menu is not ambitious – the main attraction of the evening is baked potatoes. The range of beers includes Guinness, Heineken, and Żywiec.

Pod Baryłką

Garbarska 7. **Map** 2 D2 & 4 D5. ☎ *826 62 39.* 🕒 *11am–midnight daily.* 🪑 $

This is one of Warsaw's nicest pubs. It has a pleasant, cozy interior, with a quiet atmosphere. The food includes grilled ham and cheese sandwiches (quite tasty), and pretzels to nibble with a choice of 11 draft beers.

Café Blikle

Nowy Świat 33. **Map** 2 D5 & 6 D1. ☎ *826 66 19.* 🕒 *8am–11pm Mon–Thu, 8am–midnight Fri, 8:30am–midnight Sat, 9am–11pm Sun.* [V] ♫ 🍷 💳 $$ ★

Café Blikle is a fashionable meeting place that is helping to resurrect Warsaw's café society. Here you will find a buzzing, lively café, with many well-known Poles. The frozen yogurt and sorbet are excellent, and its famous "hollow-cheek" doughnuts are truly delicious (though other pastries can be disappointing). The café offers tempting breakfasts and good teas, with such enticements as herring dumplings; patés with chopped apricots, nuts, and prunes; and vegetarian rolls.

Literacka

Krakowskie Przedmieście 87/89. **Map** 1 D2. ☎ *635 89 95.* 🕒 *10am–until the last guest leaves daily.* ♫ 🪑 🍷 💳 $$

Situated in the legendary Dom Literata (Writer's House), the Literacka has an atmospheric café on the ground floor, but the restaurant in the cellar is not recommended. The desserts, such as apple fritters and vanilla custard, are delicious.

Przy Koperniku

Krakowskie Przedmieście 4/6. **Map** 2 D4. ☎ *828 08 52.* 🕒 *noon–1am daily.* 🪑 💳 $$

This large pub is also one of the city's latest jazz clubs, and is already rivaling the renowned Akwarium. Its vast rooms are subdivided, and there are cellar bars as well, decorated in a modern style. The pub includes a "restaurant village," with street lamps and red roof tiles. If there is no live music, recordings are played. The menu features simple, rustic dishes, which are expensive, but portions are large. We recommend *Warkocz Kopernika* (Copernicus's plait), which is three types of meat (veal, pork, and beef), elegantly "braided," grilled, and served with madeira sauce and mushrooms. There is also a wide selection of beer and vodka.

Café Bristol

Hotel Bristol, Krakowskie Przedmieście 42/44. **Map** 2 D3 & 4 D5. ☎ *625 25 25.* 🕒 *10am–9pm daily.* [V] 🍷 💳 $$$ ★

This is an exclusive, Viennese-style café, and an excellent place for breakfast, lunch, or an elegant snack at any time of the day. The interior is beautiful and stylish, complemented by professional, charming staff. Apart from delicious desserts (mousses, cream cakes, eclairs, ice creams), there are also excellent hot and cold snacks, salads, patés, club sandwiches, pancakes, and lasagna. Coffee and other drinks are expensive, but light dishes and desserts will not ruin an average budget.

Tsubame

Foksal 16. **Map** 3 E5 & 6 D1. ☎ *826 51 27.* 🕒 *noon–midnight daily.* [V] 💳 $$$ ★

This authentic Japanese restaurant offers a full range of fascinating cuisine, and includes the first sushi-bar in Poland, where you can taste specialties such as raw seafood served on a bed of rice, wrapped in a black ribbon of *nori* seaweed. Prices are high, but it offers an unforgettable experience for the gourmet. Excellent sushi provides a wide range of choice, with omelette, mackerel, tuna, salmon, yellowtail, red salmon roe, shrimp, three types of mussels, octopus, and squid. Other dishes include *maki* – attractive rolls made of rice and various ingredients, such as cucumber, pickled plums, pickled fibers of the campyo gourd, or strips of avocado. They can be accompanied by a garnish of pickled ginger and washed down with hot sake. The tea is also very good.

Da Pietro

Nowy Świat 63. **Map** 2 D5 & 6 D1. ☎ *826 58 03.* 🕒 *12:30–11pm daily.* 🪑 💳 $$$$

Although the name suggests Italian food, it is Austrian cuisine that is on the menu at Da Pietro, as the restaurant derives its name from earlier times, when this Viennese establishment was trying unsuccessfully to gain more customers by offering Italian food. Now the chefs are concentrating on what they know best: velvety garlic soup served in a large roll; consommé with small spinach rolls; a surprising pork roast accompanied by fantastic cabbage; Viennese goulash with bread-and-onion dumplings; hot apple strudel served with vanilla ice cream and whipped cream. The coffee here is excellent as well. Expensive, but delicious.

Malinowa

Hotel Bristol, Krakowskie Przedmieście 42/44. **Map** 2 D3 & 4 D5. ☎ *625 25 25.* 🕒 *6pm–until the last guest leaves daily.* [V] ♫ 🍷 💳 $$$$ ★

Malinowa is renowned as the most exclusive restaurant in Warsaw. It employs world-class chefs, including Małgorzata Marchewka, whose specialty of suckling pig with bison grass won a Silver Medal at the 1st European Cup Competition for Regional Cuisine, in 1995. The restaurant's interior, which evokes the 1920s and 1930s, is luxurious and stylish. Prices, as you might expect, are very high, but the food is not only excellent, but also beautifully presented. There are very exciting interpretations of classic dishes and innovative use of specialty ingredients, evident in some superb desserts.

Nowy Świat

Nowy Świat 63. **Map** 1 D5 & 6 D1. ☎ *826 58 03.* 🕒 *7:30am–10pm (11pm in summer) daily.* 🪑 💳 $$$$

For many years this was one of Warsaw's favorite cafés. It is large, always full, and offers a rich selection of desserts and Austrian-style dishes. As well as being a great place to eat, it also has the latest newspapers and magazines to browse through.

Restauracja Polska

Nowy Świat 21 (in the cellar of the Sculpture Gallery). **Map** 1 D5 & 6 D1. ☎ *826 38 77.* 🕒 *noon–until the last guest leaves daily.* [V] 🍷 💳 $$$$

One of the city's leading restaurants, its food is exquisite and service, excellent. The interior is stylishly decorated with antique furniture and many pictures. There is a good selection of soups, excellent chicken in a cream sauce, and reasonable dumplings in chicken broth. Also worth trying is *pierogi* (Polish ravioli) with berries.

For key to symbols, *see p205*

AROUND MARSHAL STREET

Batida

Nowogrodzka 1/3. **Map** 5 B2. ☎ 621 45 34. ◯ 7am–8pm Mon–Fri, 7am–3pm Sat, 9am–3pm Sun. Ⓥ Ⓢ

Batida is a snack bar attached to a shop and is modeled on a typical Parisian *croissanterie*, with the best French bakery in Warsaw. The hot dishes are uninteresting on the whole, but a major attraction is provided by the good coffee and cakes. At Batida, you will find a plethora of tarts, meringues, eclairs, buns, and French croissants.

Krokiecik

Zgoda 1. **Map** 2 D5 & 6 D1. ☎ 827 30 37. ◯ 9am–8pm Mon–Sat. Ⓥ Ⓢ

This self-service bar, which has survived many changes of fortune, is an ideal place for a quick and inexpensive meal. The café includes Hungarian influences in its repertoire, and you are likely to find fantastic fried cabbage or mushrooms here, as well as pancakes *(krokiety)*, soups, including borscht (beet soup) and *bogracz* (goulash soup), plus Chinese-style chicken. And for dessert, there are tasty cold pancakes with fruit and whipped cream.

Café Brama

Marszałkowska 8. **Map** 6 D3. ☎ 629 65 36. ◯ 2pm–until the last guest leaves daily. ☒ Ⓟ ☒ Ⓢ Ⓢ

Located near the Variety Theater (Teatr Rozmaitości), Café Brama has a Modern European style, with a nonchalant, bohemian atmosphere. The menu is limited but excellent, with very good dishes from the grill. There is also a great choice of alcoholic drinks. Minimalist interiors provide a tasteful backdrop, but the atmosphere is most notably provided by the music (progressive jazz), which is live in the evening.

Ha Long

Emilii Plater 36. **Map** 1 B5 & 5 C2. ☎ 620 15 23. ◯ 11am–10pm. Ⓥ ☒ Ⓟ ☒ Ⓢ Ⓢ

Two small, air-conditioned rooms with fitted carpets, an aquarium, and some attractive graphics on the walls create the atmosphere of a small, Asian restaurant. The Chinese-Vietnamese cuisine includes duck prepared in a variety of ways, such as with sizzling king prawns, or Szechwan-style, as well as the true Peking duck. This is

not just a single dish but a full menu, constituting a mega-Chinese feast that you have to order 24 hours in advance. Soup delicacies include crab, shrimp, and eel, while best of all are the "sour pike" soups.

Akwarium

Emilii Plater 49. **Map** 1 B5 & 5 C2. ☎ 620 50 72. ◯ 11am–11pm Mon–Thu, 11am–until the last guest leaves Fri & Sat. ☒ ☒ Ⓢ Ⓢ Ⓢ

This famous long-established jazz club was the best in Warsaw by virtue of being virtually the only one. It has played host to some world-famous jazz musicians over the years, and you can still hear good music here. It has a comfortable interior, but despite the attractive-looking menu, the food can be pretty awful and prices are high. Consequently, it is better to listen to the music over a cup of coffee or a glass of Polish beer, such as EB or Żywiec.

Dong Nam

Marszałkowska 45/49. **Map** 6 D2. ☎ 621 32 34. ◯ noon–11pm daily. ☒ Ⓢ Ⓢ Ⓢ

The best Thai and Vietnamese cuisine in Poland is served at Dong Nam, which also provides atmospheric interiors. Four containers on each table are filled with soy sauce, a bittersweet fruit sauce, a sharp fruit sauce, and a dark mixture of chilies, which should be used sparingly. The green curry pork is excellent, while other good dishes include fish coated in red curry sauce with coconut milk, a black soup with seafood, and Hormok-style seafood, served in the form of small soufflés with a frothy white sauce and coconut milk. The *pad thai* is also good, while an inferno on the palate is guaranteed by chicken *gai pad phet*, or a *tom yum* soup with chicken and lemon grass. The wine list is reasonably priced.

O'Hare Pub

Marriott Hotel, Aleje Jerozolimskie 65/79. **Map** 2 E5 & 5 C1. ☎ 630 51 19 & 630 74 19. ◯ 10am–midnight daily. ☒ Ⓟ ☒ Ⓢ Ⓢ Ⓢ

This chic bar is expensive, but offers good-quality food and a comfortable setting. O'Hare's serves the quintessence of American food, which includes the best hamburgers in Warsaw (Marriottburgers). The restaurant's menu includes sophisticated hamburgers and hot dogs, hot and cold sandwiches, as well as a selection of Austrian desserts. There is a good range of draft beer, including EB and Beck's.

Maharaja

Marszałkowska 34. **Map** 6 D2. ☎ 621 13 92. ◯ 11am–11pm daily. Ⓥ Ⓟ ☒ Ⓢ Ⓢ Ⓢ

Offering undoubtedly the best Indian cuisine in Warsaw, the Maharaja prepares food in a traditional tandoori clay oven. On the menu are typical breads, stuffed nan, samosas, and several chicken dishes, including maharani, vindaloo, rogan, mild spinach chicken, and tikka. Also served are delicious lamb brains and beautifully fluffy rice with caraway seeds. The many vegetarian wonders include *pakora* (fried vegetable fritters) and *kofta* (vegetable balls and grated cauliflower with peanuts, served in a cream sauce).

Mekong

Wspólna 35. **Map** 5 C2. ☎ 621 18 81. ◯ noon–11pm daily. Ⓥ Ⓟ ☒ Ⓢ Ⓢ Ⓢ

Mekong, offering Chinese cuisine, is the most beautifully furnished Asian restaurant in Warsaw. The food smells exceptional, building up a sense of expectation, while soy sauce stands ready on each table. However, attempts to serve more ambitious cuisine are not always successful. Wines and spirits are expensive here, but the green tea is a delight and obviously far less expensive.

Metromilano

Marszałkowska 99a. **Map** 6 D2. ☎ 625 27 30. ◯ 8am–midnight daily. Ⓥ Ⓟ ☒ Ⓢ Ⓢ

Metromilano is a combination restaurant, comprising spaghetti house, pizzeria, and grill bar. Despite stretching itself in three directions, the food is very good, and on the menu you will find pasta with a variety of delicious sauces, as well as good pizzas and an excellent risotto, prepared with white wine. Żywiec is the main draft beer.

Ugarit

Plac Konstytucji 1. **Map** 6 D2. ☎ 621 62 11 ext. 185. ◯ 24 hours daily. Ⓥ ☒ ☒ Ⓢ Ⓢ Ⓢ

Ugarit offers the best Arab cuisine in Warsaw, at quite reasonable prices. Its marble interior, with columns and a high ceiling, creates the impression of a railroad station, but the food is excellent. Meat dishes, cooked in a charcoal oven, include lamb and veal kabobs, chicken, ribs, and giblets. Best of all, however, are the appetizers: hummus, *muttabal* (smoked, puréed eggplant), vegetarian "Syrian steak," *basturma* (spiced meat sausage), and the warm *marija* (kabob in a roll).

U Szwejka

MDM Hotel, Plac Konstytucji 1. **Map** 6 D2. ☎ *621 87 55.* 🕒 *10am–1am Mon–Fri, 10am–2am Sat–Sun.*
[V] ♫ ☂ 💳 $$$

Noisy and full of atmosphere, here you will find the best pub food in town. Alongside a variety of beers, the chef's specials include grilled meat, such as *pleskawica* (a large, spicy chopped steak with herb butter), served with excellent fries. Hot fried mussels are also a specialty, as are cold mussels, marinated and sprinkled with grated sheeps' cheese. Deep-fried Camembert with cranberry sauce is another excellent choice on the menu. There are a number of draft beers, including Budweiser, EB, Żywiec, and Kilkenny.

Chicago Grill

Marriott Hotel, Aleje Jerozolimskie 65/79. **Map** 2 E5 & 5 C1. ☎ *630 51 75.* 🕒 *6–11:30pm daily.*
[V] ☂ 🍷 💳 $$$$

This is the only upscale restaurant in town that specializes in American cuisine. The Chicago Grill serves steaks and ribs, with draft EB and Beck's.

Kahlenberg

Koszykowa 54. **Map** 5 B2. ☎ *630 88 51.* 🕒 *11am–11pm Mon–Sat, 1–11pm Sun.* ☂ 🍷 💳 $$$$$

This excellent restaurant, offering Austrian and Polish cuisine, serves relatively inexpensive lunches. On the menu are such delights as cream collared herring stuffed with apple, Viennese beef tongue, tripe *à la Varsovie* with liver meatballs, and bread-coated meat loaf. Among the skillfully prepared fish dishes are mint-baked trout in cream sauce and carp in dried wild-mushroom sauce. The chef's specialty is, however, a dessert – hot strudel with vanilla ice cream. Kahlenberg also has a large selection of reasonably priced wines and beers.

Le Balzac

Hotel Mercure, Aleja Jana Pawła II 22. **Map** 1 A2 & 3 A3. ☎ *620 02 01.* 🕒 *noon–2:30pm, 6:30–10:30pm, daily.* ♫ 🍷 💳 $$$$

Le Balzac serves good-quality French cuisine, while the atmosphere and guests are typical of a hotel. This is a very expensive but luxurious place, which is ideal for business lunches. The menu offers a large variety of fish and seafood, and exemplary frogs and snails. There is a tempting morel *velouté*, and a fabulous confit of duck.

Lila Weneda

Marriott Hotel, Aleje Jerozolimskie 65/79. **Map** 2 E5 & 6 C1. ☎ *630 51 76.* 🕒 *6:30pm–midnight daily.*
[V] ♫ 🍷 💳 $$$$

This fashionable and comfortable restaurant is suitable for lunch or early dinner, but not ideal for a romantic evening. It offers an excellent buffet lunch, which is free to children of up to eight years of age, and before 11pm there is a different "theme buffet" each night (Indian, Polish, Asian, Mexican, seafood, and American). The menu includes fantastic fried mushrooms in blue cheese sauce, Lebanese grilled chicken, leg of lamb with mint sauce, and a variety of very tasty potato dishes. You will also find American-style club sandwiches, rarely seen in Poland, and a selection of draft beers.

Parmiggiano

Hotel Marriott, Aleje Jerozolimskie 65/79. **Map** 2 E5 & 6 C1. ☎ *630 50 96.* 🕒 *noon–10:30pm daily.*
[V] ♫ 🍷 💳 $$$$

Parmiggiano is the best Italian restaurant in town, and offers a wide selection of tasty dishes, from antipasti, through pastas, risotto, fish, and meat dishes, to delicious tiramisu for dessert. There is a friendly atmosphere, and the service is excellent. The chef's specialties include tagliatelle in basil sauce, spaghetti carbonara, risotto with wild mushrooms, swordfish in tomato sauce, veal scallops with sage *(saltimbocca)*, and saddle of lamb with olives. But leave room for the desserts.

The Former Jewish Ghetto

Valencia

Smocza 27. **Map** 3 A4. ☎ *38 32 17.* 🕒 *1pm–until the last guest leaves daily.* [V] 💳 $$$

This Spanish restaurant, located in the cellars of the Business Club and financed by the Crafts' Association, is bright and colorful. While it is expensive, only a few of the dishes are really good. Specialties include paella and (for the affluent) fresh seafood.

Malibu

Chmielna 132/134. **Map** 2 D5, 5 B2. ☎ *686 20 43.* 🕒 *noon–11pm Mon–Fri, Sat 6pm–11pm.* [V] ☂ 🍷 💳 $$$$

This is the first California restaurant in Poland. The interiors have a marine theme (decorated with shells), but this is not overly endearing. However, the food is excellent, and dishes are prepared with zest and imagination. The range of interesting sauces includes caramelized ginger, rosemary, mango, and curried coconut, and accompany grills, meats, and pasta. There is always an excellent soup of the day, along with attractive salads and fabulous brie dumplings coated with field mushrooms. The desserts are elegant, and include a white chocolate cheesecake. However, this all comes at a price, and Malibu is mainly frequented by businesspeople.

Around Łazienki Park

Czytelnik

Wiejska 12a. **Map** 6 E2. ☎ *628 14 41 ext. 304.* 🕒 *9am–4pm Mon–Fri.* $

The self-service canteen-bar of the Czytelnik publishing house is open to all. It serves inexpensive bar food and lunches, and reasonable coffee and cakes. It is quite an elitist place, however, where local people come not so much to eat (for the food is mediocre), but rather to see some famous writers, newspaper editors, and theater people.

Zielona Budka

Puławska 11. **Map** 6 D4. ☎ *49 89 38.* 🕒 *10am–10pm daily.* $

Zielona Budka is the best ice-cream parlor in town, although it has no tables. You can buy the same ice creams in many other shops and restaurants in Warsaw, but here, at their source, they seem to taste their best.

Adler

Mokotwska 69. **Map** 6 E2. ☎ *628 73 84.* 🕒 *noon–midnight daily.*
☂ 💳 $$

Adler's is Warsaw's first German restaurant. It is expensive and has pretensions to elegance. Diners choose from an extensive menu that borders on excessive, but the dishes sound authentically German, and a good selection of beer is served from barrels. In the rotunda, which was formerly a coffee bar, there is a stylized beer hall, with chairs and tables made of heavy wood, an old-fashioned tiled stove, and brickwork. Highly recommended are the cèpes in cream sauce, Bavarian dumplings, and herrings Kashubian style. A great attraction for beer lovers is a glass in the form of a boot, which holds two quarts of Beck's.

For key to symbols, *see p205*

Da Elio

Żurawia 20. **Map** 6 D1. **C** *625 54 17.* ○ *noon–midnight daily.*
V ♫ 🖼 $$

This buzzing Italian restaurant is not pretty, but is comfortable. It serves good pizzas, lasagna, can-neloni, *vitello tonnato*, and *bistecca alla pirata*. Their ice creams and sorbet are delicious, and good Italian wines are inexpensive.

Qchnia Artystyczna

Modern Art Center (Centrum Sztuki Współczesnej), Ujazdowski Castle, Aleje Ujazdowskie 6. **Map** 6 E2. **C** *625 76 27.* ○ *noon–until late daily.* V 🖼 🍴 🍷 🖼 $$ ★

This is one of the most original restaurants in town, with an eccentric interior in (what is claimed to be) a Postmodern style. With a witty menu, good atmosphere, and excellent com-pany (the center hosts many exhibitions, shows, concerts, symposiums, and modern art workshops), it lacks only an excellent chef to make it into the top grade. But the food is reason-able (if inconsistent), particularly if you are a vegetarian.

Klub Aktora

Aleje Ujazdowskie 45. **Map** 6 E2. **C** *628 93 66.* ○ *noon–until the last guest leaves daily.* ♫ 🖼 $$$$

The legendary SPATiF was the meeting place of Poland's film, theater, and literary circles. The food was not bad, and the drinks were affordable. Now it is just a faint shadow of its former self: prices have risen, and the food is mediocre, but you can still spot some well-known Polish faces here.

London Steak House

Aleje Jerozolimskie 42. **Map** 2 E5 & 5 C1. **C** *827 00 20.* ○ *noon–midnight daily.* 🖼 🖼 $$$

This restaurant offers excellent grills and a selection of English food, in a setting that is reminiscent of a pub, but with higher prices. It serves a delicious roast beef with Yorkshire pudding, a stylish T-bone steak, steak Diane, as well as tasty potatoes and quite good soups. Żywiec is the draft beer.

Belvedere

Łazienki Królewskie. **Map** 6 E5 & 6 F4. **C** *41 22 50 & 41 48 06 (bookings).* ○ *noon–until the last guest leaves daily.* V ♫ 🖼 🍴 🖼 $$$$ ★

With tables set among exotic plants of the former conservatory, this is probably the most expensive

restaurant in Poland. It offers two main specialties. The first is the classic Polish menu, such as *żurek* (fermented soup) with ham and mushrooms, roast sirloin prepared to the old recipes of Tremo (master chef at the court of King Stanisław August Poniatowski), saddle of venison in prune sauce, and rasp-berry ravioli. The second is a French menu with all the embellish-ments, such as truffles, foie gras, caviar, and oysters. The servings are small, but delicious and elegant.

Casa Valdemar

Piękna 7/9. **Map** 6 D2. **C** *628 81 40 & 628 45 43.* ○ *10am–until the last guest leaves daily.* V ♫ 🖼 🍴 🖼 $$$$$ ★

This luxurious Spanish (Castilian) restaurant, with its tastefully furn-ished interior, combines elegance with panache, spiced with a little exuberance. It offers a splendid atmosphere and delicious food. Pride of place is given to various herb-scented dishes, cooked in the clay oven, including lamb, suckling pig, poultry, Spanish sausages, and tortilla. Besides the classic gazpacho, there is also a sensational *ajo blanco* – a thick cold soup made with ground almonds and garlic; it is seasoned with oil and white sherry vinegar, and includes whole green grapes.

Montmartre

Nowy Świat 7. **Map** 2 D5 & 6 D1. **C** *628 63 15.* ○ *10am–until the last guest leaves daily.* V 🍴 🖼 $$$$

Montmartre is an excellent French restaurant, without aspiring to great elegance. Prices are expen-sive, but not excessive compared with those of others offering a similar menu. The appetizing dishes include green salad with hot chicken giblets, spicy Marseil-lais fish soup, calf kidneys in vermouth sauce, *côte de boeuf* (grilled beef ribs), frogs, snails, fresh oysters, and a Parisian delicacy, champagne fried oysters – all luxurious and expensive, but also unforgettable. Hot apple tart in caramel sauce, with vanilla ice cream, makes an ideal dessert to round off a meal here.

OTHER DISTRICTS

B-40

Most Poniatowskiego. **Map** 6 F1. ○ *10am–until the last guest leaves daily.* $

This pub has an unusual location, housed in one of the pillars sup-porting Poniatowski Bridge, on

the Praga side of the River Vistula. It serves beer, vodka, and Coca-Cola and is the meeting place of "rockers" and Harley-Davidson fans. The regulars are not keen on tourists, but if you have arrived in Warsaw on a Harley-Davidson, this is where you will make friends.

Boston Port

Okolska 2. **C** *44 03 15.* ○ *10am–7pm Mon–Fri.* V 🖼 $$

This small, modest, self-service bar concentrates on the food of the northeast coast of the United States. Dishes include a sensation-al New England fish chowder, which is prepared with five differ-ent varieties of fish. The restaurant also makes a surprisingly good home-made corned beef and roast Virginia ham, while European spe-cialties include filet mignon cooked in port, veal Marsala, and chicken cacciatore. The restaurant does not have a liquor license.

Fuks

Madalińskiego 38/40. **Map** 5 C5. **C** *49 87 24.* ○ *10am–until the last guest leaves daily.* V 🍴 🖼 $$ ★

This vegetarian's paradise has a sensational chef, who can turn soybeans into absolutely anything. And so you will find such dishes as soya in caper sauce, Greek soya, soya cocktail, soya tripe, goulash, *bigos*, Stroganoff, pork chop, shish kabob, *de volaille* (chicken Kiev), and cutlets in pastry, as well as Pekinese, Cantonese, Szechwan, Indian, Neapolitan, and even old-Polish style soya! Fuks also serves a good selection of soups, spinach ravioli, tasty bogus tiramisu, and a whole host of other delights.

Positano

Wołoska 74a. **C** *48 24 55* & Witosa 31 (Panorama Building). **C** *642 87 11.* ○ *noon–11pm daily.* V ♫ 🖼 🖼 $$

One of only a few pizzerias in town, Positano includes two small but pleasant sections offering thin crisp pizzas with tasty toppings. It also offers delicious *lasagna al forno* and salads.

Zielona Gęś

Aleje Niepodległości 177. **Map** 5 C4. **C** *25 20 26.* ○ *9am–2am Mon–Fri, 9am–5am Sat, Sun.* V ♫ 🖼 🖼 $$

This cowboy-style bar is *the* meet-ing place for fans of country music. It has a rancho-style decor, and offers a selection of grilled meats in keeping with the style, as well as salads and grilled sandwiches.

Zorba

Aleja Solidarności 61. **Map** 1 A3 & 3 C5. 📞 *18 52 60.* 🕐 *noon–10pm daily.* 🅅 🎵 ▦ 🄴 $$

Zorba specializes in Mediterranean and Greek cuisine. It is usually crowded, has an exuberant atmosphere, and the service is pleasant. Try the delicious cheese and olive salad, with retsina, or gyros with garlic and yogurt. The menu also offers *tzatziki*, souvlaki, crispy Seville duck, Moroccan *kefta*, and tasty salads, while the coffee is brewed in a Greek *brikia*.

ALAMO Steak House

Aleje Jerozolimskie 119. **Map** 2 E5 & 5 C1. 📞 *629 39 69.* 🕐 *noon–1am daily.* 🎵 ▦ 🍷 🄴 $$$

The ambience is not very exciting and the prices are high, but the American food here is excellent. Tuna salad, sweet roast ribs, roast pork in garlic sauce, and Boston steak are all recommended, while the bar offers a large selection of expensive spirits and a variety of international cocktails. The range of draft beers includes an excellent Czech lager.

Blue Cactus

Zajączkowska 11. 📞 *651 23 22.* 🕐 *noon–1am daily.* ▦ 🍷 🄴 $$$

Blue Cactus is Warsaw's first serious Tex-Mex restaurant. The interiors are colorful, but the atmosphere is perhaps a bit too bustling. A wide selection of steaks is offered, as well as classic chili con carne, delicious burritos, sandwiches, burgers, and salsa – quite expensive, but fun.

Ciao Maurizio

Wolska 50. **Map** 5 A1. 📞 *632 69 17.* 🕐 *1pm–until the last guest leaves daily.* 🅅 🄴 $$$

If you love Italian food, it is worth making a special trip to Wola to visit Ciao Maurizio. The dishes are excellent and the service is reasonable, though the atmosphere is rather restrained. The menu includes sensational sauces, served with a variety of pastas, excellent risotto (the best are with radicchio and asparagus), pancakes, vegetables in béchamel sauce, pork roast in orange sauce, pork loin à la Rossini, crème caramel, and tiramisu. Good coffee as well.

Flik

Puławska 43. **Map** 6 D4. 📞 *49 44 34.* 🕐 *10am–until the last guest leaves daily.* 🅅 🎵 ▦ 🍷 🄴 $$$

Flik has the most affordable prices of all luxury restaurants. Its comfortable interior is furnished with wicker furniture and offers an excellent view over Morskie Oko Park. The menu skillfully blends elements of a typically Polish menu, presenting dishes such as black pudding with apples; sauerkraut soup with potatoes; pork knuckle cooked in beer; bliny (buckwheat pancakes) with caviar, chopped spring onions, hardboiled egg, and thick cream; as well as foil-baked potatoes, caviar, and shrimp. Flik also offers the best *pierogi* (ravioli) in town, with cream cheese, cabbage, mushrooms, meat, or strawberries. In the summer, there is a grill set in a very pleasant garden. Good wines are served at affordable prices.

Mibella

Kasprowicza 56. 📞 *34 23 78.* 🕐 *11am–midnight daily.* 🅅 ▦ 🍷 🄴 $$$

This unpretentious place, offering good food and a pleasant atmosphere, is the best restaurant in this part of town. The menu offers calf's liver braised in cream, chicken nuggets served with three different sauces, and the classical *pfefferstek*. In the winter, a selection of hot punches, beer with spices, mead, and wine are served.

Rong Vang

Broniewskiego 74. 📞 *34 51 51.* 🕐 *10:30am–10pm daily.* 🅅 🄴 $$$

Rong Vang specializes in Vietnamese cuisine. The restaurant has a cozy, lively atmosphere, and the food is moderately priced. Interesting dishes include "moon-gazing carp," Tonkin duck, frogs fried in pastry, eel soup, coconut chicken, pork with bean sprouts, fried rice with shrimp or crab, and steamed vegetables with bamboo shoots. The "Rong Vang," after which the restaurant is named, is a rubbery rice tart, stuffed with dry fruit.

Santorini

Egipska 7 (in Saska Kępa). 📞 *672 05 25.* 🕐 *noon–11pm daily.* 🅅 ▦ 🍷 🄴 $$$

This Greek restaurant, slightly out of the city center, is an excellent place for a romantic dinner. Although the exterior is not very promising (the restaurant is in an office building), the interiors are like something out of a film, transporting diners a few hundred miles south, to the sunny setting of a restaurant by the Aegean Sea. Cold *meze* (appetizers) include excellent olives, feta cheese, hummus, stuffed vine leaves, and cold, cooked beet in garlic paste. These are served with warm dips, and accompanied by Greek wine such as retsina.

Chopin

Hotel Jan III Sobieski, Plac Zawiszy 1. **Map** 5 B2. 📞 *658 44 44 ext. 1008.* 🕐 *6:30am–10:30pm daily.* 🎵 ▦ 🍷 🄴 $$$$

This expensive, luxury restaurant, set in a modern hotel, has a tastefully arranged interior, with an atrium and verdant plants. The "Royal Table" dishes, prepared according to old Polish recipes, include excellent venison fillets à la Jagiellon, together with a rich selection of dishes from all around the world, including Austrian *tafelspitz*, Florentine veal, Alpine pork knuckle, Mexican *puntas de filete*, spicy Thai salad, and Nile perch in balsamic sauce. Some are delicious, but the standard is inconsistent. The fried ice cream, however, is a must for dessert.

Shogun

Migdałowa 42. 📞 *648 74 78.* 🕐 *noon–11pm daily.* 🅅 ▦ $$$$

This luxurious Japanese restaurant in the outlying Natolin district is incredibly expensive and frequented mainly by the executives of large international electronic and car companies. Its specialty is sukiyaki – a Japanese fondue.

Zajazd Napoleoński

Płowiecka 83. 📞 *15 30 68.* 🕐 *1pm–until the last guest leaves daily.* 🅅 ▦ 🍷 🄴 $$$$

Set in a country manor house, this restaurant offers good Polish and French cuisine, using frogs, snails, wild mushrooms, cream asparagus, veal knuckle braised in honey, rolled fillets of venison, roast duck, and veal scallops in cèpe sauce. For dessert, try vanilla ice cream smothered in hot raspberries. Only the overly ornate decor may take the edge off your appetite.

FARTHER AFIELD

Pod Złotym Linem

In Wierzbica, past Serock, on the road to Olsztyn. 📞 *782 74 73.* 🕐 *8am–9pm (10pm in summer) daily.* ▦ $$

This first-class and relatively inexpensive restaurant offers a huge selection of fish: tench, crucian carp, zander, catfish, trout, carp, eel, and pike. The fish is fresh, and mainly fried, braised in cream, or served in cold jelly. Another specialty is eel in dill sauce.

For key to symbols, *see p205*

SHOPPING IN WARSAW

SHOPPING HAS BECOME a completely different experience in Warsaw ever since privatization began in 1989. After years of shortages, which encompassed foodstuffs as well as various consumer goods, it is now possible to buy virtually everything in Warsaw. Many Western retailers have opened branches here, and international brand-name products are widely available. Polish manufacturers and retailers, spurred by this competition, are now matching the quality and range of imported goods. A growing number of department stores, shopping centers, and pedestrian areas are ideal for leisurely browsing, while a traditional bustling atmosphere continues in the city's bazaars.

A traditional
paper cut-out

Ballantine's, a liquor store that specializes in whisky

OPENING HOURS

SHOPS IN CENTRAL WARSAW are usually open from 10am until 7pm on Monday to Friday, and from 9am until 2pm or 3pm on Saturday. Delicatessens and many of the supermarkets often open earlier, and stay open until 8pm or even 10pm.

Department stores and large shopping centers also have longer opening hours, while at least one or two shops in each district of Warsaw are open 24 hours a day.

Large shopping centers are open on Sundays, as are many of the souvenir shops during the tourist season. On the last Sunday before Christmas and Easter, virtually all of the city's stores stay open for shoppers who need to make last-minute purchases.

In the center of Warsaw, stores are at their busiest on Saturdays and during the afternoon, so aim to shop early in the day if you want to avoid the crowds.

HOW TO PAY

NOT SURPRISINGLY, cash is the preferred method of payment in Poland. Although certain stores used to accept hard currency from tourists, this no longer applies, so all transactions are now handled in złoty.

Do not be surprised if store clerks ask you for the exact sum when you pay for goods, as a shortage of change seems to be a constant problem.

Many retail outlets, particularly department stores, accept checks, but only from Polish bank accounts.

Western-owned as well as Polish shops selling luxury goods and souvenirs for the tourist trade take all the more popular credit cards. Look for the logos of accepted credit cards, which are usually prominently displayed.

All prices in Poland include tax, which cannot be reclaimed when taking goods out of the country. There are several duty-free shops at Warsaw's Okęcie Airport.

Fukier Decoration, located on Mokotowska Street

SALES

THE PHENOMENON of sales has been known in Poland for only a few years. Initially only large department stores and Western-owned shops offered seasonal price reductions. Polish-owned stores

Marshal, a popular clothes shop on Nowy Świat Street

were slower to adopt this new pattern of trading, particularly as the word "sale" was previously associated with the cut-price and sub-standard goods that used to clutter many shops during the Communist era.

Now, however, sales are an accepted part of the shopping calendar. As in most other European countries, sales are usually held twice a year, just after Christmas and during the summer.

Perfumery on Chmielna Street

DEPARTMENT STORES AND SHOPPING CENTERS

W ARSAW has several good department stores, which provide a comprehensive range of merchandise. Moreover, a number of stores have recently been refurbished, making them more attractive and user-friendly.

The most popular department stores belong to the Domy "Centrum" group. This group's principal outlets are **Junior**, **Sawa**, and **Wars**, which specialize in clothes for all age groups, but also stock a wide range of other goods. While the stores do not sell foodstuffs, they are available from the nearby **Sezam**, which is also on Marshal Street (Marszałkowska).

The best place to go when shopping for children and expectant mothers is a shop called **Smyk** (see p132).

Also worth visiting is the **Arka** shopping center. It occupies an attractive Secessionist building that was

City Center shopping center

formerly the Jabłkowski Brothers' department store (see p131). Its range of boutiques offers leading European brand-name merchandise, including clothes, shoes, cosmetics, and interior-design items.

Among Warsaw's modern, purpose-built shopping centers are **City Center**, **Lim** at the Marriott Hotel, and **Panorama**, all of which provide a choice of individual shops, cafés, and dining areas. Panorama, in particular, has spacious interiors, featuring a fountain and patio (see p105).

MARKETS

M ANY OF WARSAW'S locals consider markets to be the only place to shop, if you are looking for low prices.

The largest of Warsaw's markets is the **Saxon Market** (Jarmark Saski), held at the Dziesięciolecie Stadium. This once impressive sports arena is now one of the biggest open-air markets in Europe. Street vendors and Russian traders are among those who

Arka shopping center

and Science. A good place to buy fresh fruit and vegetables is the **Mirowski Halls** (Hale Mirowskie). Extending along both sides of John Paul II Avenue, this market offers a vast assortment of foodstuffs, including meat and dairy produce. Warsaw's most

Blikle's famous patisserie on Nowy Świat

set up stalls here, offering an astonishing range of goods.

Nearby on Targowa Street is **Różycki Market** (see p174). During the Communist era, this was a haven for private trade and an important source of consumer goods that were unavailable in Poland's state shops. Trade continues to flourish, and now Gypsies, Romanians, and Russians join the Polish traders at the bazaar.

Another market frequented by locals is at **Defilad Square**, next to the Palace of Culture

famous food market is situated on **Polna Street**. This long-standing institution, where it has always been possible to find international delicacies, survived every attempt by the Communists to nationalize and regulate trade. Even now, its shabby kiosks stock top-quality culinary items, including a choice of exotic fruit and vegetables from all over the world. The clientele at Polna Street market is said to include many of the city's diplomats.

Where to Shop

Warsaw's stores offer a wide selection of both designer and brand-name apparel, as well as Polish specialties such as amber jewelry, Silesian crystal glass, leather goods, tableware, folk art, and contemporary art. Several department stores provide "one-stop shopping," while plenty of boutiques, bookstores, galleries, and souvenir shops are also excellent for browsing. The greatest concentration of stores is in the Old Town and New Town, on Nowy Świat Street, and around Marshal Street.

POLISH FOLK ART

Polish handicrafts and folk arts are renowned for their quality and beauty. Among the most popular items are embroidered tablecloths, pottery, leather goods, painted wooden Easter eggs (pisanki), and Christmas tree decorations fashioned from straw. Other specialties are colorful paper cutouts of rustic motifs, naive art such as paintings on glass, and carved religious figures.

The **Cepelia** retail chain specializes in folk art, with beautiful hand-woven kilims, textiles, wickerwork, and leather goods such as the unique moccasins (kierpce) produced by Polish highlanders from Zakopane, in the south of Poland.

Other shops in the city center that sell folk arts and crafts include **Folk Art and Handicrafts** and the **Folk Art and Crafts Gallery**.

CONTEMPORARY ARTS AND CRAFTS

Numerous art galleries and interior-design shops throughout the city provide a comprehensive choice of items of modern Polish and European design.

The finest handblown glass and crystal can be found in **Galeria MP**, located in the Old Town Market Square. In addition, the **Opera** shop in the New Town has a wide selection of attractive artifacts produced mainly by Polish artists and craftsmen. Fans of modern Italian design will find items from the Alessi range in **Gallery Aina Progetti**, on Krakowskie Przedmieście. The flamboyant interiors of

Fukier Decoration, on Mokotowska Street, are an inspiring showcase for an extensive choice of top-quality soft furnishings, glassware, pottery, and other decorative items.

While Gdańsk is the capital of Poland's historic amber trade, Warsaw also has several galleries that specialize in amber jewelry and objets d'art, particularly in the Old Town and along the Royal Route.

Among central Warsaw's more prestigious contemporary art galleries are **Zapiecek** and **Plac Zamkowy**, both in the Old Town, **ZPAP** on Krakowskie Przedmieście, and **Posters and Graphic Arts** on Hoża Street.

Original paintings are also available at far more affordable prices from stalls and street artists in the Old Town Market Square, on Nowomiejska Street, and by the Barbican.

ANTIQUES

While warsaw has a growing number of antique shops, strict regulations limit the export of any works of art produced before 1945.

Antiques can be exported only with a special government license, which is issued only in exceptional circumstances. This protectionist policy is a result of the enormous losses suffered during World War II.

Many good antique shops are located in the Old Town and along the Royal Route. Some of the best known among them are **Desa** (which is a state-owned chain of antique shops) and **Rempex**. The Sunday **Antique Market** is held every week in Koło.

It is worth arriving early for the best choice, as the market usually begins to wind down in the afternoon, at around 2pm. The **Saxon Market** (see p191) is also worth a visit, if you enjoy sifting through an assortment of bric-a-brac.

BOOKS AND RECORDS

Although it is possible to buy guidebooks and illustrated books in English, German, and French, they are still something of a rarity in Warsaw. The widest range of foreign-language books is available at the city's largest bookstores: **Empik in Junior**, **Odeon**, **Leksykon**, and **Joseph Conrad Bookshop**.

Impressive selections of fiction and reference books can be found in **Bolesław Prus** and **Liber** bookstores, while the widest variety of books covering fine art is provided by the **Royal Castle** shop on Świętojańska Street.

If you are interested in collecting prints and books you should make sure you visit the city's numerous second-hand bookshops (look for shop signs saying Antykwariat). A good "itinerary" is to follow the Royal Route, starting at **Kosmos i Logos** on Ujazdowskie Avenue, and continuing into the Old and New towns, particularly via Nowomiejska and Freta streets.

Digital is the best place to buy records while various collectors' items can also be found in the small shops scattered around the center of Warsaw. **Odeon** and **By the Opera** have a wide selection of records, and a large stock of sheet music.

CLOTHING AND SHOES

The choice and quality of clothes and footwear have improved dramatically over the past few years. Several world-famous fashion houses, including **Pierre Cardin**, have opened boutiques in Warsaw. Similarly, a typical range of denim jeans and jackets can now be found in the **Wrangler** and **Levi Strauss** shops.

Meanwhile, clothes designed by Warsaw's own growing band of young fashion designers are available in boutiques such as **Hanaoka** and **Grażyna Hase**.

Department stores also sell good-quality, yet inexpensive designs manufactured in Poland, under their own label. Two of the best known shops for women are **Cora** and **Telimena**. Among menswear, **Bytom** is good for suits and **Próchnik** for coats, while **Wólczanka** is the best place to buy shirts.

Shops and boutiques in the city center carry a range of brand names catering to most budgets. At the sophisticated end of the market are **Dantex** and **Lord**, while **House of Carli Gry** and **Marshal** are mid-range outlets. **India Market**, selling a variety of Indian clothes, is relatively inexpensive and popular with younger consumers.

Shoe stores include **Bata** and **Salamander**, as well as the ubiquitous **Adidas** and **Reebok** stores.

Poland is renowned for the quality and design of leather goods, including handbags, purses, jackets, and belts. A good selection is available in **Pekar**, on Jerozolimskie Avenue, and **Pantera** on Nowy Świat Street, as well as the eponymous boutique owned by the celebrated leather-goods designer **Andrzej Kłoda**.

PERFUMES

A COMPREHENSIVE selection of the world's leading perfumes is available from **J Powierza**, which is located on Chmielna Street, as well as **Marguerite** on Nowy Świat Street, which specializes in French perfumes.

Moreover, **Christian Dior**, **Estée Lauder**, and **Guerlain** have opened branches in Warsaw that stock their full range of products. The Guerlain shop also includes a beauty salon.

Cosmetics and toiletries, whether international or Polish brand names, are readily available in most pharmacies, larger supermarkets, and department stores.

FOOD AND DRINK

THE CITY CENTER has plenty of delicatessens where you can stock up on various supplies. Fresh fruit and vegetables can be bought at markets or from numerous stalls scattered around the center of town. Some shops and mini-supermarkets are open 24 hours a day, seven days a week. Among the larger stores with a comprehensive selection are **Sezam**, **Rema 100**, and **Supersam**, with **Luxus** conveniently situated in Powiśle and open every day.

A recent addition is the huge **Szalony Max** (Mad Max) supermarket, located in the basement of Dom Słowa Polskiego on the western edge of the city center. It has a large parking area and forms part of a shopping center. The largest supermarkets tend to be located on the outskirts of town, catering to shoppers who drive there to do their weekly shopping. These include Globi, Billa, Leclerc, and Robert.

Imported wines and spirits are expensive in Poland, and while there is no local wine production, there is a good selection of beer and vodka. The largest selection is stocked by **Alcoholic Drinks of the World**, while spirits, particularly whisky, are a specialty of **Ballantine's**. A large choice of coffees is available in **Farewell to Africa** (Pożegnanie z Afryką), a café that also has a shop.

PATISSERIES AND CONFECTIONERS

WARSAW OFFERS plenty of opportunities to indulge to anyone with a sweet tooth. The **Hortex** chain, for instance, has an array of cakes at branches throughout the city. There are, of course many smaller patisseries, many of which also have a café on the premises. Warsaw's "institutions" include **Blikle** (see p124), which is famous for its doughnuts. Blikle has its main outlet on Nowy Świat Street, as well as branches on Hoża Street and Wilcza Street.

Other specialties include a very good *sękacz* (knobbly cake) at the **Pomianowski** patisserie, excellent cream slices at the **Hotel Europejski's** patisserie, and the best apple strudel in town at the **Café Bristol**.

Zielona Budka (Green Kiosk) specializes in ice cream, and its products can be found throughout Warsaw.

For a taste of the finest chocolates, try **Staroświecki firmowy E Wedel** (Old-fashioned Shop of E Wedel), where a charming café specializes in hot chocolate and chocolate cake.

PHARMACIES

IN LINE with international practice, many types of medication and drugs can be purchased only with a doctor's prescription. However, many nonprescription drugs (under international brand names) are readily available over the counter at very competitive prices.

Each district in Warsaw has a 24-hour pharmacy. The city center is served by a pharmacy in the **Central Railroad Station** (Dworzec Centralny). Other convenient pharmacies are on Widok and Freta streets.

Two of Warsaw's most attractive pharmacies feature splendid 19th-century interiors. There is a shop at No. 18 Nowy Świat Street where the decor is English Gothic, while at No. 19 Krakowskie Przedmieście, the interiors are Neo-Renaissance in style.

FLORISTS

ONE OF WARSAW's largest florists is **Tulipan** (Tulip), on Jerozolimskie Avenue, with another store on Nowy Świat Street.

Also on Nowy Świat Street is **Sonia Interflora**, which delivers flowers to every country that is part of the Interflora network.

According to local superstition, a wedding bouquet ordered from **Glorioza** brings good luck to newlyweds.

Flower shops can also be found at various hotels, railroad stations, and the airport.

DIRECTORY

DEPARTMENT STORES AND SHOPPING CENTERS (DOMY TOWAROWE I CENTRA HANDLOWE)

Arka
Bracka 25.
Map 2 D5 & 6 D1.
『 827 60 21.

City Center
Złota 44/46.
Map 1 B5 & 5 C1.
『 625 25 24.

Panorama
Witosa 31.
『 642 06 66.

Shopping Center (comprising Junior, Sawa, and Wars)
Marszałkowska 104/122.
Map 1 C5 & 5 C1.
『 827 92 61.

Smyk
Krucza 50.
Map 2 D5 & 6 D1.
『 827 93 95.

BAZAARS AND MARKETS (BAZARY I TARGOWISKA)

Defilad Square (Na placu Defilad)
Plac Defilad.
Map 1 C5 & 5 C1.

Market by Mirowski Halls (Przy halach Mirowskich)
Aleja Jana Pawła II.
Map 1 B4.

Polna Street (Na Polnej)
Polna.
Map 6 D3.

Różycki Market
Targowa 54.
Map 4 F4.
『 619 03 44.

Saxon Market (Jarmark Saski)
Stadion Dziesięciolecia.
Map 4 F4.
『 617 29 00.

POLISH FOLK ART (FOLKLOR POLSKI)

Cepelia
Nowy Świat 35.
Map 2 D5 & 6 D1.
『 826 42 73.

Plac Konstytucji 5.
Map 6 D2.
『 621 26 18.

Bracka 3.
Map 2 D5 & 6 D1.
『 621 58 38.

Krucza 23/31.
Map 6 D2.
『 621 96 94.

Folk Art and Handicrafts (Rękodzieło Ludowe i Artystyczne)
Chmielna 8.
Map 2 D5 & 6 D1.
『 826 60 31.

Folk Arts and Crafts Gallery (Galeria Sztuki Ludowej i Artystycznej)
Plac Konstytucji 2.
Map 6 D2.
『 621 66 69.

Other Folk Art shop
Marszałkowska 99/101.
Map 5 C1.
『 628 33 50.

CONTEMPORARY ARTS AND CRAFTS (RĘKODZIEŁO ARTYSTYCZNE I GALERIE SZTUKI WSPÓŁCZESNEJ)

Aina Progetti
Krakowskie Przedmieście 17.
Map 2 D3 & 4 D5.
『 47 03 72.

Fukier Decoration
Mokotowska 39.
Map 6 D2.
『 625 77 22.

Galeria MP
Rynek Starego Miasta 9/11.
Map 2 D1 & 4 D4.
『 831 69 61.

Opera
Freta 14.
Map 1 C1 & 3 C4.
『 831 73 28.

Plac Zamkowy
Plac Zamkowy 1/13.
Map 2 D2 & 4 D4.
『 831 06 84.

Posters and Graphic Arts (Grafiki i Plakatu)
Hoża 40. **Map** 6 D2.
『 621 40 77.

Zapiecek
Zapiecek 1.
Map 2 D2 & 4 D4.
『 831 99 18.

ZPAP
Krakowskie Przedmieście 15/17.
Map 2 D3 & 4 D5.
『 635 51 70.

ANTIQUES (ANTYKI)

Antique Market (Targ Staroci na Kole)
Obozowa 99.
『 36 23 51.

Desa
Nowy Świat 48.
Map 6 D1 & 2 D5.
『 826 44 66.

Rynek Starego Miasta.
Map 2 D1 & 4 D4.
『 831 16 81.

Nadine
Plac Trzech Krzyży 18.
Map 6 E1.
『 621 63 18.

Rempex
Senatorska 11.
Map 1 C3.
『 826 22 71.

BOOKS AND RECORDS (KSIĘGARNIE)

Bolesław Prus Bookstore (Księgarnia im B Prusa)
Krakowskie Przedmieście 7.
Map 2 D3 & 4 D5.
『 826 18 35.

By the Opera (Przy Operze)
Moliera 8.
Map 2 D3 & 4 D5.
『 826 46 48.

Digital
Aleje Jerozolimskie 2.
Map 2 E5 & 6 E1.
『 827 87 73.

Empik in Junior
Marszałkowska 104/122.
Map 1 C5 & 5 C1.
『 827 92 61.

Joseph Conrad Bookshop (Księgarnia im J Conrada)
Aleje Jerozolimskie 28.
Map 2 D5 & 6 D1.
『 827 05 38.

Kosmos i Logos
Aleje Ujazdowskie 16.
Map 6 E2.
『 628 65 82.
『 621 38 67.

Leksykon
Nowy Świat 41.
Map 2 D5 & 6 D1.
『 826 45 33.

Liber
Krakowskie Przedmieście 24.
Map 2 D3.
『 826 30 91.

Odeon
Hoża 19.
Map 6 D2.
『 621 80 69.

Royal Castle (Zamku Królewskiego)
Świętojańska 2.
Map 2 D2 & 4 D4.
『 657 22 64.

CLOTHING AND SHOES (ODZIEŻ I OBUWIE)

Adidas
Aleje Jerozolimskie 56c.
Map 5 B2.
『 630 22 37.

Andrzej Kłoda
Krakowskie Przedmieście 81.
Map 2 D3 & 4 D5.
『 827 07 40.

Bata
Marszałkowska 87.
Map 6 D2.
『 629 15 94.

Bytom
Bytom has a boutique in Wars Department Store, Marszałkowska 104/122.
Map 1 C5 & 5 C1.

Cora
Marszałkowska 82.
Map 6 D2.
『 625 16 94.

Dantex
Aleje Jerozolimskie
11/19.
Map 2 D5 & 6 D1.
C 621 67 94.

Galeria Hanaoka
Freta 19.
Map 1 C1 & 3 C4.
C 831 06 03.

Grażyny Hase
Marszałkowska 6 m. 2.
Map 6 D3.
C 628 21 59.

**House of
Carli Gry**
Marszałkowska
86/92.
Map 6 D2.
C 621 29 36.

India Market
Hoża 5/7.
Map 6 D2.
C 629 61 68.

Krakowskie
Przedmieście 31.
Map 2 D3.

Levi Strauss
Plac Konstytcji 6.
Map 6 D2.
C 621 59 51.

Aleje Jerozolimskie 51.
Map 5 C1.
C 621 75 71.

Lord
Marszałkowska 87.
Map 6 D2.
C 625 34 96.

Marshal
Nowy Świat 49.
Map 2 D5 & 6 D1.
C 627 99 07.

Pantera
Nowy Świat 21.
Map 2 D5 & 6 D1.
C 826 46 58.

Pekar
Aleje Jerozolimskie 29.
Map 2 D5 & 6 D1.
C 621 90 82.

Pierre Cardin
Aleje Jerozolimskie 31.
Map 2 D5 & 6 D1.
C 622 30 01.

Próchnik
Aleja Jana Pawła II 18.
Map 1 B5 & 5 B1.
C 620 34 16.

Reebok
Marszałkowska 2.
Map 6 D3.
C 625 62 56.

Salamander
Aleje Jerozolimskie 42.
Map 2 D5 & 6 D1.
C 827 02 67.

Telimena
Marszałkowska 82.
Map 6 D2.
C 623 63 37.

Wólczanka
Marszałkowska 82.
Map 6 D2.
C 623 63 37.

Wrangler
Aleje Jerozolimskie 109.
Map 5 B2.
C 629 74 07.

**PERFUMES
(PERFUMERIE)**

Christian Dior
Nowy Świat 45.
Map 2 D5 & 6 D1.
C 827 11 04.

Estée Lauder
Nowy Świat 47.
Map 2 D5 & 6 D1.
C 826 01 84.

Guerlain
Krakowskie
Przedmieście 42/44.
Map 2 D3 & 4 D3.
C 625 25 25.

J Powierza
Chmielna 18.
Map 2 D5 & 6 D1.
C 827 75 83.

Marguerite
Nowy Świat 30.
Map 2 D5 & 6 D1.
C 826 54 47.

**FOOD AND DRINK
(SKLEPY
SPOŻYWCZE)**

**Alcoholic Drinks
of the World
(Alkohole Świata)**
Aleja Solidarności 84.
Map 1 A3.
C 38 52 40.

Ballantine's
Krucza 47a.
Map 6 D2.
C 625 48 32.

**Farewell to Africa
(Pożegnanie
z Afryką)**
Freta 4/6.
Map 1 C1 & 3 C4.

**French Wine Shop
(Sklep win
francuskich)**
Marszałkowska 104a.
Map 6 D2.
C 827 65 61.

Luxus
Solec 32/34.
Map 6 F4.
C 625 36 06.

Rema 100
Krucza 50.
Map 6 D2.
C 827 08 68.

Sezam
Marszałkowska 126/134.
Map 1 C5 & 5 C1.
C 827 45 26.

Supersam
Puławska 2.
Map 6 D4.
C 25 24 74.

Szalony Max
Miedziana 11 (entrance
on Towarowa Street).
Map 5 B1.
C 620 71 39.

**PATISSERIES AND
CONFECTIONERS
(CUKIERNIE)**

Blikle
Nowy Świat 35.
Map 2 D5 & 6 D1.
C 826 45 68.

Café Bristol
Krakowskie
Przedmieście 42/44.
Map 2 D3.
C 625 25 25.

Hortex
Rynek Starego
Miasta 3/7.
Map 2 D1 & 4 D4.
C 831 63 47.

Plac Konstytucji 7.
Map 6 D2.
C 628 76 78.

Hotel Europejski
Krakowskie
Przedmieście 13.
Map 2 D3 & 4 D5.
C 826 50 51.

Pomianowski
Krakowskie Przedmieście 8.
Map 2 D3 & 4 D5.
C 826 77 25.

**Staroświecki
firmowy E Wedel**
Szpitalna 8.
Map 2 D5 & 6 D1.
C 827 29 16.

Zielona Budka
Puławska 11.
Map 6 D4.
C 49 89 38.

**PHARMACIES
(APTEKI)**

**Central Station
(Na Dworcu
Centralnym)**
Aleje Jerozolimskie.
Map 5 C1.
C 25 69 84.

Kosma i Damian
Rynek Starego Miasta
17/19. **Map** 2 D1 & 4 D4.
C 831 17 84.

Other Pharmacies
Freta 13/15.
Map 1 C1 & 3 C4.
C 831 50 91.

Widok 19.
Map 2 D5 & 6 D1.
C 827 35 93.

Krakowskie
Przedmieście 19.
Map 2 D3 & 4 D5.
C 826 18 03.

Nowy Świat 18.
Map 6 D1 & 2 E5.
C 826 53 82.

**FLORISTS
(KWIACARNIE)**

Glorioza
Wilcza 19.
Map 6 D2.
C 629 63 86.

Sonia Interflora
Nowy Świat 40.
Map 2 D5 & 6 D1.
C 826 32 27.

Tulipan
Aleje Jerozolimskie 21.
Map 2 D5 & 6 D1.
C 628 04 95.

Nowy Świat 19.
Map 6 D1.
C 826 44 58.

ENTERTAINMENT IN WARSAW

WARSAW has become a much livelier city over the past few years, and while not yet matching New York or London in the diversity of entertainment available, there is still plenty to interest visitors. Two opera houses and the Philharmonic offer programs that will please even the most discerning classical music lovers. Jazz fans can choose from several excellent clubs, while devotees of other types of popular music can enjoy a variety of venues, from palaces and museums to stadiums, bars, and clubs. Theaters show major films from around the world, usually in their original language with Polish subtitles, and English-language plays are also staged. Moreover, Warsaw holds various cultural festivals throughout the year, including music, film, theater, art, and jazz.

Saxophone player

Finale of Małgorzata Potocka's glamorous review at the Tango Club nightspot

PRACTICAL INFORMATION

THE MOST comprehensive and up-to-the-minute information on what is happening in Warsaw can be found in the monthly magazine *Kalejdoskop Kulturalny (Cultural Kaleidoscope)*, which is available from Ruch kiosks and other newsstands. *Cultural Kaleidoscope* has an English section with information on museums, galleries, exhibitions, theater events, music, and films, with details of foreign culture centers, antique shops, auction houses and features on life in the capital.

Additionally, there are a couple of English-language publications: *Warszawa What, Where, When* and *Welcome to Warsaw*. Both are published monthly, and are available free from many of the city's hotels. Together with features on topical events, both magazines provide comprehensive listings, including museums and exhibitions, films and theaters, as well as times of religious services. The English-language weekly *Warsaw Voice* contains some listings. Warsaw's main tourist office *(see p237)* is also a good source of up-to-date entertainment information.

Roulette table at Orbis Casino in the Victoria Hotel

A scene from Stefan Moniuszko's opera the *Haunted Manor*, at the Grand Theater (Teatr Wielki)

central point on Emilii Plater Street, which makes it very convenient to change bus routes. Tickets for night buses can be bought on board from the driver *(see p255)*.

FESTIVALS

Warsaw is an established city for various annual festivals *(see p52)* and competitions, where some of the world's finest performers can be seen. Opera lovers, for instance, can attend the annual Mozart Festival, which is held in June and July.

By far the largest number of festivals are held in the autumn. If you are a fan of jazz music, the best time to visit Warsaw is in October, when you can attend the

BOOKING TICKETS

Tickets for productions at all of Warsaw's theaters can be purchased up to two weeks in advance, at the theater booking offices. Reservations can be made by mail or over the telephone, and all reserved tickets must be picked up a short time before the performance is due to start.

Tickets to theater productions, concerts, and special events, together with festival passes, can also be purchased from the **ZASP** booking office. The company charges only a modest commission on its ticket transactions.

Tickets can also be obtained through travel agencies that service visitors to Warsaw *(see p237)*. Some travel agents, such as **Mazurkas Travel**, organize evening visits to concerts and the opera that include transportation and a

Interior of the 18th-century Łazienki Theater

glass of champagne during the intermission.

Hotels also offer help booking tickets, through either the concierge or reception.

TICKET PRICES

Ticket prices in Poland are generally lower than in Western Europe, although the cost of tickets to see world-class stars may be comparable. Important festivals, such as the Warsaw Autumn, the Mozart Festival, and the Jazz Jamboree, attract major names, although ticket prices are affordable for the general public, due to generous sponsorship.

Movie tickets are inexpensive, with theater and opera tickets significantly cheaper than in many Western cities, though opera tickets can be moderately expensive, depending on the production.

In some instances, students can buy passes to sit in the aisles for a nominal fee.

NIGHT TRANSPORTATION

The easiest and safest way of returning to your hotel after a night out is, of course, by taking a taxi. However, there are many bogus taxi drivers touting for business, and you should either take a taxi from a stand or telephone for a radio taxi *(see p252)*. Licensed radio taxis are the least expensive option.

While Warsaw's "daytime" public transportation services end at around 11pm, there are night buses running every 30 minutes throughout the night. These buses stop at one

A horse race at the Służewiec Racetrack

concerts of the popular, yearly Jazz Jamboree.

There are also classical music festivals at this time, including the Warsaw Autumn. Additionally, Renaissance and Baroque music is performed at the Festival of Early Music, which is held in October.

USEFUL ADDRESSES

Mazurkas Travel, Forum Hotel
Nowogrodska 24/26.
Map 6 D1. 629 12 49.
Długa 8/14.
Map 3 C4. 635 50 91.

Polish Landscape
Cegłowska 28. 34 18 12.

Tourist Information
Plac Zamkowy 1/3.
Map 4 D4. 635 18 81.

ZASP
Aleje Jerozolimskie 25.
Map 2 D5. 621 94 54.

Entertainment in Warsaw

Warsaw has long-standing theatrical and musical traditions. Many celebrated musicians have given concerts here, including Niccolò Paganini, Franz Liszt, and Polish composers such as Stanisław Moniuszko. The greatest source of pride, however, is Frederic Chopin, who studied and performed in Warsaw.

The first theater open to the public, the Operalnia, was built in 1748, and the city now has a thriving repertoire of opera, ballet, musicals, movies, and concerts. In addition, Warsaw's program of annual festivals includes organ music, jazz, and street theater.

FOREIGN-LANGUAGE PERFORMANCES

Warsaw is proud of its **Jewish National Theater**, which is unique in Europe. Performances are given in Yiddish, accompanied by translations into Polish and English. This provides an excellent opportunity to experience Jewish culture and a sense of Jewish life in Poland, which has all but vanished. The company's repertoire includes various plays and musicals based on several centuries of Jewish tradition.

English-language performances are staged at the **English Theater Company**, a venue that often plays host to British artists. Some of their productions are bilingual.

Occasionally, other theaters offer English-speaking productions as well, while once a month, the **Espero** theater company performs plays in the Esperanto language.

THEATERS

The city's long-standing theatrical tradition dates from the end of the 16th century when Warsaw became the capital of Poland.

Theater companies are now free to choose from a wide range of classical and modern plays. During the Communist era, the choice of productions was always state-controlled.

Among the most popular venues with Varsovians are the **Powszechny**, **Ateneum**, and **Współczesny** theaters. They all feature the best actors and the best directors, and each opening night is a major social event. The **Polski**, **Dramatyczny**, **Rozmaitości**, **Nowy**, and **Na Woli** theaters specialize in drama, while comedies are often staged at the **Kwadrat** and **Komedia** theaters.

Teatr Studio is renowned for staging highly original works that frequently border on experimental theater. Avant-garde productions, as well as audio and video art, can be seen at the Modern Art Center (Centrum Sztuki Współczesnej, *see p159*).

Interesting productions are held at the **Teatr Adekwatny** and the **Teatr Jestem**, within Warsaw's historic Stara Prochownia (Old Gunpowder Depository, *see p89*).

Teatr Ochoty provides for audiences of a younger age group, while four other theaters also offer entertainment for children (*see p233*).

OPERA AND BALLET

Warsaw's two opera companies are the **National Opera**, which is based at the Grand Theater (Teatr Wielki), and the **Warsaw Chamber Opera** (Warszawska Opera Kameralna).

The National Opera is associated with the staging of monumental works, with huge casts and world-class soloists. The company's varied program includes Polish operas and classics from other countries.

The Warsaw Chamber Opera, as its name suggests, stages mainly courtly Baroque operas. The company is particularly known for its productions of the music of Mozart. These performances form part of Warsaw's annual Mozart Festival (*see p53*) and feature Mozart's work in its entirety, including his very early works.

The Warsaw Ballet Company, based at the Grand Theater, alternates its shows with those of the National Opera.

MUSICAL THEATERS

Among the wide choice of musical theaters to be found in Warsaw, one of the most popular is **Roma–Teatr Muzyczny**, which stages classical operettas and musicals.

For lighter musical entertainment, try **Rampa**, **Buffo**, or **Syrena**. These theaters stage musicals and reviews, as well as satirical cabarets and comedies, using established performers. Syrena's productions are generally more traditional than those of Rampa and Buffo, which aim at a younger audience.

Various musicals based on Jewish life, which are performed in Yiddish, can be seen at the **Jewish National Theater** (Teatr Żydowski).

Musicals and revues are also included in the repertoires of other theaters.

CLASSICAL MUSIC

The most established of Warsaw's concert halls is the **National Philharmonic** (Filharmonia Narodowa, *see p131*). Its two auditoriums serve as venues for various classical music festivals, most notably the Warsaw Autumn (*see p54*), and competitions such as the Chopin International Piano Competition (*see p54*), held every five years.

The Philharmonic also stages so-called Thursday Concerts, which are aimed at youth audiences, while on Sunday morning concerts of classical music are held for children.

Classical music can be heard in the **Polish Radio Concert Studio** (Studio Koncertowe Polskiego Radia), and also in the Academy of Music's concert hall. The Warsaw Music Society (Warszawskie Towarzystwo Muzyczne) also hosts concerts in Szuster Palace, while the Chopin Society organizes performances in Ostrogski Palace.

CONCERTS IN PALACES, CHURCHES, AND MUSEUMS

MANY CLASSICAL concerts are held in Warsaw's palaces, churches, and museums. These historic settings, which often have excellent acoustics, provide a memorable experience for the audience.

Chamber music is a regular attraction at the **Royal Castle**, **Wilanów Palace**, and various venues within Łazienki Park, including the **Palace on the Water**, **Myślewicki Palace**, the **Theater on the Island**, and the **Stanisławowski Theater** in the **Old Orangerie**.

Among the museums providing concert venues are the National Museum and the Former Bank of Poland and Stock Exchange, which houses the John Paul II Art Collection. Concerts held at Staromiejski Dom Kultury and the Archdiocese Museum are also extremely popular.

Organ music can be enjoyed in various churches in Warsaw, but particularly at the following places: Holy Trinity Church (Przenajświętszej Trójcy), St. John's Cathedral (katedra św. Jana), St. Joseph's Church (św. Józefa), St. Savior's (Zbawiciela), and Holy Mary, Queen of the World (Matki Boskiej Królowej Świata).

During the summer, Chopin concerts are held in Żelazowa Wola and by the Chopin monument in Łazienki Park.

MOVIE THEATERS

MOST OF Warsaw's movie theaters are around Marshal Street (Marszałkowska). These include the **Capitol**, **Luna**, **Muranów**, **Palladium**, **Bajka**, and **Relax**, while the **Kultura** and **Skarpa** are located on the capital's Royal Route.

A popular studio theater in Warsaw that shows mainly Polish films is **Rejs**. Classic movies are screened at **Iluzjon**, while interesting films can be seen at the theater in the Palace of Culture and Science. Many films are premiered in the conveniently situated, although somewhat dilapidated, Kultura. **Femina**

is Warsaw's first "Multiplex" theater, although others are currently under construction in the city center.

Additionally, every autumn a film festival is held. At this, an international selection of films is usually previewed.

MUSIC CLUBS

THE NUMBER of music clubs in Warsaw has increased considerably over the past few years, with the current total in excess of 50.

The unquestionable leader of the jazz scene is the long-established **Aquarium Jazz Club**. It has a loyal audience and live music every night.

Other popular jazz venues are **Rynek Jazz Club**, **Stodoła**, and **Riviera-Remont**. However, these jazz clubs also provide various other types of popular music, and hold discos on weekends.

More varied repertoires are offered by **Blue Velvet**, **Empik Club Pub**, and **Klub Giovanni**. Meanwhile, the **Irish Pub** specializes in country, folk, and rock music, while the **Blues Bar** provides a wide range of blues. Other popular pubs in central Warsaw offering live music include **Piwnica Architektów** and **Falcon Pub**.

NIGHTCLUBS AND DISCOTHEQUES

NIGHTLIFE has greatly improved over the past few years. However, the most active venues still tend to be student discos, which means of course that the clientele is young. These discos include **Riviera-Remont**, **Stodoła**, **Park**, **Hades**, **Hybrydy**, and **Klub Medyka**.

Equally popular are the discos held at **Dekadent** and **Dziekanka**. Additionally, **Ground Zero** offers a novel setting, being housed within a bunker that dates from the Stalinist era. Fans of techno music should try **Trend**.

Among the most exclusive and expensive nightclubs in Warsaw are **Tango**, **Cul de Sac**, and **Yesterday**, though the most prominent of all is **Orpheus**. Some nightclubs

also offer light entertainment. Anyone who enjoys watching women's mud wrestling should try **Arena**; if you enjoy the sight of men's biceps, then visit **Ufo Club**.

GAY AND LESBIAN CLUBS

WHILE there are not many gay and lesbian clubs in Warsaw, they are undoubtedly on the increase and no longer create a sensation when they open. Among the casual venues where you can have a cup of coffee or a glass of beer are **Koźla Club** and the **Między Nami** café.

Discos are held at nightclubs, such as **Rudawka**, which also has a reasonable restaurant. Additionally, the **Centrum Fantom** club provides a gym and many other forms of entertainment.

SPORTS

WARSAW OFFERS sports enthusiasts a reasonable range of choices. Swimmers can use the pools at Namysłowska or Inflancka Street, while tennis players can play all year round at the **City Tennis Club**, **Solec**, the **Mera** sports hall, and the **Legia** sports stadium.

Soccer matches are also held at the Legia stadium, with ice hockey and figure skating in **Torwar**. Speed skating is available at the **Stegna** rink.

The best water-sports facilities are provided outside the city on Zegrzyński Reservoir (Zalew Zegrzyński). Similarly, horseback riding is offered by many out-of-town clubs, such as those in Kanie and Podkowa Leśna, with a round of golf available at the **First Warsaw Golf and Country Club**.

The surrounding countryside is also ideal for walking and cycling. These activities can be undertaken as part of an escorted group, with various groups meeting on weekends. Joining such a group is free, with the times and places of meetings advertised in newspapers.

If you are a horse-racing enthusiast, you can spend a very enjoyable Sunday at the **Służewiec Racetrack**.

DIRECTORY

FOREIGN-LANGUAGE PERFORMANCES

English Theater Company
Państwowa Szkoła
Baletowa, Moliera 4.
Map 2 D3.
[619 98 17.

Espero
Galeria Nusantara,
Nowogrodzka 18a.
Map 4 D1.
[629 24 41.

Jewish National Theater (Teatr Żydowski)
Plac Grzybowski
12/16.
Map 1 B4.
[620 62 81.

THEATERS

Ateneum
Jaracza 2.
Map 2 F4.
[625 73 30.

Dramatyczny
Palace of Culture and
Science.
Map 1 C5 & 5 C1.
[656 68 44.

Kameralny (Scena Teatru Polskiego)
Foksal 16.
Map 2 E5 & 6 D1.
[826 49 18.

Komedia
Północne Centrum
Sztuki,
Słowackiego 19a.
[33 68 80.

Kwadrat
Czackiego 15/17.
Map 2 D4.
[826 23 89.

Mały
Marszałkowska 122.
Map 1 C5.
[827 50 22.

Na Woli
Kasprzaka 22.
[632 24 78.

Nowy
Puławska 37/39.
Map 6 E5.
[49 35 51.

Polski
Karasia 2.
Map 2 E4.
[826 79 92.

Powszechny
Zamoyskiego 20.
[18 25 16.

Rozmaitości
Marszałkowska 8.
Map 6 D3.
[629 45 54.

Scena Prezentacje
Żelazna 51/53.
Map 1 A5 & 5 B1.
[620 82 88.

Staromiejski
Jezuicka 4.
Map 2 D2 & 4 D4.
[635 80 15.

Teatr Adekwatny
Biuro Obsługi Widzów,
Kanonia 8/1.
Map 2 D2 & 4 D4.
[831 85 67.

Teatr Jestem
Stara Prochownia,
Boleść 2.
Map 2 D1.
[658 05 62.

Teatr Ochoty
Reja 9.
Map 5 B3.
[25 85 44.

Teatr Studio
Palace of Culture and
Science.
Map 1 C5 & 5 C1.
[620 21 02.

Współczesny
Mokotowska 13.
Map 6 D3.
[25 59 79.

OPERA AND BALLET

National Opera (Teatr Narodowy–Opera)
Teatr Wielki,
Plac Teatralny 1.
Map 1 C3 & 3 C5.
[826 50 19.

Warsaw Chamber Opera (Warszawska Opera Kameralna)
Aleja Solidarności 76b.
Map 3 B5 & 1 A3.
[831 22 40.

MUSICAL THEATERS

Buffo
Konopnickiej 6.
Map 6 E2.
[625 47 09.

Rampa
Kołowa 20.
[679 89 76.

Roma–Teatr Muzyczny
Nowogrodzka 49.
Map 5 C2.
[628 03 60.

Syrena
Litewska 3.
Map 6 D3.
[628 06 74.

CLASSICAL MUSIC

Academy of Music Dedicated to Frederic Chopin (Akademia Muzyczna im. F Chopina)
Okólnik 2.
Map 2 E4 & 6 D1.
[827 83 08.

Frederic Chopin Fellowship (Towarzystwo im. Fryderyka Chopina)
Okólnik 1.
Map 2 E4 & 6 D1.
[827 54 71.

National Philharmonic (Filharmonia Narodowa)
Sienkiewicza 10.
Map 1 C5 & 5 C1.
[826 57 12.

Polish Radio Concert Studio (Studio Koncertowe Polskiego Radia)
Woronicza 17.
[645 52 52.

Warsaw Fellowship of Music (Warszawskie Towarzystwo Muzyczne)
Pałac Szustra,
Morskie Oko 2.
Map 6 E5.
[49 65 51.

MOVIE THEATERS

Agrafka
Plac Żelaznej
Bramy 2.
Map 1 B3.
[628 10 26.

Atlantic
Chmielna 33.
Map 2 D5 & 6 D1.
[827 08 94.

Bajka
Marszałkowska
138.
Map 1 C4.
[826 69 66.

Capitol
Marszałkowska
115.
Map 1 B3 & 3 C5.
[827 35 00.

Femina
Aleja Solidarności
115.
Map 3 B5 & 1 A3.
[620 18 10.

Foksal
Foksal 3/5.
Map 2 E5 & 6 D1.
[826 59 72.

Iluzjon
Narbutta 55a.
Map 5 C5.
[48 33 33.

Kultura
Krakowskie
Przedmieście
21/23.
Map 2 D3 & 4 D5.
[826 33 35.

Luna
Marszałkowska 28.
Map 6 D3.
[621 78 28.

Muranów
Andersa 1.
Map 1 B2 & 3 B5.
[831 03 58.

Ochota
Grójecka 65.
Map 5 A2.
[22 24 73.

Palladium
Złota 7/9.
Map 2 D5 & 6 D1.
[826 64 68.

Paradiso
Aleja Solidarności 62.
Map 3 C5 & 1 C2.
[826 90 93.

Polonia
Marszałkowska 56.
Map 6 D2.
(628 58 22.

Rejs
Krakowskie
Przedmieście 21.
Map 2 D3.
(826 33 35.

Relax
Złota 8.
Map 1 C5 & 5 C1.
(827 77 62.

Skarpa
Kopernika 7/9.
Map 2 E5 & 6 D1.
(826 48 96.

Tęcza
Suzina 6.
(33 79 58.

Wars
Rynek Nowego
Miasta 5/7.
Map 1 C1 & 3 C4.
(831 44 88.

Wiedza
Pałace of Culture and
Science.
Map 1 C5 & 5 C1.
(656 67 95.

MUSIC CLUBS

**Aquarium Jazz
Club**
Emilii Plater 49.
Map 1 B5 & 5 C1.
(620 50 72.

Blues Bar
Agrykoli 1.
Map 6 E3.
(628 57 47.

Blue Velvet
Krakowskie
Przedmieście 5.
Map 2 D3.
(826 62 51.

Empik Club Pub
Nowy Świat 15/17.
Map 2 E5 & 6 D1.
(826 12 18.

Falcon Pub
Marszałkowska 55/57.
Map 6 D2.
(621 96 75.

Harenda
Krakowskie
Przedmieście 4/6.
Map 2 D3 & 4 D5.
(826 31 37.

Irish Pub
Miodowa 3.
Map 1 C2.
(826 25 33.

**Klub
Giovanni**
Krakowskie
Przedmieście
24/28.
Map 2 D3 &
4 D5.
(826 92 39.

Opus One
Plac Emila
Młynarskiego.
Map 1 C5 & 5 C1.
(827 23 47.

**Piwnica
Architektów**
Koszykowa 55.
Map 5 C2.
(660 52 06.

**Riviera-
Remont**
Waryńskiego 12.
Map 6 D3.
(25 74 97.

**Rynek Jazz
Club**
Rynek Starego
Miasto 2.
Map 2 D1 & 4 D4.

Stodoła
Batorego 10.
Map 5 C4.
(25 86 25.

Viking
Mazowiecka 12.
Map 2 D4.
(827 31 51.

NIGHTCLUBS
AND DISCO-
THEQUES

Arena
Marszałkowska 104.
Map 6 D3.
(827 50 91.

Cul de Sac
Foksal 2.
Map 2 E5 & 6 D1.
(827 54 11.

Dekadent
Leszno 19.
(632 53 52.

Dziekanka
Krakowskie
Przedmieście 56.
Map 2 D3 & 4 D5.
(635 87 44.

**Ground
Zero**
Wspólna 62.
Map 5 C2.
(625 52 80.

Hades
Aleja Niepodległości
162.
Map 5 C4.
(49 12 51.

Hybrydy
Złota 7/9.
Map 2 D5 & 5 C1.
(827 37 63.

Klub Medyka
Oczki 5/7.
Map 5 C2.
(628 33 76.

Loch
Rynek Starego
Miasto 29/31.
Map 2 D1 & 4 D4.
(831 02 63.

Orpheus
Hotel Marriott,
Aleje Jerozolimskie
65/79.
Map 5 C2.
(630 54 16.

Park
Aleje Niepodległości
196.
Map 5 C4.
(25 71 99.

Relax
Marymoncka 34.
(827 42 46.

Tango
Smolna 15.
Map 2 E5 & 6 E1.
(827 86 39.

Trend
Aleja Krakowska
171.
(846 09 94.

Ufo Club
Rzeźbiarska 80.
(15 22 00.

Yesterday
Szkolna 2/4.
Map 1 C4.
(826 10 60.

GAY AND
LESBIAN CLUBS

**Centrum
Fantom**
Bracka 20a.
Map 2 D5 & 6 D1.
(630 54 16.

Koźla Club
Koźla 10/12.
Map 1 C1 & 3 C4.

**Między Nami
(Entre Nous)**
Bracka 20.
Map 2 D5 & 6 D1.
(827 94 41.

Rudawka
Elbląska 53.
(633 19 99.

SPORTS

**City Tennis
Club**
Wybrzeże
Kościuszkowskie 2.
Map 2 F4.
(693 43 43.

**First Warsaw
Golf & Country
Club
(Rajszewo)**
Rajszew 70.
(774 06 55.

Inflancka
Inflancka 8.
(831 92 29.

Legia
Łazienkowska 3.
Map 6 F2.
(628 13 60.

Mera
Bohaterów Września
6/12.
(22 93 82.

Namysłowska
Namysłowska 8.
Map 4 E2.
(619 27 59.

**Służewiec
Racetrack
(Tor Wyścigów
Konnych)**
Puławska 266.
(43 14 41.

Solec
Solec 71.
(621 68 93.

**Stegny
Skating
Rink (Tor
Łyżwiarski
Stegny)**
Inspektowa 1.
(42 21 92.

Torwar
Łazienkowska 8.
Map 6 F2.
(621 44 71.

CHILDREN'S WARSAW

WARSAW OFFERS many attractions for both children and teenagers, and you can easily spend several days in the city without any fear of your children getting bored. There are amusement parks, playgrounds, puppet theaters, and toy stores, as well as adventure parks and the zoo. Other options include riding in a horse-drawn carriage or a

Playing in the Warsaw snow

miniature train around the Old Town. There are also tourist attractions that are not specifically aimed at children, but that nevertheless appeal to them. For instance, children enjoy the view from the observation terrace at the Palace of Culture and Science *(see p135)*, while the Museum of Technology *(see p134)* is educational and entertaining.

PRACTICAL TIPS

CHILDREN are warmly welcomed in Poland, and numerous hotels will either offer a reduced rate for children or even allow them to stay free of charge *(see p195)*.

Visitor attractions that usually charge admission fees, such as museums, theaters, and the zoo, also offer special entrance charges for children. Additionally, many museums allocate certain days (during school holidays) when admission is

A carriage ride through the streets of the Old Town

free. Children are also eligible for reduced-rate tickets on public transportation *(see p251)*, and those below the age of four usually travel for free.

SHOPPING

THE BEST PLACE for shopping with children in Warsaw is the Smyk department store *(see p132)*. Occupying five levels, Smyk provides most things that a child (from a baby to a teenager) will want or need. These include a wide range of toys and sports equipment, together with a variety of clothes and shoes.

Sign for Kidiland toy store

Children's clothes are also available at **5 10 15** and at **Panorama** department store, while **Świat Dziecka** (Children's World) has a good selection of clothes and toys for young children. When

shopping specifically for toys, the widest choice is at **Kidiland**, **Baba Jaga** (The Wicked Witch), and **Disney**. If you are near the New Town, it is worth going to **Kleofas**, which is in the area.

SHOP ADDRESSES

Baba Jaga
Marszałkowska 76. **Map** 6 D2.

Disney
Emilii Plater 47. **Map** 1 B5 & 5 C2.

5 10 15
Bracka 22. **Map** 2 D5 & 6 D1.

Kidiland
Plac Konstytucji 5. **Map** 6 D2.

Kleofas
Mostowa 32. **Map** 1 C1 & 3 C4.

Panorama
Witosa 31.

Świat Dziecka
Puławska 2. **Map** 6 D4.

MUSEUMS

MANY OF WARSAW's museums are of great interest to children, as well as adults. This certainly applies to the Museum of Technology (Muzeum Techniki, *see p134*), where

A lion and lioness in Warsaw's zoo

numerous active displays and working models engage children's interest. The opening times for these museums are listed under the museum entries in this guide.

THEATERS, CONCERTS, AND CIRCUSES

WARSAW HAS four children's theaters, each with a repertoire that is aimed solely at the youngest members of the audience. These theaters are **Baj**, **Lalka**, **Guliwer**, and **Scena im Tove Jansson**. Additionally, there are several theaters and opera houses that stage performances especially for children.

Classical music is particularly accessible to children at the Philharmonic (Filharmonia Narodowa), where special "child-friendly" performances are led by Aunty Jadzia. This entertaining character can introduce children as young as two years old to the enchanting world of music.

Although Warsaw does not have a permanent circus, visiting circuses often pitch their tents in various parts of the city, providing shows at most times of the year.

PARKS, PLAYGROUNDS, AND THE ZOO

AN IDEAL PLACE to take children for a walk is Łazienki Park, where they can feed ducks, various birds, and squirrels, and admire the

A typical performance at the Guliwer children's theater

colorful displays by peacocks. Additionally, on Sunday mornings children can ride ponies in the park.

An outing to one of the city's **Botanical Gardens** (Ogród Botaniczny) provides a pleasurable expedition (see p160). The main garden near Łazienki Park is open from May to October; another on the outskirts of town is open between April and October.

The **Zoo** (Ogród Zoologiczny, see p174) is situated on the picturesque Right Bank of the River Vistula.

Among Warsaw's many playgrounds and play centers, the most popular are **Orlando** in the Bródno district, and **Kolorado** in Jelonki. Both have numerous games involving tunnels, slides, and pools. Fans of merry-go-rounds, shooting galleries, and cable cars should visit **Cricoland**, Warsaw's most exciting amusement park.

The "Choo-choo" miniature train that runs through the Old Town

SURVIVAL
GUIDE

PRACTICAL INFORMATION

Warsaw has become far more accessible to visitors over the past few years. New and refurbished hotels, restaurants, and cafés have led the way in raising standards of service to Western levels and broadening the choice considerably. Travel agents have also extended their range of services, while other considerations such as public transportation, currency exchange, and shopping facilities have greatly improved as well.

A carriage in the Old Town

All of the city's most popular attractions can easily be reached by public transportation, but the center of the city is best visited on foot. Although the cost of living in Warsaw is generally lower than in other European cities, prices in the finest restaurants and hotels are comparable. Warsaw is relatively safe, though as in any city visitors should be on their guard against thieves, and cars should be left only in guarded parking lots.

The charming tourist information office in the Old Town

TOURIST INFORMATION

The most comprehensive tourist information office (Informacja Turystyczna) is located in Castle Square (Plac Zamkowy). It offers advice on visiting the city as well as maps and guidebooks. Information on bed-and-breakfast accommodations is available from a kiosk in the Central Railroad Station (Dworzec Centralny).

Anyone traveling farther afield can purchase maps at the Atlas bookshop on Aleja Jana Pawła II (John Paul II Avenue). Hotels and guided tours in other Polish cities can be booked through **Orbis**.

ORBIS

Orbis logo

LANGUAGES SPOKEN

English is widely spoken, particularly in hotels, restaurants, cafés, stores, and other tourist places, but it is less common at Polish railroad stations. Many Varsovians speak at least some English, with German often spoken as a second language. It should be possible, for instance, to get directions from local people in the capital, though not always on the first attempt.

WHEN TO VISIT

Spring, summer, or early autumn are equally enjoyable times to visit Warsaw, and the month of May is often when it is at its best. However, this is also a favorite month for school trips, so the city is full of schoolchildren.

During the summer, the city has an abundance of fast-food and ice cream stalls, and sidewalks and squares are lined with cafés, some offering live music and dancing.

OPENING HOURS

Opening times of museums and galleries are detailed in this guide. In general, they are closed on Mondays. There are exceptions, such as Wilanów, which is closed on Tuesdays. Most tourist attractions are usually open from 9am to 5pm. However, out-of-season (from October 1 to April 30) museum opening hours are shorter. There are some locations, such as the Botanical Gardens and Arkadia Park in Nieborów, that are closed during the winter.

Churches are open from early morning mass until the last evening mass (typically

Bus used by Mazurkas Travel

from 6am to 10pm). Monasteries have irregular visiting hours, but are usually open to the public on Sunday afternoons. Delicatessens and food shops are usually open from 7am to 7pm, Monday to Saturday. Supermarkets have longer opening hours, sometimes to 10pm, and often on Sunday mornings as well.

Department stores are open from 9am to 8pm, with most other stores open from 10am to 7pm, Monday to Friday, and 9am to 2pm on Saturday. All-night drugstores, which are also open on Sundays, can be found in every district *(see p239)*. All the banks in Poland are open from 8am to 6pm, Monday to Friday.

Bars, cafés, and restaurants have the flexibility to set their own opening times. Restaurants tend to open at about noon and remain open, without an afternoon break, until late at night. In practice, they usually do not close until the last customers leave.

ZASP theater booking office

LISTINGS MAGAZINES

WARSAW PROVIDES a wide range of cultural activities, with a variety of galleries and museums, as well as theaters and concert halls.

There are two English-language listings magazines: *Warszawa, What, Where, When*, and *Welcome to Warsaw*. Both are available free of charge and are published once a month. They can be obtained from hotel reception desks and tourist offices. There are, of course, many Polish listings magazines, including the comprehensive *Warszawski Informator Kulturalny*. Theater and concert tickets can be bought in advance from **ZASP** booking offices.

ADMISSION CHARGES

ADMISSION TO MUSEUMS is relatively inexpensive. In addition, each museum also operates its own system of reduced prices for children, students, and senior citizens.

Admission is not charged when visiting churches or the cathedral, though a contribution can be left in the offertory box. This box is usually to be found in the vestibule.

SIGHTSEEING

THE EASIEST WAY to see Warsaw's sights is through the services offered by travel agents. **Mazurkas Travel** organizes sightseeing tours of Warsaw with experienced guides, including visits to the Royal Castle *(see pp70–73)* and Wilanów Palace *(see pp168–71)*. Day trips to outlying attractions such as Żelazowa Wola, the manor house where Frederic Chopin was born *(see p182)*, and the Baroque Nieborów Palace, adjacent to the romantic park of Arkadia *(see p180)*, are also available. More extensive trips can be arranged to other historic cities, such as Kraków and Gdańsk.

Similar tours can be booked with the **Polish Landscape** travel agency, while guided city tours of Warsaw can also be arranged through **Trakt**.

Budget travelers can join less expensive tours organized by **PTTK** (Polish Tourist Organization). These include group walks around the city, as well as weekend excursions outside Warsaw.

One delightful option is a ride on the "Choo-choo" miniature train. Its route runs from Castle Square through the Old Town and New Town and along the Royal Route. Alternatively, horse-drawn carriages can be found in the Old Town Market Square, for a leisurely tour of the city.

Admission ticket to Wilanów

DIRECTORY

TOURIST OFFICES AND TRAVEL AGENTS

American Express
Krakowskie Przedmieście 11.
Map 2 D3.
(635 20 02.

Mazurkas Travel
Nowogrodzka 24/26.
Map 6 D1.
(629 12 49.

Orbis
Marszałkowska 142.
Map 1 C4.
(827 67 66.
Dubois 9.
Map 1 A1.
(635 63 16.

Polish Landscape
Cegłowska 28.
(34 18 12.

Logo of the Polish tourist office

PTTK
Litewska 11/13.
Map 6 D3.
(629 39 47.
Kasprowicza 40.
(34 68 25.
Tarczyńska 1/59.
Map 5 B2.
(22 14 35.
Brzeska 3.
Map 4 F4.
(619 38 59.

Tourist Information
Plac Zamkowy 1/13.
Map 2 D2 & 4 D5.
(635 18 81.

Trakt
Kredytowa 6.
Map 1 C4.
(827 80 68.

ZASP
Aleje Jerozolimskie 25.
Map 2 D5 & 6 D1.
(621 94 54.

Security and Health

Warsaw's streets are generally safe for tourists, and this applies especially within the central area, although sensible precautions should always be taken. Many Varsovians complain that there are too few police officers to deal with the rise in crime in the capital, which includes the activities of organized syndicates. Anyone suffering a minor health problem should seek advice at a pharmacy, while hotels can usually arrange a doctor's visit. Visitors from the US should check with their insurance companies before leaving home to be sure they are covered if medical care is needed.

PERSONAL SECURITY

Tourists can visit most of Warsaw without anxiety, as it is very rare that tourists are attacked. However, as in all major cities, visitors should be aware of possible dangers, and should avoid taking unnecessary risks.

Sign outside police stations

Women are advised not to walk around unaccompanied late at night, and there are areas where visitors should either be on their guard or avoid completely. This includes the Praga district, on the Right Bank of the Vistula, and particularly the area around Brzeska Street.

The atmosphere at the Eastern Station (Dworzec Wschodni) may be threatening, especially if traveling alone, and this also applies to Stadion Station and Różycki Market. Gambling at the market, such as the card and dice games, should be avoided, as they are run dishonestly.

The most common street crime, however, is pickpocketing. Operating in gangs, the pickpockets often crowd unsuspecting victims. Handbags should be kept securely fastened, and always maintain a grasp on purses you are carrying. Also, do not carry valuables or your passport in trouser pockets (though carrying identification is advisable). Extra care should always be taken at stations and when traveling by train, streetcar, or bus.

Badge worn by traffic wardens

Valuables should not be left unattended in cars, and it is safer to remove car radios if possible. Cars should be left in guarded parking lots (which are now becoming the norm). Western cars, such as BMW, Volkswagen Golf, Mercedes, and Audi are those most prone to theft. Public transportation is best avoided late at night – it is safer to use official taxis, with a lit-up sign.

BEGGARS

Beggars have become a widespread sight in Warsaw. They are frequently encountered on the city center's principal streets, many having arrived from neighboring countries, such as Romania. While not dangerous, they can be extremely persistent. The best way to ward off unwanted advances is simply by saying a firm "no."

POLICE AND SECURITY SERVICES

Warsaw is patrolled by policemen and -women, who belong to the various branches of the Polish police force. Private security firms also perform a similar role. Police officers patrol the city on foot and in clearly marked blue and white police cars. They are armed and have the power to stop anyone they regard as suspicious.

Any criminal acts and related incidents should be reported immediately at a police station. The main police stations are indicated on the Street Finder maps (*see pp260–65*).

Traffic police are principally concerned with driving offenses and making sure that traffic flows as smoothly as possible. They act decisively in any cases of drunk-driving, since it is illegal in Poland to drive with any alcohol present in the bloodstream. Penalties for breaking this law are severe (*see p249*), and random breath tests are conducted regularly. Similarly, penalties for speeding and parking offenses are considerable. Anyone who is involved in a serious road accident is required by law to contact the traffic police, as well as call for an ambulance and the fire department.

In addition to the regular police force, there are traffic wardens (*straż miejska*), who enforce parking regulations.

Finally, you may see private security guards, usually dressed in black uniforms, who frequently patrol private property, as well as many public events. Many of Warsaw's private security guards were formerly police officers.

Policeman   **Policewoman**   **Traffic warden**

Standard police car

Warsaw ambulance

LOST PROPERTY

GREAT CARE should be taken with personal property at all times. Luggage should never be left unattended, particularly at the airport and at the train and bus stations. Valuables should not be carried when sightseeing. Similarly, take only as much money as you think you will need, ideally using a money belt. Traveler's checks are the safest method of carrying larger sums of money.

Although the chances of recovering lost property are usually minimal, any losses should still be reported to the city's Lost Property Office (Biuro Rzeczy Znalezionych).

Lost property should also be reported to the police and a reference number or an official receipt obtained in order to make an insurance claim.

Lost or stolen passports should be reported immediately to your country's embassy in Warsaw (see p244).

HEALTH CARE

MEDICAL TREATMENT can be obtained in Warsaw, either under the national health service or privately.

For minor health problems, there are pharmacies situated

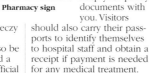

Pharmacy sign

throughout the city. A selection of 24-hour pharmacies is also included on this page.

First aid is provided free of charge in hospitals, but other types of hospital treatment may incur a charge. In more serious cases or in the event of a medical emergency, the ambulance service is on call 24 hours a day.

Hospitals with emergency rooms are indicated on the Street Finder (see pp260–65). However, it is advisable to take out fully comprehensive insurance prior to arriving in Warsaw and to keep your policy documents with you. Visitors should also carry their passports to identify themselves to hospital staff and obtain a receipt if payment is needed for any medical treatment.

Travelers may wish to take out additional, private travel insurance against the cost of emergency hospital care, doctors' fees, and repatriation. If you carry private travel insurance, make sure you have your policy with you when requesting medical assistance.

Visitors who are concerned about the levels of traffic pollution or ozone in the air can see both totals on an electronic display in front of the Smyk department store (see p132).

DIRECTORY

EMERGENCY SERVICES

Ambulance
999.

Fire
998.

Police
997.

MEDICAL ASSISTANCE

General Medical Inquiries
831 31 14 & 627 89 62.

Information on Hospital Rosters
826 27 61 & 826 83 00.
7:30am–7:30pm daily, 8am–3pm public hols.

24-Hour Dental Clinic
Ludna 10.
Map 6 F1.
625 01 02 & 625 01 05.

24-Hour Pharmacies
Dworzec Centralny.
Map 6 C1.
25 69 84.

Freta 13/15.
Map 1 C1.
831 50 91.

Widok 19.
Map 2 D5.
827 35 93.

OTHER USEFUL NUMBERS

Car Accidents
628 13 13 & 628 33 13.

City Information
General information on cultural events and local services.
913.

Lost Property
Floriańska 10.
Map 2 F1. 619 56 68.

Personal Helpline
628 36 36.

Vehicle Assistance
981.

Wake-up Calls
917.

Banking and Local Currency

PKO Bank logo

Warsaw's banks and currency-exchange facilities have become far more user-friendly to visitors since the democratic elections in 1989. Currency-exchange offices can be found easily throughout the city, and they frequently offer a more favorable exchange rate than banks. At the same time, credit cards and traveler's checks are increasingly widely accepted, particularly by hotels, restaurants, travel agents, and stores.

Sign for an exchange office

BANKS AND CURRENCY-EXCHANGE OFFICES

Central Warsaw has plenty of banks offering a broad range of financial services. The usual opening hours are from 8am to 6pm. During the lunch hour (around 1–2pm) fewer offices generally operate, which obviously means that service is a little slower.

In addition to the exchange facilities provided by banks, there are exchange offices all over the city. Rates vary between outlets, but these offices generally offer better rates than banks.

Some currency-exchange offices offer a 24-hour service, but this option is usually reflected in a higher commission. One such office is located at the Central Railroad Station (Dworzec Centralny). However, the station is a notorious low-life haunt late at night, and so it is not advisable to go there then.

Hotels also offer currency exchange, though their charges are usually higher. Currency should not be exchanged with "operators" in the street, as they are likely to be using counterfeit money.

CREDIT CARDS

Credit cards, such as American Express, VISA, and MasterCard, are increasingly accepted by local establishments – hotels, restaurants, nightclubs, car-rental firms, travel agents, and more exclusive shops.

The logos of any accepted credit cards are usually displayed prominently by the entrance and at cash registers.

Bankomat cash dispenser

However, when paying by credit card it is advisable to be sure that no extra conditions apply, such as a minimum purchasing amount. In privately owned shops, a small discount is sometimes offered to customers who are able to pay in cash.

Major international credit cards can also be used to make cash withdrawals from banks. Additionally, American Express cards can be used to withdraw cash from the relevant Bankomat automatic teller machines, and at the American Express office.

DIRECTORY

BANKS

Bank Gdański S.A.
Karowa 20. **Map** 2 D3.
826 04 61.

Bank Handlowy
Chałubińskiego 8.
Map 5 C2.
830 03 04.
Aleje Jerozolimskie 65/79.
Map 5 A2.
830 06 76.

Bank Polska Kasa Opieki S.A. (PKO S.A.)
Plac Bankowy 2. **Map** 1 B3.
637 10 61.
Czackiego 21/23. **Map** 2 D4.
661 27 18.

Narodowy Bank Polski
Plac Powstańców Warszawy 4.
Map 2 D4.
620 03 21.

Powszechny Bank Kredytowy
Aleje Jerozolimskie 7.
Map 6 E1.
621 00 66.
Jasna 8.
Map 1 C4 & 6 D1.
622 01 00.

CURRENCY EXCHANGE

ABA-International
Piękna 20. **Map** 6 D2.
625 14 25.

American Express Travel
Krakowskie Przedmieście 11.
Map 2 D2. 635 20 02.

Kantor
Rynek Starego Miasta 25.
Map 2 D2. 635 79 88.

Nora
Krakowskie Przedmieście 20/22.
Map 2 D3. 826 64 02.

Podziemia Dworca Centralnego
Box 45. 630 29 66.
Box 75. 630 29 90.

LOST CREDIT CARDS

Polcard, Dział Autoryzacji
For MasterCard and VISA.
611 30 00 & 612 25 52.

Triangular pediment on the PKO S.A. Bank headquarters

BANK POLSKA KASA OPIEKI SA

CASH AND TRAVELER'S CHECKS

Тhe polish unit of currency is the złoty, which literally means "golden," and it is generally abbreviated to "zł." There is also a smaller unit: the grosz. One hundred groszy are equivalent to one złoty. Traveler's checks can be cashed in currency-exchange offices, as well as most hotels and many (but not all) banks. **American Express** and **Thomas Cook** are perhaps the best known brands, and both have offices in Warsaw.

Bank Notes
Bank notes are issued in denominations of 10, 20, 50, 100, and 200 złoty. All bills portray important Polish kings.

200 złoty

100 złoty

50 złoty

10 złoty

20 złoty

Coins
Coins are issued in these denominations: 1, 2, 5, 10, 20, and 50 groszy, and 1, 2, and 5 złoty. All coins feature an emblem of the Polish eagle on the reverse side.

5 złoty

2 złoty

1 złoty

5 groszy

10 groszy

20 groszy

50 groszy

1 grosz

2 groszy

BANK NOTES

Formerly, bank notes featured celebrated Poles, such as Tadeusz Kościuszko, Frederic Chopin, and Nicholas Copernicus. Notes from recent years feature Polish kings: Zygmunt I Stary (200 zł), Władysław Jagiełło (100 zł), Kazimierz Wielki (50 zł), Bolesław Chrobry (20 zł), and Mieszko I (10 zł).

Telephone and Postal Services

THE POLISH TELECOMMUNICATIONS AGENCY is called Telekomunikacja Polska, and the postal service is Poczta Polska. Various improvements have been made to both services in the past few years. However, lines in post offices can still be long and slow-moving, while finding a public telephone that works can also be a time-consuming endeavor.

USING THE TELEPHONE

THE BEST PLACE to find a public telephone in working order is in a post office. Hotels also provide public telephones in their lobbies. This is also a far less expensive option than phoning from your room. All modern phones are push-button, though older dial telephones are not uncommon.

There are no coin-operated public telephone booths in Poland. Public phones accept either tokens (*żetony*) or telephone cards (*karty*). Telephone tokens and cards can be purchased at post offices or newspaper kiosks.

Different types of telephone tokens are available. Token A is sufficient for only a three-minute local call. For long-distance calls, use either token C or a telephone card. Telephone cards are usually the more convenient option whatever type of call you wish to make.

Three rates are charged for intercity calls within Poland. The highest rate is between 8am–6pm. From 6pm–10pm the charge is 25 percent lower, while the charge is 50 percent lower between 10pm–8am. Calls made on the weekend are even less expensive. For international calls, a single rate is charged

Logo of the Polish Postal Service

for each country, regardless of the time of day.

To make a call from a public phone, first check that on lifting the receiver there is a continuous tone. After dialing there is a short initial tone, followed by a longer intermittent tone. A short, rapidly repeating tone indicates that the number is busy.

To call Warsaw from the US, dial 011 48 22, and then the number. When calling the US, dial 00 1, the area code (omitting the first 0), and then the number.

USING TELEPHONE TOKENS

1 Lift the receiver and wait for the dial tone.

2 Insert the token in the slot.

3 Dial the number and wait to be connected.

4 On hearing instructions, insert the next token.

5 When you have finished speaking, replace the receiver. Unused tokens will be returned to you.

USING A TELEPHONE CARD

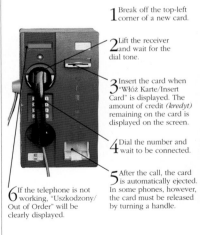

1 Break off the top-left corner of a new card.

2 Lift the receiver and wait for the dial tone.

3 Insert the card when "Włóż Kartę/Insert Card" is displayed. The amount of credit (*kredyt*) remaining on the card is displayed on the screen.

4 Dial the number and wait to be connected.

5 After the call, the card is automatically ejected. In some phones, however, the card must be released by turning a handle.

6 If the telephone is not working, "Uszkodzony/Out of Order" will be clearly displayed.

C-type telephone token, for long-distance calls

Logo of Polish Telecommunications

This corner must be broken off before the telephone card can be used.

Telephone card for 100 units

Customers inside the main post office in Warsaw

POSTAL SERVICES

POST OFFICES offer an increasingly comprehensive and varied range of services.

There are post offices throughout the city, though Warsaw's main post office, **Poczta Główna**, is located

Red mailbox, found throughout the city outside post offices, for all mail outside Warsaw

on Świętokrzyska Street. It is open 24 hours a day, seven days a week. As well as the usual services – sending letters, packages, and telegrams; selling and mailing money orders (within Poland); and providing telephone directories – this post office offers customers telex, fax, and telephone booths. Additionally, it can provide a poste restante service, for holding mail on your behalf.

At a special counter, stamp collectors can also purchase commemorative sets of stamps (Polish stamps are among the most decorative).

Lines operate according to numbered tickets. On entering the post office, collect a numbered ticket from a computerized machine. You must then wait until this number is displayed above a counter, indicating when and where you will be served.

MAILING LETTERS

STAMPS ARE SOLD at newspaper kiosks as well as in post offices, though newsdealers will sell stamps only with postcards.

Around Warsaw are green mailboxes, which are for mail being sent within the city

Mailbox for national and overseas mail

itself. For mail to other destinations within Poland, and for all overseas mail, use red mailboxes. Deliveries within Poland usually take two or three days, while overseas mail can take up to seven days. An express postal service is available for urgent deliveries, together with a special courier service (at a much higher price). International courier companies, such as **DHL**, also have offices in Warsaw.

USEFUL ADDRESSES

American Express
Krakowskie Przedmieście 11.
Map 2 D3.
(635 20 02.

DHL
Aleje Jerozolimskie 11/19. **Map** 2 E5.
(622 14 09.

Poczta Główna
Świętokrzyska 31/33. **Map** 1 C4.
(826 60 01.

Decorative Polish postage stamps

USEFUL TELEPHONE NUMBERS

- Local (Warsaw) directory inquiries: dial 913.
- National (Poland) directory inquiries: dial 912.
- International operator: dial 901.
- Warsaw city code: dial 022 in Poland, 22 from abroad.

To call overseas:
• Dial 0 and wait for signal. Dial 0 again and follow it with code of the country, the city code (minus the initial 0), followed by the number.

Additional Information

DISABLED TRAVELERS

FACILITIES for the disabled are still limited in Warsaw. Special elevators operate at air terminals and at subway stations, but access to most offices and shops is still difficult for those in a wheelchair. The number of cars parked on sidewalks throughout the city can also present serious obstacles.

There are, however, some hotels that have rooms specially equipped for disabled travelers (see pp201–3). Among the many organizations that can provide assistance, the best are listed below. Information for disabled travelers is also available from the **National Council for the Disabled**, and there are a number of companies that offer special transportation.

USEFUL ADDRESSES

National Council for the Disabled (Krajowa Rada Osób Niepełnosprawnych)
Konwiktorska 9.
℩ 831 22 72.

Polish Association for the Blind (Polski Związek Niewidomych)
Konwiktorska 9.
℩ 831 85 32.

Polish Association for the Deaf (Polski Związek Głuchych)
Podwale 23.
℩ 831 08 96.

Polish Society for the Fight Against Disability (Polskie Towarzystwo Walki z Kalectwem)
Oleandrów 4.
℩ 25 70 80.

Transport for Disabled People
Alians Falck SOS.
℩ 635 68 24.
Taxi service for disabled passengers.
℩ 919.
Tus – transport service for disabled people.
℩ 831 93 31.

CUSTOMS AND CURRENCY REGULATIONS

CITIZENS of most European countries, and many outside Europe (including the US), need a passport valid for six months after the date of arrival to enter Poland. Visitors from other countries must first obtain a visa.

There is no duty on purchases of personal items or gifts to the value of $100. Duty is charged on cigarettes and alcohol. A special permit is needed to export antiques. Firearms need special permission. You can bring unlimited foreign currency into Poland, but a form must be completed on arrival, as

An ISIC

you cannot depart with more money than you brought in.

If you have any inquiries regarding imports and exports, contact the **Customs Information Office** ℩ 694 31 94.

STUDENTS

IT IS WORTH having a valid ISIC (International Student Identity Card) if you are visiting Warsaw. This entitles the bearer to reduced rates in museums and international students' hostels (which are open during vacation periods), as well as reduced fares on international rail and air travel. Reductions are not available, however, on Warsaw's public transportation system.

Almatur specializes in student travel (see p196).

Holders of IYHF (International Youth Hostel Federation) cards are entitled to reduced charges at youth hostels (see pp194–5).

USEFUL ADDRESS

Almatur
Kopernika 15.
℩ 826 26 39.

TELEVISION AND RADIO

VARIOUS satellite channels – such as CNN, Sky, and MTV – are generally available to visitors staying in larger and more expensive hotels. These channels show news, films, and other feature programs in several languages. The most popular television

---

EMBASSIES AND CONSULATES

Australia
Estońska 3/54.
℩ 617 60 81.

Austria
Gagarina 34. Map 6 F4.
℩ 41 00 81.

Canada
Matejki 1/5. Map 6 E2.
℩ 629 80 51.

France
Piękna 1. Map 6 D2.
℩ 623 84 01.

Germany
Dąbrowiecka 30.
℩ 617 30 11.

Israel
Krzywickiego 24. Map 5 C3.
℩ 25 09 23.

Italy
Plac Dąbrowskiego 6.
Map 3 C5 & 1 C4.
℩ 826 34 71.

Russia
Belwederska 49. Map 6 E4.
℩ 621 34 53.

United Kingdom
Aleja Róż 1. Map 6 D2.
℩ 628 10 01.

United States
Al. Ujazdowskie 29/31. Map 6 E2.
℩ 628 30 41.

channels in Warsaw are broadcast in Polish. This includes stations 1 and 2, the citywide channel WOT, and the national POLSAT.

The most popular music programs are broadcast by Radio Z (107.5 FM), RMF (91.0 FM), Radio Kolor (103 FM), and Wa-Wa (89.8 FM). Interesting music programs are broadcast by "Trójka" (98.8 FM).

However, the state-run Polish Radio (Polskie Radio) is the main broadcaster in Poland. Its two main stations are PR1, which is on 92.0 FM, and PR2, on 70.2 FM. Other stations broadcasting in the Warsaw area include Radio Bis (102.4 FM), Radio Eska (102.0 FM), Radio dla Ciebie (101.0 FM), Rozgłosnia Harcerska (101.5 FM), and a Catholic radio station, Radio

The listings magazine *Warszawa What, Where, When*

NEWSPAPERS AND MAGAZINES

FOREIGN NEWSPAPERS are readily available throughout Warsaw in hotel kiosks, certain bookstores, and the many Ruch kiosks.

Among the English-language publications published in Warsaw are *Warsaw Voice* and *Warsaw Business Journal*. There are also monthly listings magazines, such as *Warszawa What, Where, When* (written in both English and German), *Welcome to Warsaw* (English), *Spotkania z Warszawą* (English), and *Kalejdoskop Kulturalny (Cultural Kaleidoscope).*

Among Polish newspapers the most popular are *Życie Warszawy, Gazeta Wyborcza, Rzeczpospolita,* and *Życie.*

Warsaw Voice, the most popular English paper in Warsaw

ELECTRICAL APPLIANCES

WARSAW'S ELECTRICITY supply is 220 V. Plugs are the standard continental type, featuring two round pins.

A travel adapter will enable you to use electrical appliances (this should ideally be purchased prior to your arrival in Warsaw).

WARSAW TIME

WARSAW is six hours ahead of Eastern Standard Time. During summer time, which runs from the end of March until the end of September, clocks go forward by 1 hour to daylight saving time.

PLACES OF WORSHIP

Methodist Church (Kościół Ewangelicki-Metodystyczny)
Mokotowska 12.
Map 6 D3.
☎ 628 53 28.
✝ 11am Sun.

Mosque (Muzułmańskie)
Wiertnicza 103.
☎ 1pm (winter), noon (summer) Fri.

Polish Autocephalic Orthodox Church (Polski Autokefaliczny Kościół Prawosławny)
Aleja Solidarności 52.
Map 1 A3, 3 B5. ☎ 619 08 86.
✝ 9am and 5pm Mon–Fri; 8am and 10am Sun.

Polish National Church (Kościół Polskokatolicki)
Szwoleżerów 2. **Map** 6 F3
☎ 41 37 43.
✝ 11am Sun.

Protestant Calvinist Church (Kościół Ewangelicko-Augsburski)
Plac Małachowskiego 1. **Map** 2 D4.
☎ 827 68 17.
✝ 10:30am Sun.

Protestant Reformed Church (Kościół Ewangelicko-Reformowany)
Aleja Solidarności 76a. **Map** 1 B3.
☎ 831 45 22.
✝ 10am Sun.

Seventh-Day Adventists Church (Kościół Adwentystów Dnia Siódmego)
Foskal 8. **Map** 2 E5, 6 D1.
☎ 826 25 06.
✝ 9:30am–noon Sat; 5–6:30pm Sun.

Synagogue (Żydowskie)
Twarda 6. **Map** 1 B5, 5 B1.
☎ 620 43 24.
✡ 9:30am Sat.

Whitsuntide Church (Kościół Zielonoświątkowy)
Sienna 68/70. **Map** 1 A5, 5 B1.
☎ 24 85 75.
✝ 6pm Fri; 11am Sun.

A Roman Catholic priest conducting the celebration of Mass

GETTING TO WARSAW

WARSAW lies at the heart of Europe and has excellent rail and air links with the rest of the continent. The airport is close to the city center, and there are regular flights from major European cities, as well as from the US, Southeast Asia, and the Middle East. LOT Polish Airlines, the national carrier, offers flights from many countries. Poland's railroad system is both efficient and inexpensive, with Warsaw's main station centrally located in the capital. The cheapest, though slowest, way to reach Warsaw is by bus. However, the number of highways under construction in Poland means road travel, by bus or car, is also improving rapidly.

LOT airplane

AIR TRAVEL

WARSAW has direct air links with 44 cities in 34 countries. These include daily connections with many European cities, and regular flights from North American cities such as Chicago, New York, Montreal, and Toronto. There are no direct flights from Australia, but there are connections via Southeast Asia or several European cities, such as London and Paris.

Flights from London take 2 hours, 15 minutes; from Paris 2 hours; and from New York, about 9 hours, 40 minutes.

Twenty-five airlines use Okęcie Airport, including **British Airways**, **Delta Airlines**, **Lufthansa**, and **Air France**. In addition to international flights, **LOT** offers internal flights to cities such as Gdańsk and Wrocław.

TICKETS

APEX TICKETS usually offers the best value, with savings of 30–40 percent on the economy fare. However, these tickets must be booked up to one month in advance, and have a fixed return date. Discount agencies also offer reduced fares, while students, children, and senior citizens usually qualify for discounts.

AIRLINES

Aeroflot
Aleje Jerozolimskie 29.
Map 6 D1.
(628 17 10.

Air France
Krucza 21.
Map 6 D2.
(628 12 81.

British Airways
Krucza 49.
Map 6 D1.
(628 94 31.

Delta Air Lines
Królewska 11.
Map 1 C4.
(827 84 61.

KLM
Plac Konstytucji 1.
Map 6 D2.
(621 70 41.

LOT
Aleje Jerozolimskie 65/79.
Map 5 C2.
(952, 953.

Lufthansa
Aleje Jerozolimskie 56c.
Map 5 C2.
(630 25 55.

SAS
Nowy Świat 19.
Map 6 D1.
(826 12 11.

LOT flight attendant at Okęcie Airport

OKĘCIE AIRPORT

OKĘCIE IS WARSAW'S only airport handling international air traffic, and is conveniently situated just 6 km (4 miles) south of the city center. The airport originally dates from 1933, but the present terminals were built in 1992, and have the capacity to handle approximately 3.5 million passengers annually.

The new airport building is easy to negotiate, with one terminal for international flights and an adjacent terminal for domestic flights.

Facilities at the airport include airline offices, travel agents, banks and currency-exchange counters, duty-free shops, a post office, souvenir shops, restaurants, cafés, bars, and car rental counters.

The logo of City Line buses, serving Okęcie from the city center

CITY CONNECTIONS

REGULAR BUS SERVICES link Okęcie Airport with the center of Warsaw and the outlying suburbs. Bus 175 operates between the airport and the city center, with bus 188 operating between the airport and Praga. These are Warsaw City Transport buses, for which tickets are bought at newspaper kiosks, and canceled in a ticket machine on boarding the bus.

There is also a special City Line service connecting Warsaw with Okęcie. This service runs every 20 minutes (30 minutes on Sundays and public holidays) from 5:30am to 10:30pm. The City Line service stops at all the major hotels in the center of Warsaw. The fares are more expensive than those of regular buses, but City Line buses

Luggage trolley

Inside the terminal building at Warsaw's Okęcie Airport

are less crowded, and there is more space for luggage. The fares on this service are collected by the driver.

A more expensive, but also more comfortable, journey into the city is offered by the Fly and Drive bus company. The facilities include radiotelephones, which can be used during the journey.

A taxi from the airport can prove very expensive. It is best to avoid taxis waiting outside the terminal building,

or drivers touting for business within it, as they are far more expensive than radio taxis (if you do take one of these taxis, agree to a price in advance). Radio taxis can be booked at the airport (see p252).

LOT Airlines-sponsored taxi

WARSAW'S AIR LINKS WITH EUROPE

Warsaw has good air links not only with numerous European cities, but also with countries of the former Soviet Union and the Balkan states.

Traveling by Rail

WARSAW can be reached by train from the major European cities, and its central location makes the city an ideal base from which to explore the rest of Poland.

Tickets for intercity trains in Poland are inexpensive. Visitors can purchase the Polrailpass and Junior Polrailpass (for those under 26 years of age). They are available for both first- and second-class seats, with an additional ticket required for a sleeping berth or sleeping car. These passes allow unlimited travel on all Polish trains for the duration of the ticket: 8, 15, 21 days, or one month.

The extensive Polish railroad network is operated by the state-owned PKP (Polskie Koleje Państwowe). The trains fall into several categories: express trains for long-distance journeys with few stops; fast trains offering a

PKP railroadman

before the departure time, as lines for tickets are often long. Most trains have two classes of accommodation. First class is 50 percent more expensive than second class. Similarly, express and intercity trains are about twice the price of standard trains. The letter R on a timetable indicates trains on which you need to reserve a seat (passengers without reservations are fined).

Railroad Stations

WARSAW'S Central Railroad Station (Dworzec Centralny, *see p136*) is the largest and busiest railroad station in the whole of Poland.

Almost all international trains pass through this station, which is located in the city center by the Palace of Culture and Science. All the station platforms are belowground, with the main hall and ticket office on the ground level. Passageways between the two levels contain a baggage-check room, as well as 24-hour currency-exchange counters, stores, and some snack bars.

To the west of the city center is Warszawa Zachodnia. This station is a departure point for many trains heading north and east, and is linked to the adjacent bus station. Similarly, trains heading west generally depart from Warszawa Wschodnia, in the Praga district, to the east of the city center.

Traveling by Bus

BUSES are the cheapest form of public transportation, whether you are traveling to Warsaw from other European countries or traveling within Poland. Routes between Warsaw and the major European cities are provided by a company called **Pekaes**.

In Poland buses offer the most comprehensive public

transportation network, reaching almost every town, as well as many country villages.

The state-owned company **PKS** (Państwowa Komunikacja Samochodowa) has the largest number of routes and offers three types of service: local, intercity, and long-distance. There are two PKS terminals in Warsaw: the main one, Warsaw Central, is adjacent to the Central Railroad Station; while the second, Warszawa Zachodnia, is situated southwest of the city center, in the district of Ochota.

Polski Express bus

The privately owned **Polski Express** is the principal alternative for longer routes. Although the company offers fewer destinations than PKS, the buses tend to be newer and more comfortable, and journey times are usually faster and tickets are cheaper. Polski Express buses operate from Okęcie Airport, but all services also stop by the Central Railroad Station.

Pekaes
📞 23 63 94–96.
PKS
📞 23 63 94.
Polski Express
📞 620 03 30.

Ticket hall at the Central Railroad Station

greater number of stops; and local services, which stop fairly frequently.

Intercity trains also operate on principal routes. They are more comfortable and faster than express services, but they require tickets to be reserved when buying the ticket.

Buying Tickets

TICKETS CAN BE BOUGHT at railroad stations or in advance from Orbis travel offices (*see pp236–7*). When buying tickets at the station, allow at least half an hour

Zachodni bus station

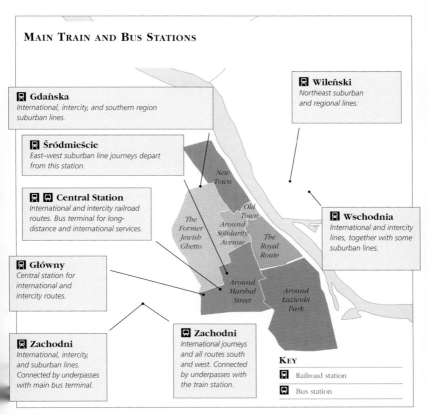

MAIN TRAIN AND BUS STATIONS

Gdańska
International, intercity, and southern region suburban lines.

Wileński
Northeast suburban and regional lines.

Śródmieście
East–west suburban line journeys depart from this station.

Central Station
International and intercity railroad routes. Bus terminal for long-distance and international services.

Wschodnia
International and intercity lines, together with some suburban lines.

Główny
Central station for international and intercity routes.

New Town

Old Town

Around Solidarity Avenue

The Former Jewish Ghetto

The Royal Route

Around Marshal Street

Around Łazienki Park

Zachodni
International, intercity, and suburban lines. Connected by underpasses with main bus terminal.

Zachodni
International journeys and all routes south and west. Connected by underpasses with the train station.

KEY

🚆 Railroad station

🚌 Bus station

TRAVELING BY CAR

Traveling to warsaw by car offers the most flexiblility for your itinerary, and Poland is well connected via international highways to many cities in the north of Europe. Poland imposes the usual restrictions on overseas drivers: a valid driving license must always be carried, together with car registration documents, car stickers bearing initials that identify the country of origin, and a Green Card (an international certificate of insurance).

Within Warsaw, there are several car-rental agencies, including international companies such as Hertz and Avis *(see p250)*. Prices are usually higher than in Western Europe, and it is also best to book at least a week in advance.

The minimum driving age in Poland is 18. Seat belts must be worn at all times, and children under the age of 12 are not allowed in the front passenger seat. Between November 1 and March 1, all drivers are required by law to keep the car headlights turned on at all times, day and night. Speed limits indicated on road signs are shown in kilometers. Polish police continually monitor speed limits, and offenders are required to pay on-the-spot fines. Drunk-driving laws are also strict, and the limit is so low that alcohol should be completely avoided when driving.

The price of gasoline is relatively low in Poland, but except at the main gas stations in Warsaw, credit cards are seldom accepted.

The Polish road system is extensive, but many roads are in poor condition. This is the case even in Warsaw, where an occasional pothole is not unknown. Although parking is free in most of the city, car theft is common, so use only guarded parking lots if possible.

A road sign for the center of Warsaw

GETTING AROUND WARSAW

THE CENTER of Warsaw is compact enough for visitors to explore on foot. Most areas beyond the center can easily be reached using the city's bus and streetcar system. While Warsaw's metro system is being developed, currently it links only the Polytechnic in the city center with the suburbs to the south, including Ursynów, the

Visitors on foot

largest residential suburb. Beyond pedestrian areas, a car is the best way of getting around. Throughout this guide, there are suggested routes for sightseeing, with streetcar and bus numbers indicated for each sight described. City maps that show bus and streetcar routes are available at Ruch kiosks, newsstands, and tourist offices.

DRIVING IN TOWN

DRIVING IN WARSAW is still relatively relaxed compared with in most other European capital cities. While traffic jams do occur, they are usually only during rush hours (which are between 7–8am and 2–5pm). However, the roads are not always in good condition, with uneven surfaces and potholes not unknown, particularly outside the center of Warsaw.

No stopping on the street

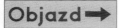

No stopping on the road and no parking on the sidewalk

Traveling by car is obviously the most convenient way to

Dotyczy także chodnika

Objazd ➡
Detour

get around the city, particularly if you are planning to visit outlying attractions.

There are a number of car rental firms with branches in Warsaw. However, prices tend to be slightly more expensive than those in Western Europe. Major international companies, such as **Avis**, **Budget**, and **Hertz**, all have offices at

Okęcie Airport as well as in Warsaw's city center.

The Old Town and New Town are both closed to traffic, but are easy and enjoyable to explore on foot.

PARKING

P
Płatny

TOWING
PARKING
PŁATNY STRZEŻONY

Sign for a secure parking lot

PARKING IS PERMITTED on most Warsaw streets, and even on the sidewalks, as long as there is no sign to indicate

otherwise. Although the parking regulations in the city center are fairly relaxed, there is a constant threat of break-ins and vehicle theft. Consequently, you are strongly advised always to leave your car in a guarded parking lot. Several of them are in central Warsaw, and they have been indicated on the Street Finder maps in this guide (see pp256–65).

CAR RENTAL FIRMS

Avis
Marriott Hotel.
⦿ 630 73 16.

Budget
Marriott Hotel.
⦿ 630 72 80.

Hertz
Nowogrodzka 27.
⦿ 621 13 60.

WARSAW ON FOOT

Sightseeing in Warsaw is an enjoyable experience on foot, as many of the city's historic sights are within easy walking distance of one another. This particularly applies to the Old and New Town areas, where many interesting buildings are located and cars are banned. However, as with Warsaw's roads, sidewalks can also be in a state of disrepair, while pedestrian areas often feature cobbled streets. If you intend to spend any length of time walking around the city, wear comfortable shoes that can cope with this type of terrain. Also, it is advisable to take great care when crossing streets, even at crosswalks, as drivers in Warsaw are not known for their willingness to stop for pedestrians.

Pedestrian crossing

Street name in a historic area

Plac Zamkowy
Typical street sign

PARKING PENALTIES

IF YOU LEAVE your car in a no-parking zone, you will have to pay a hefty penalty. A car that is parked dangerously and left unattended will be towed away by the vigilant traffic police. You will then have to reclaim your car, probably from a distant police compound. This is time-consuming and entails a fine (plus towing charges), which must be paid on the spot. Cars can also be wheel-clamped. In this case, you must telephone a traffic warden to remove the clamps, after the fine is paid (instructions are left on your car).

A wheel clamp

WARSAW TRANSPORTATION

THE PUBLIC TRANSPORT system includes the extensive streetcar and bus network, while the metro is mainly used by commuters *(see p253)*. While not particularly modern, buses and streetcars are inexpensive and frequent (operating between 5am and 11pm). Night buses augment the service, operating every half hour from behind the Palace of Culture and Science.

There is a flat-rate fare for bus, streetcar, and metro trips, regardless of distance. However, for fast buses you need to use two tickets, and for night buses you need three. A ticket is also needed for any luggage.

There are about 100 bus routes and 30 streetcar routes operating around Warsaw. Streetcars are most useful for making short trips in the city center *(see pp254–5)*.

STREETCAR, BUS, AND METRO TICKETS

One type of ticket is valid for use on streetcars, buses, and the metro. Tickets must be bought before boarding, and are available at all Ruch kiosks, newsstands, and metro stations. As the majority of tickets are sold at kiosks, they can be difficult to purchase on weekends and in the evening, when the kiosks tend to be shut.

Ruch kiosk, selling public transportation tickets

Single-fare ticket

It is often best to buy a pack of ten tickets at a time. When traveling by streetcar and bus, passengers must "cancel" tickets, once on board, by punching them in a machine (on the metro, it is located on the station platform). It is important to always travel with a valid ticket – one that has been canceled – as Warsaw has strict transport police, known as controllers, who are to some extent motivated by a share of the fines. Controllers operate in plainclothes, but carry identification. Fines must be paid on the spot, and are not negotiable. Routes most scrupulously controlled are streetcars between the Central Station and the market at the 10th Anniversary Stadium, and the No. 175 buses. If you carry any luggage (including all but the smallest suitcase or backpack), you must buy an additional ticket; fines are also imposed for carrying luggage without a ticket. Children below the age of 4, and people over the age of 75, travel free.

Single reduced-fare ticket

Travel passes that are valid for a day, a week, or a month can be obtained only at the ZTM office, at 37 Senatorska Street, or at any of the city's main transport terminals. These passes do not need canceling.

Weekly and monthly tickets

Getting Around by Taxi

Taxis provide the most efficient and comfortable means of traveling around Warsaw, and fares are not high by international standards. There are numerous reliable taxi firms based in Warsaw but, as in any major city, watch out for drivers who overcharge or take a circuitous route to your destination. It is best to either book a taxi or take one from an official stand.

Taxi-stand sign

taxi stands, indicated by a blue sign. It is also possible to book taxis to pick you up at a pre-arranged time. Most taxi companies employ telephone operators who speak English.

Do not take taxis with drivers who solicit at Okęcie Airport, Castle Square, the Central Railroad Station, or other main tourist locations. If in doubt, ask at your hotel what the fare to a specific destination is likely to be.

TYPES OF TAXIS

There is no official color for taxis in Warsaw. However, all taxis feature a distinctive yellow and red stripe, together with the city's crest, an official number marked on the doors, and a "taxi" sign on the roof. Most also display the name and telephone number of their company.

Warsaw's largest and most established taxi company is **MPT-Radio Taxi** but many other reliable companies also provide a good level

kilometer traveled. Warsaw is divided into two zones, and taxi fares vary according to which one you travel through. Zone one covers the city center, and journeys to districts outside this zone will be more expensive. It should be possible to negotiate a rate for a long journey, which should be done before you set off. Fares also operate at a higher rate during the night (from 10pm to 6am).

Some taxis may have meters that predate the devaluation of the złoty (and will

Warsaw taxi

of service, among them **Korpo-Taxi**, **Super-Taxi**, **Tele-Taxi**, and **Volfra-Taxi**.

Some leading hotels provide their own car services, but they can be far more expensive than regular taxis. There is also a special car service from the airport, called "Fly and Drive with LOT," which is offered by LOT Polish Airlines (see p247).

TAXI FARES

When you start a journey by taxi, make sure that the meter has been switched on and is displaying the current minimum standard charge, above the word opłata (fare). Once you set off, the fare will increase after each

indicate a fare that runs into thousands). In these cases, the driver converts the fare to its current equivalent. If you are concerned about the fare charged, ask for a receipt and check the amount with the taxi company concerned.

HOW TO AVOID BEING OVERCHARGED

Avoid using any cab that does not display the name of a recognized taxi company (listed on this page). The best place to find a taxi is at one of the many official

Taxi meter

RADIO TAXI COMPANIES

Express-Taxi
96 36.

Halo-Taxi
96 23.

Korpo-Taxi
96 24.

MPT-Radio Taxi
919.

OK Taxi
96 28.

Sawa-Taxi
644 44 44.

Super-Taxi
96 22.

Super-Taxi 2
96 61.

Taxi-Lux
96 66.

Taxi Plus
96 21.

Tele-Taxi
96 27.

Top-Taxi 2
96 64.

Trans-Taxi
96 29.

Volfra-Taxi
96 25.

Wa Wa Taxi
96 44.

Getting Around by Metro

Metro sign

W ARSAW'S METRO SYSTEM currently has only one line. It operates from the city center, from a station by Warsaw Polytechnic *(see p136)*, and extends south for 11 km (7 miles) through districts such as Mokotów and Ursynów, before terminating at Kabaty. The metro is the fastest and most efficient means of transportation to these areas. The next stations on the line are now under construction. So in the next few years, the metro will reach as far as the Zoliborz district.

USING THE METRO

M ETRO STATION ENTRANCES are indicated by yellow signs bearing a large red letter *M*, with an arrow at the center of the letter. Entrances include stairs and ramps, and at each station there is also an elevator solely for the use of the elderly, disabled people, and people traveling with small children. To use the elevator, ask the station staff for assistance.

Tickets are available from the ticket office at each station. They are the same tickets that are used on streetcars and buses *(see p251)*.

Metro stations have a single platform, which is situated between the tracks, so that you can board a train going in either direction. The destination of the trains stopping on each side of the platform is indicated by a blue sign with an arrow and the name of the final stop on the line. To go toward Warsaw Polytechnic and the city center, take the train from the platform marked "Centrum."

The edge of each platform is painted with an unbroken white line. For safety reasons, passengers are not permitted to cross this line until the train has come to a halt. When a train arrives, the doors open and close automatically. A recorded warning sounds just before the doors close, and there is also an announcement of the next stop.

As a security precaution, there are no trash baskets on the metro, either in cars or at stations. Used tickets and any other litter must be disposed of outside the stations. Smoking is forbidden anywhere in metro stations and on trains. Anyone who is found smoking is liable to pay a hefty fine.

Platform at Wilanówska station on Warsaw's metro system

TRAVELING BY METRO

The metro system (including stations under construction). Maps are also displayed in metro cars and on station platforms.

1 Before crossing the yellow line onto the platform, you must cancel single tickets by punching the side of the ticket, using the red machines near the stairs to the platform. Daily, weekly, and monthly tickets do not need canceling.

2 An uncanceled ticket is not valid, and passengers found in the yellow zone with invalid tickets are liable to be fined. Keep canceled tickets until you leave the station.

Machine for canceling tickets

Sign showing streetcar connection

3 To reach your destination, you may also need to use other means of transportation. Look out for blue signs at metro station exits, which indicate streetcar and bus connections.

Traveling by Streetcar

T HE STREETCAR SYSTEM is Warsaw's oldest form of public transportation. The first horse-drawn cars appeared in 1866, and were replaced in 1908 by electric streetcars. Warsaw's streetcars usually comprise two or three cars, which fill up during the rush hours (approximately 7–8am and 2–5pm). Despite the crowds, streetcars still provide one of the city's fastest forms of public transportation, taking the most direct routes along Warsaw's principal thoroughfares. There are around 30 streetcar routes, which criss-cross the city on a grid pattern, running on either a north–south or an east–west axis. As in any major city, pickpockets operate in crowded places, so take care of your belongings when traveling by streetcar. Smoking is forbidden on streetcars.

USEFUL ROUTES

O N THE EAST–WEST axis, various routes pass through the city center, along Jerozolimskie Avenue and across the Vistula to the Praga district. These routes are also handy for the Palace of Culture and Science, the Royal Route, and the National Museum. On the north–south axis, a route along Marszałkowska Street, from Bank Square (Plac Bankowy) to Zbawiciela Square, is useful for the Grand Theater, Saxon Gardens, and the Palace of Culture and Science.

STREETCAR TIMES AND ROUTES

S TREETCARS OPERATE between 5am–11pm daily, and run every few minutes; unlike buses, they do not operate at night. Each streetcar stop displays the numbers and routes of the streetcars that it serves. The routes are also marked on city maps, which are available from Ruch kiosks.

Streetcar at an intersection in the center of Warsaw

Name of steetcar stop

KRÓLEWSKA 05

2
4
15
18
31
35

36

Logo denoting a streetcar stop

Streetcar routes that use the stop

Timetable

A typical streetcar stop in Warsaw, providing route information

STREETCAR TICKETS

O NE TYPE of ticket is valid for use on the buses and streetcars throughout the city. Tickets must be bought before boarding a vehicle and are available from Ruch kiosks or similar outlets. There is a choice of single-journey, daily, or weekly tickets. A single-journey ticket is valid for one journey only, no matter what the distance, but if you change streetcar routes you need to use another ticket.

On boarding the streetcar, you must cancel a single-journey ticket by punching it in one of the small machines. Insert the end of the ticket marked with an arrow and the letter *N*. Anyone traveling who has not canceled the ticket is liable to an on-the-spot fine imposed by plain-clothes controllers. If you are carrying luggage, you must cancel an extra ticket.

WARSAW TOURS

A SIGHTSEEING STREETCAR, the so-called Berlinka, marked with the letter *T*, operates on Saturdays, Sundays, and public holidays. It departs every 40 minutes from 10am–5pm, and stops frequently so the tour can be joined throughout the city. A conductor collects the fare, which is higher than the usual one, but the tour is a great introduction to Warsaw.

Beginning at Narutowicza Square, the route follows Grójecka Street and Jerozolimskie Avenue, before crossing Poniatowski Bridge to reach Praga. It returns via Śląsko-Dąbrowski Bridge, Bank Square, Marszałkowska Street, and Zbawiciela Square, before terminating at Narutowicza Square.

A single-journey ticket

Traveling by Bus

BUSES SERVE every district of Warsaw, as well as the outlying regions. Buses operate more extensive routes than streetcars, with over 100 routes in operation, providing a frequent, if not particularly speedy, service. The majority of buses are state-owned and sport distinctive red and yellow paintwork.

Sign indicating a bus stop

TIMES AND ROUTES

THERE ARE four principal types of public bus service in Warsaw: buses for traveling around the city center; buses that link the center with the outlying suburbs; night buses; and buses serving Warsaw's suburbs and farther afield.

The four types can easily be distinguished by their route numbers. Buses with numbers from 101–199 operate within the city center and stop frequently. Those numbered between 400–500 make fewer stops between the center and the suburbs. Express buses are a subsection of this service, and are indicated by the letter *E* in front of the number. Night buses are numbered from 600–699, while green-line buses, serving the outskirts of the city, are numbered from 700 onward.

All bus stops display timetables of buses that stop there. Frequency varies from 5–20 minutes. On weekends and public holidays, bus service is less frequent. A few private lines also operate from terminals on Marszałkowska Street and Jerozolimskie Avenue.

NIGHT BUSES

NIGHT SERVICES operate between 11pm–5am. Fares are higher at night, and tickets can be bought from the driver. Night lines link the center with major suburbs, and depart every half hour from the junction of Emilii

Reduced-fare ticket

Plater and Świętokrzyska streets (the latter is easily found just behind the Palace of Culture and Science).

TICKETS

BUS TICKETS are the same as those used on streetcars and the metro. They must be purchased before you travel and are available at Ruch kiosks, newsstands, and metro stations. Single-journey tickets must be canceled on boarding the bus and are valid for only one journey on one vehicle, regardless of distance. Plainclothes controllers check that you have canceled your ticket, and hefty fines are imposed if you have not. You should also bear in mind that an extra ticket must be used for each item of luggage, such as a suitcase or backpack. On private buses, tickets are purchased from the driver when boarding.

USEFUL ROUTES

THE NUMBER 175 bus is ideal for getting around the city center. The route links Krakowskie Przedmieście and Jerozolimskie Avenue with Warsaw's main railroad stations, before heading to Okęcie Airport. Along the way, this route passes Warsaw University and the Royal Castle, and is handy for the Grand Theater as well.

Routes 116, 122, and 195 are useful for traveling south of the city center, as they continue along Miodowa Street, Krakowskie Przedmieście, Nowy Świat, and Ujazdowskie Avenue. They therefore provide a fast link between the Old Town and

Weekly ticket

Łazienki Park, as well as passing sights such as Prymasowski Palace along the way.

The most useful buses within the former Jewish Ghetto area are 180 and 166. The 180 passes the Path of Remembrance and the Jewish History Institute Museum, while 166 is useful for the Warsaw Chamber Opera and Mostowski Palace.

INFORMATION

Komunikacja Miejska ZTM (City Communications)

☎ 827 37 47.
◻ 7am–3:30pm Mon–Fri.

Characteristic red and yellow Warsaw bus

STREET FINDER

THE BLACK GRID superimposed on the *Area by Area* map opposite shows which parts of Warsaw are covered in the *Street Finder*. The map references given throughout this guide for all sights, hotels, restaurants, shopping, and entertainment venues refer to the numbered maps in this section. The key lists the features that are indicated on the maps, including transportation terminals, emergency services, and tourist information points. All the major sights are clearly marked. A complete index of the street names and places of interest that appear on the maps follows on pages 258–9. Street names that include numbers are indexed under the first word; for example "3 May Street" will be found under "May."

Façade of Wilanów Palace *(see pp168–71)*

KEY TO STREET FINDER

▢	Major sight
▢	Other sight
Ⓜ	Metro station
▤	Railroad station
▤	Bus terminal
▥	Streetcar stop
▭	Bus stop
P	Parking
i	Tourist information point
✚	Hospital
▦	Police station
✝	Church
✡	Synagogue
⊠	Post office
▬	Railroad line
→	One-way street
⌐⌐	City walls

SCALE OF MAPS 1–2

0 meters	250	
		1:10,000
0 yards	250	

SCALE OF MAPS 3–6

0 meters	400	
		1:14,000
0 yards	400	

Strolling through the Old Town *(see pp64–83)*

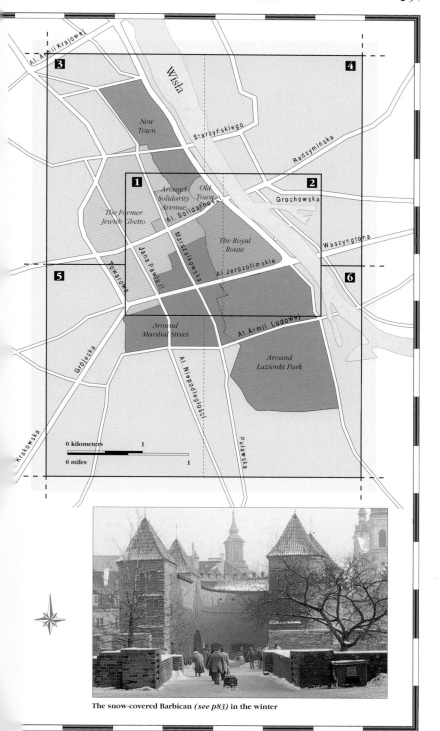

The snow-covered Barbican *(see p83)* in the winter

Street Finder Index

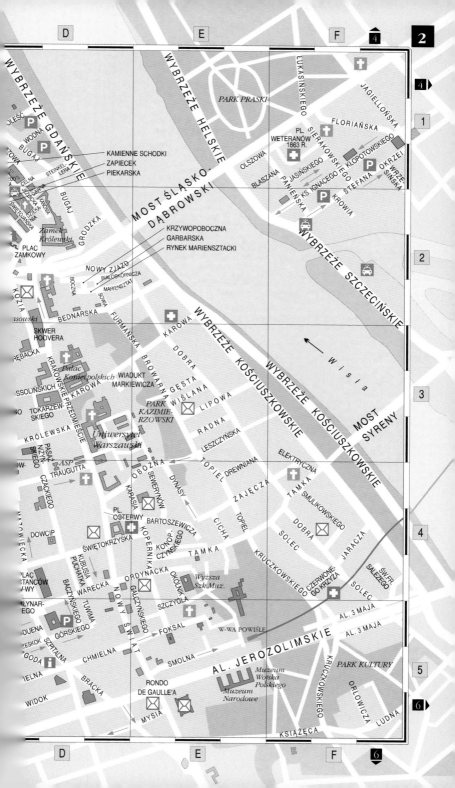

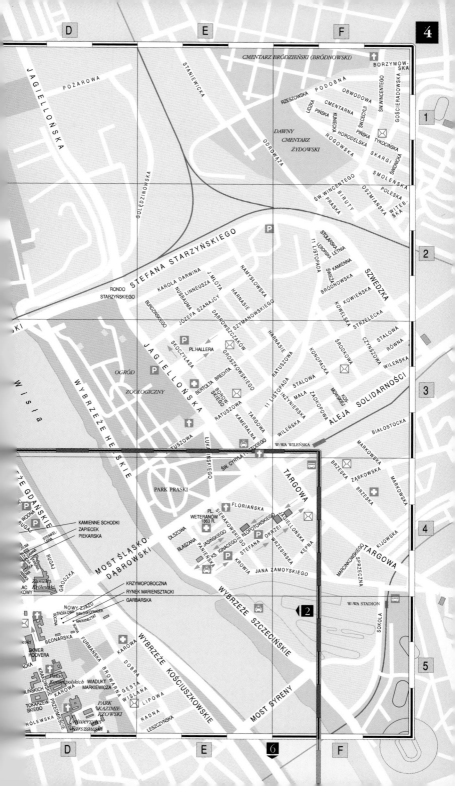

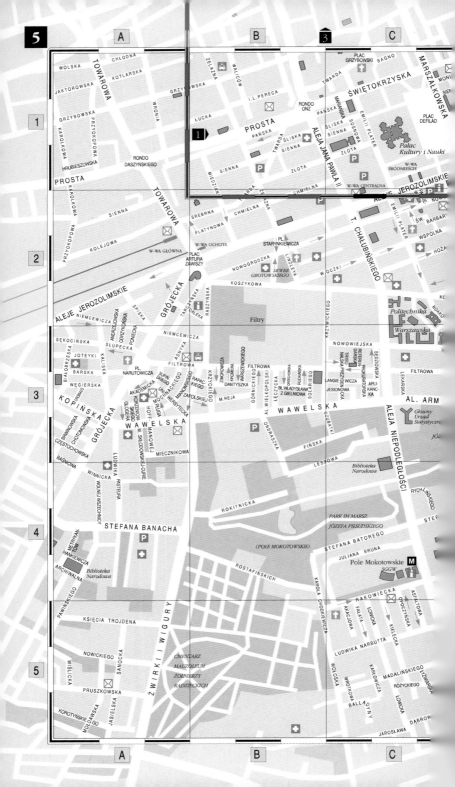

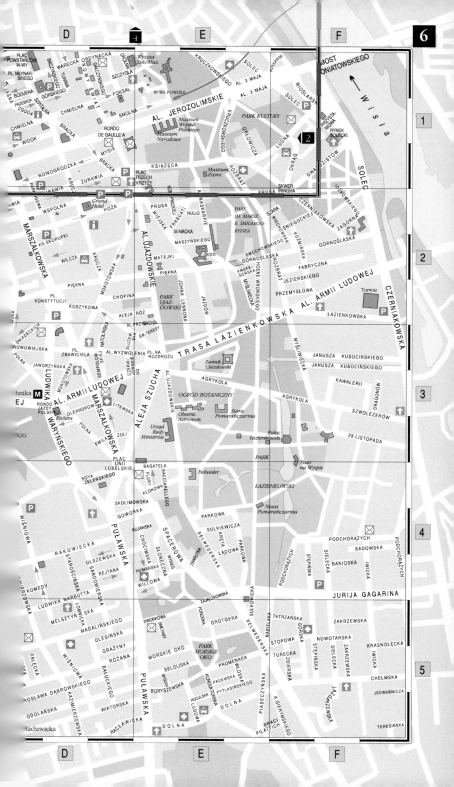

General Index

Acknowledgments

DORLING KINDERSLEY would like to thank the following people whose contributions and assistance have made the preparation of this book possible.

CARTOGRAPHY
The Institute of Land Surveying and Cartography in Warsaw for the map of Warsaw; the Meteorological Institute in Warsaw for supplying meteorological data.

ADDITIONAL ILLUSTRATIONS
Marek Górka for the Palace on the Water; Dominik Bosekand for the Szuster Palace.

DESIGN AND EDITORIAL ASSISTANCE
Guy Dimond, Sarah Martin, Adam Moore, Lee Redmond, Harvey de Roemer, Nick Ryder, Andrew Szudek.

PHOTOGRAPHY PERMISSIONS
The publisher would like to thank the following for their permission to photograph:
Central Archive of Historic Documents, Warsaw; Central Photographic Agency (PAP), Warsaw.

PICTURE CREDITS
Every effort has been made to trace the copyright holders. Dorling Kindersley apologizes for any unintentional omissions and would be pleased, in such cases, to add an acknowledgment in future editions.

The publisher would like to thank the following individuals, companies, and picture libraries for kind permission to reproduce their photographs:

J BARANOWSKI (W Gomułka on plac Defilad).

JERZY BRONARSKI, ORLĘTA AGENCY (Royal Castle).

MACIEJ BRZOZOWSKI (Czeslaw Miłosz; chamber in the Sejm, Polish Parliament).

PAWEL KOPCZYŃSKI (Warsaw on *Śmigus Dyngus*).

WOJCIECH KRYŃSKI AND TOMASZ PRAZMOWSKI (Płock).

STEFAN KRZESZEWSKI (Senate Chamber in the Sejm).

J KUŚMIERSKI (baboons in the zoo).

DAMAZY KWIATKOWSKI (mass celebrated by the Pope).

JERZY MYSZKOWSKI (paintings by Bellotto).

ANDRZEJ PAWLISZEWSKI (Warsaw airport).

IRENEUSZ RADKIEWICZ (Lech Wałęsa).

HENRYK ROSIAK (marshal's mace).

WITOLD ROZMYSŁOWICZ (Dzierżyński's monument being destroyed).

JERZY SABARZ (Archdiocese Museum).

JAKUB SITO (Pułtusk).

MARIAN SOKOŁOWSKI (Syrena car).

WOJCIECH STEIN (Cardinal Glemp; Jazz Jamboree).

JANUSZ UKLEWSKI (Anna German).

TEODOR WALCZAK (horse races; lions in the zoo).

BARBARA WOŁOSZ (Natolin).

The publishers would also like to thank the following institutions:

Administration of the Main Post Office, Warsaw
Botanical Gardens, Warsaw
Czartoryski Museum, Kraków
Earth Sciences Museum, Warsaw
Ethnographic Museum, Warsaw
Frederic Chopin Society, Warsaw
Grand Theater, Warsaw
Guild of Leather Crafts Museum dedicated to J Kiliński, Warsaw
Gulliver's Theater, Warsaw
Handicraft and Precision Craft Museum, Warsaw
Historical Buildings Institute, Warsaw
Historical Museum of the City of Warsaw
Institute of Land Surveying and Cartography, Warsaw
Jewish Historical Institute, Warsaw
Jewish Theater dedicated to Estera Kaminska, Warsaw
Literature Museum, Warsaw
LOT Polish National Airlines
Maria Skłodowska-Curie Museum, Warsaw
Museum of Fine Arts, Łódz
National Museum, Warsaw
Nieborów and Arkadia Museums
Palace of Culture and Science, Warsaw
Palace on the Water, Warsaw
PAN Fine Art Institute, Warsaw
Pavilion X of the Citadel Museum, Warsaw
Polfilm advertising and photographic agency, Warsaw
Polish Military Museum, Warsaw
Pope John Paul II Collection, Warsaw
Poster Museum, Wilanów, Warsaw
Royal Castle, Warsaw
Technology Museum, Warsaw
Theater Museum, Warsaw
Traffic Wardens Association, Warsaw
Union of Jewish Communes
Warsaw Chamber Opera
Wilanów Palace and Park, Warsaw
Xawery Dunikowski Museum within the Królikarnia, Warsaw.

Phrase Book

SUMMARY OF PRONUNCIATION IN POLISH

ą a nasal *"awn"* as in *"sawn"* or *"an"* as in the French *"Anjou"* but barely sounded

c *"ts"* as in *"cats"*

ć, cz *"ch"* as in *"challenge"*

ch *"ch"* as in Scottish *"loch"*

dz *"j"* as in *"jeans"* when followed by **i** or **e** but otherwise *"dz"* as in *"adze"*

dź *"j"* as in *"jeans"*

dż *"d"* as in *"dog"* followed by *"s"* as in *"leisure"*

ę similar to *"en"* in *"end"* only nasal and barely sounded, but if at the end of the word pronounced *"e"* as in *"bed"*

h "ch" as in Scottish "Loch"

i *"ee"* as in *"teeth"*

j *"y'* as in yes

ł *"w"* as in *"window"*

ń similar to the *"ni"* in *"companion"*

ó *"oo"* as in *"soot"*

rz similar to the *"s"* in *"leisure"* or, when it follows **p, t,** or **k,** *"sh"* as in *"shut"*

ś, sz *"sh"* as in *"shut"*

w *"v"* as in *"vine"*

y similar to the *"i"* in *"bit"*

ź, ż similar to the *"s"* in *"leisure"*

EMERGENCIES

Help!
Pomocy!
pomotsi

Call a doctor!
Zawołać doktora!
zawowach doctora

Call an ambulance!
Zadzwonić po pogotowie!
zadzvoneech po pogotovee

Police!
Policja!
poleetsya

Call the fire department!
Zadzwonić po straż pożarną!
zadzvoneech po stras posarnAWN

Where is the nearest phone?
Gdzie jest najbliższa budka telefoniczna?
gjeh yest nIbleezhsha boodka telefoneechna

Where is the hospital?
Gdzie jest szpital?
gjeh yest shpeetal

Where is the police station?
Gdzie jest posterunek policji?
gjeh yest posterunek politsyee

COMMUNICATION ESSENTIALS

Yes
Tak
tak

No
Nie
n-yeh

Thank you.
Dziękuję.
jENkoo-yeh

No thank you.
Nie, dziękuję.
n-yej jENkoo-yeh

Please
Proszę
prosheh

I don't understand.
Nie rozumiem.
n-yeh rozoom-yem

Do you speak English? (to a man)
Czy mówi pan po angielsku?
chi moovee pan po ang-yelskoo

Do you speak English? (to a woman)
Czy mówi pani po angielsku?
chi moovee panee po ang-yelskoo

Please speak more slowly.
Proszę mówić wolniej.
prosheh mooveech voln-yay

Please write it down for me.
Proszę mi to napisać.
prosheh mee to napeesach

My name is . . .
Nazywam się . . .
nazivam sheh

USEFUL WORDS AND PHRASES

Pleased to meet you (to a man)
Bardzo mi miło pana poznać.
bardzo mee meewo pana poznach

Pleased to meet you (to a woman)
Bardzo mi miło panią poznać.
bardzo mee meewo pan-yAWN poznach

Good morning
Dzień dobry
jen-yuh dobri

Good afternoon
Dzień dobry
jen-yuh dobri

Good evening
Dobry wieczór
dobri v-yechoor

Good night
Dobranoc
dobranots

Goodbye
Do widzenia
do veedzen-ya

What time is it?
Która jest godzima?
ktoora yest gojeena

Cheers!
Na zdrowie!
na zdrov-yeh

Excellent!
Wspaniale!
wspan-yaleh

SHOPPING

Do you have . . . ? (to a man)
Czy ma pan . . . ?
che ma pan

Do you have . . . ? (to a woman)
Czy ma pani . . . ?
che ma panee

How much is this?
Ile to kosztuje?
eeleh to koshtoo-yeh

Where is the . . . department?
Gdzie jest dział z . . . ?
gjeh yest jawuh z

Do you take credit cards? (to a man)
Czy przyjmuje pan karty kredytowe?
chi pshi-yuhmoo-yeh pan karti kreditoveh

Do you take credit cards? (to a woman)
Czy przyjmuje pani karty kredytowe?
chi pshi-yuhmoo-yeh panee karti kreditoveh

bakery
piekarnia
p-yekarn-ya

bookshop
księgarnia
kshENgarn-ya

department store
dom towarowy
dom tovarovi

exchange office
kantor walutowy
kantor valootovi

pharmacist
apteka
apteka

post office
poczta, urząd pocztowy
pochta, ooZHAWNd pochtovi

postcard
pocztówka
pochtoovka

stamp
znaczek
znachek

travel agent
biuro podróży
b-yooro podroozhi

How much is a postcard to . . . ?
Ile kosztuje pocztówka do . . . ?
eeleh koshtoo-yeh pochtoovka do

airmail
poczta lotnicza
pochta lotneecha

STAYING IN A HOTEL

Have you any vacancies? (to a man)
Czy ma pan wolne pokoje?
chi ma pan volneh poko-yeh

Have you any vacancies? (to a woman)
Czy ma pani wolne pokoje?
chi ma panee volneh poko-yeh

What is the charge per night?
Ile kosztuje za dobę?
eeleh koshtoo-yeh za dobeh

I'd like a single room.
Poproszę pokój jednoosobowy.
poprosheh pokoo-yuh yedno-osobovi

I'd like a double room.
Poproszę pokój dwuosobowy.
poprosheh pokoo-yuh dvoo-osobovi

I'd like a twin room.
Poproszę pokój z dwoma łóżkami.
poprosheh pokoo-yuh z dvoma
woozhkamee

I'd like a room with a bathroom.
Poproszę pokój z łazienką.
poprosheh pokoo-yuh z
wazhenkAWN

bathroom
łazienka
wazhenka

bed
łóżko
woozhko

bill
rachunek
raHoonek

breakfast
śniadanie
shn-yadan-yeh

dinner
kolacja
kolats-ya

double room
pokój dwuosobowy
pokoo-yuh dvoo-osobovi

full board
pełne utrzymanie
pewuhneh ootzhiman-yeh

guest house
zajazd
za-yazd

half board
dwa posiłki dziennie
dva posheewuhkee jen-yeh

key
klucz
klooch

restaurant
restauracja
restawrats-ya

shower
prysznic
prishneets

single room
pokój jednoosobowy
pokoo-yuh yedno-osobovi

toilet
toaleta
to-aleta

EATING OUT

A table for one, please.
Stolik dla jednej osoby proszę.
stoleek dla yednay osobi prosheh

A table for two, please.
Stolik dla dwóch osób proszę.
stoleek dla dvooh osoob prosheh

May I see the menu?
Mogę prosić jadłospis?
mogeh prosheech yadwospees

May I see the wine list?
Mogę prosić kartę win?
mogeh prosheech karteh veen

I'd like . . .
Proszę . . .
prosheh

May we have the bill, please?
Proszę rachunek?
prosheh raHoonek

Where is the toilet?
Gdzie jest toaleta?
gjeh yest to-aleta

MENU DECODER

baranina
mutton, lamb

barszcz czerwony
beet soup

bażant
pheasant

befsztyk
beef steak

bigos
hunter's stew (sweet and sour
cabbage with a variety of meats
and seasonings)

bukiet z jarzyn
variety of raw and pickled vegetables

ciasto
cake, pastry

cielęcina
veal

cukier
sugar

cukierek
sweet, confectionery

dania mięsne
meat dishes

dania rybne
fish dishes

dania z drobiu
poultry dishes

deser
dessert

flaki
tripe

grzybki marynowane
marinated mushrooms

herbata
tea

jarzyny
vegetables

kabanos
dry, smoked pork sausage

kaczka
duck

kapusta
cabbage

kartofle
potatoes

kasza gryczana
buckwheat

kaszanka
black pudding

kawa
coffee

kiełbasa
sausage

klopsiki
meat balls

lody
ice cream

łosoś
salmon

łosoś wędzony
smoked salmon

makowiec
poppy-seed cake

naleśniki
pancakes

piernik
spiced honeycake

pierogi
ravioli-like dumplings

piwo
beer

prawdziwki
cèpes (type of mushroom)

przystawki
entrées

pstrąg
trout

rolmopsy
rollmop herrings

sałatka
salad

salatka owocowa
fruit salad

sok
juice

sok jabłkowy
apple juice

sok owocowy
fruit juice

sól
salt

śledź
herring

tort
cake

wieprzowina
pork

wino
wine

woda
water

ziemniaki
potatoes

zupa
soup

HEALTH

I do not feel well.
Źle się czuję.
zhleh sheh choo-yeh

I need a prescription for . . .
Potrzebuję receptę na . . .
potzheboo-yeh retsepteh na

cold
przeziębienie
pshef-yENb-yen-yeh

cough (noun)
kaszel
kashel

cut
skaleczenie
skalechen-yeh

flu
grypa
gripa

hay fever
katar sienny
katar shyiennny

headache pills
proszki od bólu głowy
proshkee od booloo gwovi

hospital
szpital
shpeetal

nausea
mdłości
mudwosh-che

sore throat
ból gardła
bool gardwa

TRAVEL AND TRANSPORTATION

When is the next train to . . . ?
Kiedy jest następny pociąg do . . . ?
k-yedi yest nastENpni pochAWNg do

What is the fare to . . . ?
Ile kosztuje bilet do . . . ?
eeleh koshtoo-yeh beelet do

A one-way ticket to . . . please
Proszę bilet w jedną strone bilet do . . .
prosheh beelet v yednAWN stroneh beelet do

A round-trip ticket to . . . please
Proszę bilet w obie strony do . . .
prosheh beelet v obye strony do

Where is the bus station?
Gdzie jest dworzec autobusowy?
gjeh yest dvozhets awtoboosovi

Where is there a bus stop?
Gdzie jest przystanek autobusowy?
gjeh yest pshistanek awtoboosovi

Where is there a tram stop?
Gdzie jest przystanek tramwajowy?
gjeh yest pshistanek tramvl-yovi

booking office
kasa biletowa
kasa beeletova

station
stacja
stats-ya

timetable
rozkład jazdy
rozkwad yazdi

baggage room
przechowalnia bagażu
psheHovaln-ya bagazhoo

platform
peron
peron

first class
pierwsza klasa
p-yervsha klasa

second class
druga klasa
drooga klasa

one-way ticket
bilet w jedną stronę
beelet v yednAWN
stroneh

round-trip ticket
bilet powrotny
beelet povrotni

airline
linia lotnicza
leen-ya lotna-yeecha

airport
lotnisko
lotn-yeesko

arrival
przylot
pshilot

flight number
numer lotu
noomer lotoo

gate
przejście
pshaysh-cheh

bus
autokar
awtokar

NUMBERS

0
zero
zero

1
jeden
yeden

2
dwa
dva

3
trzy
tshi

4
cztery
chteri

5
pięć
p-yENch

6
sześć
shesh-ch

7
siedem
sh-yedem

8
osiem
oshem

9
dziewięć
jev-yENch

10
dziesięć
jeshENch

11
jedenaście
yedenash-cheh

12
dwanaście
dvanash-cheh

13
trzynaście
tshinash-cheh

14
czternaście
chternash-cheh

15
piętnaście
p-yEntnash-cheh

16
szesnaście
shesnash-cheh

17
siedemnaście
shedemnash-cheh

18
osiemnaście
oshemnash-cheh

19
dziewiętnaście
jev-yENtnash-cheh

20
dwadzieścia
dvajesh-cha

21
dwadzieścia jeden
dvajesh-cha yeden

22
dwadzieścia dwa
dvajesh-cha dva

30
trzydzieści
tshijesh-chee

40
czterdzieści
chterjesh-chee

50
pięćdziesiąt
p-yENchjeshAWNt

100
sto
sto

200
dwieście
dv-yesh-cheh

500
pięćset
p-yENchset

1,000
tysiąc
tishAWNts

1,000,000
milion
meel-yon

TIME

today
dzisiaj
jeeshl

yesterday
wczoraj
vchorl

tomorrow
jutro
yootro

tonight
dzisiejszej nocy
jeeshAYshay notsi

one minute
jedna minuta
yedna meenoota

half an hour
pół godziny
poowuh gojeeni

hour
godzina
gojeena

DAYS OF THE WEEK

Sunday
niedziela
n-yejela

Monday
poniedziałek
pon-yejawek

Tuesday
wtorek
vtorek

Wednesday
środa
shroda

Thursday
czwartek
chvartek

Friday
piątek
p-yAWNtek

Saturday
sobota
sobota

Warsaw's Railroad and Metro System

Młociny
Wawrzyszew
Bielany
Kaskada
Marymont
Plac Wilsona

Dworzec Gdański

Ratusz
Świętokrzyska
Centrum

Politechnika

Pole Mokotowskie

Racławicka

Wierzbno

Wilanowska
Służew
Ursynów
Stokłosy
Imielin
Natolin
Kabaty

○—○ Existing metro station
○—○ Planned metro station

KEY

Metro line

Railroad line

🚉 Main railroad station

🚌 Bus station

Warszawa
Gdańska

Warszawa
Koło

Warszawa
Kasprzaka

Warszawa
Ochota

Warszawa
Wola

Warszawa
Zachodnia

0 kilometers   1

0 miles   1